SERVICE
MANAGEMENT
EFFECTIVENESS

David E. Bowen
Richard B. Chase
Thomas G. Cummings
and Associates

SERVICE
MANAGEMENT
EFFECTIVENESS

Balancing Strategy,
Organization and Human Resources,
Operations, and Marketing

 Jossey-Bass Publishers
San Francisco • Oxford • 1990

SERVICE MANAGEMENT EFFECTIVENESS
Balancing Strategy, Organization and Human Resources, Operations, and Marketing
by David E. Bowen, Richard B. Chase, Thomas G. Cummings,
and Associates

Library of Congress Cataloging-in-Publication Data

Bowen, David E.
    Service management effectiveness : balancing strategy,
organization and human resources, operations, and marketing / David
E. Bowen, Richard B. Chase, Thomas G. Cummings, and associations.
        p.   cm. — (The Jossey-Bass management series)
    Includes bibliographical references.
    ISBN 1-55542-222-5
    1. Service industries—Management.   I. Chase, Richard B.
II. Cummings, Thomas G.   III. Title.   IV. Series.
HD9980.5.B68   1990   90-4047
658—dc20   CIP

Manufactured in the United States of America

The paper in this book meets the guidelines for
permanence and durability of the Committee on
Production Guidelines for Book Longevity of the
Council on Library Resources.

JACKET DESIGN BY WILLI BAUM

FIRST EDITION

Code 9031

The Jossey-Bass
Management Series

Contents

Preface

Service Management Effectiveness emerged from a desire to provide leading academic experts on service organizations with a vehicle through which they could "sing their songs." We wanted to give the contributors an opportunity to speak their minds about service in any way they chose, such as through overviews of their past work, suggestions for new directions, case reports, or whatever other way they felt they could best express the message they wanted to communicate.

As editors, we established only a couple of boundaries for the contributors: (1) The topics they chose were to be of interest and accessible to both academics and sophisticated practitioners, and (2) although asked to write from the perspective of their own fields, the contributors also were requested to address how service issues in their fields meshed with issues in the fields of the other contributors. A central theme of the book, introduced in the first chapter and developed throughout, is that service management effectiveness requires a cross-functional perspective. The functions, or disciplines, represented are: strategic management, organization and human resource management, operations management, and marketing.

Genesis of the Book

Our original plan for *Service Management Effectiveness* was to bring the contributors together for a conference at the University of Southern California, hosted by the Center for Operations Management, Education and Research. The center is one of only two or three research centers in the country that has the study of service operations as a central objective. The book then would have emerged from the presentations and discussions at that conference. Schedule conflicts ultimately made the conference idea unworkable. We decided, however, that the book would have considerable merit even without the conference. Publications of academic thinking about service are few in number compared to the proliferation of popular books from authors such as Karl Albrecht, Chip Bell, Tom Peters, and Ron Zemke. (Their books are all quite good, but they are written from a different perspective.)

We invited to be contributors those academics who had helped energize thinking about service in their fields through sustained exploration of the subject, which was visible in their research and writing. Only Fred Luthans and Tim R. V. Davis are exceptions in that they are relative newcomers to the study of service management effectiveness. They are old hands, however, in the application of behavioral management, a potentially useful technology for shaping the behavior of service employees.

Overview of the Contents

An illustrative glimpse of the contributions follows; more is said about them in Chapter One, in which a complete description of the chapter contents is tied to an overview of some basic issues surrounding service management effectiveness.

In Part One, which covers the field of strategic management:

- James L. Heskett (Chapter Two) reviews the unique nature of strategy in a service context, emphasizing how the multifunctional nature of service affects strategy.
- Dorothy I. Riddle (Chapter Three) describes the key variables and functionally integrated processes associated with strategic decision making in service firms.
- James Brian Quinn and Penny C. Paquette (Chapter Four) examine the interface between service and manufacturing and describe how service technologies can be factors in manufacturing.

In Part Two, regarding the field of organization and human resource management:

- Peter K. Mills and Dennis J. Moberg (Chapter Five) describe the nature of customer participation in the technology of service firms and its impact on firms' strategic options.
- Benjamin Schneider (Chapter Six) proposes alternative strategies and tactics for enhancing a firm's service orientation.
- David A. Tansik (Chapter Seven) examines the human resource management activities firms must utilize to ensure that their customer contact personnel have the necessary skills, knowledge, and abilities.
- Fred Luthans and Tim R. V. Davis (Chapter Eight) detail the application of behavioral management techniques within service firms.

In Part Three, which examines the field of operations management:

- W. Earl Sasser and William E. Fulmer (Chapter Nine) describe how new information technologies can be used for customized, but efficient, service delivery.
- David A. Collier (Chapter Ten) maps out the operational steps management must follow to deliver service quality.
- Albert H. Rubenstein and Eliezer Geisler (Chapter Eleven)

share what they have learned from a long-term study of the role of information technology in service firms.

- James A. Fitzsimmons (Chapter Twelve) looks at the application of just-in-time inventory control systems in service firms as an example of what the service sector can learn from the manufacturing sector.

In Part Four, which concerns the field of marketing:

- John A. Czepiel (Chapter Thirteen) examines the need for service firms to recognize and enhance the social and relational nature of their exchanges with customers in order to market effectively.
- John E. G. Bateson (Chapter Fourteen) analyzes the contingencies affecting service firms' need for a marketing department and where a marketing department fits within an organization's structure.
- Christopher H. Lovelock (Chapter Fifteen) describes how to balance the often competing priorities of marketing and operations management.
- Valarie A. Zeithaml (Chapter Sixteen) shows how marketing, operations management, and human resources management need to be integrated to develop and deliver realistic service quality communications to customers.
- Richard B. Chase and Deborah L. Kellogg (Chapter Seventeen) close by overviewing the present state of knowledge about service management effectiveness. They provide suggestions for building on this knowledge base in the future.

Acknowledgments

We would like to acknowledge the work of our academic colleagues who are not included in this volume but who have tackled issues of service management effectiveness in recent years. Any listing of them would be inherently incomplete, but certainly deserving of mention are: Leonard L. Berry, Texas A&M University; Stephen Brown, Arizona State University; Christopher Hart, Harvard University; John Haywood-Farmer,

University of Western Ontario; Robert Johnston, University of Warwick (England); Eric Langeard, Universite d'Aix-Marseille (France); Vince Mabert, Indiana University; David I. Maister, private consultant; Newton Margulies, University of California, Irvine; A. "Parsu" Parasuraman, Texas A&M University; Anat Rafaeli, Hebrew University of Jerusalem; Aleda Roth, Duke University; Roger W. Schmenner, Indiana University; and G. Lynn Shostack, Coveport Group, Inc.

David Bowen would like to thank Benjamin Schneider for getting him interested in service when they were together at Michigan State University. Schneider has led the way in showing how organizational work conditions not only affect employees but spill over to affect customers as well. He remains a terrific colleague and friend. Bowen also wishes to thank Gareth Jones, Texas A&M University, and Caren Siehl, INSEAD, for stimulating his thinking about service, organizational behavior, and the quality of life.

Richard Chase would like to thank Ted Levitt for setting the stage for service operations in his famous "McDonald's hamburger" article (a description that he hates but with which he is nonetheless stuck), Earl Sasser for building the first data base on services through his case writing, and the late James D. Thompson for providing the powerful concept of the technical core, around which much of Chase's work has been drawn.

Thomas Cummings would like to thank Eric Trist, who showed that there is "organizational choice" in designing both manufacturing and service work, and Edward E. Lawler III for showing the critical link between employee involvement and service management effectiveness.

Los Angeles, California   David E. Bowen
March 1990   Richard B. Chase
      Thomas G. Cummings

The Authors

David E. Bowen is associate professor of management and organization in the School of Business Administration at the University of Southern California. He received his B.A. degree (1973) from Alma College in political science, his M.B.A. degree (1977) from Michigan State University, and his Ph.D. degree (1983) from Michigan State University in business administration. Bowen's main research activities have been in the human resource management practices of service organizations, the socialization of customers, and service-oriented manufacturing. In 1988, he was designated an Ascendant Scholar of the Western Academy of Management for his work on service. His recent publications in the service area include *A Framework for Analyzing Customer Service Orientations in Manufacturing* (1989, with C. Siehl and B. Schneider), *Organization and Customer: Managing Design and Coordination of Services* (1989, with R. Larsson), and *The Interdisciplinary Study of Service: Some Progress, Some Prospects* (1990).

Richard B. Chase is professor of operations management and director of the Center for Operations Management, Education and Research in the School of Business Administration at the University of Southern California. He received his B.S. degree (1962), his M.B.A. degree (1963), and his Ph.D. degree (1966), all from the University of California, Los Angeles, in business administration. Chase's main research activities have been in service system design, service quality, and service-based manufacturing strategy. His experience with quality includes being an examiner for the Malcolm Baldrige National Quality award. In 1985 he was elected a Fellow in the Academy of Management and in 1987 he was elected a Fellow in the Decision Sciences Institute. Chase's books include *Management: A Life Cycle Approach* (1983, with others) and *Production and Operations Management: A Life Cycle Approach* (5th ed., 1989, with N. J. Aquilano). Other publications include "Where Does the Customer Fit in a Service Operation?" (1978), "The Customer Contact Model for Organization Design" (1983, with D. A. Tansik), and "The Service Factory" (1989, with D. A. Garvin). Chase was visiting professor of production and operations management at the Harvard Business School in 1988–89 and is on the editorial boards of five journals, including *Management Science, Journal of Operations and Production Management*, and *Decision Sciences*.

Thomas G. Cummings is professor of management and organization in the School of Business Administration at the University of Southern California. He received his B.S. degree (1966) in agricultural economics and his M.B.A. degree (1967), both from Cornell University. He received his Ph.D. degree (1970) from the University of California, Los Angeles, in business administration. Cummings's main research activities have been in designing high-performing organizations, planned organizational change, and transorganizational systems. His most recent books include *Large-Scale Organizational Change* (1989, with others), *Organization Development and Change* (4th ed., 1989, with E. Huse), and *Self-Designing Organizations* (forthcoming, with S. Mohrman). Other publications include "Managing Organizational Decline: The Case for Transorganizational Systems" (1983, with J. Blumenthal and L. Greiner) and "Future Directions in Socio-Technical Systems Theory and Research" (1987). Cummings is associate editor of the *Journal of Organizational Behavior* and is on the editorial boards of *Academy of Management Review, Consultation*, and the *Journal of Organizational Change Management*.

John E. G. Bateson is senior lecturer in marketing and Ernst and Whinney Research Fellow at the London Business School and a principal of the MAC Consulting Group. He received his B.S. degree (1970) from Imperial College in chemistry, his M.B.A. degree (1972) from the London Business School, and his D.B.A. degree (1980) from the Harvard Business School. Bateson was previously marketing manager with Philips Industries, Ltd., and brand manager with Lever Brothers. In 1984 he was visiting associate professor at the Stanford Business School. He has published extensively on services marketing and in the *Journal of Marketing Research and Marketing Science*. He is author of *Marketing Public Transit* (1988) and *Managing Services Marketing* (1989).

David A. Collier is a member of the faculty of management science at The Ohio State University. He received his B.S. degree (1970) from the University of Kentucky in mechanical engineering, his M.B.A. degree (1972) from the University of Kentucky, and his Ph.D. degree (1978) from The Ohio State University in operations management. Collier has taught in the Fuqua School of Business at Duke University, in the Colgate Darden Graduate School of Business at the University of Virginia, and in numerous executive management programs. He has received several awards for outstanding journal articles; more recently, he has been awarded major grants to study service quality. He is president of Service Management Systems, Inc., which specializes in management education and consulting for organizations that provide services. Collier is author of *Service Management: The Automation of Services* (1985) and *Service Management: Operating Decisions* (1987).

John A. Czepiel is associate professor of marketing in the Graduate School of Business Administration at New York University. He received his B.S. degree (1964) from the Illinois Institute of

Technology in business and economics. His M.S. degree (1972) in management and his Ph.D. degree (1972) in marketing are both from Northwestern University. Czepiel has been an active researcher in services marketing and is particularly interested in the social processes that underlie marketplace behavior.

Tim R. V. Davis is associate professor of management at Cleveland State University. He received his B.A. degree (1974) from Bowling Green State University in behavioral sciences. His M.A. degree (1975) in management and organizational communication and his Ph.D. degree (1978) in business administration, management, personnel, and labor relations are both from the University of Nebraska. Davis is on the editorial boards of *Organizational Dynamics* and *The Academy of Management Executive*. Author of numerous articles and book chapters, he is conducting research on various aspects of service management.

James A. Fitzsimmons is William H. Seay centennial professor of business at the University of Texas. He received his B.S.E. degree (1960) from the University of Michigan in industrial engineering, his M.B.A. degree (1965) from Western Michigan University, and his Ph.D. degree (1970) from the University of California, Los Angeles, in operations management. His principal research interest is in the area of service operations management. As a registered, professional industrial engineer, Fitzsimmons has held positions at Corning Glass Works and Hughes Aircraft Company. He is associate editor of *Management Science* and coauthor of a widely adopted text, *Service Operations Management* (1982). Fitzsimmons has published extensively in journals such as *Management Science, Socio-Economic Planning Sciences, Journal of Operations Management*, and *Interfaces*.

William E. Fulmer is Floyd Gottwald Professor of Business Administration at the William and Mary Graduate School of Business Administration. Previously he was visiting professor at Harvard University's Graduate School of Business and professor of business administration in the Colgate Darden Graduate School of Business Administration of the University of Virginia.

Fulmer received his B.A. degree (1967) from David Lipscomb College in business and economics and his M.A. and Ph.D. degrees (1974) from the University of Pennsylvania in business and applied economics. He also holds an M.B.A. degree (1968) from Florida State University in management. He is author of *Problems in Labor Relations* (1980), *Union Organizing* (1982), and the soon-to-be-published *Strategic Management: Text and Cases*. He is also coauthor of *The Objective Selection of Supervisors* (1978, with H. R. Northrup) and *Readings in Strategic Management* (1987, with A. A. Thompson and A. J. Strickland).

Eliezer Geisler is professor of management in the College of Business and Economics at the University of Wisconsin, Whitewater. He received his B.A. degree (1970) in political science and labor economics and his M.B.A. degree (1973) from Tel Aviv University. His Ph.D. degree (1979) is from the Kellogg School of Management at Northwestern University in organizational behavior. Geisler is an honorary member of the Society for the Advancement of Management. His main research activities have been in the management of technology and innovation.

James L. Heskett is UPS Foundation Professor of Business Logistics in the Graduate School of Business Administration at Harvard University. He was formerly a member of the faculty of The Ohio State University. He received his B.A. degree (1954) from Iowa State Teachers College in business education, his M.A. degree (1958) from Stanford University, and his Ph.D. degree (1960) from Stanford University in business administration. Heskett is on the board of directors of Cardinal Distribution, Inc.; Sepratech, Inc.; and the Equitable of Iowa companies. He serves on the scientific advisory board of ISTUD, a business school in Italy, and the advisory boards of IPADE, a business school in Mexico, and INCAE, a business school in Central America. Heskett is author of *Marketing* (1976) and *Managing in the Service Economy* (1986), and coauthor of *Business Logistics* (rev. ed., 1974, with N. Glaskowsky, Jr., and R. M. Ivie) and *Logistics Strategy: Cases and Concepts* (1985, with R. Shapiro). He was on the editorial board of the *Journal of Marketing Research* for a number of years and is now a member of the editorial boards of the *Journal of Business Logistics* and the *Transportation Journal*.

Deborah L. Kellogg is a Ph.D. candidate at the University of Southern California in the field of operations management. She received her B.S. degree (1975) from Pacific Lutheran University in nursing and her M.S. degree (1985) from the University of Colorado in management science and information systems.

Christopher H. Lovelock is visiting senior lecturer in the Sloan School of Management at Massachusetts Institute of Technology, where he teaches in the Alfred P. Sloan Fellows Program. He was previously a professor in the Harvard Business School, and he has also taught at Stanford University; the University of California, Berkeley; the Wharton School of the University of Pennsylvania; and INSEAD in France. He is principal of Christopher Lovelock & Associates. Lovelock received both his M.A. degree (1962) in economics and his B.Com. degree (1963) from the University of Edinburgh. He also holds an M.B.A. degree (1969) from Harvard University and a Ph.D. degree (1973) from Stanford University in marketing. He is author or coauthor of twelve books, including *Services Marketing* (1984), *Managing Services: Marketing, Operations, and Human Resources* (1988), and *Public and Nonprofit Marketing* (1989). He is currently writing a new book on the management of service businesses. His articles have appeared in such publications as *Harvard Business Review, Business Horizons, Service Industries Journal, Journal of Marketing Research, Sloan Management Review, The Wall Street Journal,* and *Financial Times*.

Fred Luthans is George Holmes Professor of Management at the University of Nebraska. He received his B.A. degree (1961) in mathematics, his M.B.A. degree (1962), and his Ph.D. degree (1965) in management and organizational behavior all from the University of Iowa. Luthans was president of the Academy of Management in 1986 and is currently editor of *Organizational Dynamics*, consulting editor of the McGraw-Hill management series, and associate editor of *Decision Sciences*. Author or coauthor of over a dozen books and 100 articles, he currently is conducting research on the delivery of service by front-line employees in a variety of organizational settings.

Peter K. Mills is associate professor of management in the Graduate School of Business at Indiana University. He received his B.A. degree (1970) in business management and his M.B.A. degree (1971) from Long Beach State University. He received a Ph.D. degree (1978) from the University of Stockholm in business administration and a Ph.D. degree (1980) from the University of California, Irvine, in organizational behavior. Mills is author of *Managing Service Industries: Organizational Practices in a Post-Industrial Economy* (1986), and he continues to do research in this area. He has published articles in such journals as the *Academy of Management Journal, Academy of Management Review, Journal of Management,* and *Human Relations and Organization Dynamics.*

Dennis J. Moberg is associate professor of management in the Leavey School of Business and Administration at Santa Clara University. He received his B.S. degree (1966) from the University of Wisconsin, Madison, in chemistry, his M.B.A. degree (1968) from the University of South Dakota, and his D.B.A. degree (1975) from the University of Southern California in management. His main research activities are in the area of the ethics of intraorganizational influence. He is a Fellow of the Center for Applied Ethics at Santa Clara University. Moberg's books include *Interactive Cases in Organizational Behavior* (1988) and *Interactive Cases in Management* (1989) (both with D. Caldwell).

Penny C. Paquette is research associate for James Brian Quinn in the Amos Tuck School of Business Administration at Dartmouth College. She received her B.A. degree (1970) from Smith College in history and her M.B.A. degree (1976) from the Amos Tuck School of Business Administration. Paquette is coauthor of the instructor's manual for *The Strategy Process* (1988), a business policy textbook, and of recent articles in *Scientific American* and *Sloan Management Review.*

James Brian Quinn is William and Josephine Buchanan Professor of Management in the Amos Tuck School of Business Administration at Dartmouth College. He holds a B.S. degree (1949) from Yale University in engineering, an M.B.A. degree (1951) from Harvard University, and a Ph.D. degree (1958) from Columbia University in economics. Quinn is an authority in the fields of strategic planning, the management of technological change, and entrepreneurial innovation. His current research is centered around technology and the service sector. He is chairman of the National Academy of Engineering's Committee on Impacts of Technology in the Service Sector.

Dorothy I. Riddle is professor at the Centre for International Business Studies at Dalhousie University, Halifax, Nova Scotia. She is president of International Services Institute, Inc., a member of the Services World Forum, and on the editorial board of the *Journal of Services Marketing*. She received her B.A. degree (1964) from the University of Colorado in psychology, her Ph.D. degree (1968) from Duke University in psychology, and her M.B.A. degree (1981) from the University of Arizona.

Albert H. Rubenstein is Walter P. Murphy Professor of Industrial Engineering and Management Sciences at Northwestern University, where he established and heads the Organization Theory Area and the Program of Research on the Management of Research and Development. He is also director of the Master of Engineering Management program and the Center for Information and Telecommunication Technology. Rubenstein received his B.S. degree (1949) from Lehigh University and his M.S. degree (1950) and his Ph.D. degree (1954) from Columbia University, all in industrial engineering. He has been on the industrial engineering staff at Columbia University and on the faculty of the School of Industrial Management at Massachusetts Institute of Technology. He is president of International Applied Science and Technology Associates, Inc. He was editor of *I.E.E.E. Transactions on Engineering Management* from 1960 through 1985. Rubenstein is author of over 150 articles on research and technology management, organization theory, and the innovation process.

W. Earl Sasser is professor at Harvard Business School, where he is chairman of the M.B.A. program and teaches "Decisionmaking and Ethical Values" in the first-year segment of the M.B.A. program and "Service Management" in the second-year segment. He developed the school's first course on the management of service operations. Sasser received his B.A. degree (1965) from Duke University in mathematics, his M.B.A. degree (1967) from the University of North Carolina, and his Ph.D. degree (1969) from Duke University in economics. With his colleague Daryl Wyckoff, Sasser has coauthored several books in the field of service management. He is currently involved with James L. Heskett and Christopher Hart in a course development and research project on a variety of topics of relevance to service managers, including service quality and productivity.

Benjamin Schneider is professor of psychology and of business management at the University of Maryland, College Park. He received his B.A. degree (1960) from Alfred University in psychology and business administration, his M.B.A. degree (1962) from the Baruch School of the University of the City of New York, and his Ph.D. degree (1967) from the University of Maryland, College Park, in industrial and social psychology. Schneider's professional experience includes a faculty position at Yale University, a Fulbright to Israel, and a chaired professorship at Michigan State University. He has been president of both the Organizational Behavior Division of the Academy of Management and the Society for Industrial and Organizational Psychology. He is author of more than seventy articles and book chapters, as well as four books. Schneider is vice-president of Organizational and Personnel Research, Inc., a consulting firm that specializes in the design and implementation of human resource approaches to organizational effectiveness.

David A. Tansik is associate professor of management and policy in the Karl Eller Graduate School of Management at the University of Arizona, where he is also faculty coordinator for executive programs. He is on the editorial board of, and book review editor for, the *Journal of Technology Transfer*. Tansik received his B.B.A. degree (1965) from the University of Texas, Austin, in personnel administration, his M.A. degree (1968) in sociology and his Ph.D. degree (1970) in organization theory from Northwestern University.

Valarie A. Zeithaml is associate professor in the Fuqua School of Business at Duke University and was previously on the faculty at Texas A&M University. She received her B.A. degree (1970) from Gettysburg College in psychology, and her M.B.A. degree (1977) and her Ph.D. degree (1980) from the University of Maryland. She has taught advertising and marketing for over ten years and has received several distinguished teaching awards. Zeithaml formerly was account executive for Torrieri-Meyers Advertising. She received the 1981 Consumer Research Award from the *Journal of Consumer Research* for the best interdisciplinary manuscript on consumer behavior written from a doctoral dissertation. Her articles have appeared in the *Journal of Consumer Research*, *Journal of Marketing*, *Journal of Consumer Affairs*, *Journal of Retailing*, and *Management Accounting*. Zeithaml serves on the editorial review board of the *Journal of Marketing* and the *Journal of Consumer Research*.

SERVICE
MANAGEMENT
EFFECTIVENESS

1

Suppose We Took Service Seriously?

David E. Bowen
Thomas G. Cummings

"Using industrial models to manage service-based corporations makes as little sense as using farm models to run factories" (Davis, 1983). Davis's viewpoint suggests two questions worth considering at the outset of a book on service management effectiveness. First, is service important enough to warrant spending time developing models of service management effec-tiveness, whatever their form? Second, are service businesses different enough from manufacturing businesses that the two really require different models of management?

The Importance of Service

Harold J. Leavitt once posed the question "Suppose we took groups seriously?" to get people thinking about the idea of groups replacing individuals as the basic building blocks of organizations. In the same spirit, a case can be made that services should replace products as the basic building blocks in management thought and practice — or, at a minimum, that they should be taken more seriously. According to Bureau of Economic Analysis data (Bureau of Economic Analysis, 1988), the service sector in 1988 accounted for 72 percent of gross national product (GNP) and 76 percent of employment in the United

1

States. These figures actually understate the full amount of service economic activity, as Quinn and Paquette report in Chapter Four of this volume. If performed within manufacturing firms, services such as product design, research and development (R&D), market research, accounting, and data processing are captured as manufacturing costs. Alarming in light of this is the reminder from Luthans and Davis (Chapter Eight) that most reports still indicate that the productivity of the service sector is poor (see, for example, Chipello, 1988; Clark, 1986). Concern has been expressed that service in the United States is experiencing the same decline in quality that has plagued manufacturing over the last few decades (Quinn and Gagnon, 1986).

The evidence indicates that good service enhances bottom-line returns. Benjamin Schneider's research on climate for service in a chain of private-sector medical supply stores showed that it was significantly related to unit profitability (Moeller and Schneider, 1986); significant relationships have also been found between dimensions of climate for service and indices of unit effectiveness in financial sales and customer satisfaction in university teaching (Moeller, Schneider, Schoorman, and Berney, 1988). And a significant positive relationship has been found between bank-branch customers and employees' perceptions of service quality and their intentions to remain with the service organization (Parkington and Schneider, 1979; Schneider, 1973).

Service pays in manufacturing as well. This is clear in the profit impact of market strategy (PIMS) data collected by the Strategic Planning Institute of Cambridge, Massachusetts (Buzzell and Gale, 1987). The data come from tens of thousands of product lines in industries around the world. Among the findings are that sustainable market share is related most clearly to perceived product or service quality and that those organizations rated above average on service charged an average of 9 to 10 percent more for their basic products and services than those rated below average. Furthermore, market share for the above-average organizations grew by 6 percent a year; it declined by 2 percent a year for the below-average firms. Finally, the above-average companies had an average return on sales of 12 percent, compared to 1 percent for the below-average firms.

Techniques for implementing a service orientation in manufacturing are appearing in both the popular media and academic publications. Heskett (1987) has elaborated how a "service vision" and the requirements of implementing it can be usefully applied in manufacturing; Chase and Erikson (1988) and Chase and Garvin (1989) have described the workings of what they termed a "service factory" in which the factory creates direct links with the customer to compete through service. Bowen, Siehl, and Schneider (1989) provide a "framework for analyzing customer-service orientations in manufacturing," describing the configuration of strategic choices, organizational arrangements, and customer-service activities necessary to infuse a service mentality within a manufacturing organization.

The service and manufacturing sectors continue to learn from one another. In the 1970s, Levitt provided descriptions of how to apply manufacturing logic and techniques to service organizations in the form of the "production line approach to service" (Levitt, 1972) and "the industrialization of service" (Levitt, 1976). More recent articles describe how to apply service logic and techniques to manufacturing organizations. And now we are seeing descriptions of how to apply contemporary manufacturing operations techniques such as just-in-time (JIT) and Taguchi methods to service organizations. The transferability of technologies across service and manufacturing sectors is discussed by Quinn and Paquette in Chapter Four.

The futurists tell us that intangibles will be the primary source of value added in the new economy (Davis, 1987). With "hollow" corporations (those that contract out their goods-producing functions), knowledge industries, sophisticated product technologies, and so on dominating the new economy, service intangibles will increasingly become a competitive arena.

This overview underscores the need to take services seriously. We now turn our attention to the question of whether services need to be managed differently than products.

The Unique Nature of Service

In *The Coming of Post-Industrial Society*, Bell (1973) uses the metaphor of a game to describe how the nature of work has changed as the economy has evolved. Work was initially a "game against nature" in which brawn and energy were the skills required to work the land and sea. Next came a "game against fabricated nature," in which efficiency and organization were used to produce a stream of goods from people and machines. This was followed by the emergence of a services-dominated postindustrial economy in which work became a "game between persons"—between teacher and student, bureaucrat and client, hotel clerk and guest—in which interpersonal skills must supplement technical skills if the game is to be played well.

The nature of work in the services game differs from that in manufacturing in terms of both *what* is exchanged—services versus goods—and *how* exchange typically occurs—the roles played by the organization and the customers in production and consumption. These differences can be summarized in terms of three defining attributes of service listed by Bowen and Schneider (1988), who drew on the pioneering efforts of authors in a number of disciplines (for example, Chase, 1978; Bateson, 1977; Lovelock, 1981; Schneider, 1973). These are presented as "prototypical" differences in the sense that one can best understand them by thinking of a relatively pure example of services, such as professional services, at one extreme and long-linked mass manufacturers at the other extreme.

The first defining attribute of services is that they tend to be intangible. Services are experiences that are rendered, while products are objects that are possessed. Intangibility makes it difficult for management, employees, and customers to assess service output and service quality. Consequently, an organization's overall "climate for service," the atmospherics or feel of the setting, is very important in shaping both customers' and frontline employees' attitudes about the process and outcome of service delivery.

The second defining attribute is that services tend to be produced and consumed simultaneously. There typically are no intermediate distribution linkages between the production of a service and its consumption by a customer. Particularly in labor-intensive services, quality is created during the service encounter between service provider and customer. This simultaneity complicates the process of managing the supply of and demand for services. It also transforms low-level, often low-paid, customer-contact personnel, such as bank tellers and hotel clerks, into key factors in a company's overall effectiveness. These personnel often carry out management, operations, and marketing functions as they do their jobs.

The third defining attribute is that customers tend to participate in the production and delivery of the services they consume. Service customers often act as producers as well as consumers. They act as "coproducers" of their service when they describe their symptoms to the doctor and then take their medicine as prescribed or when they fill their own shopping carts and then unload them for checkout by the grocery clerk. Service customers can even be "sole producers" when they use coin-operated car washes and assorted automated teller machine options. It is because customers perform these tasks that they have been labeled as "partial employees" of the service organization (Mills, Chase, and Margulies, 1983) or as part of the "human resources" mix of the service organization (Bowen, 1986). The participation of the customer in the service operation makes it difficult to maximize the efficiency of the operation or to provide a consistent offering over time and across customers. When customers act as producers, service managers must control both employee and customer behavior in order to operate effectively.

Although these three defining attributes of service help to illustrate how the services game differs from the manufacturing game, they offer only a glimpse of some of the many differences. More comprehensive treatments are presented elsewhere (for example, Bowen and Schneider, 1988; Bateson, 1989; Lovelock, 1988; Heskett, 1986; Zeithaml, Parasuraman, and Berry, 1985; Riddle, 1986; Mills, 1986). Even this brief overview, however, suggests the unique appearance in service of management issues in a number of areas: (1) corporate strategy and such issues as how competitive advantage is gained in the exchange of intangibles in the marketplace; (2) organization design and human resources and such issues as what human resource practices create favorable climates for service; (3) operations management and such issues as how to personalize service production and delivery without compromising operations efficiency; and (4) marketing and such issues as how to balance the differing orientations of marketing and operations toward the on-site customer.

Service Management Effectiveness: An Interdisciplinary Perspective

The chapters that follow further develop the ways that the differences between services and goods must be reflected in how service businesses formulate and implement business strategy, organize themselves, manage their operations and human resources, and market their offerings. The chapters present and integrate the work of leading service management experts from a variety of disciplines in order to stimulate theory building and research on service management effectiveness across disciplines. A common starting point for all contributors is the theme expressed in Davis's statement quoted at the beginning of this chapter — that management models developed for manufacturing cannot be extended to services without substantial modification. It *is* time to start taking service seriously. The authors offer theory- and research-based direction to the sophisticated practitioner concerned with service management issues and effectiveness.

One reason an interdisciplinary perspective is provided in these chapters is the fact that functional integration is so essential for managing service organizations effectively. Figure 1.1 is provided to highlight this perspective. Although we are applying this framework to *service* organizations, functional integration is a desirable feature of manufacturing organizations as well. Service organizations are particularly dependent on functional integration, however. For example, customer contact personnel not only produce the service but are also directly

Figure 1.1. Service Management Effectiveness:
An Interdisciplinary Perspective.

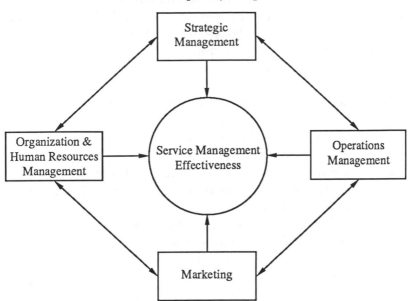

involved in marketing it. In turn, marketing services is very much a human resource activity, because the quality of the selection and training of services personnel spills over to affect customers' perceptions of the quality of the service they receive. These are some of the reasons why much of the published work on service emphasizes the need for all levels and functions of the organization to collaborate in achieving service quality.

This book embodies the theme of functional integration by presenting contributions from the various disciplines associated with each function—strategy, organization and human resources, operations management, and marketing. Each contributor was encouraged to address how his or her own area interacts with other areas. The authors were also encouraged to present their message at a level that would be meaningful to both an academic and a practitioner audience. The result is a set of chapters that overview state-of-the-art thinking about service management effectiveness in each of the academic disciplines and also provide numerous examples from such companies as Federal Express, Humana, ADP Services, Ford Motor Company, IBM, McDonald's, SAS Airlines, American Airlines, Ramada Inns, and Seattle Metro. Following is a brief overview of each chapter by discipline or function.

Strategy. In Chapter Two, "Rethinking Strategy for Service Management," James L. Heskett reviews and integrates previous work about strategy formulation for service firms and suggests dimensions on which future management planning and research should focus. He makes the important observation that services are inherently multifunctional and that consequently we need a strategic, as opposed to a functional, orientation for managing and studying service business.

Dorothy I. Riddle addresses "Key Strategic Decisions for Service Firms" in Chapter Three. She shows that strategic decision making in service organizations needs to go beyond concerns about external growth or markets to include strategic issues related to the design of the service, the internal service system, and internal capacity constraints. Making these strategic decisions needs to be an interactive process, including personnel from operations, human resource management, marketing, and strategic planning.

In Chapter Four, "Service Technologies: Key Factors in Manufacturing Strategy," James Brian Quinn and Penny C. Paquette discuss the role of service technologies in the economy and show how the services and manufacturing sectors mutually influence each other. They provide numerous examples of how service technologies can significantly enhance manufacturing and marketing performance and how manufacturing can become a service provider.

Organization and Human Resource Management. Peter K. Mills and Dennis J. Moberg discuss "Strategic Implications of Service Technologies" in Chapter Five. Writing from an organization-theory perspective that serves to bridge the marketing and operations points of view, they develop the relationship between the unique nature of service technologies and the strategic options available to service organizations. A central focus is on the social, relational aspect of these technologies and the differing roles that customers play within them.

In Chapter Six, "Alternative Strategies for Creating Service-Oriented Organizations," Benjamin Schneider describes how an organization can become more service oriented. He presents case studies of two organizations' very different approaches to becoming more service oriented and presents selection and training approaches that support a service orientation. Schneider integrates the issue of changing to a service orientation with the broader, more established literature of organization development and strategic change.

David A. Tansik identifies "Managing Human Resource Issues for High-Contact Service Personnel" in Chapter Seven. He addresses the unique role of human resource management in service organizations, describing the skills, knowledge, and abilities required for customer-contact personnel in different types of services and reviewing implications for recruitment, selection, training, control and evaluation, rewarding, and development.

In Chapter Eight, "Applying Behavioral Management Techniques in Service Organizations," Fred Luthans and Tim R. V. Davis describe the use of behavioral management to produce observable improvements in service delivery by both front-office and back-office employees. They present detailed descriptions of the application of behavioral management to a variety of settings, including banking, fast food, and real estate. The authors emphasize that specific programs aimed at shaping service behaviors via their consequences (feedback and rewards) are more effective than vague attempts to improve the interpersonal skills of employees.

Operations Management. In Chapter Nine, "Creating Personalized Service Delivery Systems," W. Earl Sasser and William E. Fulmer describe how the new information and communication technologies offer significant benefits for service organizations. These new technologies typically increase the speed and reliability of service transactions and enable service firms to offer a greater range of mass-customized services with enhanced quality and efficiency.

David A. Collier discusses the important topic of "Measuring and Managing Service Quality" in Chapter Ten. He examines how managers define, measure, establish standards for, monitor and control, and evaluate quality service. Collier presents a powerful method for combining internal and external measures of service quality called a "service quality map."

In Chapter Eleven, "The Impact of Information Technologies on Service Operations," Albert H. Rubenstein and Eliezer Geisler describe a long-term program of research into the role and effectiveness of information technology in service firms. They discuss the intricacies of measuring the impact of information technology on service firms' performance and present survey data on the information-system practices of service companies. The authors argue strongly that decisions about information technology should be integrated with decisions about corporate strategy in service firms.

James A. Fitzsimmons proposes "Making Continual Improvement a Competitive Strategy for Service Firms" in Chapter Twelve. He suggests that service productivity can be improved through the process of learning and experience typically applied in manufacturing settings. He applies the Japanese technique of just-in-time inventory control to the waiting lines often seen in service firms. Focusing service personnel on waiting-line reduction can create an ongoing problem-solving climate. However, the full benefits of this technique may require supporting changes in management style and organizational structure, thus leading to a potential revolution in how work is managed and organized in service organizations.

Marketing. In Chapter Thirteen, "Managing Relationships with Customers: A Differentiating Philosophy of Marketing," John A. Czepiel emphasizes the need for service businesses to view their exchanges with customers as "relationships" rather than merely "transactions." Managing from this relational perspective involves recognizing the social as well as the economic aspects of exchange. Managing relationships is a means by which firms can strategically differentiate themselves from others; it also results in customers being not only attracted but retained as well. Czepiel also describes how firms can map their relational philosophy in terms of their "portfolio" of different types of customer relationships.

John E. G. Bateson discusses "Evaluating the Role and Place of Marketing in Service Firms" in Chapter Fourteen. He presents a contingency model of the role and place of the marketing department within a service organization, examining how different mixes of environmental characteristics, management objectives, and service technologies call for alternatives ranging from no marketing department at all to a strong, centralized marketing department. Two central themes are the tension that arises between the operations and marketing functions with increased marketplace competition and whether firms really need a marketing department per se in order to implement a marketing orientation.

In Chapter Fifteen, "Managing Interactions Between Operations and Marketing and Their Impact on Customers," Christopher H. Lovelock presents key operations management issucs, describes how different decisions on these issues may affect customers, and suggests the role that marketing can play to best deal with the situation regardless of the operational choice. He addresses ways to strike a balance between the typically opposing concerns of marketing and operations and how this balance will be struck differently under alternate corporate strategies of cost leadership, differentiation, or focus.

Valarie A. Zeithaml discusses "Communicating with Customers About Service Quality" in Chapter Sixteen. She emphasizes that accurately and effectively communicating service quality to customers requires the functionally integrated efforts of marketing, operations, human resources, and finance. She presents several research propositions around this notion in which service quality can be measured using SERVQUAL, a survey instrument that she has developed with colleagues. SERVQUAL works from a definition of service quality as the extent to which customer perceptions of service meet or exceed their expectations. This definition of service quality is used to underscore the importance of advertising only those services that operations can actually deliver—that is, marketing should not create unrealistic expectations that result in customers viewing service quality as poor.

The book concludes with Chapter Seventeen, in which Richard B. Chase and Deborah L. Kellogg assess "The State of Service Management Knowledge." Using a framework depicting different stages of knowledge development, they assess the service management field, including the contributions in this book. Although they conclude that our knowledge of service management is still in its infancy, the material in this book represents the kinds of cross-functional perspectives that are needed to advance knowledge of service management effectiveness.

References

Bateson, J.E.G. "Do We Need Services Marketing?" In P. Eiglier (ed.), *Marketing Consumer Services: New Insights.* Report no. 77-115. Cambridge, Mass.: Marketing Science Institute, 1977.

Bateson, J.E.G. *Managing Services Marketing: Text and Readings.* Chicago: Dryden Press, 1989.

Bell, D. *The Coming of Post-Industrial Society: A Venture in Social Forecasting.* New York: Basic Books, 1973.

Bowen, D. E. "Managing Customers as Human Resources in Service Organizations." *Human Resource Management,* 1986, *25,* 371–384.

Bowen, D. E., and Schneider, B. "Services Marketing and Management: Implications for Organizational Behavior." In B. M. Staw and L. L. Cummings (eds.), *Research in Organizational Behavior.* Vol. 10. Greenwich, Conn.: JAI Press, 1988.

Bowen, D. E., Siehl, C., and Schneider, B. "A Framework for Analyzing Customer Service Organizations in Manufacturing." *Academy of Management Review,* 1989, *14,* 75–95.

Bureau of Economic Analysis. "The National Income and Product Accounts of the United States." *Survey of Current Business,* July 1988, pp. 78, 81.

Buzzell, R. D., and Gale, B. T. *The PIMS Principles: Linking Strategy to Performance.* New York: Free Press, 1987.

Chase, R. B. "Where Does the Customer Fit in a Service Operation?" *Harvard Business Review*, 1978, *56* (6), 137–142.

Chase, R. B., and Erikson, W. "The Service Factory." *Academy of Management Executive*, 1988, *2*, 191–196.

Chase, R. B., and Garvin, D. A. "The Service Factory." *Harvard Business Review*, 1989, *62*, 61–69.

Chipello, C. J. "Foreign Rivals Imperil U.S. Firms' Leadership in the Service Sector." *Wall Street Journal*, Mar. 21, 1988, pp. 1, 10.

Clark, L. H. "Manufactures Grew Much More Efficient, but Employment Lags." *Wall Street Journal*, Dec. 4, 1986, p. 1.

Davis, S. M. "Management Models for the Future." *New Management*, Spring 1983, pp. 12–15.

Davis, S. M. *Future Perfect.* Reading, Mass.: Addison-Wesley, 1987.

Heskett, J. L. *Managing in the Service Economy.* Boston: Harvard Business School Press, 1986.

Heskett, J. L. "Lessons in the Service Sector." *Harvard Business Review*, 1987, *65*, 118–126.

Levitt, T. "Production-Line Approach to Service." *Harvard Business Review*, 1972, *50* (5), 41–52.

Levitt, T. "The Industrialization of Service." *Harvard Business Review*, 1976, *54*, 63–74.

Lovelock, C. H. "Why Marketing Management Needs to Be Different for Services." In J. H. Donnelly and W. R. George (eds.), *Marketing of Services.* Chicago: American Marketing Association, 1981.

Lovelock, C. H. *Managing Services: Marketing, Operations, and Human Resources.* Englewood Cliffs, N.J.: Prentice-Hall, 1988.

Mills, P. K. *Managing Service Industries: Organizational Practices in a Post-Industrial Society.* Cambridge, Mass.: Ballinger, 1986.

Mills, P. K., Chase, R. B., and Margulies, N. "Motivating the Client/Employee System as a Service Production Strategy." *Academy of Management Review*, 1983, *8*, 301–310.

Moeller, A., and Schneider, B. "Climate for Service and the Bottom Line." In M. Venkatsen, D. M. Schmalensee, and C. Marshall (eds.), *Creativity in Services Marketing.* Chicago: American Marketing Association, 1986.

Moeller, A., Schneider, B., Schoorman, F. D., and Berney, E. "Operationalization of the Katz and Kahn Subsystem Model of Unit Effectiveness: Development, Reliability, and Validity of the Work Facilitation Diagnostic." In F. D. Schoorman and B. Schneider (eds.), *Facilitating Work Effectiveness*. Lexington, Mass.: Lexington Books, 1988.

Parkington, J. J., and Schneider, B. "Some Correlates of Experienced Job Stress: A Boundary Role Study." *Academy of Management Journal*, 1979, *22*, 270–281.

Quinn, J. B., and Gagnon, C. E. "Will Services Follow Manufacturing in Decline?" *Harvard Business Review*, 1986, *64* (6), 95–105.

Riddle, D. I. *Service-Led Growth: The Role of the Service Sector in World Development*. New York: Praeger, 1986.

Schneider, B. "The Perception of Organizational Climate: The Customer's View." *Journal of Applied Psychology*, 1973, *57*, 248–256.

Zeithaml, V. A., Parasuraman, A., and Berry, L. L. "Problems and Strategies in Services Marketing." *Journal of Marketing*, 1985, *49*, 33–46.

Part One

Strategic Management in Service Firms

2

Rethinking Strategy
for Service Management

James L. Heskett

Implementing and researching strategy in the service sector are equally difficult. We have moved beyond issues such as whether strategic options are different in manufacturing and services (Shostack, 1977; Thomas, 1978; Bateson, 1979; Berry, 1980; Enis and Roering, 1981) without fully comprehending the significance of such differences. Given this as well as the growing body of well-documented practice and research, it is perhaps appropriate to explore types of efforts that may be most fruitful in examining and implementing strategies in the service industries. The purposes of this chapter therefore are to synthesize previous work about strategy formulation for service enterprises, underline the need for new ways of thinking about services, and suggest dimensions around which future management planning and research may usefully be centered.

Efforts to Delineate Services

A number of efforts have been made to establish taxonomies of importance for strategic decision making as well as to differentiate services from other types of endeavor. These go back at least as far as Adam Smith ([1776] 1977), who established the taxonomy, for purposes of economic analysis, of productive

17

activities (creating tangible product) and nonproductive activities (creating intangible services) and along with it a stigma
that has attached itself to services to the present day. Clark
(1940), in a landmark work setting forth stages in the transition
of economies, described sectors of economies as primary (ex-
tractive), secondary (manufacturing), and tertiary (services).
Gersuny and Rosengren (1973) further divided the tertiary sector into three parts, consisting of quasi-domestic services (food
and lodging), whether performed in the home or elsewhere;
business services; and a "quinary" group including recreation,
health care, and education, in which a central purpose is to
involve and improve the customer. Fuchs's early analysis of the
service economy, which seems somewhat superficial in view of
subsequent thinking on the subject, declared "that most of the
industries in it are manned by white-collar workers, that most of
the industries are labor intensive, that most deal with the consumer, and that nearly all of them produce an intangible product" (Fuchs, 1969, p. 16). Perhaps the most remarkable aspect of
this comment is that it was advanced barely two decades ago.

Since then, efforts have been made to counter sweeping
generalizations that, for example, all or most services are
people-intensive, require lower levels of capital than other types
of business (and thus are attractive as start-ups by poorly cap-
italized entrepreneurs), involve higher value added than manufacturing activities, are a drag on productivity in developed
economies, and are homogeneous in most respects. Information presented in Table 2.1 suggests the importance of laying
these assumptions to rest. The table presents basic profit models
for the largest firms in each of several types of service and
manufacturing industries and suggests that on many important
dimensions there is greater diversity among the service than
among the manufacturing industries. Further, there is no pattern other than extreme diversity that distinguishes service industries from manufacturing industries in general on any one
of these dimensions. This should emphasize the importance of
understanding basic profit models for a particular industry.
Managers take this for granted. And researchers must as well,
especially if the orientation of their research crosses service

Table 2.1. Profit Models for the Five Largest Firms in Selected Service and Manufacturing Industries, 1987.

Industry	$\dfrac{Revenues}{Assets}$	×	$\dfrac{Profit}{Revenues}$	×	$\dfrac{Assets}{Equity}$	=	$\dfrac{Profit}{Equity}$	Revenues per Employee
Service sector								
Retailing	1.25		2.2%		4.8		13.0%	$ 95,000
Wholesaling	4.53		1.0%		3.0		13.1%	$376,000
Air transport	.99		0.7%		4.3		2.9%	$121,000
Highway transport	1.71		1.9%		2.5		8.0%	$ 72,000
Electric utilities	.32		12.9%		2.8		11.5%	$269,000
Telephone communications	.48		10.9%		2.6		13.7%	$115,000
Medical	.82		2.4%		3.5		6.8%	$ 47,000
Broadcasting/entertainment	.80		10.1%		2.5		19.6%	$176,000
Diversified financial services	.16		3.5%		22.8		12.7%	$366,000
Manufacturing sector								
Food	2.18		3.3%		2.9		20.6%	$164,000
Aerospace	1.34		3.9%		2.8		14.3%	$104,000
Pharmaceuticals	1.02		12.2%		1.9		24.0%	$119,000
Chemicals	1.00		8.1%		2.0		16.4%	$195,000
Automotive	1.32		4.7%		2.6		16.1%	$155,000
Computers	.92		9.2%		1.7		14.3%	$118,000
Forest/paper products	1.03		6.1%		2.1		13.5%	$168,000
Textiles	1.49		3.6%		2.1		11.1%	$ 73,000
Petroleum[a]	.96		4.8%		2.2		10.3%	$571,000

[a] Excluding Texaco, the third largest petroleum company, which reported very heavy losses in 1987.
Sources: Adapted from "The Fortune 500," 1988; "The Service 500," 1988.

industry boundaries. This understanding is the basis for developing competitive strategy and positioning a firm in relation to its customers and competitors. It is the basis for determining, for example, whether superior performance will be achieved by doing the same things that competitors do better than they do them or by attempting to be as different as possible from competitors on important dimensions.

More recent efforts have attempted to delineate characteristics of service endeavors that set them apart both from manufacturing and from each other. It is important to remind ourselves that the focus of this effort is on understanding differences in strategic options, as opposed to the process of strategy formulation, which is presumed to have more general application across industries and economic sectors. Both Judd (1964) and Rathmell (1974) pointed out for us the importance of redefining services for purposes of both practicing and researching strategy delineation. But neither offered more than general guidelines. Shostack (1977) ushered in what might be termed the modern era of service delineation with her suggestion that various services be categorized for study and practice in terms of the proportion of physical goods and intangible services that each product package might contain. Hill (1977) set forth a taxonomy that is of importance particularly for understanding the impact of services on those served by suggesting that services might usefully be regarded as those that (1) affect people as opposed to goods, (2) produce permanent or temporary effects on people or things, (3) create reversible or nonreversible effects, (4) deal with physical or mental effects, and (5) involve individuals or groups of people.

Thomas (1978) suggested the value of viewing services primarily as either equipment-based or people-based. Chase (1978) emphasized the importance of determining the significance of customer contact in the delivery process in order to take advantage of opportunities to divorce customer-contact functions from processing functions to achieve advantages of functional "buffering" often enjoyed by manufacturing firms. Kotler (1980), in addition to echoing earlier statements, suggested that services could usefully be delineated in terms of the degree to which they meet personal or business needs, are public or private, and are for-profit or nonprofit.

Lovelock (1980) developed the first of several matrix schemes whereby various characteristics might be arrayed against each other when he proposed categorizing services by (1) basic demand characteristics, such as service to people or property, demand-supply relationships, and whether relationships with customers are discrete or continuous; (2) the nature of the service and its benefits, including the relative importance of goods or physical service in the package, whether a service is made up of a bundle of features, and the timing and duration of benefits; and (3) service delivery procedures, including the need for multisite delivery, methods of allocating capacity, the necessity of customer presence during service delivery, the extent to which transactions are time-defined as opposed to task-defined, and whether consumption is independent or collective.

A simple matrix that has become particularly useful in explaining differences in approaches to a wide array of policies ranging from the design of the service delivery system to the selection and development of service employees is one that links the degree of customer contact with the degree of customization of the product in a service setting (Maister and Lovelock, 1982). Lovelock (1984) has expanded this approach with a series of matrices linking (1) direct recipients of services (people or things) with the degree to which the service act involves tangible or intangible actions; (2) the degree to which customers enjoy a "membership" relationship with the service provider with whether service delivery is continuous over time or discrete; (3) the extent to which demand fluctuates over time with the degree to which peak demands can be met; and (4) whether service is delivered through multiple or single sites with the nature of the interaction between the customer and the service organization, expressed in terms of the physical effort that each must expend to consummate the service. In addition, cross-functional relationships linking marketing and operations have been addressed specifically by Chase (1985). While matrix representations have serious limitations, they have helped us begin to comprehend the nature of at least some simple relationships underlying various services.

Research concerning customer behavior in the purchase of services has begun to yield additional insights of importance for strategy formulation. Zeithaml (1981), extending the ideas of Nelson (1970) and Darby and Karni (1973), has suggested that if one regards products and services as possessing search qualities (which a customer can determine prior to purchase), experience qualities (which can be determined only after purchase), and credence qualities (which a customer cannot determine, even after purchase and use), services generally possess higher proportions of credence qualities than do products. As a result, Zeithaml has hypothesized higher perceived risks for customers and related phenomena in the purchase of services as opposed to goods that have served to lend direction to research on the subject.

There are several curious features of this body of work, which has been carried out primarily to understand important characteristics of services. First, most of it has been done under one functional banner or another, with a particular concentration on marketing, operations, or human behavior. At the same time, journals fostering cross-functional thought on strategy, such as the *Journal of Business Strategy*, contain precious little of this kind of work. This is of special note for a sector of economic activity that is distinguished from manufacturing activity in part by the inability to define a marketing or an operations strategy per se, given the inability to buffer one function from another in many service industries. It is hard to find a management policy in services that does not cross functional lines, which suggests the difficulty of approaching questions of strategy in service firms from a purely functional perspective.

Second, the work itself suggests the large number of variables associated with performance in a typical service firm. This represents a daunting challenge to research on service strategy. It has led researchers to develop a base from which they can work in venturing into the murky waters of the more holistic service firm. Thus, we see recent work centered around industries (Roth and Van der Velde, 1988); important events in the service delivery process (Czepiel, Solomon, and Surprenant, 1985; Collier, 1989); problems of particular importance for service firms, such as the management of quality (Berry, Bennett, and Brown, 1988); the design of the service delivery process (Shostack, 1987); the players in the service encounter (Parkington and Schneider, 1979; Hochschild, 1983; Schneider and Bowen, 1985; Johnson and Seymour, 1985); and methods that have a high impact on more than one function of the firm (Sasser, 1987; Hart, 1988).

Third, consideration of issues of finance and control has been strangely lacking in efforts to understand the makeup of service industries. And yet these are at the very heart of some of our measurement problems in many service firms. Dearden (1978) states the nature of the problem most clearly by pointing out that in services in which joint costs predominate, profit measurements are highly difficult and questionable. Thomas (1978) and, more recently, Johnson and Kaplan (1987) have raised the same issue. Without reliable measures of profit, the outcomes of strategic actions become hard to determine. This is of particular importance in asset-intensive service industries in which two or more well-defined services draw on the same set of assets. There are indications that services are becoming more asset-intensive, with Roach (1988) estimating, for example, that the amount of capital invested in high-technology (especially computing and communication) equipment per information worker tripled between 1970 and 1986 and now exceeds that for workers in basic industrial activities. For example, rather than try to measure the margins of its consumer information and its network services, which draw on the same central computing and network facilities, CompuServe, Inc., tries to price its products to achieve balanced around-the-clock usage and maximum capacity utilization of its resources. This type of behavior has considerable significance for the study of strategy in asset-intensive service firms.

Among the finance issues of great importance (but given relatively short shrift in the strategic literature) are those of ownership of assets as opposed to contracting or franchising, particularly in multisite services in which physical assets play a major role.

Finally, there is a strange absence of any reference to the role of information in the strategic mix of services that we have attempted to categorize. In services in general, the "product" contains a higher information content than do manufactures. And many make much more intensive use of information in the process of service creation, particularly where it is important to anticipate customers' needs as a means of minimizing investment in fixed facilities and labor and substituting information for assets. Cleveland (1985) suggests the importance of this oversight by pointing out that organizations that deal in information as opposed to products have an entirely different mind set concerning strategy. This is directly traceable to the differences between information and goods. Information is expandable without any obvious limits; compressible into summaries for easier handling; substitutable for capital, labor, or physical materials; transportable at least at the speed of light; diffusive and hard to contain, especially when it contains high proprietary value; and shared rather than exchanged among people, with an expansion of the total as it is shared. Goods have none of these characteristics, greatly constraining strategic options for manufacturers. The implications of these differences for strategy in service firms are of great moment and deserve more attention.

Evaluating and Formulating Strategy

Having said this, we have developed a number of criteria for the formulation and evaluation of strategy. There is reasonable agreement, for example, that effective strategies are comprehensive, not functional (Heskett, 1986); are aimed at relatively attractive market opportunities, according to the degree to which needs of significant groups of customers are not being met by existing alternatives; are focused around a customer group, a service concept, an operating strategy or process, a geographical area or specific service delivery site, or a particular group of service providers (Heskett, Sasser, and Hart, 1990);

are internally consistent in the "position" that they create in relation to customers and competitors (Shostack, 1987); develop customer switching costs that encourage loyalty; and are hard to duplicate.

While it may appear that there is little here that distinguishes strategy for services from that for manufacturers, the cross-functional intricacies of services give certain of these criteria particular importance, beginning with the caveat that strategies are not unifunctional. Practitioners instinctively know and practice this. For example, when Herbert Kelleher, CEO of Southwest Airlines, announces that he will not fly airplanes east of Cleveland, Ohio, in order to avoid the congestion of the eastern U.S. air routes and preserve the tight scheduling, high aircraft utilization, and low cost of his airline, he is describing both marketing and operations strategy (Taylor, 1988).

Positioning in relation to market opportunities and competitors' offerings of a service as opposed to a product is different primarily in terms of the dimensions on which the positioning is based. Rather than product attributes, the positioning of a service most often is based on features having more to do with tangible evidence often associated with an intangible service, such as the intensity of staffing (service), location, and the "image" of the service delivery facility in a customer's mind, as well as price. For both tangible and intangible aspects of a service, mapping (Lovelock, 1984) has been shown to be as useful for services as for products.

In addition to those providing tangible evidence to customers, a number of other dimensions on which a service strategy can be differentiated from its competition are suggested by work associated with the typing of service businesses. These dimensions include the following:

Designing the Service Product

- Providing tangible evidence for an essentially intangible service
- Customizing a typically standard service
- Standardizing a typically customized service

Managing the Customer

- Seeking ways to manage demand
- Managing customers' expectations of quality in a service
- Helping reduce customers' perceived risks associated with a service
- Involving customers in the delivery of the service
- Developing "membership" relationships with customers
- Requiring customer efforts to qualify for a service
- Seeking to either reduce or increase personal contact in the delivery of a service
- Managing loyalties between customers, servers, and the firm

Developing the Operating Strategy to Realize Sources of Leverage

- Managing the asset intensity of the business
- Emphasizing the use of technology in a people-intensive business
- Developing networks of routes, communications, or relationships
- Developing effective recovery mechanisms for service failures
- Developing methods of controlling operations without owning assets
- Substituting information for assets through information-base development
- Distinguishing regulated and nonregulated business opportunities
- Divorcing the customer from the service delivery process
- Seeking ways to inventory a service
- Managing capacity to accommodate or discourage certain types of demand
- Pricing for capacity utilization versus service-by-service profit
- Effectively using shared resources for two or more services

Integrating the Service Delivery System with the Operating Strategy

- Clustering locations to achieve market impact, advertising economies, or effective control

- Locating facilities in proximity to customers
- Designing the service delivery system as a quality-control device
- Developing low-investment alternatives to facility ownership
- Designing facilities for high customer visibility
- Emphasizing ease of supervision in facility design
- Designing the customer encounter "site" to channel customer behavior

Developing an Internal Human Resource Strategy

- Targeting groups of employees as carefully as groups of customers
- Positioning the service to meet employees' needs more effectively than do competitors
- Empowering servers within limits
- Designing support systems to help servers solve customer problems
- Eliminating unnecessary emphasis on rigid policies that interfere with the ability of servers to solve customers' problems
- Seeking to reduce the degree or improve the quality of individual judgment in the service delivery process
- Leveraging the highest and scarcest skills in the organization through supporting mechanisms
- Spending for human development versus turnover and training costs
- Developing positive incentives, such as "well pay" versus "sick pay"
- Creating opportunities for unusual levels of compensation

On each of these dimensions, it is possible to determine the location of the major competitors in relation to various concentrations of customer needs as a basis for formulating and implementing important elements of strategy.

Focus has benefited service firms in many ways. It can be centered around one or more of the five elements shown in Figure 2.1: customer (procurer), service concept (product), op-

Figure 2.1. Important Points of Focus in Service Strategies.

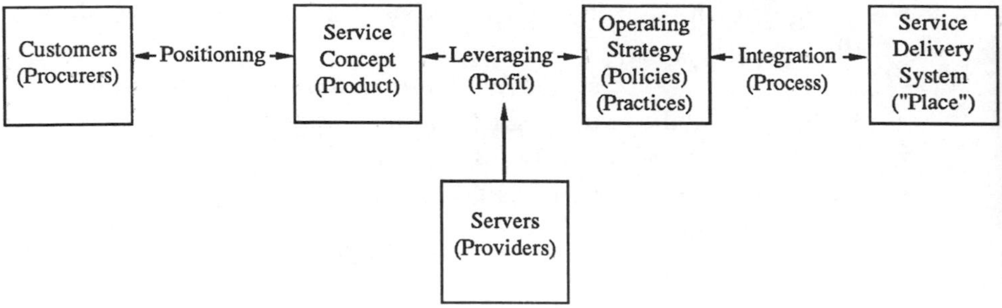

```
┌───────────┐         ┌───────────┐          ┌───────────┐          ┌───────────┐
│ Customers │←Positioning→│ Service │←Leveraging→│ Operating │←Integration→│  Service  │
│(Procurers)│         │  Concept  │ (Profit)   │  Strategy │ (Process)  │ Delivery  │
│           │         │ (Product) │            │ (Policies)│            │  System   │
│           │         │           │            │(Practices)│            │ ("Place") │
└───────────┘         └───────────┘            └───────────┘            └───────────┘
                                        ↑
                                  ┌───────────┐
                                  │  Servers  │
                                  │(Providers)│
                                  └───────────┘
```

Source: Adapted from Heskett, 1986.

erating strategy (policies and practices), service delivery system ("place"), and server (provider). Merrill Lynch developed the Cash Management Account to serve a broader range of needs of a particular targeted customer group (procurers), individuals with substantial amounts to invest. Club Med developed a focused service concept (product) designed to help its customers achieve truly carefree vacations. United Parcel Service has focused its package delivery services around an operating strategy (policies and practices) that is designed to handle only packages of up to seventy pounds. McDonald's has designed its service delivery system (place) around a combination of facilities and food preparation devices that, when combined with a limited menu, produce both acceptable quality and low cost. And the Marriott Corporation hires many of its people (providers) on the basis of their ability to work with each other and with customers. In truly effective service strategies such as these, focus is not confined to one of the five elements. This makes it particularly important that the elements of strategy are internally consistent.

Shostack (1987) has probably taken the most detailed look at the matter of internal consistency, applying it to each stage of the service delivery process. In this process, each step is assessed in terms of whether it permits customer options that are more or less divergent from a norm and whether it requires higher or lower complexity in the service delivery process. The implication here is that more highly focused services communicate to the customer a consistent message in terms of both range of choice and the level of expected customer participation in the service delivery process (with a low range of choice and significant customer participation often associated with lower levels of complexity in the service). The development of customer switching costs has to do both with the design of the service and the strategy associated with its delivery and with the way in which it is delivered. Thus, frequent-flyer programs encourage customer loyalty among airline customers. But unless the service offered is timely and the employees of the airline are competent and courteous in their delivery of the service, the customer is lost to another airline.

The ease of duplication of a service strategy, another way of stating the difficulty with which barriers to competitive entry may be fashioned, depends a great deal on the sources of leverage that are employed in its design and implementation. Significant sources of leverage, as shown in Figure 2.2, include customers themselves, servers, networks, relationships, information banks, real estate, technology, and financing. The development of these sources of leverage lies at the very heart of the strategy implementation process and requires closer examination than we have given it to date.

Sources of Competitive Leverage

Significant sources of leverage (with the possible exception of customers) are listed in the likely order of their effectiveness in discouraging successful competitive emulation in Figure 2.2. It is useful to note several aspects of this diagram, which in itself represents a hypothesis based on general experience. First, it features several sources that are of particular relevance for services as opposed to manufacturing: networks, relationships, density of business patterns, and information banks. Second, the sources of competitive leverage that are most effective in terms of the difficulty with which they can be emulated by competitors also are likely to be the hardest and most time-consuming to implement. Finally, it is perhaps surprising that

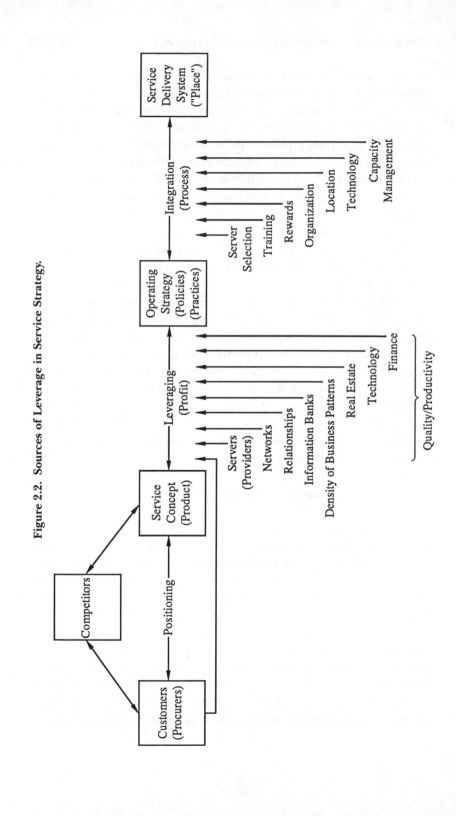

Figure 2.2. Sources of Leverage in Service Strategy.

technology and financing are outranked by so many of the other sources of leverage. It is useful to consider each in turn.

Networks take a number of forms, including operating locations linked by transport routes, reservation and communications systems, and the need to maintain a common standard of service quality. They require time and extensive investments to build. They are a substantial discouragement to would-be operators of new airlines, telephone companies, hotel chains, or other network-based services. As Eccles and Crane (1988) have pointed out, relationships are a form of network. They are of particular importance, for example, in financial and other brokered services in which the majority of employees are exposed not only to customers but also to competitors and suppliers and rely on relationships with all of them for new business, information with which to enhance service to clients, and job opportunities. Such relationships are developed over time and with proven capability to both perform and reciprocate.

Many services are composed primarily of information. They are enhanced by the development of an information bank, again often over long periods of time. For services, the information bank is the closest equivalent to the learning curve in manufacturing. The effect often is different, however. The learning curve is a concept that leads to lower costs per unit of product over time. The information bank produces services of greater value, regardless of the effect on the cost of the delivery of the service.

Density of business patterns is especially critical in influencing the economics of service businesses in which the service is taken to the customer by the provider. This is particularly true of repair and other industrially oriented services. In consumer services, the clustering of facilities, particularly in multisite service businesses such as hospitality, medicine, and entertainment, can contribute to the more cost-effective use of advertising as well as the business-building impact of repeated contact by customers with a business's facilities, leading to higher overall use of available capacity.

Real estate is of particular importance in consumer services in which the customer comes to the service site; for example, retailing, hospitality, and related services. The acquisition of the best sites can represent significant barriers to competition in these industries. Ease of acquisition grows with the success of a business, as illustrated by the close relationship between shopping mall developers and the owners of successful retail chains. Thus, the barrier to competitive entry is built over time. At times, the capacity for new sites may be exhausted, absolutely precluding entry, as several budding airline entrepreneurs who have attempted to gain access to boarding gates at the nation's crowded airports have discovered.

In relation to these sources of leverage, technology and financial capability are relatively insignificant in many nonfinancial service industries. Further, there often is little that is proprietary for significant periods of time about either of these sources, further distinguishing services from manufacturing at least in regard to the use of technology. While not true of all services, this somewhat counterintuitive conclusion may well be characteristic of many. It remains to be tested and appraised by future research.

Customers themselves are, of course, important sources of leverage in service strategies, as noted in Figure 2.2. This is particularly true when lasting relationships can be established with them, their expectations and perceived risks can be managed, and they can be encouraged to participate in the service delivery process in useful and customer-empowering ways. The permanence of this source and the resulting barrier to competition that it represents vary with the nature of the service. But we need to understand more fully its importance.

In total, these sources of leverage produce the quality and productivity achieved by leading firms. Value-enhancing quality and cost-reducing productivity create margins for profit. We do not yet sufficiently understand how these sources of leverage interact, leading us to speculate, for example, why significant recent investments by information-intensive service firms in technology have not produced expected productivity gains (Roach, 1988).

Future Directions

What purposes have efforts to study strategy formulation in service businesses served? First, they have encouraged us to think more broadly about strategic alternatives for services than merely how they might emulate "industrial" practice (Levitt, 1972, 1976), a not altogether inspiring model from the beginning of the Industrial Revolution through the era of Taylorism to the present day. They have even suggested lessons that the service sector holds for manufacturing (Heskett, 1987). Second, they have led us from a focus on particular service industries to one on cross-industry similarities, suggesting opportunities for strategic planners to take cues from other service industries. And, third, they have raised questions about the feasibility or even relevance of a strict functional orientation among either practitioners or researchers. The interfunctional nature of almost any strategic statement renders questionable a strictly functional approach to a study of service firm strategy, especially in service industries requiring the involvement of the customer in the service production and delivery process, so-called high-encounter industries.

Where do we go from here? What avenues will prove most fruitful for researching phenomena that managers have to deal with on an ongoing basis? Given the complexity of strategic issues, legitimate questions can be raised as to whether they are researchable. Determinants of performance can never be singled out. We can attempt, with multivariate analysis, to develop a sense of the importance of such determinants. But the combined effects of such determinants rarely can be assessed adequately. Too often, factors in the environment mask the true effectiveness or even appropriateness of managerial actions. Further, managers seek differentiation of their strategies from competitors as often as they emulate them. This makes the identification and analysis of patterns of action even more difficult.

At the very least, we seek to define pieces of the puzzle that can be examined and establish points of view or starting points from which to examine determinants of performance or survey practice and perceptions. These starting points have included business functions, industries, problems, events, players, and methods associated with service delivery. They vary significantly in terms of their breadth, their research tractability, and the likely results that we may obtain from them that are of significance in understanding strategy.

Business functions and industries perhaps provided the earliest starting point for research in services. In particular, those interested primarily in marketing or operations have developed a body of work emanating from concepts, many of them applied to product marketing or production, previously developed in those fields. Given the interfunctional nature of services, however, this work often has lost its functional identity, encouraging many researchers to turn to an industry focus.

Financial services, and banking in particular, have received greater scrutiny to date than other service industries. Much of this work is broad-based, with the industry used as a surrogate for services in general. As a result, it has been difficult to focus much of it on specific issues and initiatives. The work, however, has included not only surveys of practice and perceptions but also efforts to measure determinants of performance (Roth and Van der Velde, 1988). It will be important to concentrate our efforts in one or more industries that provide a willing laboratory for research, recognizing, of course, the nontransferability of much of this work to other service industries, as suggested by the extreme differences shown in Table 2.1.

Problem-oriented research, centered around issues such as quality, productivity, employee turnover, and relationship management, is defined by a focus first on results, then on causes. But again, the influencing factors bearing on each of these problems in services are often so diffuse that a comprehensive research effort faces formidable challenges in sorting them out. By selecting a result (an effect) rather than a cause as the focus of research, we inherently face questions as to what kind of causes (independent variables) to include in our examination. Nevertheless, certain problem areas, such as the management of quality, are sufficiently different in services to warrant the scrutiny that they are getting (Berry, Parasuraman, and Zeithaml, 1988).

The remaining research bases, because they start from a focus on causes of performance, may well provide the most definitive insights into ways of improving such performance. In particular, an extensive examination of an important event in the service delivery process, the encounter between the server and the served, is beginning to yield real results (Czepiel, Solomon, and Surprenant, 1985). In combination with research into attitudes and performance of parties to the encounter (Parkington and Schneider, 1979; Johnson and Seymour, 1985; Schneider and Bowen, 1985), it is yielding important information about, for example, relationships between employee attitude, customer perceptions and satisfaction, volume of business, and profit performance, particularly in high-encounter services.

Finally, we are beginning to develop a body of research in services around methods or concepts that have strategic significance. They involve the development of a method or concept, its actual implementation, and the measurement of results, most often on a before-and-after basis. Two of these efforts are worth noting.

The first involves the concept of the unconditional service guarantee. Through observation of management practice, it has been documented (Hart, 1988) and is being implemented in a number of organizations. This, in turn, provides the opportunity for a measurement of the impact of the guarantee on sales, the price (or value) of the service, customer attitudes, the quality of service, server attitudes, and, ultimately, profit.

A second example of this type of research involves the concept of the partner-manager introduced by Au Bon Pain, a French bakery restaurant chain (Sasser, 1987). It involves a combination of empowering policies under which unit managers are given greater latitude to earn incentives without upper limits through a profit-sharing arrangement with the company, within the bounds established by the company's "moments of truth" quality-control system. It has had a significant favorable impact on measures such as employee attitude, turnover, and compensation; company profits; operating organization; and quality. More important, these dimensions are measurable.

There are several reasons why we will be seeing significant progress made with research based on methods or concepts. First, generally it is much easier to experiment with service concepts than with manufactured products. It often requires fewer resources and much less fixed investment. For many such experiments, the risk is limited. And service managers, with fewer traditions and entrenched practices, often are more willing to engage in such experiments. Second, the multisite nature of many service industries provides the ideal setting in which to test ideas and practices. Again, the risk can be limited to one or a few sites. But more important, comparative data with which to measure the impact of an independent variable on results are readily available. It is quite possible that findings associated with methods- or concepts-centered research will be found to be transferable to a number of service industries. This already appears to be the case with the concept of the unconditional service guarantee, for example.

Conclusion

Avenues of importance for both managers seeking to obtain competitive advantage and researchers examining strategy in service enterprises have been reviewed briefly in this chapter. In the process, several significant opportunities for both have been suggested. This kind of discussion raises the questions of what strategy is and how it is bounded, in terms of types of problems or issues that fall inside and outside its limits. In fact, depending on point of view, it can be argued that a number of research efforts and discussions referred to earlier do not represent examinations of strategic importance. But in every instance, the implications of the work, if not the scope of the immediate research objectives themselves, were multifunctional, suggesting strategic importance. This is inherently true of much practice in services. It is what provides constant challenges to general managers, many more of whom are required in services than in the more highly functionalized manufacturing organization. And it represents unparalleled research opportunities to those willing to drop traditional mantles, assume greater risks, and learn to live with the uncertainty and ambiguities associated with the research of strategy in the service industries.

References

Bateson, J.E.G. "Why We Need Service Marketing." In O. C. Ferrell, S. W. Brown, and C. W. Lamb, Jr. (eds.), *Conceptual and Theoretical Developments in Marketing*. Chicago: American Marketing Association, 1979.

Berry, L. L. "Services Marketing Is Different." *Business Week*, May–June 1980, pp. 24–29.

Berry, L. L., Bennett, D. R., and Brown, C. W. *Service Quality: A Profit Strategy for Financial Institutions*. Homewood, Ill.: Dow Jones–Irwin, 1988.

Berry, L. L., Parasuraman, A., and Zeithaml, V. A. "The Service-Quality Puzzle." *Business Horizons*, Sept.–Oct. 1988, pp. 35–43.

Chase, R. B. "Where Does the Customer Fit in a Service Operation?" *Harvard Business Review*, 1978, *56* (6), 137–142.

Chase, R. B. "A Matrix for Linking Marketing and Production Variables in Service System Design." In B. Hartman and J. Ringuest (eds.), *Proceedings of the 1985 American Institute for Decision Sciences Conference*. Atlanta, Ga.: 1985.

Clark, C. *The Conditions of Economic Progress*. London: Macmillan, 1940.

Cleveland, H. "The Twilight of Hierarchy: Speculations on the Global Information Society." *Public Administration Review*, Jan–Feb. 1985, pp. 185–195.

Collier, D. A. "Process Moments of Trust: Analysis and Strategy." *Service Industries Journal*, 1989, *9* (2), 205–221.

Czepiel, J. A., Solomon, M. R., and Surprenant, C. F. (eds.). *The Service Encounter: Managing Employee/Customer Interaction in Service Businesses*. Lexington, Mass.: Lexington Books, 1985.

Darby, M.R., and Karni, E. "Free Competition and the Optimal

Amount of Fraud." *Journal of Law and Economics*, Apr. 1973, pp. 67–86.

Dearden, J. "Cost Accounting Comes to Service Industries." *Harvard Business Review*, 1978, *56*, 132–140.

Eccles, R. G., and Crane, D. B. *Doing Deals*. Boston: Harvard Business School Press, 1988.

Enis, B. M., and Roering, K. J. "Services Marketing: Different Products, Similar Strategies." In J. H. Donnelly and W. R. George (eds.), *Marketing of Services*. Chicago: American Marketing Association, 1981.

"The Fortune 500." *Fortune*, Apr. 25, 1988, pp. D1–417.

Fuchs, V. *The Service Economy*. New York: Columbia University Press, 1969.

Gersuny, C., and Rosengren, W. R. *The Service Society*. Cambridge, Mass.: Schenkman, 1973.

Hart, C. "The Power of Unconditional Service Guarantees." *Harvard Business Review*, 1988, *66*, 54–62.

Heskett, J. L. *Managing in the Service Economy*. Boston: Harvard Business School Press, 1986.

Heskett, J. L. "Lessons in the Service Sector." *Harvard Business Review*, 1987, *65*, 118–126.

Heskett, J. L., Sasser, W. E., and Hart, C. *Service Breakthroughs*. New York: Free Press, 1990.

Hill, T. P. "On Goods and Services." *Review of Income and Wealth*, 1977, *23* (Dec.), 315–338.

Hochschild, A. R. *The Managed Heart: Commercialization of Human Feeling*. Berkeley: University of California Press, 1983.

Johnson, E. M., and Seymour, D. T. "The Impact of Cross-Selling on the Service Encounter in Retail Banking." In J. A. Czepiel, M. R. Solomon, and C. F. Surprenant (eds.), *The Service Encounter: Managing Employee/Customer Interaction in Service Businesses*. Lexington, Mass.: Lexington Books, 1985.

Johnson, H. T., and Kaplan, R. S. *Relevance Lost*. Boston: Harvard Business School Press, 1987.

Judd, R. C. "The Case for Redefining Services." *Journal of Marketing*, 1964, *28* (Jan.), 59.

Kotler, P. *Principles of Marketing*. Englewood Cliffs, N.J.: Prentice-Hall, 1980.

Levitt, T. "Production-Line Approach to Service." *Harvard Business Review*, 1972, *50* (5), 41–52.

Levitt, T. "The Industrialization of Service." *Harvard Business Review*, 1976, *54*, 63–74.

Lovelock, C. H. "Towards a Classification of Services." In C. W. Lamb and P. M. Dunne (eds.), *Theoretical Developments in Marketing*. Chicago: American Marketing Association, 1980.

Lovelock, C. H. *Services Marketing*. Englewood Cliffs, N.J.: Prentice-Hall, 1984.

Maister, D. H., and Lovelock, C. H. "Managing Facilitator Services." *Sloan Management Review*, 1982, *23* (4), 19–31.

Nelson, P. "Advertising as Information." *Journal of Political Economy*, July–Aug. 1970, pp. 729–754.

Parkington, J. J., and Schneider, B. "Some Correlates of Experienced Job Stress: A Boundary Role Study." *Academy of Management Journal*, 1979, *22*, 270–281.

Rathmell, J. M. *Marketing in the Service Sector*. Cambridge, Mass.: Winthrop, 1974.

Roach, S. S. "Technology and the Service Sector: America's Hidden Competitive Challenge." In B. R. Guile and J. B. Quinn (eds.), *Technology in Services: Policies for Growth, Trade, and Employment*. Washington, D.C.: National Academy Press, 1988.

Roth, A. V., and Van der Velde, M. *The Future of Retail Banking Delivery Systems*. Rolling Meadows, Ill.: Bank Administration Institute, 1988.

Sasser, W. E. "Au Bon Pain." Case no. 9-687-063, Harvard Business School Case Services, 1987.

Schneider, B., and Bowen, D. E. "New Services Design, Development and Implementation and the Employee." In W. R. George and C. Marshall (eds.), *New Services*. Chicago: American Marketing Association, 1985.

"The Service 500." *Fortune*, June 6, 1988, pp. D1–317.

Shostack, G. L. "Breaking Free from Product Marketing." *Journal of Marketing*, 1977, *41* (Apr.), 73–80.

Shostack, G. L. "Service Positioning Through Structural Change." *Journal of Marketing*, 1987, *51* (Jan.), 34–43.

Smith, A. *The Wealth of Nations*. New York: Dutton, 1977. (Originally published 1776.)

Taylor, J. H. "Risk Taker." *Forbes*, Nov. 14, 1988, p. 108.

Thomas, D.R.E. "Strategy Is Different in Service Businesses." *Harvard Business Review*, 1978, *56*, 158–165.

Zeithaml, V. A. "How Consumer Evaluation Processes Differ Between Goods and Services." In J. H. Donnelly and W. R. George (eds.), *Marketing of Services*. Chicago: American Marketing Association, 1981.

3

Key Strategic Decisions
for Service Firms

Dorothy I. Riddle

Literature on the effective management of service firms has proliferated rapidly (Albrecht, 1988; Carlzon, 1987; Lovelock, 1988; Mills, 1986; Moores, 1986), leaving the concerned service manager with a bewildering array of variables that must be considered. Selecting the correct variables for managerial attention has become particularly important as the competitive focus on service quality has increased (Berry, Zeithaml, and Parasuraman, 1985; Rabin, 1983; Uttal, 1987), with perceived higher quality translating into substantially higher profits (Luchs, 1986; Thompson, DeSouza, and Gale, 1985).

In order to ensure success, the service manager must be able to differentiate effectively between those variables generic to successful competitive positioning in services and those linked to the implementation of a particular competitive strategy. Generic variables must be addressed by all service firms, while managing variables specific to a particular competitive strategy depend first on the careful articulation of the desired competitive position.

On the basis of the model depicted in Figure 3.1, this chapter will address in turn the variables involved in four categories of strategic issues for decision making: delivery issues, core issues, and both internal and external growth issues. Deliv-

Figure 3.1. Types of Strategic Issues in Services Management.

ery issues occur at the juncture of *operations* and *marketing,* blending internal and external operational considerations in the design of the service itself. Core issues occur at the juncture of *operations* and *human resource management* and address the basic nature of the internal firm environment. Internal growth issues occur at the juncture of *strategy* and *human resource management* and are concerned with constraints posed by the internal system. External growth issues occur at the juncture of *strategy* and *marketing* and address externalities affecting the firm.

In the development of each decision variable in this chapter, the assumption will be that a service firm, even if targeting only domestic markets, must view itself as operating in an international environment with regard to both multicultural customer groups and potential foreign competitors. The specific focus of the following discussion will be on the elements of strategy formulation and implementation that are either unique or in some way particularly salient to service firms as outlined in Table 3.1. For each of the strategic questions posed in this chapter, Table 3.1 summarizes the key variables involved and the range of implementation options available to the service manager.

The primary reason why services have unique strategic issues is because of their intangibility. Customers must commit to purchasing before service production, and the services themselves are to a large extent ephemeral, making the evaluation process primarily subjective and customer dependent (Riddle, 1988b). Because of the intimate relationship between perception, evaluation, and experience, the roles of production and marketing are inextricably intertwined for employees just as human resource management and internal marketing (Berry, 1981; Gronroos, 1985) are for supervisors.

Contextual Issues for Strategic Decision Making

In order to identify correctly the key strategic decisions that must be addressed by a given service firm, the first task for service managers is to identify accurately the service type descriptive of their firm. Three types of service firm categorization are particularly relevant to strategic decision making: accountability focus, career track options, and types of staff training needed. Given the type of service firm, the managerial consequences follow automatically.

Accountability Focus. Most commonly, service firms are categorized as either for-profit or not-for-profit. For purposes of strategic analysis, further refinement of the not-for-profit category into public agencies, private not-for-profit firms, and membership organizations is often helpful. The major strategic issue is who will judge success and thus control the direction of growth. While the customer might be assumed to be the final arbiter in the marketplace, in fact the customer has direct influence only in the membership organization, where customer and member are one and the same. In for-profit firms, it is the shareholders or owner who must ultimately be satisfied with any management decisions. Similarly, in public agencies and private not-for-profit firms, continued success is controlled by the funders—either political-legislative or private donors. Successful service management depends on identifying the concerns and vested interests represented in the oversight bodies

Table 3.1. Matrix of Strategic Issues.

	Strategic Question	Key Decision Variables	Implementation Implications
Strategic context	1. Accountability focus	For-profit firm Public agency Private not-for-profit firm Membership organization	Satisfy shareholders Satisfy politicians Satisfy funders Satisfy members
	2. Career track options	Customer service organization Professional service organization	Manage single career track Manage dual career tracks
	3. Types of training needed	Low-complexity service High-complexity service	Train in basic routines Train in intricate routines Train customer for role
		High-divergence service	Train in contingency planning
Delivery issues	4. Tailoring availability	Implicit need(s) targeted[a]	Optimize capacity management Select range of hours Ensure phone accessibility Select site(s)
	5. Tailoring environment	Implicit need(s) targeted[a]	Select high or low load Determine physical decor Determine security level Determine staff appearance
	6. Tailoring style	Implicit need(s) targeted[a]	Determine how formal Determine how personalized Determine how much self-service Determine the queuing protocol Select relationship versus transaction marketing
	7. Tailoring range	Implicit need(s) targeted[a]	Determine which products Determine how customized Select network or stand-alone
Core issues	8. Guaranteeing consistency	Production-line organization } Job-shop organization	Blueprint system(s) Design facility layout Manage inventory Design jobs Optimize decoupling Optimize technical quality Optimize integrative quality

Internal growth issues	9. Guaranteeing *attentiveness*	Ensuring courtesy Ensuring helpfulness Ensuring noninterruption Ensuring respect	Specify context Operationalize behaviors Train behaviors Market internally
	10. Guaranteeing *recoverability*	Anticipation of problems Problem identification Problem management	Optimize crisis planning Train in problem solving Give authority to improvise
	11. Guaranteeing *evaluation*	Internal evaluation External evaluation	Review, revise, reward Optimize functional quality
	12. Assessing excess capacity	Proprietary skills Nonproprietary skills	Add target groups Integrate horizontally Add complementary services Integrate vertically
	13. Identifying specialties	Industry-specific specialty Industry-general specialty	Target new markets Diversify to similar industries
	14. Management cycle stage	Entrepreneurial Professional management	Justify new ventures Consolidate gains
	15. Cultural factors	Certainty of service outcome Length of customer contact Type of customer contact Type of service task	Emphasize respective differences Design tolerance for ambiguity Design open system Train for cultural adaptation Train in cultural values Train in cultural customs
External growth issues	16. Integrating telematics	Importance of customer flexibility Importance of employee flexibility	Create continuous access Create personalized delivery Decouple service production Create telecommuting options
	17. Externalization options	Buy versus make Expand competitive domain	Control quality for contracted services Shape new preferences
	18. Managing public services	Cost-inefficient public service Excess demand for public service Monopoly unnecessary	Supply contracted management Supply complementary capacity Acquire the public service

a Implicit needs possible to target include convenience, security, belonging, status, autonomy, and self-actualization.

and reassuring them that the management decisions made are in their best interest.

Career Track Options. Another common way to classify service firms is into customer service organizations (CSOs) or professional service organizations (PSOs) (Sasser, Olsen, and Wyckoff, 1978). The distinguishing feature is whether career track options within the firm are continuous. In a CSO, employees can presumably start at the bottom and work their way up, using company-sponsored training programs. In PSOs, however, there is a stratum of staff that has received external professional training and licensing. Professional staff are seldom hired as support staff, and support staff can never become professional staff without external training and licensing.

As a consequence, in PSOs there is a dual career system with ceilings on the promotion of support staff. In order to ensure highly motivated support staff in PSOs, the service manager must exercise ingenuity and creativity in devising reward alternatives to traditional promotion for senior support staff. In addition, the manager must carefully address the fact that professional staff typically have a primary loyalty to their profession, whose code of conduct, rather than the firm's policies and procedures, typically controls their behavior.

Types of Staff Training Needed. A less common but very useful way to categorize service firms is by degree of complexity of task sequence and degree of divergence necessary (Shostack, 1987). Here, *complexity* refers to the number and intricacy of the tasks to be performed, while *divergence* refers to the degree of discretion that can or must be exercised by employees.

Strategic decision making in the present competitive environment of necessity involves three parties—management, employees, and customers. Successful strategic conceptualization and implementation depend on addressing the needs and concerns of each party in an integrated manner. For example, customers may be most satisfied with complete customization of service delivery. However, extensive customization in a price-sensitive market may erode profits, a prime concern of management, and leave employees feeling unpleasantly at the mercy of customer whims (Riddle, 1988c). Some middle ground must be found that balances these concerns effectively.

In a service firm, professional staff are typically seen as the key players and rewarded financially for the discretionary judgment they must exercise. However, the front-line support staff (receptionists, telephone operators, secretaries) often must exercise as much or more discretion in handling the initial customer interaction. To ensure that employees exercise appropriate judgment in firms where divergence is high, contingency planning needs to be an important part of the employee training program.

In many service production systems, whether or not there is direct interaction, the customer plays an important role as a "partial employee" (Mills, Chase, and Margulies, 1983). As the complexity of the service delivery system increases, it can become more difficult for customers to understand the behaviors required of them in the service production process and what role they should adopt. For example, they may need to play an active role in supplying information, initiating follow-up, or participating promptly in scheduled activities. Or they may need to be content with a more passive role, reacting to options posed or merely waiting for service completion. In each instance, satisfaction is tied to the feeling of having acted appropriately (Zeithaml, Berry, and Parasuraman, 1988). Thus, an important part of strategic management is how best to convey to customers the appropriate role behaviors.

Management Decisions Regarding Delivery Issues

In positioning a service firm competitively in the market, there are a range of "delivery" issues that must be considered whose resolution matrix will be unique to the firm's competitive strategy. That matrix represents the design of the service as perceived by the customer and illustrates the fact that employees of service firms commonly perform production and marketing functions simultaneously.

The key to successful differentiation in competitive strat-

egy is to link the design of the service product (service purchase
bundle) to the targeted implicit customer needs (Riddle,
1988b)—that is, those needs that can be met most effectively by
the services of the firm. One cannot be all things to all people,
and correct focus is essential to profitability. Typically, the successful firm targets one (or at most two) of the implicit needs of
the customer—convenience, security, belonging, status, autonomy, or self-actualization (Riddle, 1986b). For example, two
different types of stores may be able to charge a price premium
successfully—both a Circle K that targets convenience and a
gourmet specialty story that caters to status or prestige needs.

Strategic design factors encompass every aspect of how
the service is experienced by the customer and can be divided
into four major elements: availability, environment, style, and
range.

Availability. One important aspect of the customer's perception of service adequacy is whether and how easily the customer can acquire the service. From a capacity management
perspective, the customer is typically interested in minimizing
effort costs, while the producer wishes to ensure a steady stream
of demand for optimal use of production capacity.

Customers with strong convenience needs are often willing to pay a premium for the ability to access the service at will
and expect in return that their effort costs will be minimal.
Service delivery would need to be available at numerous sites
within easy distance, with plenty of parking (if arrival by car is
anticipated), long or continuous hours of access, and immediate
(walk-in) services.

By contrast, customers with strong status needs are usually willing to absorb greater effort costs in return for a feeling
of exclusivity about the service received—that it is either unavailable to or not affordable by a wide range of persons. Service
delivery may then be restricted to prestigious locations, with less
extensive open hours and the use of a reservation system.

Environment. The first impression received by customers
of the service delivery environment begins to shape judgments

of how adequate the service delivery will be. Customers for whom belonging is an important need, for example, will respond most positively to more informal, less pretentious physical surroundings. The environment can be relatively "high-load" (Booms and Bitner, 1982) — that is, with multiple activities or higher noise level — and the staff can be more casually dressed.

For customers with strong security needs, though, especially when the service outcome is uncertain (for example, surgery), the initial impression needs to be one of control and professionalism. A "low-load" environment, with muted colors and a uniformed staff, will be more reassuring.

Style. Both in initially approaching the service delivery system and in receiving the service, the manner in which the customer is treated needs to be matched to the customer's needs. Customers with strong autonomy needs, for example, will respond well to delivery systems with a large component of self-service and a "first come, first served" queuing protocol so that they feel in control of the pacing of the delivery process. Such customers typically have little interest in relationship building or paying for personalized service touches.

By contrast, customers with strong status needs will expect individualized attention, little if any self-service, and a friendly but formal environment where their superior status is clearly underlined. They would expect a queuing protocol that provides then with a separate, streamlined queue and would respond well to relationship marketing (Berry, 1983) if focused on their uniqueness.

Range. Customer groups also vary according to the range of service products that they expect to find in a given service firm. Customers with strong self-actualization needs may be less concerned about the quantity of service options than about the quality of experience that they can expect to receive. Customers with strong convenience needs will tend to select service firms where they can "one-stop" shop with certainty that the services needed will be available. Standardized service products will be more acceptable to customers oriented to belonging than to customers oriented to status, who expect more customization.

A newer trend among service firms is to create "networks" in which a wide range of services are available without diluting the focus of any one service firm in its arena of expertise. Thus, the property buyer may select a realty firm in which he or she has confidence, which in turn will provide (through referral) the financing company, the title company, the insurance company, and so on. Or the service firm may choose a "service supermarket" approach in which boutique services are run—an approach adopted by Sears so that its reputation as a retailer was extended to a range of services such as finance, optometry, insurance, and so on.

Management Decisions Regarding Core Issues

Decisions regarding core issues are ones that are primarily controlled by the management of the service firm and that concern the internal systems design. Such decisions are generic in nature—that is, they must be addressed by all service firms regardless of competitive strategy.

To underline the necessity for an overall customer service orientation, we can think of the systems design as a "CARE" package with four components: Consistency, Attentiveness, Recoverability, and Evaluation.

Consistency. One of the biggest difficulties to overcome in services is the fact that, from the customer's perspective, services are a risky purchase. Given the nature of the service production process, there is little assurance that the quality of the service will be the same from time to time. Standardized service delivery systems, such as fast-food chains, owe much of their success to the fact that the service product is relatively predictable both in the food preparation and in the timing of delivery.

The basic tools of the operations analyst to enhance production efficiency—for example, system blueprinting (Shostack, 1984), facility design, inventory management, job design, quality control—can be used to ensure predictable production procedures. The end result needs to be a service production process that is consistent over time, place, employee, customer, and service product.

Attention must be paid to the development of standard service routines for both back-office and front-office staff, supplemented by training to ensure proper "technical" service quality (Gronroos, 1982). In addition, since the decoupling (separation) of production and consumption increases the degree of control that management can exercise over the production process (Chase, 1978), new opportunities for decoupling need to be identified that will allow additional service functions to be moved into the "back office."

For more complex service delivery systems, care must be taken to ensure not only clear routines within tasks but also the smooth linking between tasks and/or departments. Such an internal service orientation involves having employees or departments view each other as "customers" in order to enhance "integrative" service quality (Lehtinen and Lehtinen, 1982; Riddle, 1988b).

For the front-office staff, there are additional considerations beyond standardization, especially where the degree of divergence is great. Staff members who regularly interact with customers are a valuable marketing asset as well as the primary service providers. In their marketing role, the "emotional labor" content is high (Hochschild, 1983), resulting in a potential for feeling a lack of control and in a heightened propensity for "burnout." Thus, the human resource management issues for front-office staff become particularly acute as the need for consistency of interaction with customers must be weighed against the realities of human emotions.

The role played by the customer also needs careful attention. Frustration for both the customer and the employee can result where the behaviors needed from the customer are unclear to the customer (Solomon, Surprenant, Czepiel, and Gutman, 1985). "Boundary-spanning" employees (Bowen and Schneider, 1985) need to have built into their job descriptions the responsibility for "socializing" the customer to required behaviors.

Attentiveness. Basic to any successful service is the quality of the interaction with the customer, or the "functional" quality (Gronroos, 1982) of the service. While aspects of the interactive style may be specific to the particular competitive strategy, there are basic employee behaviors linked to customer satisfaction across a wide variety of services and business strategies.

Generalized friendliness, especially out of context, may be interpreted negatively by the customer (Surprenant and Solomon, 1987). Attentive behavior needs, rather, to be specific and relevant to the task at hand. Successful service firms, such as Disneyland, have learned the importance of codifying and training employees in such basics as the specific verbal and nonverbal behaviors that denote courtesy, helpfulness, and respect to customers.

One specific dimension worth noting is the importance to customers of the sense of "uninterrupted" service delivery. Once the service process has begun, customers value being able to retain the employee's attention until service has been completed.

Recoverability. Crisis-management skills are particularly important in services where environmental uncertainty is typically high. Unfortunately, many managers assume that careful system design will result in a problem-free delivery system. In actuality, problem situations provide a service firm with an opportunity to excel — with careful planning. Despite the inconvenience of the problem, customers are likely to feel even more favorably toward a firm that they view as having done everything humanly possible to minimize difficulties from problem situations (Parasuraman, 1987).

Given the variability of customer input as well as other externalities (such as weather or political conditions), it is crucial to devise an "early warning system" that will help spot likely problems before they occur so that preventive measures may be taken. For example, airlines can create alternate plans for passenger transport when labor strikes are threatened or serious weather disturbances are predicted, just as hotels can schedule extra staff or ensure that all preventive maintenance is completed in anticipation of conventions or tour groups.

All staff responsible for customers need problem-solving skill training to help identify both problems that occur and the particular reasons for customer dissatisfaction. In order to offer effective solutions, for example, staff must be able to differentiate between a customer who feels merely annoyed and one who feels victimized (Bell and Zemke, 1987). If a flight delay causes missed connections, for example, one passenger might be satisfied with a free ticket for a later direct flight while another (who is about to miss an important meeting) would be more satisfied with the inconvenience of a more circuitous routing in order to arrive in time.

The most important innovation in service crisis management has been the willingness to delegate authority to front-line staff so that they can improvise on the spot (Leonard, 1987). One of the most frustrating experiences for the customer is to battle through corporate red tape simply to get the firm to correct *its* mistake. One U.S. bank has been very successful, for example, by authorizing bank tellers to accept customers' versions of what should have happened to their accounts, apologize, and promise an immediate correction. Follow-up research has shown that, in the vast majority of instances, the customer *was* in fact right.

Evaluation. A common issue among service firms is the failure to quantify behavioral expectations in ways that can be measured and rewarded. American Airlines owes some of its success to its attention to measurable objectives, ranging from how quickly the phone should be answered through how quickly the beverage service should begin after flight takeoff to how quickly the plane door should be opened once the plane is parked at the airport gate.

Singapore's Changi Airport is another example of the consequences of specifying performance requirements. To the delight of the weary traveler, it has imposed strict time limits on the baggage-handling companies that are monitored by computerized conveyor belts. If the companies wish to retain their contract, the first bag must be on the belt within twelve minutes of the plane's parking at the gate, and the last bag (even from the large 747s) must be on the belt within twenty-five minutes.

Management Decisions Regarding Internal Growth Issues

Internal growth decisions are concerned with evaluating external threats and opportunities in light of the firm's strengths and weaknesses. Their purpose is to determine how the firm can expand most effectively through either increased markets or increased product offerings.

Assessing Excess Capacity. In order to expand, a firm needs to ensure that expansion builds on areas where excess production capacity is present rather than stressing functions that are already overloaded. Such excess capacity may comprise proprietary skills essential to the production of that particular service or general skills that can be extended to related service functions. The basic expansion decision to be made is whether to offer the same service to more customer groups or to offer different services to the same customers.

The first alternative (increased customer groups) can be implemented either through marketing or through horizontal integration. For example, an insurance firm with excess capacity in its claims department may be able to handle more insurance customers — that is, target additional customer groups — or might merge with an insurance firm whose claims processing is inadequate. Its growth strategy is based on exploiting precisely the specialized skills most abundant in the company.

The second alternative (increased services) can be implemented through either developing related services or integrating with related service firms. For example, a restaurant with excellent food-handling service might be able to add a variety of new complementary services — for example, catering. But if the insurance firm referred to above chose to add related financial services, the claims staff available might well not be able to handle the work effectively. Only if the excess skills available are general in nature can one effectively expand the range of services managed.

Identifying Specialties. One important service growth strategy in both service and nonservice firms can be to identify a particular skill that is not abundant in the market and focus growth around that skill. When the skill is industry-specific, the challenge is to look for new markets where the skill is scarce. For example, Tunisian phosphate companies have successfully exported their managerial skills in that industry. Similarly, the Chinese have consciously first imported technical expertise in a given industry and then reexported that skill (repackaged for a developing-country environment) to countries in Africa.

On the other hand, when the skill is one that can be applied across industries, the firm can consider diversifying into industries where that skill is required. For example, companies such as Movenpick successfully operate firms in a range of hospitality industries.

Management Cycle Stage. There is considerable difference between the operational patterns and constraints of a firm run by an entrepreneur and those of one run by a professional manager. Typically, the entrepreneur is interested in start-ups and new ventures. A firm run by an entrepreneur needs to consider carefully whether proposals for new ventures stem simply from boredom with routine or from a legitimate identification of a market opportunity.

One of the most difficult strategic shifts to make is from management by the original entrepreneur to professional management by someone dedicated to the follow-through necessary to make initially successful ventures continue to grow. Unless the shift is made, employees will gradually become burdened and ineffective as expansion moves too quickly.

Cultural Factors. Cultural factors are one of the most complex topics in service management. Few studies other than that of Hofstede (1984) have attempted the type of massive cross-cultural analysis within multinational corporations that is necessary to determine the precise role played by culture. It is clear, though, that culture affects the structure of the firm, the design of role behaviors, the shaping of customer expectations, and the evaluation of satisfaction (Edvardsson and Gustavsson, 1988; Lublin, 1988; Riddle, 1988a).

No service firm environment is free of cultural influences, and the corporate culture itself is shaped by cultural values (Adler and Jelinek, 1986). Typically, a firm creates its own corporate culture, ignoring where necessary the external cultural environment. Unless the corporate culture is oriented to customer needs and therefore to some degree of adaptation, entry into foreign markets is unlikely to be successful.

Transferring a service concept to a new external cultural environment can be done most effectively when the service to be provided is relatively discrete, with a low-risk outcome and minimal customer contact (Riddle, 1986a). As soon as uncertainty increases, for example, customers will respond differently depending on whether they are culturally conditioned to accept risks. Similarly, when contact with the customer increases or becomes ongoing, then successful service delivery must be attuned to the cultural factors that put a particular customer at ease in a service encounter.

Firms wishing to expand internationally need to assess how willing they are to design open delivery systems that tolerate ambiguity in what is expected and acceptable. In addition, those firms will need to invest in training their staff to adapt culturally, respect value differences, and adopt local customs and behavior where appropriate.

Management Decisions Regarding External Growth Issues

External growth decisions are focused more exclusively on new market opportunities, concerned primarily with external factors — domestic and international. Regardless of whether a service firm wishes to enter the international arena, that arena will affect the firm. Foreign investment is increasingly shifting from manufacturing to the service sector. With the goal of integration within the European Community by 1992, consolidation among European firms is already occurring. Those firms will pose a challenge to both the U.S. service transnationals that have traditionally controlled over half the international markets and the rising Japanese service transnationals.

Integrating Telematics. One of the competitive changes made possible by new telematic (computers + telecommunications) technology is increased flexibility for customers. As customers become accustomed to using or receiving services from interactive data bases and on-line real-time services, their expectations about availability shift. They become more demanding of continuous and immediate access to services. For example, a client may now legitimately expect to pose a specialized legal question to his or her attorney one afternoon and receive an answer the next day — assuming that the law firm is connected to law offices around the world that could be working on the problem "overnight."

Similarly, videotext services providing customers with a wide range of services heighten one's expectations of the extent to which a range of personal needs can be met. The use of computer-aided design can enable architects to include the customer in the design process, with immediate feedback on cost and schedule implications. Thus, the firm that wishes to retain customers must be sure that appropriate technology is being incorporated into the service delivery process.

For employees, too, telematics can increase flexibility and hence both employee morale and employer attractiveness. With an increased decoupling of service production and delivery to the customer, employees are less likely to feel controlled by customer demands and more able to schedule work efficiently.

Of particular benefit when designed appropriately is the ability for employees to "telecommute" — that is, work at a computer terminal in a different location from the main office but connected by modem. Originally, this innovation was seen as ideal for people working at home, but people quickly realized that the employee then felt isolated from other workers and pressed by home demands. Sweden has pioneered in establishing "telecommute" centers in small communities where employees of different firms work together in one office and hence provide the requisite social atmosphere of conviviality and support. Such a procedure has the benefit to the firm of widening its recruiting beyond those present in the main-office community.

Externalization Options. For services, there is an important variant of the traditional "make-buy" decision known as the externalization of "producer" services. This refers to the establishment of specialty service firms that provide to companies a range of support and professional services often provided in house by large companies. The importance of such a phenomenon has been denigrated in the media by terms such as the "hollow corporation," applied negatively to the capacity to contract out all service functions. But the cost flexibility inherent in such a design is immense.

There are two different strategic issues here for firms. One is whether, given the fact that producer services is a high-growth area, the firm wishes to "externalize" one of its own service functions, as a number of U.S. manufacturing firms have done. Another is whether, instead of using resources to support an internal department (such as advertising), the firm would wish to free resources for growth by contracting for such services externally as needed. If the latter strategy is adopted, then the firm must concern itself with ensuring that the quality of service delivered is up to its own standards.

Another externalized growth option open to firms is, rather than establishing a producer services firm in a traditional area, to develop a new service by identifying a portion of the distribution channel where specialized skills can be applied. For example, traditional messenger services have branched into obtaining visas on short notice for personnel traveling abroad.

"Privatized" Public Services. The move to privatize public services has been quite popular, though the success rate of actually providing opportunities for private-sector firms to acquire ready markets is still questionable (Vernon, 1988). It is common for governments to wish to retain profitable monopolies while divesting themselves of unprofitable ones. Whether

those unprofitable ones would be of interest to anyone is a real issue encountered by a range of countries.

More commonly now, though, rather than privatizing public services, governments are contracting out their management. If a firm has an efficient and cost-conscious managerial style with excess managerial talent, it might very profitably contract for the management of a cost-inefficient public service. For example, U.S. waste management firms have acquired such contracts in Latin American countries.

Private-sector contracts are particularly common now for public services where there is excess demand that cannot be met within the existing system. Privately managed prisons are an interesting and unusual example.

Research Questions Regarding Strategy

In essence, all of the implementation implications listed in Table 3.1 lend themselves to empirical testing. There are a few basic research issues, however, that deserve special mention:

1. What is the optimal method for involving both managers and employees in the strategic decision-making process?
2. What are the best empirical correlates in service delivery design for each of the implicit needs expressed by customers?
3. Given the importance of consistency in reducing perceived risk for customers, what degree of variability is permissible in franchise chains from one site to another?
4. How can one best operationalize "attentive" behavior?
5. What are the ingredients of effective crisis management for service firms?
6. How can one best balance control by customers and by employees?
7. What is the impact of cultural variables on each of the strategic options?
8. What criteria should be used to determine whether to "make" or "buy" support services?

Conclusion

Strategic decision making in services will gain in importance as the competition for market share and profits intensifies. In an effective service firm, strategic decision making cannot be focused only at the management level or restricted to a "strategy" department. If that happens, usually only external growth issues are addressed. However, the service manager needs also to consider strategic issues related to the design of the service (delivery issues), the internal service system (core issues), and internal capacity constraints (internal growth issues).

In a service firm, all strategic decisions typically involve at least two traditionally defined departments or functions, rather than being restricted to a given department. Thus, strategic decision making in services needs to be an interactive process, including operations, human resource management, and marketing functions as well as strategic planning.

Integral to all decisions is the issue of the type of service firm in question, which will in turn dictate the type of strategies open to the firm. Only a few of the crucial factors (for example, core issues) can be addressed generically. The rest depend on a thorough understanding of the nature of the particular service firm and the rationale behind its competitive positioning.

References

Adler, N., and Jelinek, M. "Is 'Organization Culture' Culture Bound?" *Human Resource Management*, 1986, *25* (1), 73–90.

Albrecht, K. *At America's Service*. Homewood, Ill.: Dow Jones–Irwin, 1988.

Bell, C. R., and Zemke, R. E. "Service Breakdown: The Road to Recovery." *Management Review*, Oct. 1987, pp. 32–35.

Berry, L. L. "The Employee as Customer." *Journal of Retail Banking*, 1981, *3* (3), 33–40.

Berry, L. L. "Relationship Marketing." In L. L. Berry, G. L. Shostack, and G. D. Upah (eds.), *Emerging Perspectives on Ser-*

vices Marketing. Chicago: American Marketing Association, 1983.

Berry, L. L., Zeithaml, V. A., and Parasuraman, A. "Quality Counts in Services Too." *Business Horizons*, 1985, *28*, 44–52.

Booms, B. H., and Bitner, M. J. "Marketing Services by Managing the Environment." *Cornell Hotel and Restaurant Administration Quarterly*, 1982, *23* (1), 35–39.

Bowen, D. E., and Schneider, B. "Boundary-Spanning-Role Employees and the Service Encounter." In J. A. Czepiel, M. R. Solomon, and C. F. Surprenant (eds.), *The Service Encounter: Managing Employee/Customer Interaction in Service Businesses*. Lexington, Mass.: Lexington Books, 1985.

Carlzon, J. *Moments of Truth: New Strategies for Today's Customer-Driven Economy*. Cambridge, Mass.: Ballinger, 1987.

Chase, R. B. "Where Does the Customer Fit in a Service Operation?" *Harvard Business Review*, 1978, *56* (6), 137–142.

Edvardsson, B., and Gustavsson, B. *Quality in Services and Quality in Service Organizations: A Model for Quality Assessment*. Working Paper 88:5. Karlstad, Sweden: Service Research Centre, 1988.

Gronroos, C. *Strategic Management and Marketing in the Service Sector*. Helsinki, Finland: Swedish School of Economics, 1982.

Gronroos, C. "Internal Marketing—Theory and Practice." In T. M. Bloch, G. D. Upah, and V. A. Zeithaml (eds.), *Service Marketing in a Changing Environment*. Chicago: American Marketing Association, 1985.

Hochschild, A. R. *The Managed Heart: Commercialization of Human Feeling*. Berkeley: University of California Press, 1983.

Hofstede, G. *Culture's Consequences*. Beverly Hills, Calif.: Sage, 1984.

Lehtinen, U., and Lehtinen, J. R. *Service Quality: A Study of Quality Dimensions*. Helsinki, Finland: Service Management Institute, 1982.

Leonard, S. "Love That Customer!" *Management Review*, Oct. 1987, pp. 36–39.

Lovelock, C. H. *Managing Services: Marketing, Operations, and Human Resources*. Englewood Cliffs, N. J.: Prentice-Hall, 1988.

Lublin, J. "U.S. Franchisers Learn Britain Isn't Easy." *Wall Street Journal*, Aug. 16, 1988, p. 18.

Luchs, R. "Successful Businesses Compete on Quality—Not Costs." *Long Range Planning*, 1986, *19* (1), 12–17.

Mills, P. K. *Managing Service Industries: Organizational Practices in a Post-Industrial Society*. Cambridge, Mass.: Ballinger, 1986.

Mills, P. K., Chase, R. B., and Margulies, N. "Motivating the Client/Employee System as a Service Production Strategy." *Academy of Management Review*, 1983, *8*, 301–310.

Moores, B. (ed.). *Are They Being Served?* Oxford, England: Philip Allan, 1986.

Parasuraman, A. "An Attributional Framework for Assessing the Perceived Value of Services." In C. F. Surprenant (ed.), *Add Value to Your Service*. Chicago: American Marketing Association, 1987.

Rabin, J. H. "Accent Is on Quality in Consumer Services This Decade." *Marketing News*, Mar. 12, 1983, p. 12.

Riddle, D. I. "Innovative Management of the Customer-Employee Relationship in International Service Firms." In *Proceedings of the Annual Meeting of the Decision Science Institute*. Honolulu, 1986a.

Riddle, D. I. *Service-Led Growth: The Role of the Service Sector in World Development*. New York: Praeger, 1986b.

Riddle, D. I. "Cultural Aspects of Services Technology Transfer." In R. Johnson (ed.), *The Management of Service Operations*. Coventry, England: University of Warwick, 1988a.

Riddle, D. I. "Culturally Determined Aspects of Service Quality." Paper presented at the Quality in Services Symposium, University of Karlstad, Sweden, Aug. 14–17, 1988b.

Riddle, D. I. "Public Sector Productivity and Role Conflicts." In R. M. Kelly (ed.), *Promoting Productivity in the Public Sector: Problems, Strategies and Prospects*. New York: St. Martin's Press, 1988c.

Sasser, W. E., Olsen, R. P., and Wyckoff, D. D. *Management of Service Operations: Text, Cases, and Readings*. Boston: Allyn & Bacon, 1978.

Shostack, G. L. "Designing Systems That Deliver." *Harvard Business Review*, 1984, *62* (1), 133–139.

Shostack, G. L. "Service Positioning Through Structural Change." *Journal of Marketing*, 1987, *51*, 34–43.

Solomon, M. R., Surprenant, C., Czepiel, J. A., and Gutman, E. G. "A Role Theory Perspective on Dyadic Interactions: The Service Encounter." *Journal of Marketing,*1985, *49* (4), 99–111.

Surprenant, C. F., and Solomon, M. R. "Predictability and Personalization in the Service Encounter." *Journal of Marketing*, 1987, *51* (4), 86–96.

Thompson, P., DeSouza, G., and Gale, B. T. *The Strategic Management of Service Quality.* PIMSLETTER no. 33. Cambridge, Mass.: Strategic Planning Institute, 1985.

Uttal, B. "Companies That Serve You Best." *Fortune,* Dec. 7, 1987, pp. 98–116.

Vernon, R. (ed.). *The Promise of Privatization.* New York: Council on Foreign Relations, 1988.

Zeithaml, V. A., Berry, L. L., and Parasuraman, A. "Communication and Control Processes in the Delivery of Service Quality." *Journal of Marketing*, 1988, *52* (4), 35–48.

4

Service Technologies: Key Factors in Manufacturing Strategy

James Brian Quinn
Penny C. Paquette

In the recent past, technology has played just as vital a role in the development of the service sector as it has elsewhere in the economy. Services technologies will continue to create even more new challenges and opportunities for both service providers and manufacturers. We use the broad definition of technology as "knowledge, usually about physical and chemical relationships, systematically applied to useful purposes." "Services technologies" include the wide range of technologies specifically developed for or applied in service activities. Services technologies may appear at the level of systems interfaces to the outside world, at the integrated-operations or general-management level, in incremental operations-productivity improvements, or as specialized equipment or software for specific service functions.

Over the past three and a half years we have conducted research into the impacts of technology in the service sector.

Note: The authors gratefully acknowledge the generous support of the Bell & Howell, Bell Atlanticom, Bankers Trust, Royal Bank of Canada, Braxton Associates, and American Express companies in this project.

Our studies have embraced not just the "information technologies," important as they are. Other services technologies have been instrumental in improving performance and opening new markets in virtually all service industries. Jet aircraft have made long-haul passenger and freight handling much more efficient and convenient—extending the import and export of many perishable goods worldwide. New diagnostics, life-support systems, drug therapies, and surgical procedures have revolutionized medical practice. By making it possible to transport virtually all goods safely, new containerization, loading, refrigeration, and handling techniques for volatile liquids have vastly extended international trade in manufactures. And, of course, information technologies have stimulated new initiatives in almost all service areas—most notably in retailing and wholesale trade, engineering design, financial services, communications, and entertainment. As will be apparent, many of the technologies are themselves embedded in manufactured products; others are software or applied knowledge systems—such as those of medical diagnosis or operations research.

In terms of their economic and structural impacts, major new technologies in services seem to generate certain distinctive and repetitive patterns:

1. *New economies of scale* appear that cause many service activities to centralize into larger institutions, at first concentrating activities into fewer large units, then allowing renewed decentralization as smaller units in more dispersed locations link into networks with larger companies and deliver services to more distant locations. This pattern has recurred in health care, air transport, insurance, ground transport, banking and financial services, communications, and so on. Midsized service enterprises, unable to afford the new technologies themselves, have often been forced to merge upward in scale, niche radically, or go out of business. Porter and others (Porter, 1980; Booz, Allen & Hamilton, n.d.) have recognized the effects of this pressure on midsized firms as "being caught in the middle." Profit Impact of Market Strategy (PIMS) data (Strategic Planning Institute, 1985) show that technologies have allowed the scale and concentration of reporting strategic business units (SBUs) in

services to become just as great as those of reporting manufacturing SBUs. While the proportion of sales held by the top four firms in manufacturing industries is on average about 72 percent, the average in service industries is about 68 percent.

2. *New economies of scope* (Goldhar and Burnham, 1983) frequently provide powerful second-order effects. Once properly installed, the same technologies that created new scale economies allow service enterprises to handle a much wider set of data, output functions, or customers without significant cost increases — and often with cost decreases through allocating technology development or equipment costs over a greater variety of operations. Thus, banks (Citicorp), airlines (American), retailers (Sears), and travel-bank services (American Express) use their installed facilities and networks to grow by extending their presence into a broad range of new activities.

3. *Increased complexity* can often be economically handled by the new technologies. Electronic systems and computer models have been the main enabling technologies but are by no means alone in permitting management of much greater complexity. A variety of new sensing, telecommunications, information handling, materials, and processing technologies now routinely design, build, and test radical new designs for boat hulls and aircraft; specify structures for new molecules and predict their performance; suggest and test hypotheses for medical research; access and analyze global and astronomical data bases; run remote factories and processes; handle worldwide monetary and securities transactions; control effluents in water supplies; monitor environmental and political events; and manage huge transportation systems with a precision and speed previously impossible. As this occurs, PIMS data show that technology allows value added per employee in large services units (SBUs) to be as high as that in similar manufacturing SBUs — on average about $26,000 per employee.

4. *A breakdown of traditional industry demarcations* has accompanied the changes such services technologies have wrought. Functional and cross-competition within and among individual service industries and between service and manufacturing enterprises has significantly increased (Faulhaber, Noam,

and Tasley, 1986). The well-documented changes in the "financial services" industry provide a powerful example of this impact (Quinn, 1988b). Technology ultimately forced deregulation of the communications, banking, and financial services industries as competing institutions' products (electronic bits) became ever more indistinguishable and easier to transmit, switch, and store. Retailers such as Sears integrated backward and forward into insurance and finance, manufacturers such as General Motors and Ford became major national players in consumer credit, the airlines invaded other travel services and retailing, Goodyear developed its auto repair network, Federal Express revolutionized competition with the U.S. government in message delivery, and so on.

A single integrated example will dramatize some of the ways services technologies—and these four modes of impact—interact to restructure competitive relations within and among companies, industries, and even nations.

• In the mid-1960s and early 1970s, securities trading houses found that they were being overwhelmed by the need to physically handle the 10–12 million shares then being transferred daily. The major Wall Street firms formed what became the Depository Trust Company to concentrate—and immobilize—virtually all traded certificates under one roof and to automate what had been the back-office handling of such certificates. This technology forced many small and midsized brokerage houses, which could not afford their own automation, to merge or affiliate with the large houses.

As the surviving houses developed their own in-house electronic systems for automated trading, they found that they not only could handle the system's increased transaction volumes (now sometimes more than 500 million shares some days) but could also introduce a variety of new products, such as mutual funds, cash management accounts, deferred insurance annuities, and so on, tailored to individual customers' needs. To exploit these potentials, they consolidated and developed networks of decentralized local offices all over the country. A second wave of small affiliated brokerage houses then formed to deliver the economies of scope and capabilities for handling complexity that the new technologies permitted.

Later, as European exchanges and brokerage houses automated, international electronic monetary transactions (now running well over $100 trillion per year) forced world financial markets into a new integration. Countries generally found that they must harmonize their trading rules with those of other nations or risk losing their competitive positions in these new markets. Large industrial companies increasingly began to place their own securities (commercial paper) directly on world markets, and financiers created new instruments (such as swaps and junk bonds) to exploit the new opportunities that the markets permitted. Now the finances of all advanced economies have become so intimately interlinked that, as we shall explain later, the very nature of international manufacturing (as well as services) competition has been revolutionized. Combined with the cross-competition described above, this has created whole new matrices of external opportunities and threats for individual companies and options for obtaining strategic advantage.

Services in the Economy

Dispelling Myths. While most are generally aware of services' importance in the economy, few seem to realize the scale of that dominance, at least statistically. (A single service industry category, financial services and real estate, is almost as large as all of manufacturing; see Table 4.1.) There are several widely held misconceptions that hamper understanding of this fact and its implications for business and public policy decisions. It is essential that the service sector be put into the proper perspective.

High value added per employee can be created in large service enterprises—as high as that in manufacturing units. On an aggregate value-added basis, the contribution of the service sector is even more impressive, rising from $555 billion in 1976 to more than $1 trillion in 1986 in real terms, while that in manufacturing leveled out at around $290 billion (in 1972 dol-

Table 4.1. U.S. Gross National Product and Employment by Industry, 1987.

	GNP (in Billions of Dollars)	Percentage of Total GNP	Employment (in Millions)	Percentage of Total Employment
Total economy	$4,527	100%	110.8	100%
Agriculture, forestry, fisheries	95		1.8	
Mining and construction	304		5.8	
Manufacturing	854		19.1	
Total goods sector	$1,253	28%	26.7	24%
Finance, insurance, real estate	$ 776		6.8	
Retail trade	427		19.0	
Wholesale trade	313		5.9	
Transportation and public utilities	287		4.1	
Communications	121		1.3	
Other services	794		26.1	
Total private services	$2,718	60%	63.2	57%
Government and government enterprises	535		20.9	
Total service sector	$3,252	72%	84.1	76%

Source: Bureau of Economic Analysis, 1988.

lars). The fact that, for the whole nation, average value added per employee in services is somewhat lower than that in manufacturing—contrasted to the PIMS data for larger concerns—indicates that technology can provide significant economies of scale to larger services enterprises.

Service industries are capital intensive. While certain small-scale retail, domestic services, or restaurant activities clearly do not require much capital, major service industries such as communications, transportation, pipelines, and electric utilities are among the most capital intensive of all industries. Increasingly, the banking, entertainment, health care, financial services, auto rental, message delivery, and retailing industries also qualify.

Kutscher and Mark's (1983) data show that certain service industries—notably, railroads, pipelines, broadcasting, communications, utilities, and air transport—were among the most capital
intensive of all industries, while few service industries were
found in the lowest capital-intensity deciles. Roach (1988) also
notes that total capital investment per "information worker"
(dominantly services) now exceeds that for workers in basic
industrial activities.

Service companies are large-scale. Both PIMS and *Fortune* 500
data confirm that the size and concentration of large service
units are at least comparable to those of manufacturing. Large
service companies, such as airlines and hospital chains, are
increasingly becoming the lead customers for those introducing
new technologies and play a major role in specifying and shaping the technologies themselves. Some large banks, utilities,
financial institutions, communications companies, and hotel,
distribution, and rental chains have the scale to conduct research, development, and major innovation programs in house.
Companies such as AT&T, Citicorp, Humana, Federal Express,
McKesson, ServiceMaster, National Car Rental, and American
Airlines are innovators in their own right, as well as major
customers, coalition partners, and suppliers for manufacturers
and other services companies.

Services substitute directly for manufactures. Far from being
inferior economic outputs, services are directly interchangeable
with manufactured goods in a wide variety of situations (Levitt,
1976). Few customers care whether a refrigerator manufacturer,
for example, implements a particular feature by using a hardware circuit or by using internal software. Improved transportation or materials handling services can lower a manufacturer's
costs as effectively as cutting direct labor or materials inputs.
Computer-aided design and manufacturing software can increase quality or decrease costs as easily as can new equipment.
Such "service" investments improve productivity or add value
just as investments in physical-handling machinery or product
features would. But other forms of substitution are even more
impressive, restructuring entire industries.

Fluid Boundaries Between Services and Manufacturing Products. Unfortunately, data anomalies in how the "service" and "product" sectors of the economy are measured ("Measuring the Service Economy," 1985) obscure how fluid the boundaries are between the "services-producing" and "goods-producing" sectors. Specialized services such as product design, research and development, market research, accounting, or data analyses are captured as "manufacturing" costs if performed within manufacturing concerns but as "services" if provided externally. Internal salespeople are reflected in manufacturing employment, but external sales representatives and wholesalers are considered services. If a farmer harvests his or her own grain, the costs become "production" costs; if the farmer hires a professional combine operator, the activity is a service. Home cooking and clothes washing are not measured as service activities, but restaurants and automatic laundries are. The oil that provides a home's heat is a product sale, but electricity for the same purpose may come from a "service sector" utility. And so on.

Even more fundamentally, products themselves are only physical embodiments of the services they deliver. As Theodore Levitt (1969, p. 343) explains, "People do not buy or consume things. . . . They buy the expectation of benefits . . . not quarter-inch drills but quarter-inch holes." A diskette delivers a software program or data set, services. An automobile delivers flexible transportation, a service. Electrical appliances deliver entertainment, dishwashing, clothes cleaning and drying, or convenient cooking or food storage, all services. In fact, most products merely provide a more convenient or less costly form in which to purchase services. All "services" or "products" are really just means for providing satisfactions to customers.

Because technology constantly creates new potentials for substitutions — and the capacity to eliminate unneeded intermediaries — the boundary between services and manufactured goods is extremely fluid and varies widely over time. Recognizing this, manufacturers can extend the scope of their operations, lower their costs, and expand their margins by eliminating or taking over adjacent service functions — sometimes opening up whole new markets for themselves and new support industries for others. Consider the following two examples.

• In the early days of computers, a high priesthood controlled access to the huge machines that could run only in special, environmentally controlled temples. Programmers or others "submitted" punched cards or tapes for processing, often at inconvenient times determined by the priesthood. By designing their machines and software to be more "user friendly," manufacturers slowly eliminated the priesthood and expanded their markets. The success of Apple and the IBM PC was essentially due to this process, which (oddly enough) later opened more service and product opportunities through clever use of the computers and design of software.

• "Permanent press" and crease-resistant fabrics, which were manufacturing innovations, have significantly restructured the white goods, apparel, and personal service industries. In the past, those who could afford it sent their tablecloths, bed linens, and dress clothing (especially men's trousers and shirts) to the laundry, getting them back neatly ironed in a week or so. Others spent hours tediously ironing in their own homes. Permanent press and "wash and wear" fabrics shrank the commercial laundry business, increased the attractiveness of home washers, dryers, and "touch-up" irons, and freed domestic workers and homemakers for other tasks. To fully exploit permanent press possibilities, new detergents, whiteners, and home laundry equipment designs soon appeared—changing the nature of competition in those fields as well.

The potential for substitutions of products for services (and vice versa) abounds. Automated communication systems have eliminated tiers of banking, brokerage, and insurance personnel. Increased quality in home appliances and automobiles has decreased the time, cost, and frustration that consumers expend on maintenance and repair. Prepared gourmet foods, convenience mixes, and microwave dinners substitute for restaurant sales and home-cooking time. Conversely, cable network services replace home antenna sales and provide more of what the customer is really buying—increased quality in reception and choice in programs. Computer-aided design and manufacturing software substitutes for added production machinery. And so on.

Firms that recognize the fluidity of the boundaries between "products" and "services" and between the "services-producing" and "goods-producing" sectors of the economy will be in a position to take advantage of the implications. The strategies of different firms reflect their perceptions of where they lie along the spectrum from service to product. With service activities within a manufacturing firm today representing more than 75 percent of its costs—and generally more of its value added—some "manufacturing" firms are beginning to think of the factory itself as a service. Ge van Schaik, president of Heineken's, has been known to say, "We are just a marketing company with a production facility as a service."

Other entire industries that might traditionally be considered "manufacturing" industries are now looking more like "service" industries as technology encourages such specialization that each producing unit in the industry is essentially providing a "service" to the others with whom it forms various coalitions. This may be becoming the case for whole segments of the semiconductor and pharmaceuticals-biotechnology industries. Much of the former is structuring itself around design, silicon foundry, systems assembly, and/or distribution entities, each dominantly providing services for other levels of the chain. Much of the biotechnology industry is now in the form of independent research, cell line creating, process developing, clinical testing, and distribution (service) companies that create most of the value added for particular "products."

Services-Manufacturing Interface

Major Power Shifts

The examples mentioned above are only indicators of the intimate, mutually interacting, constantly changing relationships between manufacturing and services. At the macrolevel, services technologies have already profoundly changed much of the power balance between the "service" and "manufacturing" sectors as they are traditionally defined. At a micro, or individual enterprise level, the implications for manufacturing strategies are enormous. Figure 4.1 suggests the full range of the complex and often overlooked interrelationships between service and manufacturing firms. Using a classical "industry analysis" approach (Porter, 1980) within this framework can suggest how in many instances service companies have increased their bargaining power as lead customers, as major buyers and through buyers' coalitions, as product codevelopers, and as suppliers to manufacturing firms. More detailed analysis shows how this has affected individual manufacturers' strategies.

As Lead Customers. Because the number of major trunk airlines (service providers) declined with deregulation and the introduction of wide-bodied jets, aircraft manufacturers had to modify their strategies. The number of U.S. lead customers for a firm such as Boeing shrank to a handful of large "megacarriers," each with a more powerful bargaining position than before. The military could no longer provide the "first-order" volumes necessary to launch a commercial aircraft. Consequently, to obtain essential economies of scale and yet satisfy each customer, Boeing invested heavily (over $800 million) in flexible automation, allowing it to modify internal seating, baggage storage, maintenance systems, and customer convenience patterns to suit virtually any requirement its major (services) customers might demand over the useful life of the aircraft. Boeing is now even investigating whether and how to restructure the overall cabin configuration of its 747 aircraft in response to the recommendation of Scandinavian Air's president—that aircraft seating patterns would be optimized for business passengers if the cabin cross section were a horizontal ellipse rather than a circle or vertical ellipse. Continued or extended deregulation in the United States and in Europe could lead to further concentrations in the domestic and world airline industry, with even greater power shifts occurring.

Even when buyers have not consolidated into large individual units, services technologies allow them to achieve similar bargaining power.

Figure 4.1. Some Mutual Interactions Among Manufacturing and Service Activities.

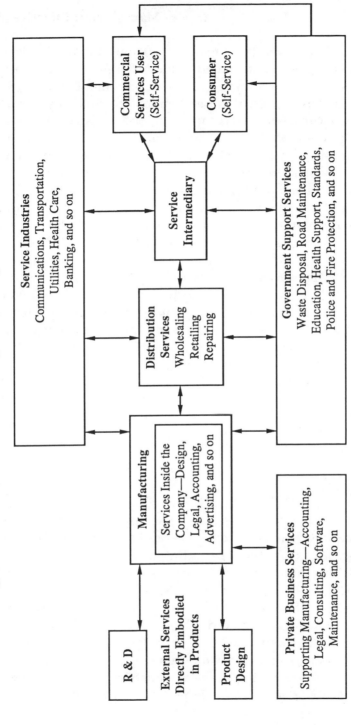

⟶ = The fact of trade means that each party benefits from the presence of the other.

• For example, a team of airline and manufacturer-supplier experts, coordinated by the Air Transport Association, has created an automated parts procurement system (Spec 2000) that is expected to save millions of dollars yet can be accessed with a personal computer. Spec 2000 is a computerized compendium of manufacturers' catalogues including more than a million part numbers and an automated computer-to-computer ordering system. The system not only allows an airline to get comparative specification and quotation data but also gives information about how vendors meet their delivery and performance criteria, thus increasing the information leverage of all potential purchasers ("Spec 2000 . . . ," 1987).

As Major Buyers. A large retailer (such as Sears, IKEA, or Toys R Us) can offer instant distribution, powerful presentation, and financial support for any consumer product specialty or innovation it chooses to carry. Thus, overseas producers have immediate access to advanced U.S. (or European) markets without creating the costly distribution channels they once had to build. Access to large retail computer chains thus provided rapid penetration for many Asian "clones" and intense competition for U.S. manufacturers, restructuring the entire computer industry. Similarly, Super Valu (in foods) and McKesson (in pharmaceuticals) have become true "channel commanders," controlling the linkage between their suppliers and retail customers.

• Super Valu can provide full support for a grocery store's point-of-sale scanning system, its shelf price verification needs, its receiving function, even for goods from direct delivery suppliers, and so on. By performing its distribution task so efficiently that even some chain grocers use its services instead of buying directly, Super Valu offers small independents the same advantages of scale that major chains have. Using the same approaches, McKesson and other drug wholesalers in the last ten years have increased the percentage of pharmaceuticals going through their distribution systems from 45 percent to more than 65 percent (with more than 85 percent estimated for the mid-1990s) as manufacturers increasingly recognize that such groups can simultaneously service their retail customers more efficiently and share the gains to the benefit of both manufacturers and retailers.

As Product Codevelopers. Hospital chains such as Humana, with its $4 billion in revenues and eighty-five hospital care units (with a total of more than 17,500 beds), have become important standard setters in medical care — and major targets for medical products and equipment manufacturers. To attract doctors to practice in its system, Humana must have the most current available equipment, while meeting the requirements of state certificate-of-need processes and the government's Diagnosis Related Group (DRG) payment system, which limits the amounts that can be reimbursed for individual procedures. To meet these conflicting specifications, manufacturers have had to undertake much more targeted development strategies than they used in the past. To assist them in its own interest, Humana has created a corporate-level group working with manufacturers, helping to specify and develop new products, sometimes providing clinical testing facilities, and occasionally even taking a venture capital position in newer companies. When a new technology proves effective, Humana can quickly roll it out to all its hospital and outpatient facilities — and with its volume require the producer to provide needed educational, training, or supplies support.

As Suppliers. Service companies' cost leverages have also increased significantly because of new technologies. For example, many manufacturers now find that their medical care or insurance outlays for employees are higher than their own profits. Hence, new strategies creating coalitions with providers, insurers, or major hospital chains have emerged as key elements in cost control and profitability. Deregulation has created much more powerful intermodal transportation companies with handling capabilities that increase shipping efficiencies enormously — but at a strategic cost. The transportation companies have greatly enhanced their bargaining power versus manufacturers or other shippers. Some companies have maintained their private trucking fleets primarily to counterbalance that

increased power (Johnson and Schneider, 1988). Similarly, large
money-center banks have increased their effectiveness and bargaining power through their information systems. They now
have the information, instant capital access, and worldwide
connections to manage a company's financial assets with a
knowledge base and leverage that few manufacturers can equal.
And, increasingly, they can efficiently offer selected accounting,
credit, and bill-paying services that the producers might have
performed in the past. Other examples of supplier leverage
abound.

• ServiceMaster ($1.4 billion in revenues) can lower its
customers' costs by managing the complete maintenance of
their complex equipment. Or it will, on occasion, redesign the
customer's physical plant, provide capital for the plant, operate
it, and share resulting gains with its customer. Giant Bechtel
($4.5 billion in revenues) has a new unit, Bechtel Development
Corporation, that will coordinate the complete design, construction, financing, and development of large-scale projects
such as major buildings, harbor facilities, industrial parks, and
health care centers. In selected cases, it will take a profit-sharing
or equity position in lieu of part of its fee. Verax, a world leader
in developing immobilized mammalian cell processes for biotechnology, can eliminate the complex process-engineering
step for its customers, provide the full production process on a
license basis, or take over the manufacturing itself for a part-
nership or royalty position.

Scale and Stability in Service Markets

Such relationships between manufacturers and service
companies are far from coincidental. It has often been asserted
that service companies are very dependent on manufacturers;
that is, many service firms primarily handle manufacturers'
products or sell a majority of their services (such as freight
handling, advertising, and so on) to producers. However, it is
equally true that many manufacturers sell their products principally to service firms (as do producers of aircraft, medical
equipment, computer systems, textbooks, and so on). While

complete intersectoral sales figures are not available, the simple facts are that 76 percent of all employment is in services and 72 percent of GNP is generated by the service sector. This clearly indicates that the service sector and its employees are the major markets for most consumer and "commercial" products. One particularly extensive study by Stephen Roach (1985) of Morgan Stanley estimates that 85 percent of all high-technology communications and related equipment sold in the U.S. in 1985 went to industries (predominantly services) whose primary output is knowledge or information.

It should also be noted that the markets that the service sector provides for manufactured goods are growing more rapidly and more stable than manufacturing markets. There is substantial evidence (Urquart, 1981; Moore, 1987) that the service sector has a stabilizing effect on the economy as a whole and since the early 1950s has helped lessen the severity and shorten the duration of recessionary periods. Bureau of Labor Statistics data show that in business cycles from 1948 to 1980, U.S. services employment increased at an average annual rate of 2.1 percent during economic contractions as well as 4.8 percent during expansions (Urquart, 1981). In contrast, employment in the goods-producing sector *declined* at an average annual rate of 8.3 percent during recessions and advanced at a rate of only 3.8 percent during expansions. Further, the highly decentralized nature of service employment means that future consumer buying power is likely to be more dispersed geographically and less driven by cyclical swings of large manufacturing industries—or the communities they dominate. Analysis of the Bureau of Labor Statistics establishment data base for states and selected areas shows that every state now has more service jobs than it has manufacturing, mining, construction, and agricultural jobs combined. Such dispersion of economic activity has clearly been brought about by the technologies that allow service enterprises to be located and efficiently managed in many decentralized locations.

Expanded Manufacturing Markets

While changes brought about by technology have shifted economic power balances away from manufacturers and toward their service customers and suppliers, they also offer manufacturers significant opportunities to expand their markets and improve the value added and competitiveness of their products.

• For example, they offer a rich new array of channels through which manufacturers can reach specialized market segments. Electronic home shopping, telemarketing, and interactive video terminals located in banks, airports, hotels, airplanes, and shopping malls allow manufacturers to contact whole new groupings of customers in comfortable psychological situations where they are likely to buy. Adaptations of these technologies in retail showrooms allow customers to see and select from a manufacturer's complete product line when the retailer—for example, a shoe or furniture outlet—cannot carry all possible sizes and variations in current stocks. Some technologies allow personalized design of products such as shoes or ski boots to the customer's unique dimensions or desires by directly linking the retail floor to the factory's cutting room.

More significantly, marketing strategists have documented that as personal affluence or the sheer size of markets grow, there is an increasing demand for differentiated, individualized, or customized products (McKenna, 1988). Manufacturers have begun to adopt flexible, automated production systems in order to produce the necessary variety at reasonable costs. But the key to sales in such markets today is fastest response time at lowest system costs. U.S.-based manufacturers that are able to link flexible production systems directly to their customers' market intelligence networks should have very real competitive advantages (in timing, inventory, and transportation costs) over foreign producers. In heavy, bulky, or complex products such as automobiles, it could become impossible for overseas producers of more standardized lines to compete against responsive, integrated U.S. manufacturing-distribution systems. Already, foreign firms are investing in manufacturing capacity in the United States to get closer to its huge, highly variable marketplace, in the process helping to generate a genuine "remanufacturing" of the United States for certain products. And the number and range of goods that it pays to produce in the United States (or closer to their markets anywhere) rather than overseas will continue to expand.

• Such considerations seem to be an important factor in Honda's rapid proliferation of automobile models and options, its increased emphasis on U.S. production, and the importation of its own "just-in-time" suppliers to the United States (when U.S. manufacturers proved unwilling or unable to meet Honda's service and quality demands). Honda now offers a much wider variety of styles and options and faster delivery to the U.S. marketplace than it ever could have from a solely Japanese base. Increasingly, it will have to obtain more of its components and subassemblies from nearby, U.S.-based producers to obtain the response time it needs without escalating inventory costs.

• The U.S. textile and apparel manufacturing industries that were decimated by foreign competition have begun a resurgence because of these changes ("American Textiles...," 1988). "Quick response" reordering systems linking retailers to apparel manufacturers and textile mills can provide significant competitive advantages. Fabric can be delivered in the United States in one-third the time it takes from Taiwan, and computer-aided design and manufacturing links between cutters on Seventh Avenue and southeastern mills can halve the time from design to delivery—a critical factor in fashion goods ("Taking Control in the Rag Trade," 1987). By affixing uniform product code (UPC bar code) labels on its products at the factory and offering electronic ordering systems, Levi Strauss now lowers system costs by providing quick replenishment of stocks from its U.S. factories to retailers who connect their checkout registers' bar-code scanners directly to their (and Strauss's) inventory reordering computer systems ("How Levi Strauss...," 1987).

Services as Manufacturing Inputs

Many aspects of a manufacturer's cost competitiveness depend intimately on service activities, whether performed within the firm or purchased from vendors. Greater efficiencies in communication, transportation, financing, distribution,

Table 4.2. U.S. Versus Japanese Productivity in Services.

	Japan		United States		U.S. Output per Hour as a Percentage of Japanese Output per Hour
	1970	1980	1970	1980	1980
Private domestic business	3.59	6.01	9.40	10.06	167%
Agriculture	1.37	2.38	16.53	18.36	771%
Selected services					
Transportation and communications	3.86	5.66	9.29	13.14	232%
Electricity, gas, water	14.01	19.74	21.98	25.38	129%
Trade	2.88	4.53	6.88	7.92	175%
Finance and insurance	6.69	12.03	8.21	8.20	68%
Business services	3.39	3.60	7.69	7.59	211%
Manufacturing	3.91	8.00	7.92	10.17	127%

Note: Productivity is measured as output per hour in 1975 dollars.
Source: UNIPUB, 1984, p. 67.

health care, or waste handling (service industries) can markedly affect a manufacturer's direct costs. To the extent that these and other services can be more efficiently provided because of services technologies, they lower living costs for workers and improve the quality of life they can enjoy at any given wage level— thus controlling wage demands in countries where services are most efficiently provided. In most areas, the efficiency of U.S. services industries has been more than competitive with our international trading partners—even compared with Japan (see Table 4.2). Although output-per-hour statistics are hard to evaluate and some changes have undoubtedly occurred since, 1980 data indicate that except in the area of finance and insurance, the U.S. was significantly more efficient than Japan in all major service industries (Quinn, Baruch, and Paquette, 1987).

Aggressively managing their service inputs can provide manufacturing enterprises a major attack point for improving their competitiveness in the future. Because of the sophistication, scale, and scope economies that service companies can now bring to bear, manufacturers increasingly find that they can gain competitive advantage—in both efficiency and effectiveness—by having specialized service enterprises handle their accounting, legal, payroll, employee benefits, maintenance, repair, or even research and design functions. This is one of the factors contributing to the rapid growth of the business-services industry in recent years—in 1982, business services accounted for $90.7 million of GNP and employed 3.4 million people; by 1986, they provided $162.8 million of GNP and 4.9 million jobs (Tschetter, 1987).

As technology creates new capabilities, manufacturers and service providers will constantly have to reassess when to produce their own services and when to buy them externally. By offering manufacturers the option of buying services from the outside, external service groups provide the benefits of a competitive benchmark for controlling functions that otherwise can become bloated internal monopolies. Even without actual outsourcing, the implicit threat of outside service competitors can be a powerful motivator for internal groups to innovate, control costs, and increase the quality of their outputs. Few other management techniques have proved as useful for this purpose.

• For example, ADP Services developed a flexible payroll-handling system that was so low in cost that ADP soon took over payrolls for 10 percent of the potential client base in its geographical areas. From this vantage point, it expanded into routine bank accounting and tax filings for its customers and their employees. In a logical extension, it took over Employment Retirement Income Security Act (ERISA) reporting, certain personnel records and analysis functions, and even personalized communication functions by printing slogans, messages, or logos on checks or notes included with payroll checks to employees. All this allowed producers a check on their own costs for these functions, access to economies of scale and lowered overhead costs, and expertise that they might not be able to afford in-house.

Such service companies have also become major innovators. Independent service providers are motivated and able to provide imaginative technology investments that their individual customers could not afford in-house. Thus, they begin to set new competitive standards for the quality, range, and flexibility of their offerings. Fortunately for their customers, because of intense competition, service companies often cannot translate their product improvements into higher margins. As a consequence, productivity improvements in services often show up in measured data only as productivity increases for their customers—frequently manufacturers. Unless manufacturers and others seek out these innovations, they can miss out on important sources of competitive advantage. For example:

• Federal Express has long been a leader in the development of package sorting, handling, and control systems and equipment. Using this expertise, the company now offers its COSMOS and supporting systems as part of a service to help customers automate and manage their own shipping docks and package or message-handling functions ("Casebook: NCR Corp.," 1988).

• Michigan Bell has created innovative new "facilitating" services, such as those that improve communications among the big three automakers and their suppliers, coordinating hardware and software vendors in developing and exchanging engineering drawings and specifications between job shops and factories. Although Michigan Bell started with such large company networking projects, it should be able to roll this experience out to other areas. It can offer a shared service (with a standard interface system) providing state-of-the-art design and specification coordination to large and small manufacturers alike ("Ameritech Has Promises...," 1987).

Converting Overhead into Value Added

External service groups may also be instrumental in helping companies convert today's seemingly intransigent overhead cost escalation into increased value added. As flexible manufacturing systems (FMS) and computer-integrated manufacturing (CIM) drive variable production costs ever lower, the percentage of costs represented by service support and other fixed costs will increase (Gunn, 1987). Consequently, in the future there should be even more incentives for effective use of service suppliers' innovative capabilities. In fact, FMS and CIM installations themselves are unlikely to be effective unless proper attention is given in advance to service-support arrangements such as training, cost accounting, organization, communication, and control systems. Because internal groups are likely to be inexperienced in such matters or biased by old ways of doing things, the proper expertise for such changeovers may often be found only in external service groups.

However, services should not be regarded simply as external or "overhead" adjuncts to the manufacturing process, bought to keep a factory going, obtain materials, or deliver products to customers. They are often significantly embodied in the product itself. The major value added to a product is typically due less to its basic commodity value (for example, producing the grain and vegetables in a processed food or the "body in white" for an automobile) than to the styling features, perceived quality, subjective taste, and marketing presentation added by "service" activities inside or outside the company (Office of the U.S. Trade Representative, 1983). In most manufacturing industries, service costs (such as planning, accounting, inventory, quality assurance, transportation, design, advertising, and distribution costs) generally outweigh direct labor costs by factors of between three and ten to one.

Yet most companies have diligently driven down direct labor costs while only cautiously attacking the greater costs and value-added potentials of service functions (Miller and Vollmann, 1985). Some examples illustrate the advantages that manufacturers can obtain from aggressively managing their product design and system complexity and properly exploiting the leverage that service functions can contribute to perceived product quality.

  • In the automobile industry, designing and introducing a new car line are major components of overhead costs and significant contributors to the value that the customer perceives. At Ford, this design cycle had taken five to six years and could cost several billion dollars. In 1980, Ford's CEO and president decided to undertake a new "simultaneous design" process for their new upper-middle line, which became the Taurus/Sable cars. To integrate design from research to marketing, they established a core group, called Team Taurus, that had a full-time representative from all of the critical groups within Ford—product design, component engineering, manufacturing, sales, marketing, purchasing, service, legal, environmental and safety engineering, and corporate headquarters (virtually all service operations). Instead of moving the design step by step along these groups to the marketplace—with numerous conflicts and design reworks—Team Taurus involved everyone from the outset. The result: Taurus/Sable's introduction cost some $250 million *less* than its design budget and was exceptionally successful in the marketplace. Future cars will probably be designed with the same process in only three to four years, potentially saving Ford hundreds of millions of dollars more and ensuring that manufacturing design is much closer to the customer (Quinn, 1988a).

   • Black and Decker (B&D), faced by both U.S. inflation and strong cost competition from overseas manufacturers, decided that it had to radically redesign its products for greater value added and lower cost. It focused on simplifying its product offerings, developing a "family" look for the 122 basic tools (with hundreds of variations) in its line, standardizing materials and components, and creating new product features specifically adapting the products to meet worldwide (non-U.S.) product specifications. In a program that took seven years to break even, B&D drove labor costs in each component down to such "trivial" levels that no competitor could obtain a meaningful competitive edge by simply having lower labor costs. Interestingly, however, B&D found that its simplification and automation programs drove out about $3 of overhead for each $1 of labor saved, and its standardization programs substantially improved the rapidity, efficiency, and effectiveness of its future product development capabilities (Lehnerd, 1987).

   The Strategic Planning Institute's PIMS data base clearly shows that financial performance is directly related to the way customers perceive the quality of a company's goods or services

(Uttal, 1987). Not surprisingly, one of the biggest determinants in perceptions of overall "product" quality is the amount and type of customer service received. As the two examples above illustrate, greater attention to product design both reduces repairs needed and provides a "halo" effect concerning the way the product actually performs. Using technology more directly to support its product in the field, Cadillac has vastly improved its service ratings by linking its dealers' mechanics with a corps of ten corporate engineers who use a computerized data base of engineering drawings, service bulletins, and data links to walk the mechanics step by step through difficult repairs — ensuring that a Cadillac gets repaired right the first time (Uttal, 1987).

Manufacturers as Service Providers

In a variety of other ways, services and service technologies are becoming vital competitive weapons for large "manufacturing" companies. For example:

• General Motors has found that financial services are an indispensable competitive weapon. General Motors Acceptance Corporation (GMAC) now manages over $75 billion in private consumer debt, has provided one-third to one-half of GM's profitability in recent years, and has allowed GM to offer 1.9 percent financing as a pricing strategy to offset competition on a "features" or production-cost basis. Ford has stated that it hopes to increase its own financial services business to 30 percent of earnings as both a growth vector and a way to balance cyclical swings in the automobile business ("Car Finance Companies...," 1988).

• At IBM, software has always been a key to success, especially in the early years, when it was "bundled" into product and rental prices. Now, with the hardware becoming extremely low-cost and competitive, IBM has been shifting its focus even more toward software, networks, and communication linkages (services) as its basis for adding value and improving profits ("Computers," 1987).

Some manufacturers initially ventured into services to

support their main product offerings, then found that the service itself became an attractive new product line. For example:

    • Because of the very high costs its customers incurred when their equipment went down for repair, Caterpillar Company developed one of the largest, fastest-response parts systems in existence. Around 1980, some of Caterpillar's customers began asking for help in managing their own parts control and distribution. Caterpillar responded and now has a lively business providing worldwide logistics and transportation service to large manufacturers interested in efficient warehousing and delivery of their own parts ("CLS Explores New Logistic Frontiers," 1987).

    Similarly, food companies such as Pillsbury have noted that their large-scale distribution and support systems can provide growth opportunities in industrial and institutional feeding. Manufacturers of complex test and measurement equipment, such as that used in the nuclear power and chemical industries, have found that they can make as much money by screening and training personnel for their customers as they can from their equipment sales. Similar creative expansions of their own services capabilities can offer other manufacturers new opportunities to share directly in the growing services market (Canton, 1984).

Global Manufacturing Competition

    One of the areas where services and service technologies affect manufacturing most markedly is international operations. About one-fifth of the total capital invested in U.S. manufacturing firms is now in facilities outside the United States (Drucker, 1987), and trade statistics indicate that the profits, royalties, and intercorporate sales that these multinational entities remit to the United States provide a favorable net balance of trade for the country. But improved telecommunications, air transport, and cargo-handling technologies have forced virtually all manufacturers (regardless of size) to consider their supply sources, markets, and competition on a worldwide scale or lose their competitive position. Effective coordination of large manufacturing enterprises'—and many much smaller companies'—international operations now depends heavily on services technologies and efficiencies.

Global information concerning exchange rates, transportation, and sourcing has become a crucial competitive weapon in manufacturing. While overhead costs tend to drop markedly with offshore manufacturing, logistics costs tend to *increase* by a factor of about 20 percent, and tariffs can become significant ("International Logistics Management," 1987). So important are these costs that before an experienced Japanese automobile manufacturer began a joint venture in the United States, it set a target of having the most cost-efficient inbound-outbound logistics system in the world. Since most of the other costs of manufacturing here and in Japan were essentially fixed, logistics control technologies became the key strategic variables.

Economies of scale in international operations today are often due more to the corporation's service capabilities—that is, technology transfer, marketing skills, financial services, logistics, and so on—than to its plant scale economies. A significant component of a multinational company's competitive edge is its capacity to handle cross-border data and services flows (Sauvant, 1986). Consequently, maintaining the freedom of these flows is a very sensitive and critical point in maintaining the international competitiveness of U.S. manufacturing as well as service enterprises. For international manufacturing operations, managing services technologies has become an increasingly vital link in obtaining competitive advantage. And the value added in what a manufacturer sells overseas is dominated by its service rather than direct production functions (Shelp, 1981). In fact, the latter (service or knowledge) components are those that the host country can least easily provide and are thus the company's critical competitive advantage over local competitors.

But it is the integration of world capital markets (service institutions) through electronic communications (service technologies) that is perhaps forcing the greatest changes in major companies' manufacturing strategies. While the total of all goods and services sold in international trade was approxi-

Table 4.3. Exchange Rate Fluctuations, February 1985 to October 1987.

Percentage Change in Value of Dollar Against Various Countries' Currencies	Country
− 50	Switzerland
− 47	West Germany
− 45	Japan
− 37	Britain
− 26	Taiwan
− 3	Canada
− 3	South Korea
+ 5	Saudi Arabia
+ 110	Israel
+ 687	Mexico

Source: Adapted from "Economic and Financial Indicators," 1987, p. 130.

mately $4 trillion in 1987, the Clearing House for International Payments (CHIPS) alone handled almost $140 trillion in international financial transactions, Euromarkets another $150 trillion, and so on. Instead of following goods, money now flows toward the highest available real interest rates or returns in safer, more stable economic situations. As a result, exchange rates have fluctuated by about 50 percent among major trading partners within a few months (see Table 4.3), principally because of fiscal or monetary, not trade or management, decisions. Such fluctuations can enormously change the relative costs of production or importing from a particular location in a short time period.

Simply targeting higher annual productivity improvements (typically in the 5 percent to 10 percent range) will not cope with changes of this magnitude. A firm now needs to manage several groups of global portfolios—of production sites, market outlets, and financial sources in different geographical locations—among which it can switch resources and management focus rapidly and flexibly. Since most firms cannot afford to own all such entities themselves, they tend to form a series of coalitions, linking their capabilities and their partners' by information, communication, and contract arrangements rather than by ownership (vertical or horizontal integration) ties. Because of their high value-added potentials, service companies are central to many of these coalitions. For years, of course, such service-production integration (of banks, producers, and export distribution companies) has been at the heart of Japan's trading power. Similar coalitions appear likely to provide an essential model for other nations, including the United States, in the future.

Future Research

Given the importance of services in the economy, the ways technology is transforming the service sector, the fluidity of the boundaries between services and manufacturing, and the intimate relationship between manufacturing and services competitiveness, it seems appropriate to investigate more closely the technology-related strategic practices of successful and unsuccessful service firms. With the support of many successful service companies, profiled as the best users or developers of technology in their fields, we are identifying patterns of management that lead to greatest effectiveness and contrasting these with firms that have failed or have been less successful. There is a strong need for more intensive research, new data bascs, and in-depth case studies in this area.

References

"American Textiles: Cutting Their Coat. . . ." *Economist*, Feb. 13, 1988, pp. 62–63.

"Ameritech Has Promises for Future Manufacturing." *Managing Automation*, Oct. 1987, pp. 48–49.

Booz, Allen & Hamilton. "From Strategic Planning to Strategic Performance: Closing the Achievement Gap." *Outlook*, n.d., p. 4.

Bureau of Economic Analysis. "The National Income and Product Accounts of the United States." *Survey of Current Business*, July 1988, pp. 78, 81.

Canton, I. "Learning to Love the Service Economy." *Harvard Business Review*, 1984, *62*, pp. 89–97.

"Car Finance Companies: A Nice Little Runner." *Economist*, Aug. 6, 1988, pp. 63–64.

"Casebook: NCR Corp." *Distribution*, Apr. 1988, p. 58.

"CLS Explores New Logistics Frontiers." *Distribution*, Sept. 1987, pp. 52–55.

"Computers: The New Look." *Business Week*, Nov. 30, 1987, pp. 78–86.

Drucker, P. "From World Trade to World Investment." *Wall Street Journal*, May 26, 1987, p. 32.

"Economic and Financial Indicators." *Economist*, Oct. 17, 1987, p. 130.

Faulhaber, G., Noam, E., and Tasley, R. (eds.). *Services in Transition: The Impact of Information Technology on the Service Sector*. Cambridge, Mass.: Ballinger, 1986.

Goldhar, J., and Burnham, D. "Changing Concepts of the Manufacturing System." In *U.S. Leadership in Manufacturing: A Symposium at the Eighteenth Annual Meeting of the National Academy of Engineering, November 4, 1982*. Washington, D.C.: National Academy Press, 1983.

Gunn, T. *Manufacturing for Competitive Advantage*. Cambridge, Mass.: Ballinger, 1987.

"How Levi Strauss Is Getting the Lead out of Its Pipeline." *Business Week*, Dec. 21, 1987, p. 92.

"International Logistics Management." *Distribution*, Oct. 1987, pp. 13–20.

Johnson, J., and Schneider, K. "Private Trucking: A Dinosaur?" *Business Horizons*, Jan. 1988, pp. 73–78.

Kutscher, R., and Mark, J. "The Services Sector: Some Common Perceptions Reviewed." *Monthly Labor Review*, Apr. 1983, pp. 21–24.

Lehnerd, A. P. "Revitalizing the Manufacture and Design of Mature Global Products." In B. Guile and H. Brooks (eds.), *Technology and Global Industry*. Washington, D.C.: National Academy Press, 1987.

Levitt, T. *The Marketing Mode: Pathways to Corporate Growth*. New York: McGraw-Hill, 1969.

Levitt, T. "The Industrialization of Service." *Harvard Business Review*, 1976, *54*, pp. 63–74.

McKenna, R. "Marketing in an Age of Diversity." *Harvard Business Review*, 1988, *66*, pp. 88–95.

"Measuring the Service Economy." *New York Times*, Oct. 27, 1985, p. F4.

Miller, J., and Vollmann, T. "The Hidden Factory." *Harvard Business Review*, 1985, *63*, pp. 142–150.

Moore, G. "The Services Industries and the Business Cycle." *Business Economics*, Apr. 1987, pp. 12–17.

Office of the U.S. Trade Representative. *U.S. National Study on Trade in Services*. Washington, D.C.: Office of the U.S. Trade Representative, 1983.

Porter, M. E. *Competitive Strategy: Techniques for Analyzing Industries and Competitors*. New York: Free Press, 1980.

Quinn, J. B. *Ford: Team Taurus*. Hanover, N.H.: Amos Tuck School of Business Administration, 1988a.

Quinn, J. B. "Reference Note on the Financial Services Industry." In J. B. Quinn, H. Mintzberg, and R. James (eds). *The Strategy Process: Concepts, Contexts, and Cases*. Englewood Cliffs, N.J.: Prentice-Hall, 1988b.

Quinn, J. B., Baruch, J., and Paquette, P. "Technology in Services." *Scientific American*, Dec. 1987, pp. 50–58.

Roach, S. S. "Information Economy Comes of Age." *Information Management Review*, Jan. 1985, pp. 9–18.

Roach, S. S. "Technology and the Service Sector: America's Hidden Competitive Challenge." In B. Guile and J. B. Quinn (eds.), *Technology in Services: Policies for Growth, Trade, and Employment*. Washington, D.C.: National Academy Press, 1988.

Sauvant, K. *International Transactions in Services: The Politics of Transborder Data Flows*. Boulder, Colo.: Westview Press, 1986.

Shelp, R. *Beyond Industrialization: Ascendency of the Global Service Economy*. New York: Praeger, 1981.

"Spec 2000 Weds Airline Procurement Systems with Automatic Technology." *Air Transport World*, Jan. 1987, p. 66.

Strategic Planning Institute. *Profit Impact of Market Strategy (PIMS) Data Base*. Cambridge, Mass.: Strategic Planning Institute, 1985.

"Taking Control in the Rag Trade." *Business Month*, Apr. 1987, pp. 48–49.

Tschetter, J. "Producer Services Industries: Why Are They Growing So Fast?" *Monthly Labor Review*, Dec. 1987, pp. 31–40.

UNIPUB. *Measuring Productivity: Trends and Comparisons from the First International Productivity Symposium, Tokyo, Japan, 1983.* New York: UNIPUB, 1984.

Urquart, M. "The Services Industry: Is It Recession Proof?" *Monthly Labor Review*, Oct. 1981, pp. 12–18.

Uttal, B. "Companies That Serve You Best." *Fortune*, Dec. 7, 1987, pp. 98–116.

Part Two

Organization and Human Resource Management in Service Firms

5

Strategic Implications
of Service Technologies

Peter K. Mills
Dennis J. Moberg

Organization theory offers a unique perspective to those who seek a better understanding of service organizations. While marketing specialists focus on the strategic questions of adapting an organization's service offerings to market realities and operations analysts concentrate on the design of effective service operations, organization theory serves as an important bridge between these two levels of analysis. Organization theory is concerned with the effectiveness of the organization as a whole. Consequently, it is more concerned with the *coordination* of marketing and operations than it is with providing answers to the dilemmas of each function.

Equally important, organization theory contains two paradigms that take perspectives similar to those of marketing and operational analysis but emphasize the effectiveness of the entire organization. One is the *outside-in*, or strategic management, paradigm. Like marketing, this concerns how organizations adapt or react to their environments; however, the outside-in paradigm also focuses on how this adaptation process should be internally managed. The other is the *inside-out*, or technology management, paradigm. Like operational analysis, this concerns the design of effective service delivery systems; however, the technology paradigm also focuses on the strategic implications of these designs.

Our intention is to draw on the technology paradigm in order to illuminate certain strategic options available to service organizations. The first section of this chapter describes service technology. Of special concern is the *relational* feature, or social transactions, of such technologies and the rather problematic role that clients play as "partial organizational members" and sources of uncertainty. The second section of the chapter deals with this client role much more systematically, disaggregating it into practically meaningful elements. Here our objective is to develop a useful scheme that practitioners can use to analyze their operations. The third section identifies three different strategies for including the client in the organization and discusses the implications of each. Since we are focusing on "technical" relationships, we do not concern ourselves with opportunities or threats in the organization's environment or with the specific nature of market niches or potential segments. Rather, we address these strategies largely from the standpoint of effectively designing service operations around their unique competencies.

Technology: The Starting Point of Strategy Formulation

Few concepts are as crucial to the functioning of organizations as technology. Several writers have underscored the importance of technology by noting that technology is a major source of productivity gain in organizations; the jobs that people actually perform within the firm are largely determined by technology—that is, if technology changes, then jobs are correspondingly changed; and the overall design of organizations is dictated by the technology (Emery and Trist, 1965; Litterer, 1973; Thompson, 1967). While such beliefs are widespread, technology remains a most enigmatic variable. Scholars have found that technology is a very elusive organizational concept, difficult to separate from other organizational properties. And practitioners have often conceived of technology in such concrete terms, as embodied in particular tools and machines, that it has taken on little analytical force.

The most widely accepted definition of technology is any activity employed in the conversion of an input into the output (Perrow, 1967). In other words, technology is problem-solving activities. Robert Dubin (1968) segmented these activities into two fundamental types: machine technology and knowledge technology. Machine technology comprises all the tools, instruments, machines, and formulas that are essential to the performance of the task. This type of technology lends itself to processes and systems where output can readily be determined and monitored for compliance with specifications. Conversely, knowledge technology comprises the set of ideas responsible for expressing the goals of the work and the importance of the rationale for the techniques employed. It includes all the academic and applied disciplines that are used in doing the work.

Whether one is dealing with machine technology or knowledge technology, organization theorists are concerned not so much with the sophistication of the technology as with its effectiveness in problem solving. From an organizational viewpoint, technologies are optimal to the extent that they are sufficient to contend with all the problems that arise, reducing each to a series of straightforward calculations and routine operations. Insufficiency of technology results in uncertainty, a lack of information about how to deal with problems of converting inputs to outputs. Uncertainty causes organizational problems not because it paralyzes action but because it requires structures and processes to contend with it (including structures and processes that coordinate marketing and operations functions). For example, to produce goods, organizations need to be structured differently when there is insufficient technology in the process (such as in the taking of spy satellite photos during sunspot periods) than when the technology is sufficient (such as in the production of hydroelectric power).

One can conceive of many instances where technology is sufficient in manufacturing, but this is not the case with services. With high-tech services (for example, computer repair), this is obvious. However, even unsophisticated service technologies have uncertainties that their manufacturing counterparts do not. In order to understand just how endemic uncertainty is to the services, we will compare their technologies with those of manufacturing.

Service Technologies Versus Manufacturing Technologies

There is presently no consensus for a sharp delineation between service and manufacturing technologies (Mills and Moberg, 1982). One reason is that most organizations produce outputs that are in part product and in part service (Sasser, Olsen, and Wyckoff, 1978). Consider a restaurant. While meals are manufactured, service amenities such as ambience and menu choice constitute a vital element of customer utility. In fact, the purest manufacturing case that one could offer involves some service production and the purest service case some manufacturing. Even human service organizations, which owe their uniqueness almost entirely to the type of service rendered to clients, manufacture consultant's reports, blueprints, and surgical corrections. An additional factor that contributes to the fuzziness of the difference between manufacturing and service technologies is that service outputs are more difficult to separate into units. Instead, we are forced to speak of a "bundle" of services that is offered (Reder, 1969), and we can only presume that they are consumed.

Clearly the "bundle" notion of service output renders service technologies a heterogeneous array of activities (Stigler, 1956). Furthermore, the essence of service technology in contrast to manufacturing technology is evident from the writings of none other than Karl Marx (who may have had a better appreciation of the services than he did of the efficacy of economic systems): "Services are consumed the moment that they are produced. The useful effect can be consumed only during the process of production. It does not exist as a utility different from the process, a use-thing which does not function as an article of commerce, does not circulate as a commodity after it has been produced" (cited in Berger, 1970, p. 54). This early conception, pointing out two distinctive characteristics of service technologies, is reflected in many current conceptions of service technologies (for example, Fuchs, 1968; Sasser, 1976; Lovelock and Young, 1979; Berry, 1984). The first distinctive characteristic is that, unlike that of manufacturing, the output of a service organization is a use-thing, a performance or an effort that tends to be *intangible* (Sabolo, 1975). The intangibility of service outputs leads to two other important features of service technologies: Clients often have few objective reference points to use in perceiving the value of the service they consume (Bowen and Jones, 1986). Relevant cues are ambiguous, and client perceptions are highly subject to social influence (Berger and Luckmann, 1966). In addition, the intangibility of services provides incentives for service operations to make relations with service providers more satisfying to clients. Thus, an important factor in the satisfactions that clients derive from the services rendered by banks is the pleasantness of tellers and loan officers, as the empirical work of Schneider and his colleagues has demonstrated (Schneider, Parkington, and Buxton, 1980; Schneider and Bowen, 1985).

A second distinctive characteristic of service technologies originally conceived by Marx is the *simultaneous production and consumption* of services (Fisher, 1935; Clark, 1940). This implies that the customer and the service producer must interact for the delivery of the service to be complete. In contrast to manufacturing workers, service employees are actually "minifactories" unto themselves, because they not only produce the output but sell it as well (Sasser, Olsen, and Wyckoff, 1978). This has several implications. Since the client must be brought into the work flow, the technology is more uncertain. Clients are typically ego-involved in the service production process, since it is they or their personal property that constitutes the raw material transformed, and there is insufficient knowledge or machinery to contend with this potential client reactivity. This is in stark contrast to the benign malleability of the inanimate raw materials transformed in manufacturing operations.

Clearly, client reactivity requires the knowledge technology used in a service operation to extend beyond materials handling. Not only is knowledge technology necessary because of the uncertainty inherent in client reactivity, but, more significantly, knowledge will be necessary to provide the rationale or explanation for the actions actually taken by the service provider. This is a form of technical justification that is undertaken solely by service providers. Technical justification is a bonding mechanism to assure customers of the service provider's competence under conditions of uncertainty. This is causal information for a decision and is also instrumental in clients' receptivity to the service being rendered. And the more reactivity expected of clients, the more technological justification can be correspondingly expected of the service provider.

Are Service Technologies Ever Sufficient?

Manufacturing technologies are occasionally sufficient. In some circumstances, there is little residual uncertainty, and this allows organizations to segregate production from marketing and to carefully control manufacturing tasks (Thompson, 1967). This is *never* the case with service technologies. Service technologies are insufficient because client contact is never totally understandable.

Services cannot be produced without the input of clients. This brings clients into the operation's work flow, where their presence is potentially disruptive. A service can be viewed as "a contract under which one or more persons (principals) engage another person (the agent) to perform some service on their behalf which involves delegating some decision making authority to the agent" (Jensen and Meckling, 1976, p. 308). In any service relationship, there is some reciprocal goal congruence because the customer gives the service provider the right or authority to do what the provider thinks is necessary to render the service. And such rights extend to how customers should behave in the operations of any "normal" service organization. Thus, although manufacturing administrators may concentrate on employee behavior, service administrators must contend with client behavior as well.

This implies that service organizations must draw on three distinct knowledge technologies instead of only two. Manufacturing organizations apply one knowledge technology to transform inanimate raw materials into finished goods and a second (management theory) to maintain an effective organization. In contrast, service organizations must apply one knowledge technology to produce the service, another to maintain the organization, and a third to manage the client. This third technology is never sufficient, since the organization's control over clients (as the principals in the contract) is never complete.

Organizational Effectiveness with Insufficient Technology

When manufacturing organizations have insufficient technologies, they can use several different techniques for managing the residual uncertainty. For instance, they can segregate the manufacturing portion of the organization from the marketing portion, or they can create elaborate control mechanisms. Yet neither of these mechanisms is open to service organizations.

Inability to Segregate Production from Marketing. As we have seen, an important characteristic of services is that production and marketing are fused—services are consumed when they are produced. It is not possible to completely seal off production from marketing. Instead, the organization is left with no alternative but to ration services, meaning that the customer must accommodate the service system (Mills and Moberg, 1982).

Difficulty of Control. Control is highly problematic in service organizations. This is especially so when there is uncertainty around the process. It is generally believed that under such conditions, the firm should adopt output controls (Ouchi and Maguire, 1975). Such controls may take the form of contracting on the outcome, such as offering the service organization's employees commissions and contingencies that serve to align the employees' self-interests with those of the organization itself by the mutual sharing of risks. But output control is hardly in the best interest of service organizations, as such risks to the

service employee are simply myths and detrimental to the organization. Lawyers, for example, carefully estimate the risk before
they accept cases and turn down high-risk, low-return ones.
Similarly, salespeople on commission learn to reduce risk of
limited customer purchases by discriminating in favor of customers who "appear" likely to buy.

Output control can work against the organization, because employees on commission can screen out potential customers and sales by stereotyping or ignoring customers or
treating different customers differently. And the firm can never
fully prove the extent to which this is actually occurring. Thus,
output control mechanisms can never really be justified — it is
not a control mechanism at all, since control suggests some type
of cybernetic process (Green and Welsh, 1988), that is, a planned
system established to respond to predictable conditions within
an environment.

Perhaps the most distinct aspect of service technologies is
the inseparability of the output of service operations from the
process necessary to produce the output, as Marx's insightful
definition notes. The technology or the production process *is*
the output. Since any technology entails a set of steps and/or
sequences, what is being sold to customers is a "bundle" of
subprocesses, and the notion of control in service operations
has to be concentrated on the steps in the technology. What this
means for managers is that it is futile to exert much effort to
control outcomes when they are surrounded by intangibility
and uncertainty. Rather, resources are better spent breaking
down the steps in the technological process and treating each
process step as an actual "product" that can be administered
independently to customers. Alternatively, control can be exercised on inputs, admitting all but the least compliant clients to
the organization.

In summary, then, service technologies seem to have several features that distinguish them from manufacturing technologies. These emerge from the intangible nature of service
outputs and the necessary contact between client and service
provider. Service technologies draw on three knowledge bases
but are never sufficient to contend with all the uncertainty

involved in the work. Moreover, the techniques of dealing with uncertainty that are available to manufacturing organizations are not useful in the services. For organization theorists, this leaves unanswered the question of how service organizations can manage the uncertainty arising from the insufficiency of its technology. One answer is *client control*. In order to keep uncertainty within manageable limits, client conduct within the service organization must be monitored and deviations from acceptable behavior minimized. To do this, however, requires a highly detailed view of what forms of client behavior are desired and what forms are not. What follows is a framework that facilitates this sort of analysis.

An implication from such earlier works is that customers have an important part to play in the technology and production of services. It is the customers' involvement in service operations that generates the notion of "technical" relationships—a series of indispensable exchanges in the technology. This is a segment of service technology that is embodied in the social interaction between service providers and clients. Within such interactions, information is generated, converted, and exchanged in the process of rendering the service to clients. The task activities necessary to convert the information in the transaction will depend largely on the kinds of relationships that exist between provider and customer-client. Consequently, the technology of the service becomes inseparable from the social relationship between provider and customer.

The social relationships inherent in the technology of service operations are largely of reciprocal interdependencies. This kind of social exchange makes it difficult to segment the transformation process into discrete subsystems along manufacturing lines. It is for this reason that services have been analyzed as bundles of activities. And it is not surprising that few attempts have been made to unbundle the technologies of such operations. But the unbundling of the technical activities that are nested in the relationships between provider and customer is not only possible but vital to the performance of the firm. "Unbundling" services essentially means segmenting the technical exchanges into subsystems in order to detect not only

Shostack's (1984) notion of "failpoints" but, more importantly, the firm's unique competencies. The way to unravel service technologies, and in so doing unbundle the lines of output that the firm has to offer, is to examine the activities performed by customers in service operations.

A Framework for Analyzing Client Roles

Earlier, we indicated that service organizations draw on three different knowledge technologies. Two of these pertain to activities that must be undertaken by clients for the service to be rendered. The third entails mechanisms necessary to secure client compliance with prescribed activities. When services are viewed as agency relationships, the client gives the service provider the right or authority to control the client's behavior. A third type of technology is therefore required to motivate, control, or regulate clients' involvement in the operations. Our analysis, however, will focus on only the first two technologies, which are related to the activities or roles required of clients within the boundaries of the organization. The framework for the following analysis entails two transformation systems within the firm, the well-known dual core transformation. Each of these transformation systems consists of its own core technologies and makes demands of clients.

The two knowledge technologies that make demands on clients are decomposed into tasks that must be completed for the service to be produced and the system maintained (Gronroos, 1986). Psychiatry (a service production knowledge technology) defines certain tasks, as does the knowledge associated with effectively operating a psychiatric clinic. Particular tasks required by each of these two knowledge technologies may be assigned to the client or the service provider. For example, gasoline service stations may require patrons to pump their own gas, or this service production task may be performed by a service provider. Similarly, a customer at a bank may be required to fill out a deposit slip, or this system maintenance task can be performed by a teller. Other tasks must be assumed by the client and cannot be delegated to the service provider (for example, providing information about service needs, making payment).

Since the two technologies used in service operations differ, so do the tasks that evolve from them. This is quite consistent with the traditional sociotechnical system perspective (Emery and Trist, 1965), which entails the interdependence of technology and other crucial organization properties. For example, nurses are expected to behave consistently with both the professional demands of nursing and the bureaucratic demands of the hospital administration (Corwin, 1969). Similarly, welfare recipients are expected to act in accord with both the practices of creating the service (presumed to be a derivation of social welfare theory) and the administrative needs of the agency (presumed to be a derivative of administrative theory). What is being suggested here is that organizations consist of multiple environments, giving rise to multiple technologies (Jelinek, 1977).

Since the knowledge germane to service operations may differ between different types of service (for example, forestry and law), there is little value in attempting to describe all the service production roles that might accrue to clients in all instances. However, service production roles do possess several commonalities. These can be inferred from studies on the interaction between service providers and clients and from other works on the nature and functioning of service delivery systems (for example, Mills, 1986). Service organizations are fundamentally information-processing entities. Information is in fact the essential raw material to be processed and transformed in service operations. Such raw material is brought to service operations by the client-customer through boundary-spanning employees of the firm. Studies have demonstrated that the interaction between the service provider and the customer influences the amount and type of information processed and the task activities performed (Mills and Turk, 1986).

Client Service Production Roles

There are very few instances in which the client is entirely passive during the creation of a service. Comatose patients are one exception, but even in that case, others may be appointed to conduct tasks such as making decisions about surgery as their surrogates. The components of the client's service production roles may be divided into three categories according to the client's position relative to the service operation's work flow: Service production roles make claims on clients before they enter the work flow (input considerations), while they are in the work flow (conversion considerations), and after they leave the work flow (output considerations) (Katz and Kahn, 1978).

Service Production Roles on the Input Side. Clients are often expected to perform several tasks before they enter the service system. They may be expected to plan for the necessary encounters with the service employees: Clients of tax accountants are encouraged to bring their records with them and come prepared to ask specific questions about particular deductions; retail customers are expected to bring their receipts with them when they return unwanted merchandise; and people who change dentists may be asked to arrange for their records to be forwarded.

Another client role in input processes is taking preventive action. Preventive action reduces the frequency with which clients need services; that is, it extends the life of the previous services. People who practice good oral hygiene will need dental care less often and will suffer less severe maladies than those who do not. Similarly, drivers who systematically follow the guidelines in their owners' manuals presumably will minimize the need for expensive repairs. Of course, preventive action may not be considered desirable by some service providers. Practicing safe driving habits is functional to insurance firms but dysfunctional to auto body shops. Consequently, some service operations do not assign clients this role.

Service Production Roles in the Operation's Work Flow. Once the client becomes part of the work flow, other behaviors facilitate the production of the service. This is where the client and the service employee are in direct interaction, and additional claims are often placed on the client during this phase.

First, clients are expected to provide honest and accurate information regarding their service need or the nature of the problem that they think the service will solve. As Duncan (1972) suggests, the more accurate the information, the easier it is for the service employee to help create the service. Thus, patients must translate a complex set of sensory stimuli into a chief complaint, investors are expected to articulate their attitudes toward risk, and estranged couples are required to describe the marital difficulties that led to the estrangement. As these examples illustrate, clients may be required to invest considerable energy in fulfilling this role requirement.

Another task performed by the client in the operation's work flow is choosing from among alternative levels or types of service. In restaurants, hungry patrons are expected to be able to determine what would best satisfy their appetites. And those seeking membership in a health spa must choose from among different levels of physical exertion. Again, the mental work required by this task should not be underestimated. Requiring clients to make choices has the effect of rendering the client partially responsible for the satisfaction derived from the service itself. This is problematic when clients lack sufficient knowledge to make a rational choice. Accordingly, when there is a significant knowledge disparity between client and service provider, an effort is generally made to assist the client in performing this role. For example, surgeons generally assist patients in making choices regarding the risks of alternative drugs, and lottery patrons are informed of the odds of winning.

Once the service employee begins producing the service, additional client tasks are often required. When the service production process is made up of sequential stages, client alertness is necessary for the provision of feedback about the progress of the service production. Many are the consumers who regret not correcting the mistakes of a service provider; falling asleep in a barber chair often produces comical errors. Other tasks required of clients can range from fairly simple ones, such as keeping one's head still during an optometric examination, to rather complex ones, such as emotionally preparing a youngster for his or her first school field trip.

Service Production Roles on the Output Side. In many cases, the client is assigned additional tasks after leaving the work flow. Bandages have to be changed, homework completed, and personal habits revised. Unless these regimens are followed, the delivery of the service will not produce client satisfaction.

Taken together, service production roles may make significant claims on the client (Lefton and Rosengren, 1966). In some cases, client efforts on the input and output side are more vital than any role assumed within the system itself. On the input side, the client may be required to master some of the knowledge used in producing the service. For example, self-help organizations often require clients to acquire the essential knowledge used in providing the service (for example, learning to operate a kidney dialysis unit) (Gartner and Riessman, 1977). In some cases, client involvement in creating a service may be quite complex; for example, when a client works with an architect to develop a blueprint for a house. In other cases, however, client involvement may be comparatively superficial. Because of a lack of relevant knowledge (Mills and Margulies, 1980) or through choice (Katz and Eisenstadt, 1960), clients may be quite inactive throughout the entire service production process. All that is required of a client to create home newspaper delivery is making a phone call and submitting monthly payments. Similarly, having a document translated requires little more than providing a legible copy and paying for the service.

Client System Maintenance Roles

The knowledge techniques employed within the administration of the service firm are multidisciplinary, encompassing operations management, economics, and behavioral, social, and political sciences. While all such knowledge is part of the same parent discipline, administrative science, it is possible to unbundle the activities within this segment of service operations and to specify the particular system maintenance roles commonly assigned to clients.

System Maintenance Roles on the Input Side. To reduce the variability of the raw materials they must deal with (Perrow,

1967; Argote, 1982), some service operations restrict membership to qualified clients. Ski lodges refuse entry to customers who do not have reservations, schools do not admit unqualified applicants, and wholesalers refuse service to customers who have no proof of an intention to resell. In addition, in order to minimize disruptions on the input side, service delivery systems often require clients to practice a form of self-triage. For example, a current development in health care is enabling the consumer to know when and when not to contact a physician. Thus, one component of the system maintenance role is applying decision rules provided by the system to determine whether one qualifies to enter the work flow.

System Maintenance Roles in the Operation's Work Flow. Most of the system maintenance claims on the behavior of clients are made in the work flow itself. Here the client is expected to perform several tasks that will enable the system to attain desired levels of sufficiency. First, timely attendance may be required of clients. Since services cannot be stored, service operations cannot create inventories of raw materials or finished goods. Instead, service operations experience periods of varying demand and during peak periods must store clients in queues. Since fluctuation in demand for services directly affects the firm's labor costs, managers have to decide whether to pursue a policy of chasing demand— adjusting the labor supply in accordance with demands— or to maintain level staffing (Sasser, 1976). Level capacity, for example, may be maintained through negotiated schedules. Restaurants suggest reservations, physicians appointments, and teachers class schedules. Thus, while clients may not be required to totally rearrange their schedules in order to meet the demand of the system, their attendance is often expected to conform with negotiated arrangements.

Second, clients are asked to follow rules that restrict their discretion once they enter the work flow. Client behavior is a major source of variability for service operations, which in most cases they wish to minimize (Perrow, 1967). Accordingly, they often promulgate rules to standardize client behavior in the work flow (Mintzberg, 1979). Such rules are an important coordinating mechanism to facilitate efficiency and ensure smooth movement through the work flow (queuing rules), care in dealing with expensive machinery (don't touch the tape recorder), concern about costs (if you break it, you buy it!), client safety (wear protective glasses), respect for fellow clients (no-smoking areas), or some combination of these.

Third, client communication with service employees may be generally restricted to episodes deemed appropriate to the maintenance of the system (Friedson, 1970). For example, a patient who asks a nurse a question about his or her progress is likely to be told, "You'll have to wait until the doctor comes by." Similarly, access to a professor is likely to be determined by "office hours."

Fourth, service operations generally prefer clients to make decisions quickly and irrevocably. To do otherwise requires delivery systems to lose control of schedules necessary for rational planning. Although the requirements placed on clients by service operations vary from situation to situation, the decisive client is generally preferred to the ambivalent one.

Fifth, most every culture has standards of commercial decorum that clients are expected to follow. There are times to barter over price, for example, and a client who attempts to do so inappropriately is disruptive to the system. Service providers in certain types of service delivery systems assume goal congruence (Bowen and Jones, 1986), and clients who react to providers as though they were engaged in simply a market transaction make the necessary transactions problematic.

Finally, the client is generally expected to comply with the organization's ideological system regarding the treatment of clients. This is termed "ideological similarity" by Bacharach and Lawler (1980). Elements of justice and client rights are inevitably tied up in how the client is treated. The integrity of these ideological issues must be respected by clients if the system is to be maintained. Some conflicts are inevitable, as in the case of distraught parents who try to get information about their children's involvement in a family planning agency or of a dying patient who begs for euthanasia (Katz and Danet, 1966). But such conflicts can be reduced if the service firm is effective in isolating an appropriate market niche and is fastidious in attracting and selecting customers with attitudes, values, and expectations that are consistent with those of the firm or with its unique competencies (Mills, 1986). This client task may be the most difficult and problematic.

System Maintenance Roles on the Output Side. Two client tasks are often required at this stage. One involves assisting in defining the termination of the relationship. This is the process of decoupling customers from the operation so that they are no longer *in* the system but instead *attached* to it for future patronage (Northcraft and Chase, 1985; Mills and Morris, 1986). For the sake of the system itself, it is very helpful if the client provides some signal as to his or her intentions to use the system again. This information can then be used by the operation for planning purposes. Welfare recipients are expected to inform the agency of a change in their economic situation, psychiatric patients are expected to participate in the decision to be released, and banks prefer customers to close accounts with zero balances if they do not intend to use them again.

Another client task that serves to maintain the system is providing feedback regarding the quality of service delivered. Given the intangibility of services (Sasser, Olsen, and Wyckoff, 1978), the lack of visibility of client-provider interaction, and the frequent delay between leaving the work flow and experiencing satisfaction, the system itself may benefit from feedback from clients. Consequently, clients who make the effort to provide feedback facilitate system control.

Differences Between Types of Client Roles

The types of client behaviors associated with service production and system maintenance roles may differ in one important respect. Client compliance with system maintenance roles is generally assessed in terms of whether clients do what they are required to do. In other words, client performance of system maintenance roles is basically nominal—one either follows the rules or does not. In contrast, service production roles place qualitative demands on clients. It is not sufficient for roles to be minimally taken; rather, the quality with which clients perform their roles is critical. For example, minimal or inappropriate client preparation (such as providing inaccurate information to a want-ad service) may actually be worse than no preparation at all. It is primarily for this reason that when client roles in service production can be routinized, these routine activities are then transferred to system maintenance. For example, rather than college students being required to seek extensive counseling with professors for completion of class registration, this activity is now largely undertaken within administration or maintenance. Similarly, with the evolution of the automatic teller machine (ATM), a set of routine functions traditionally performed by customers at the production level (in the presence of tellers) of banks is now performed within the domain of maintenance.

Conflicts Between Types of Client Roles

System maintenance and service production roles may make conflicting demands on clients. The service production role requires clients to make rational decisions in choosing from among the service options available, but system maintenance emphasizes speed and irrevocability in decision making. Therefore, the client may receive mixed messages about how to behave. For example, it appears that deferential hospital patients (those compliant with system maintenance roles) improve less quickly than assertive ones. Accordingly, while system maintenance argues for compliant patients, service production may require more reactivity (Korsch and Negrette, 1972).

Value of Identifying Required Client Role Behaviors

This framework of classifying required client role behaviors has a great deal of practical value. By meticulously defining all the client behaviors required of a service organization, one can identify (1) required client behaviors that are not being adequately socialized, (2) conflicts between system maintenance and service production roles, and (3) alternative ways of configuring the operation so as to involve the client in different ways.

Client Behaviors That Are Insufficiently Socialized. Occasionally, organizations find that they must reckon with uncertainty introduced by clients who fail to act out critical behaviors. Dentists may discover that their elderly patients lack incentives to engage in certain forms of preventive dental care. Similarly, grocers may find that certain customers routinely queue up in express lines when they have more than ten items in their baskets. Armed with this knowledge, those responsible for the design of service systems can establish client control systems if the uncertainties created cause problems.

Conflicts Between Necessary Client Role Components. Rigorous client role analysis may also reveal conflicts between the necessary behaviors expected of clients. For example, realizing that the independent thinking developed in liberal arts colleges may be negatively reinforced by the student's family during vacations and breaks, some colleges have alerted student families of this eventuality and given them alternative ways of reacting.

Strategic Configuring of the Service Delivery System. The third advantage of a careful analysis of client roles is that it reveals ways of configuring the service delivery system that may be strategically advantageous. Throughout this chapter, we have described the customer's involvement in service operations in terms of "technical" relationships involving a bundle of indispensable exchanges. By unbundling or disaggregating these transactions into their component parts, we reveal new service "product" lines. This extends beyond Shostack's (1984) notion of finding "failpoints" that serve to reduce uneven service, as a bad service can have a halo effect. Rather, it represents a significant way to detect the firm's unique competencies. In other words, by unraveling the tapestry of existing service technology, we reveal new patchworks of service offerings. It is to this inside-out, or technological, approach to strategic thinking that we now turn.

Strategic Implications: The Bundling Options

Marx's definition of services suggests that the process of production is the actual service. This view corresponds with Lovelock and Young's (1979) observation that in services the technology is the service and Marshall McLuhan's (1964) notion that process is product. It seems clear from the preceding discussion that technology in services is "relational" and entails at least two processes within the firm: production and system maintenance.

According to Porter (1980), a strategy is a set of steps taken by a firm to ensure or protect its competitive position in a market, with a focus on either price or innovation. Thus, the first step in an inside-out approach to strategy making in service organizations is to identify the specific service production and system maintenance behaviors required of customers that pertain to the technical relationships or subsystems (input, conversion, output). In a very real sense, the organization's competitive strategy consists of attempts by the firm to appraise and influence its environment. For service organizations, the most crucial environmental element is the customer, primarily because of the customer's vital role in the technological process. Thus, their strategy will consist of assessing the nature and extent of present client involvement and evaluating strategic alternatives. These strategic alternatives include moving toward larger bundles and moving toward smaller bundles. Each of these options has definite marketing and operations implications.

Moving Toward Larger Bundles

One strategic option open to any service organization is to offer more service to clients by reducing the number of behaviors expected of them. This is basically an innovation approach to strategy formulation. Examples include computerizing library book checkout, dropping the requirement of appointments, and extending daily banking hours into the evening. In the extreme, moving toward larger bundles results in a full service option eliminating all but the most necessary service

production client behaviors and virtually all the system maintenance behaviors. One would expect this strategy to entail a
highly diverse service, as almost every step in the technological
process would be unique. This is a form of "job shop," with much
customization of the service. Examples include designer dress
studios, valets, and personal secretarial services.

Clearly, service operations do not need to go this far to
decrease the behaviors that clients are required to perform;
simply decreasing system maintenance behaviors required of
them may result in significant advantages. Universities can replace walk-in registration with computerized systems, welfare
agencies can simplify the forms and documents that recipients
are required to fill out, and other service providers can reduce
waiting lines by adding clerks during peak hours. Here a complex interaction emerges between the system maintenance and
production activities: The nature of customer screening and
preparation that occurs during maintenance or administrative
encounters will determine customer receptivity or cooperation
during service production.

Operations Management Implications. In moving toward
larger bundles, client production behaviors should be reduced
very cautiously; larger bundles can be built most effectively by
reducing system maintenance demands. The more responsibility for service production is placed in the hands of the service
provider, the more likely it is that the operation will be blamed
for inadequacies in the service (Bateson, 1985; Mills, 1986). For
example, if patients do not choose to make informed decisions
about surgery and instead turn this job over to the physician,
patient expectations are frequently unmet. Conversely, greater
customer participation in service operations fosters customer
commitment and a willingness to accept some of the responsibility, so that customers have a more realistic expectation of
outcomes and more satisfaction with results: Having accepted
some of the responsibility, the customer has to accept some of
the blame when things do not work out.

The strategy of offering larger bundles focuses on innovation. The costs of this, even if not carried to an extreme, can be

very high (Shostack, 1987). One reason for this, of course, is that the organization has to absorb learning costs in constantly changing operations as it attempts to remain flexible. Further, this strategy dictates that the organization maintains a level capacity (Sasser, 1976), which implies a high ratio of service providers to customers as relatively high labor skills will be required in this type of job-shop, discretionary environment. Moreover, service employees will have to be handsomely compensated both for their increased repertoire and for being required to perform certain onerous tasks.

A second problem with the strategy of offering larger bundles is that professional service providers, such as attorneys and architects, may lack the skills or the motivation to perform more system maintenance behaviors themselves. This necessitates a second echelon of service providers whose role it is to save clients from system maintenance requirements. Some of the costs of this extra labor can be controlled by chasing demand (Sasser, 1976) — temporarily hiring low-skilled staff when demand is high, as when colleges hire students to assist new students during registration. This strategy decreases labor costs because of both the low compensation of these temporary service providers and the ease with which they can be laid off when the demand slackens. It does, however, pose potential coordination problems. For example, when college admissions officials preregister freshmen for classes, the decisions they make may cause conflict with members of the faculty.

Marketing Implications. It is not necessary to opt for larger bundles for every client; a service organization could offer a larger bundle only to those market segments that want it, keeping smaller bundles for other customers. The work of Fetter and Freeman (1986) on product lines and diagnosis-related groups (DRG) within the health care industry is an attempt at such segmentation. Here, the bundles of services delivered to customers consist of several related services that can be disaggregated into independent units. Thus, the larger-bundle service strategy can be viewed as a form of related diversification as synergistic technological modes are made accessible to customer demands.

A hospital that provides a full bundle of acute care services will also provide treatment for a full spectrum of patient pathologies.

Structural Implications. While services may adopt manufacturing strategies, such as related and unrelated diversification, to realize productivity gains, the manufacturing strategy of vertical integration is inaccessible to service operations. The intangible and relational nature of service technology makes integration virtually impossible. Vertical integration is a linear sequence of operations with value added at each phase toward the output. For example, an automobile firm takes in steel and through a series of activities converts it into cars. Each phase in the conversion process adds value to the final outcome. It is difficult to establish sequential interdependence in service operations given the simultaneous production and consumption of services output and the impossibility of determining value added with intangible technological processes.

Moving Toward Smaller Bundles

A second strategic option is to offer smaller bundles of services. The organization may choose to restrict activities of the client or customer to specific roles, thus reducing the freedom or divergence of the activities. Usually, this is most effectively employed when the organization engages in "blueprinting" the service process—mapping or documenting the steps and sequences of the technological processes required to produce a specific service (Shostack, 1984). This strategy tends to reduce divergence and generate uniformity. Further, by requiring clients to perform more system maintenance or service production behaviors, it reduces the labor required by the organization (Gartner and Riessman, 1977). The focus of this strategy is competing on price rather than on innovation.

Requiring clients to perform additional system maintenance behaviors allows the service organization to decrease the amount of uncertainty that has to be processed. The client must accommodate the efficiency needs of the organization. For example, discount telephone services require the customer to enter a much longer series of numbers to complete a call. Requiring clients to perform additional service production behaviors involves different kinds of problems. While the organization experiences much less uncertainty in general, there is the risk that clients may not sense the benefits of the organization, since they are doing so much of the work. Moreover, increasing the client's role in producing the service often requires increasing client system maintenance behaviors as well. For example, broadened client roles may require the establishment of rules regarding client use of machinery or equipment. For example, in steak houses where customers prepare their own meat on an open grill, rules may be needed to avoid crowding during peak periods.

Operations Management Implications. Offering smaller bundles has little impact on the service operation unless clients are enacting their enlarged roles within the organization's work flow. Smaller bundles may require a larger number of clients, with each encounter taking a smaller amount of time. Much more attention may have to be given to each bundle offered to ensure that each is economically justified. This is a classic issue in the grocery and fast-food business.

Offering smaller bundles may create a high degree of repetitiveness in the work of service employees. This can create morale problems and result in a detached attitude toward clients. This has a symmetrical effect, since clients who have to do many tasks themselves do not hold service providers in high esteem. For example, small-bundled medical care may involve nurse practitioners who command much less awe and respect than do physicians.

Marketing Implications. Small bundles require significant client incentives to take on the additional behaviors required of them. Service organizations that are monopolies, such as public utilities, may make extensive demands on customers, since the customers have no other viable options. For nonmonopolies, however, pricing strategies must be carefully designed to provide customers with incentives to accommodate the needs of the organization. Marketers can attempt to create identification with the service organization by emphasizing goal congruence or by helping the customer make the consumption of the service conspicuous, such as with T-shirts advertising the organization's name.

At the extreme, services that make large demands on client service creation behaviors may constitute self-service or self-help types of offerings, such as laundromats and weight-loss centers. With these, the organization is quite exposed to competitive pressures, since the barriers to entry in such markets are often quite low. To prevent the organization from being seen as superfluous, marketers may create some mystification around the tasks that the organization reserves for itself. For example, diet centers place a very large burden on their clients and thus run the risk of being seen as delivering few meaningful services. This perception is the target of a great deal of promotion aimed at creating the impression that the services that are offered (counseling, meal planning, menus) are special and exclusive.

Conclusion

Organizational theory offers a unique perspective on strategy formulation in service organizations. It tends to bridge notions from operations management and marketing by making the effectiveness of the entire organization its focus. In this chapter, we have adopted an inside-out perspective to developing strategy alternatives. Beginning with a discussion of service technologies, we first offered an analytical framework for appreciating the bundle of services presently offered by the firm. Following this, we enumerated the organization-wide implications of increasing or decreasing the bundle of services offered the client-customer.

Strategy formulation is at least as vital in service organizations as it is in manufacturing. Yet, without a clear picture of the total organizational implications of various strategic alternatives, organizations will be misled into presuming that any option has roughly the same effects on the organization.

   An organization's strategy for competing within a particular market segment may entail numerous managerial decisions. For service managers, however, the primacy of the technical processes and their ensuing relationships with customers
will determine the organization's distinctive competencies and
thus the company's strategy. Since organizations tend to vary,
distinctive competencies and strategies can also be expected to
vary.

References

Argote, L. "Input Uncertainty and Organizational Coordination
   in Hospital Emergency Units." *Administrative Science Quarterly*,
   1982, *27*, 420–434.
Bacharach, S. B., and Lawler, E. J. *Power and Politics in Organiza-
   tions: The Social Psychology of Conflict, Coalitions, and Bargaining.*
   San Francisco: Jossey-Bass, 1980.
Bateson, J.E.G. "Perceived Control and the Service Encounter."
   In J. A. Czepiel, M. R. Solomon, and C. F. Surprenant (eds.),
   *The Service Encounter: Managing Employee/Customer Interaction in
   Service Businesses.* Lexington, Mass.: Lexington Books, 1985.
Berger, A. *Economic Problems of Consumer Services.* Budapest:
   Akademai Kiado, 1970.
Berger, P., and Luckmann, T. *The Social Construction of Reality.*
   Garden City, N.Y.: Doubleday, 1966.
Berry, L. "Services Marketing Is Different." In C. Lovelock (ed.),
   Services Marketing. Englewood Cliffs, N.J.: Prentice-Hall, 1984.
Bowen, D., and Jones, G. "A Transaction Cost Analysis of Service
   Organization–Customer Exchange." *Academy of Management
   Review*, 1986, *11*, 428–441.
Clark, C. *The Conditions of Economic Progress.* London: Macmillan,
   1940.
Corwin, R. "Patterns of Organizational Conflict." *Administrative
   Science Quarterly*, 1969, *26*, 545–562.
Dubin, R. *Human Relations and Administration.* (3rd ed.) En-
   glewood Cliffs, N.J.: Prentice-Hall, 1968.
Duncan, R. "Characteristics of Organizational Environments

and Perceived Environmental Uncertainty." *Administrative Science Quarterly*, 1972, *17*, 313–327.

Emery, F., and Trist, E. "The Causal Texture of Organizational Environments." *Human Relations*, 1965, *18*, 21–32.

Fetter, R., and Freeman, J. "Diagnosis Related Groups: Productive Management Within Hospitals." *Academy of Management Review*, 1986, *11*, 41–54.

Fisher, A. *The Clash of Progress and Security*. London: Macmillan, 1935.

Friedson, E. *The Profession of Medicine*. New York: Dodd, Mead, 1970.

Fuchs, V. *The Service Economy*. New York: Columbia University Press, 1968.

Gartner, A., and Riessman, F. *Self-Help in the Human Services*. San Francisco: Jossey-Bass, 1977.

Green, S., and Welsh, A. "Cybernetics and Dependence: Reframing the Control Concept." *Academy of Management Review*, 1988, *13*, 287–301.

Gronroos, C. "Developing Service Quality: Some Managerial Implications." Research report presented at fifteenth annual conference of the European Marketing Academy, Helsinki, Finland, June 3–6, 1986.

Jelinek, M. "Technology, Organizations and Contingency." *Academy of Management Review*, 1977, *2*, 17–26.

Jensen, M., and Meckling, W. "Theory of the Firm: Managerial Behavior, Agency Costs and Ownership Structure." *Journal of Financial Economies*, 1976, *3*, 305–360.

Katz, D., and Kahn, R. L. *The Social Psychology of Organizations*. (2nd ed.) New York: Wiley, 1978.

Katz, E., and Danet, B. "Petitions and Persuasive Appeals: A Study of Official-Client Relations." *American Sociological Review*, 1966, *31*, 811–822.

Katz, E., and Eisenstadt, S. "Some Sociological Observations on the Response of Israel: Organizations to New Immigrants." *Administrative Science Quarterly*, 1960, *5*, 113–133.

Korsch, B., and Negrette, V. "Doctor-Patient Communication." *Scientific American*, 1972, *228*, 66–74.

Lefton, M., and Rosengren, W. "Organizations and Clients: Lateral and Longitudinal Dimensions." *American Sociological Review*, 1966, *31*, 802–810.

Litterer, J. *The Analysis of Organizations*. (2nd ed.) New York: Wiley, 1973.

Lovelock, C. H., and Young, R. F. "Look to Customers to Increase Productivity." *Harvard Business Review*, 1979, *57* (3), 168–178.

McLuhan, M. *Understanding Media*. New York: McGraw-Hill, 1964.

Mills, P. *Managing Service Industries: Organizational Practices in a Post-Industrial Economy*. Cambridge, Mass.: Ballinger, 1986.

Mills, P., and Margulies, N. "Toward a Core Typology of Service Organizations." *Academy of Management Review*, 1980, *5*, 255–266.

Mills, P., and Moberg, D. "Perspectives on the Technology of Service Operations." *Academy of Management Review*, 1982, *11*, 727–735.

Mills, P., and Morris, J. "Clients as 'Partial' Employees of Service Organizations." *Academy of Management Review*, 1986, *11*, 726–735.

Mills, P., and Turk, T. "A Preliminary Investigation into the Influence of Customer-Firm Interface on Information Processing and Task Activities in Service Organizations." *Journal of Management*, 1986, *12*, 91–104.

Mintzberg, H. *The Structuring of Organizations*. Englewood Cliffs, N.J.: Prentice-Hall, 1979.

Northcraft, G., and Chase, R. "Managing Service Demand at the Point of Delivery." *Academy of Management Review*, 1985, *10*, 66–75.

Ouchi, W., and Maguire, M. "Organizational Control: Two Functions." *Administrative Science Quarterly*, 1975, *20*, 559–569.

Perrow, C. "A Framework for the Comparative Analysis of Organizations." *American Sociological Review*, 1967, *32*, 196–208.

Porter, M. E. *Competitive Strategy: Techniques for Analyzing Industries and Competitors*. New York: Free Press, 1980.

Reder, M. "Some Problems in the Measurement of Productivity in the Medical Care Industry." In V. Fuchs (ed.), *Production and Productivity in the Service Industries*. New York: Columbia University Press, 1969.

Sabolo, Y. *The Service Industries*. Geneva, Switzerland: International Labor Office, 1975.

Sasser, W. E. "Match Supply and Demand in Service Industries." *Harvard Business Review*, 1976, *54* (2), 133–148.

Sasser, W. E., Olsen, R. P., and Wyckoff, D. D. *Management of Service Operations: Text, Cases, and Readings*. Boston: Allyn & Bacon, 1978.

Schneider, B., and Bowen, D. E. "Employee and Customer Perceptions of Service in Banks: Replication and Extension." *Journal of Applied Psychology*, 1985, *70*, 423–473.

Schneider, B., Parkington, J. J., and Buxton, V. M. "Employee and Customer Perceptions of Service in Banks." *Administrative Science Quarterly*, 1980, *25*, 252–267.

Shostack, G. L. "Designing Systems That Deliver." *Harvard Business Review*, 1984, *62* (1), 133–139.

Shostack, G. L. "Service Positioning Through Structural Change." *Journal of Marketing*, 1987, *51* (Jan.), 24–43.

Stigler, G. *Trends in Employment in Service Industries*. Princeton, N.J.: Princeton University Press, 1956.

Thompson, J. D. *Organization in Action*. New York: McGraw-Hill, 1967.

6

Alternative Strategies for Creating Service-Oriented Organizations

Benjamin Schneider

During the last decade, there has been considerable conceptual writing on defining the attributes of services, especially specifying ways in which prototypical services differ from prototypical goods (see, for example, Lovelock, 1983). In addition, some scholars have incorporated these conceptualizations of the differences between goods and services into the development of models of organization design. That is, the defining attributes of service have been reconceptualized into imperatives for organization design and management (Schneider, 1987a). These writings have been summarized in a series of books and articles on services management and marketing that appear to be useful to both academicians and practitioners, for they are characterized by disciplinary integration (for example, integration of psychology and marketing), functional integration (for example, integration of operations management, marketing, and human resources), and international integration—such works are ap-

Note: The author wishes to thank Michele Laliberte for her help in locating and digesting some of the literature cited in this chapter and Elizabeth Berney, Stuart Crandell, Sarah Gunnarson, and Daniel Schechter for their helpful comments on earlier drafts. Will and Ellen, the internal change agents described in the chapter, have requested anonymity, but they deserve special appreciation and thanks. They have read the chapter as a kind of "reliability check" on my description of their change programs.

pearing in England (Bateson, 1989), France (Eiglier and Langeard, 1987), Scandinavia (Gronroos, 1990), and the United States (Lovelock, 1988). Each of these works and the many papers on which they are based yield some insight into the many challenges that managers of service organizations must meet if their organizations are to deliver competitively excellent service. The appearance of a book on the 101 best service companies (Zemke and Schaff, 1989) will surely impel more companies to try to become more service-oriented—to take on service as a corporate imperative.

To become more service-oriented, however, will be more difficult than it first seems, for two reasons. First, service is more than a smile and a handshake; many issues must be attended to if change is to become a reality. Second, while there are many reasons why change is difficult in any organization, the primary reason is that it requires the people in the organization to change: They must change what they think about, how they think about it, how they spend their time and effort, what they reward and support, and so forth. What makes change difficult is that people prefer homeostasis and equilibrium, especially when that equilibrium is relatively comfortable. The problem is that if people are members of an organization, that organization is most likely relatively comfortable for them; it is well known that discomfort and/or dissatisfaction results in turnover (Porter and Steers, 1973). Indeed, some scholars have written that radical change of an organization is probably not possible without physically replacing people. People are not infinitely flexible, and if they are comfortable in an organization, they will be uncomfortable in a radically different one (Schneider, 1987b).

In fact, in most organizations, the changes sought by management are not so radical. Yet, even then, the most reasonable employee response to any managerial-initiated change may be to continue in the steady-state behavior, since organizations often announce a new initiative with a big splash (and a huge expense), but then fail to follow up with concrete steps for its implementation. This cycle of an announcement and a kickoff party followed by little else makes employees appropriately hesitant about enthusiastically embracing change and, over time, wary about becoming emotionally involved in "management's latest kick" (Beer, 1980).

Any organization desiring to change its focus to a service orientation may experience a similar pattern of employee hesitancy and wariness. But if management has a firm commitment to service excellence, whether because "customers deserve it" or because "there is a profit to be made from service superiority," some basic guidelines are adhered to. In the sections that follow, I describe two cases in which organizations have changed to become more service-oriented. In one case, the change has proceeded sequentially, one small step at a time, beginning in just one part of the organization and spreading slowly throughout other parts. In the second case, the change has proceeded simultaneously, with concurrent interventions at many locations, at many levels, and in many ways. The organizations described here are not companies that have already achieved service excellence; they are companies that are struggling to make the journey. They were not born with a service-excellence orientation or ethic; they are trying to create one. I describe some of the issues with which they struggle on this journey.

The Sequential Model of Change: Organization Alpha

Alpha is a nationwide financial services organization that markets and provides its financial services by telephone. It has been in existence for more than thirty-five years and has a reputation as a competent provider — it does what it does well; it does not try to be all things to all people; it is not at the high or low end of its industry. The company is publicly held and is highly dependent on the technology revolution (computers and telecommunication) for its competitive edge. In fact, it is a leader in the development and adoption of new technologies. In the past, Alpha has been more interested in technological innovation than product or human resources innovations.

In 1985, a decision was made at the top of the organization to split the human resources function into two elements. *HR Policies* (HRP) became responsible for all of the classic paperwork issues connected with human resources: pay policies and standards, maintaining records, and so forth. *HR Development* (HRD) was charged with exploring improved methods for the selection and training of lower-level workers and supervisors, addressing a turnover problem in the sales and service jobs, and improving the quality of customer contacts by monitoring the telephone contacts made by the different sales and service units and suggesting changes. Thus, the goal of HRD was to staff sales and service jobs with people who could handle the changing nature of jobs—people who could be trained to be technically competent as well as interpersonally competent when they dealt with the public.

Conceptualization of Change at Alpha. The new head of HRD, Will, was very clear that the model of change under which he wished to operate was to start small and see how things went. He implicitly adopted Weick's (1984) concept of seeking small wins. He sought my help as a consultant to design new selection procedures for the entry-level sales and service jobs. I pointed out to him that change would be very slow, if it occurred at all, unless he simultaneously addressed all HRD functions: creating new training programs for those he would hire, new supervisory development programs for the supervisors of the new hires, new incentive and career plans to reward these new kinds of employees, and so forth. He rejected these ideas, suggesting that producing some small effects in one area would give him the leverage to move on and tackle the other areas. He then challenged me to create a selection process that would measurably affect turnover and result in the hiring of people more qualified than those hired in the past.

As a specialist in organizational staffing (Schneider and Schmitt, 1986), I accepted the challenge. We embarked on a systematic program of personnel selection design and implementation characterized by the classic steps of job analysis, including specification of tasks and of the knowledge, skill, and ability (KSA) required; design and choice of selection procedures, using multiple methods (some paper-and-pencil tests, an interview, and a brief telephone simulation); content validation of the process; pilot testing; and implementation. To inform management about what was happening and how it would involve them (for example, in job-analysis panels, in completing task surveys, in participating in pilot testing of the process), Will prepared a videotape introducing us and the steps that we would take to design the new system. The process was presented matter of factly as simply a way to design new systems, just as one would design a new computer system. The only promise that Will made to upper-level management was that the new system would reduce turnover. The procedures by which the system was designed and some examples of the selection procedures implemented are presented in detail in Schneider and Schechter (1990) and summarized briefly below.

The entire selection system rests on a thorough job analysis identifying the tasks and the KSAs required to do them. A series of strategic job-analysis workshops were held with various panels of subject-matter experts to identify the kinds of KSAs that sales and service jobs of the future might require (Schneider and Konz, 1989). As a result of these workshops, we chose a multiple-hurdles selection procedure, each step of which is used to eliminate candidates for the job (Schneider and Schmitt, 1986). First, candidates are screened by means of two job-relevant paper-and-pencil tests that were chosen from four that were pilot tested. Those who pass the tests then participate in a semistructured interview in which they are questioned about their interests in using skills and abilities such as those required by the job and about how comfortable they are with certain requirements of the job, such as being at work on time every day, sitting for long periods of time, being closely monitored by a supervisor, and so forth. Finally, candidates who pass the interview participate in a telephone simulation, making four "calls" patterned after those typically handled by sales and service workers to determine whether they have the skills and abilities revealed as critical in the job analysis. Both the interview and the simulation were designed for Alpha's specific job requirements. The interviewers and assessors were trained by members of the HRD staff who were themselves trained by the consultants. Interviewer training and simulation training each took three

days. The interview and the simulation each could be completed in about thirty-five minutes.

The new system had the desired effects: Turnover rates for
new hires were significantly decreased (though not immediately
and not consistently), and trainers and supervisors of the people
hired through the new process found them responsive and
bright. Indeed, some trainers suggested that the old training
program be changed because "the new hires seem to grasp
things more quickly." Supervisors noted that the new hires were
becoming productive sooner after starting the job than had
been the case previously—that "the new hires are catching on
more quickly." There is some statistical evidence that these perceptions are accurate (Schneider and Schechter, 1990).

Other divisions in the organization, hearing about the
success of the new process, wanted to participate as well. However, rather than spreading himself too thin by moving to other
divisions, Will decided to pursue the process with sales and
service alone. In this way, he felt that he could show that an entire
system designed for a single function would yield even more
successes. Therefore, the next steps were to design and implement a new training program for sales and service workers and
to institute a formal supervisory promotion system using assessment centers (Konz, 1988).

At this point, fate intervened in that Alpha decided to
open a new office and to use the procedures already designed
for sales and service workers to staff it. Using the new systems for
hiring and training service workers and choosing their supervisors, the director of the new office found that his office was up
and running smoothly in a shorter period of time than expected, and initial results from the use of the new processes
looked excellent.

Conceptualization of Service at Alpha. Will's implicit understanding of service matched very well with the research program
carried out by Parasuraman, Zeithaml, and Berry (1985). Their
research shows that ten facets of service provision determine
success for a broad range of services; these ten determinants are
presented in Table 6.1.

Table 6.1. Determinants of Service Quality.

Determinants	*Definition*	*Examples*
Reliability	Consistency of performance and dependability	Accuracy of billing Keeping records Performing the service at the designated time
Responsiveness	The willingness or readiness of employees to provide service	Calling the customer back quickly Giving prompt service
Competence	Possession of the required skills and knowledge to perform the service	Knowledge and skill of the contact personnel Knowledge and skill of operational support personnel
Access	Approachability and ease of contact	Reasonable waiting time to receive service Convenient hours of operation
Courtesy	Politeness, respect, consideration, and friendliness of contact personnel	Consideration for the customer's property Clean and neat appearance of the contact personnel
Communication	Keeping customers informed in language that they can understand and listening to them	Explaining the service itself Assuring the customer that a problem will be handled
Credibility	Trustworthiness, believability, honesty	Company reputation Personal characteristics of the contact personnel
Security	Freedom from danger, risk, or doubt	Physical safety Financial security
Understanding the customer	Making the effort to understand	Learning the customer's specific requirements Providing individualized attention
Tangibles	Physical evidence	Physical facilities Appearance of personnel Tools or equipment used to provide the services Physical representations of the service

Source: Adapted from Parasuraman, Zeithaml, and Berry, 1985.

Will's implicit theory about service delivery was that the people delivering the service had to be competent, responsive, well trained, and courteous and that the organization had to provide the service deliverers with the training, tools and equipment, and supervision that would ensure reliability, access, and credibility. Finally, he believed that it was necessary to monitor service deliverers so that they would not backslide into sloppiness and lose the "smile in their voice." Thus, Will's view of service was that it was determined by personal and organizational attributes focused on a comprehensive mix of issues, all of which were necessary for the delivery of consistently excellent service. Once basically competent and courteous people were hired, Will's model of service implicitly required attention to these other facets. His model of change, however, was that these elements should be worked on sequentially, for both practical and political reasons. The practical reason was that Will did not want HRD to grow into a large, bureaucratic system with which he would lose personal touch. The political reason was that he felt that the best way to make change was to show successes.

Word continued to spread throughout the organization about Will's successes in reducing training time, turnover, and time to production after getting on the job for sales and service workers. Word also spread about the utility of the assessment center for those making promotion decisions. Other divisions began asking Will for help, and he responded, always beginning with the selection of the lowest-level workers in the division and then moving on to the supervisory jobs and training. He always knew, however, that the efforts focused on sales and service were not and never would be complete. Thus, Will viewed service quality as a journey. And, since sales and service was the source of revenue for Alpha, it was important to continually upgrade quality in that division.

As a result of Will's efforts, the organization has adopted an incentive system for sales and service, with three steps to make the jobs part of a career track, rather than the dead-end, one-step jobs they had been. This system permits excellence to be rewarded in the job rather than only through promotion. Will also was able to convince upper-level managers to participate in a shortened version of sales and service training. He argued that since sales and service is the backbone of Alpha, everyone should be able to identify with the "face" Alpha presents to the outside world.

Interpretation of Alpha's Change. Alpha and Will may not be as unique as they appear in the context of theories of organizational functioning and organizational change. Change at Alpha was not a response to a crisis or, as Nadler (1987) calls it, "pain" so much as it was an anticipation of future corporate needs (Katz and Kahn, 1978). The case of Alpha suggests, then, that change need not await crisis, that careful planning for the future (a characteristic of Alpha with regard to technological change in the past) can yield present change — without pain.

Will appears to have been correct in his original prediction; small wins (Weick, 1984) can produce big wins. The process by which the limited, targeted change program was put into place, especially the understated way in which it was introduced and the relatively meager promises that were made for its outcomes, produced a sense of normality about what was happening. My perception is that this sense of normality stands in stark contrast to the typical attempt to change organizations, where the first step is overblowing what is going to happen and how absolutely fantastic the outcome will be. Any initial exhilaration, of course, may be followed by nothing; or, if change is actually begun, it may not live up to anyone's expectations, including those of the change agent him- or herself. We will see in the next case, that of Bravo, how these issues can be effectively worked through. First, however, the issue of service and its delivery deserves attention. Will's model of service and its delivery had two important components. First, excellence in selling and providing Alpha's financial services was taken as a given. Will implicitly assumed that there is only one way to carry out business — to do it as well as it can be done. Whether contact with customers should be monitored, selection should be done carefully and well, or training be developed by experts rather than thrown together was never an issue requiring discussion; these things were simply done right. Will's model of service was a model of quality in its broadest and most multifaceted sense.

Second, Will understood that the people who make up the sales and service function were at the root of any successes that were achieved. He also knew, however, that while selecting competent people was important, the organization had great responsibility for ensuring that the training, equipment and supplies, supervision, and support necessary to facilitate effectiveness were available (Schneider and Bowen, 1985). In fact, he sponsored a basic research project on facilitators of effectiveness because of his belief in the importance of supplying people with what they need to do their jobs (Moeller, Schneider, Schoorman, and Berney, 1988). Will has also sponsored research yielding two master's theses and two doctoral dissertations. He thinks of his model of organizational change as building a brick wall, one brick at a time. Each brick is another piece in the service delivery puzzle, whether it be selection, training, supplies, supervision, or whatever; all of the bricks in the right place will make a strong wall.

Kanter (1983) would call Will a changemaster. He has vision, the ability to marshal other people's energies to his vision, and a sense of purpose and standards that are palpable to those with whom he works. But Will's model of change was not to change all of Alpha in all of its functions and in all of its parts; he was not after total organizational change. Thus, Will was not so much an incrementalist (Hage, 1980; Tushman, Newman, and Nadler, 1987) as he was a sequentialist; change was based not on a grand vision of total organizational re-creation but on a notion that evidence of success at one thing in one location might yield what he called "additional insurmountable opportunities." He was uninterested in changing, for example, relationships between marketing and sales and service or between the people who design the computer systems and those who use them. His model of change did not extend to these other divisions except insofar as they might become aware of the possibilities he demonstrated and seek him out. Will the changemaster is sequentially oriented, not simultaneously oriented; his focus is on one job at a time, not all jobs at once; his understanding of the requirements for service excellence focuses on the system as a whole rather than attributing service narrowly to either people or organizational attributes. In a real sense, he is after small wins on the way to organizational effectiveness. His sequential small wins are creating the ripples of change that just might yield total organizational redirection.

The Simultaneous Model of Change: Organization Bravo

Bravo is a financial services business that is part of an international financial services company called Finanserv. Finanserv has been in existence for more than a hundred years, but Bravo has been part of it for only about fifteen years. As a newcomer to an older organization, Bravo has experienced some of the socialization problems that newcomers encounter in any organization—surprise, ambiguity, uncertainty, and so forth (Louis, 1980). The CEO of Bravo, Ellen, was new to her job and relatively new to Bravo (three years) when the change effort began. Ellen believed implicitly in what has come to be called strategic human resources management (Hall, 1984, 1986; Schuler and Jackson, 1987; Tichy, 1983), and she was interested in creating a service organization through Bravo's human resources practices and procedures.

Ellen initiated a diagnosis project after hearing a presentation on the difficulty, challenges, and possibilities associated with creating a service-oriented organization (Schneider, 1986, 1987a). The main message of the presentation was that to be perceived by consumers as an excellent service organization, the organization must treat its human resources the way it wants its customers to be treated. This conclusion was based on two studies (Schneider, Parkington, and Buxton, 1980; Schneider and Bowen, 1985) subsequently replicated by others (Brown and Mitchell, 1988; Forum Corporation, 1988). The first step in the change process at Bravo was a diagnosis of how employees at all levels and in all functions perceived the climate of the organization and the role of service in it. The diagnosis was based on thirty-five group interviews, each group made up of employees at the same level and with the same function. The interviews each lasted two hours, and extensive notes were taken during them, frequently by two people to verify reliability. The notes were summarized and coded, and a lengthy report (almost 100 pages) with many quotations was prepared for Ellen.

At my first meeting with Ellen, I had warned her that reports such as the one prepared for her can appear negative because employees come to the sessions with ideas about how things can be improved. Even with this warning, she found the report depressing and at first did not believe that things were as bad as they were portrayed. The report identified numerous climate, service, and human resource problems that were apparently inhibiting the delivery of service excellence. These problems ranged from intense pressure resulting from poor interdepartmental coordination and poor training to insufficient systems support to handle the complexity and volume of financial transactions required by the business. In other words, the report turned up a total systems perspective on service rather than "just" a human resources system perspective.

Conceptualization of Change at Bravo. Ellen reviewed the report with some of the most trusted members of her top management team, and they concluded that the report was accurate. They had all heard the same kinds of issues raised before; what was new was that they were all collected in one place and in black and white. What troubled them was the diversity of issues identified in the diagnosis as requiring attention. These issues included tensions between different subsystems, such as operations and marketing, as well as interpersonal tensions and lack of support within those subsystems. For example, lack of systems support in operations was affecting operations' ability to respond to marketing's needs, and marketing's internal status hierarchy occasionally resulted in poor-quality paperwork going to operations, which slowed up operations' processing time.

Given the complexity of these problems, Ellen concluded that, if she was going to produce effective change, she would have to intervene simultaneously both within and between functions. She adopted Parasuraman, Zeithaml, and Berry's (1985) ten dimensions of service quality shown in Table 6.1 as the goals to be achieved for customer service and the standards to be used for internal evaluations of functional performance. Believing that service to external customers would be only as good as the service provided internally, she designed new performance appraisal procedures that had employees rate the service they received from other departments according to those ten dimensions.

From her top management team on down, Ellen felt that improvement was needed in the way managers dealt with their subordinates, and so she sought ways to increase their commitment to the training and supervision of their human resources and to taking personal responsibility for creating service improvement. Many of the top managers already perceived themselves as service-oriented; Ellen had to find ways to make them aware that internal dealings both within and across functions ultimately affect the end user's service perceptions. To develop this kind of awareness, Ellen arranged for an off-site weekend session run by two experienced organization development consultants. The consultants emphasized the need for top managers to take personal responsibility for what happened in their units and to monitor the quality of interunit relationships. These kinds of issues have remained a constant topic of open discussion. One immediate outcome of the process was the institution of an interfunction contracting mechanism whereby functions negotiate contracts with each other for provision of service, the contracts dealing with such issues as responsiveness, courtesy, and reliability.

Ellen next appointed a person to direct the service effort, with status equivalent to that of the head of marketing or operations. With his input, and the input of others on the top management team, she produced a service plan, with explicit service goals that served as the basis for the design of a new system for tracking internal and external (consumer) indices of service effectiveness. Goals in the service plan concerned such diverse issues as the time it takes to respond to customer requests, the percentage of errors made in processing customer requests, the percentage of complaints received from customers, the nature of customer complaints and inquiries, training time per employee per month, employee turnover, and the speed with which open positions are filled.

Service delivery problems and successes are now discussed in special meetings of the top management team, separate from meetings that deal with such issues as revenues and profits. While interpersonal and intergroup issues were emphasized during the diagnosis and subsequent off-site session, these discussions have yielded insights into noninterpersonal issues in the pursuit of service excellence. For example, as each function began to assume responsibility for service, the internal telephone system became an inhibitor of effectiveness. Also, Bravo's newsletter was found to be an ineffective medium for portraying the wide variety of issues about which employees should be informed; a new newsletter is planned. With the explicit statement of goals to be accomplished, it became clear that new software systems were going to be required for tracking, so these have been developed. As is to be expected in a living system, and as happened at Alpha, one change begot other changes.

Ellen commissioned the design and implementation of new hiring procedures for the entire business that focused explicitly on hiring people who were service-oriented as well as technically competent. These procedures included interviews similar to those used at Alpha. During diagnosis and job analysis, it became clear that many of the tasks required to produce service excellence involved employees' willingness and ability to work as a team, so the interviews also included a focus on accomplishing work goals through team effort. An interesting outcome of this interview process was the qualitative feedback from the newly trained interviewers about how professional they felt in conducting the interviews. Thus, as at Alpha, supervisors themselves were trained to conduct the semistructured interviews.

Ellen has tried to find ways to share accomplishments as well as problems. She held a meeting with the entire staff to ask for their help in achieving some very difficult goals for the year;

when the goals were achieved through their help, she held a party for everyone to celebrate the accomplishment. When new equipment has been installed, new work spaces have opened up, or new financial services are introduced, all staff members are invited to celebrate the event.

This description of some of the initiatives that Ellen has taken reveals the diversity of issues that she felt required simultaneous attention to raise the level of service excellence at Bravo. It also reveals her fundamental perspective on change—a focus on interacting with systems, with an emphasis on people's competencies and interpersonal relationships and provision of the necessary support, equipment, supplies, and procedures. Change, however, has been neither smooth nor always noticeable. I had cautioned Ellen that change would be slow, that she would have to invest incredible energies in the effort to do all of this simultaneously, but I also told her that if she persisted, the change would take hold. We compared the process to a rocket launch: Prior to lift-off, there is a lot of fire and energy without any movement. Eventually there is lift-off, but even that is very slow and surprisingly fragile until a certain critical speed is attained. I believe that movement is now taking place at Bravo; people at all levels of the company now clearly believe that this change is here to stay. Thus, while Bravo is still creating a lot of fire without yet clearing the stratosphere, much less achieving orbit, awareness has been created—lift-off has been achieved.

Ellen's one frustration during the change process is that, until recently, she has had inconsistent support for her initiatives from Finanserv. This lack of consistent support has not hindered the implementation of the kinds of changes noted above. However, because the changes that she hoped to see have been slow in appearing, the lack of clear supportive messages from above has sometimes left Ellen with the sense that she was in this alone. I believe that the ambiguity about support from upper levels of Finanserv could threaten the success of the change effort if it should lead Ellen to resign. As long as she is there, the change will persist, because she has installed processes and mechanisms that are internally self-sustaining. More recently, clearer interest has been shown from above in what she has been doing, how she has functioned, and how her experiences might be useful in other parts of Finanserv. This interest has enhanced the probability that the changes will actually achieve orbit.

It is important here to note that the nature of the change effort that Ellen has instituted has resulted in a certain amount of ambiguity about job tasks. While the commitment to service has been made clear, exactly how to implement it is less certain. This is common in organizations undergoing change, because old ways of doing the most mundane tasks need to be respecified and people need to be educated to new ways. At Bravo, because so many changes have been occurring simultaneously, people complain of a lack of clarity about how they are to do their jobs. For example, customer inquiries, which previously were dealt with by the customers' account managers, are now directed to operations, where they are coded and dealt with when possible. It is obvious that the mail room now requires new kinds of knowledge about what goes where, employees in operations need to understand which issues they can deal with and which the account managers need to handle, and so forth. Without this attention to every detail, change cannot occur; yet it is the very attention to detail that creates ambiguity about how things should be done.

Conceptualization of Service at Bravo. Ellen has a dual conceptualization of service: Her customers deserve it, and it is the only way to build a business in which repeat customer business is necessary for organizational survival. She became committed to service as the vehicle to success in her previous role as a marketing manager. She asks, "Have you ever tried to sell something to an unhappy customer?" She believes that a happy customer will stay with you and that it is cheaper to keep a customer than to find one.

What Ellen means by service is total dedication to anticipating and meeting client needs, with an emphasis on anticipation. Ellen is committed to the idea that no client should have a complaint and that all clients should want to recommend Bravo to a friend. She believes that this almost compulsive kind of dedication can be achieved only through an integrated service operation. This means that no one part of Bravo is more important than others: All the parts must be functioning and interacting smoothly for clients to receive consistently excellent service. Her role, she believes, is to reveal her commitment to service through what she spends money on, what she supports and rewards, and what she expects in the way of relationships among employees and between employees and customers. Like Will, she understands that behavior talks while speeches go unheard. She believes that a critical mass of simultaneous efforts is required before people get the message; her view of organizations is very complex, so her view of what is required to deliver excellent service is also complex.

Interpretation of Bravo's Change. The simultaneous model of change is a very difficult one to implement. The many issues requiring attention are almost infinite in number and infinitely complex in their multilevel relationships. Organizational change efforts can fail (Mirvis and Berg, 1977) when the "changemasters" (Kanter, 1983) set their sights too high, expect change too quickly, or assume that since they have become converts to the change idea, others will also embrace it.

Change at Bravo was begun when Ellen requested an organizational diagnosis. She must have suspected that there was a need for what Nadler (1987) calls reorientation: a change prompted not so much by external as by internal conditions (what Nadler calls re-creation) and requiring relatively complex ways of thinking and behaving. Ellen's implicit model of organizational functioning was quite comprehensive and complex, with explicit attention to the many layers and levels of relationships and issues identified in the organizational diagnosis report. It was her decision to pay attention to all of these issues simultaneously. Traditional organization development issues also attained an important status at Bravo. The nature of interpersonal relationships within and between levels and functions was seen as important for service delivery. These relationships were emphasized through the off-site session and through conscious adoption of Parasuraman, Zeithaml, and Berry's (1985) determinants of service quality as a basis for internal appraisal.

The initial uncertainty generated by the changes at Bravo was substantial. Everyone was involved in the change effort simultaneously in an attempt to permeate the entire system with a common language (through the goals and the performance appraisal) and new service-focused procedures, equipment, and systems. Ellen occasionally commented that she wished she could have stopped Bravo for a while, put in the changes, and then started it up again; she knew what everyone was experiencing. She said "it was like building an airplane in full flight."

Conclusion

In this discussion of how organizations become service-oriented, my emphasis has been on the systems nature of change and how slowly systems change. This slowness characterizes change even when the change is driven from the top and even when the approach to change attempts to grapple simultaneously with the complexity of organizations and the way they really function. Others have commented that there are numerous routes to change (Blake and Mouton, 1987), that change is not necessarily successful change (Mirvis and Berg, 1977), that change may be instigated in different ways (Nadler, 1987), and that change may occur at similar paces with different intervention strategies and at different paces with the same strategies (Lawler, 1986). What may be unique about this chapter is its focus on achieving service as a strategic initiative (Bowen, Siehl, and Schneider, 1989) and its documentation of a sequential effort for achieving service excellence.

In retrospect, I can discern no difference in the *speed* with which total organizational change is occurring in Alpha and in Bravo. There does appear to be a difference in the *depth* to which the changes have permeated the two organizations; there is more awareness at more levels at Bravo. (Bravo is a much smaller organization than Alpha.) The equivalent *rates* of change are interesting for a number of reasons. At Alpha, there was no initial goal of total organizational change; change was initiated by the human resource department, although with support from the top (see Beres and Musser, 1987). At Bravo, change is being driven from the top (albeit without the unambiguous support of Finanserv). The effort at Bravo is toward total simultaneous change, while at Alpha it is sequential. The Bravo case more closely resembles that documented by Roitman, Liker, and Roskies (1987), who ask "When is all at once too much?" While change at Alpha was not begun with the idea of total organizational transformation, at Bravo the goal was at least a reorientation. By documenting its successes along the way, Alpha has communicated its goals and methods throughout major sections of the corporation. In this way, it has become a study in incremental change (Hage, 1980) through a kind of internal action research (French and Bell, 1984) in which small successes lead to new opportunities for change in a ripple or sequential effect.

Ellen at Bravo has experienced more frustration than has Will at Alpha. This difference in frustration seems to have two facets. First, Will did not need as much active support from above as Ellen did because he proceeded just as if he were putting in a new computer system. In addition, he did not begin with high expectations for big successes, and small wins were documented. Second, Ellen had more of a sense of urgency for change and thought it more important to achieve change rapidly. She put huge amounts of energy into showing through her behavior how important she felt the change was. Her investment of energy perhaps led to unrealistic expectations about the speed with which change would occur. This, combined with ambiguous messages of support for her efforts from above, occasionally resulted in a sense of frustration and futility.

The issue of the *depth* to which change has permeated Alpha and Bravo is more difficult to describe. Perhaps the best evidence for the depth of change at Bravo is the very large number of changes made by Ellen that have become institutionalized and, paradoxically, the greater sense of initial ambiguity at Bravo about the changes. By simultaneously intervening at many levels and over many issues, Ellen raised the consciousness of more people more quickly to her service vision. While this strategy may produce initial fragility, it may also produce more total organizational change more quickly.

In this chapter, I have addressed four major themes that deserve some further attention. The first theme is *open systems*. The open-systems approach addresses multiple issues across many levels of interacting subsystems. In addition, open-systems theory emphasizes the role of feedback from the larger environment of the organization. At Bravo, Ellen was affected by the ambiguity of the larger environment (Finanserv). Will, however, revealed perhaps the classic relationship with the larger environment by trying to anticipate what was going to be required; in Katz and Kahn's (1978) terminology, Will represented the adaptive subsystem by sensing what was going to be required in the future. The view of open systems presented here suggests that, in fact, change in both Alpha and Bravo was promoted by the concept of anticipation. At Alpha, it was the idea of anticipating what the future would bring in terms of the requirements for competent people. More subtle but equally important was Ellen's concept that excellent service required anticipating customers' needs as well as meeting their expectations.

Open systems thinking is important for conceptualizing change, but, as Will demonstrated at Alpha, it is not necessary to think about the *total* system in order to initiate change and have an effect. It is instructive to note, however, that it is precisely because Alpha was an open system that small wins (Weick, 1984) in one division became known to other divisions. It may be that it is in the nature of systems to evolve to total system change when the effectiveness of the change is vouched for by someone other than the change agent him- or herself. At Alpha, this happened fortuitously when the new department was opened and the HRD procedures that had been developed were found to be useful there. Finally, Will demonstrated that a total systems change perspective is not necessary for change to begin, nor does the change need to proceed through all subsystems simultaneously for change to occur. This suggests that organizations perhaps have more choices than they think when contemplating change.

The second theme is *pain (or crisis) as the stimulus to change*. There seems to be agreement in the literature on change that felt pain is a correlate of the embracing of change; the higher the pain level, the more speedily change is embraced. A number of authors (for example, Nadler, 1987; Bartunek and Moch, 1987; Beckhard and Harris, 1977) observe that the key to change in an organization is making all its multiple constituencies aware of how much pain the organization is experiencing. Thus, from a practical standpoint, executives who identify the degree of pain that the organization is experiencing must not assume that all its constituencies are equally aware of it. The cases presented here, however, suggest that this might not always be the best advice. Ellen instituted many tangible changes as indicators of the level of pain that she felt that Bravo was experiencing, yet change was occurring no more rapidly there than at Alpha, where pain was not a public issue. Obviously, one case study does not prove a point, but the results here suggest that identifying a high level of pain may also raise expectations about the speed and degree of change to unrealistic levels. These unrealistic expectations can, in turn, create a sense of frustration, reducing the energy available to continue the change effort. I conclude from this that not all organizations should take the "raise the awareness of pain" route to change: some should take the route that requires small wins to be demonstrated prior to more wholesale acceptance of the need for change. An organization with a climate of skepticism would be the place to take this latter approach; Alpha is that kind of company. In short, the climate or culture of the setting may dictate the most appropriate form of change for that setting.

The third theme addressed here is the change agents' *conceptualizations of service*. In both cases, there was extraordinarily high commitment to service, albeit for somewhat different reasons. At Alpha, service was conceptualized broadly as quality; for Will, the only way to do things is to do them well. At Bravo, Ellen had a dual commitment to service, with her beliefs about what customers deserve and her strategic view that long-run success depends on demonstrating multifaceted service excellence. Both Will and Ellen implicitly believed that the route to excellence was through both people and the organization's assumption of responsibility for developing its capacity to deliver excellence. Both organizations had people who were deeply committed to excellence and to the belief that through good people and appropriate organizational support, excellence is achievable.

Perhaps the most interesting information presented in this chapter concerns the wide variety of ways in which Will and Ellen sent the message that they were working toward service excellence. Will never deviated from quality as his standard, and Ellen implemented a variety of programs to create a sense that the organization was services driven. In these ways, both Ellen and Will were practicing good services marketing: State your values and then reward, support, and expect the activities and behaviors that will implement them (Schneider and Gunnarson, forthcoming).

The fourth theme is the framework in which the two cases were presented: *sequential versus simultaneous change*. I have demonstrated that change can occur through either strategy and that either strategy may be appropriate for some change situations. Both strategies, however, seem to require someone deeply committed to service excellence with a very broad interpretation of what service excellence requires. The change need not occur from the top down, but top-down support will at least decrease the sense of frustration associated with the slow pace at which change always proceeds. These cases reveal that those initiating change efforts toward a service orientation might profit from exposure to experience with other kinds of strategic change presented in the literature (Kilmann, Covin, and Associates, 1987; Pennings, 1985). Perhaps the most important lesson here is that, regardless of how the change process begins, eventually it will be necessary to pay attention to the various levels, subsystems, and interactions that characterize real organizational functioning if total organization change is to happen.

References

Bartunek, J. M., and Moch, M. K. "First-Order, Second-Order, and Third-Order Change and Organizational Development

Interventions: A Cognitive Approach." *Journal of Applied Psychology*, 1987, *23*, 483–500.

Bateson, J.E.G. *Managing Services Marketing: Text and Readings.* Chicago: Dryden Press, 1989.

Beckhard, R., and Harris, R. T. *Organizational Development: Strategies and Models.* Reading, Mass.: Addison-Wesley, 1977.

Beer, M. *Organizational Change and Development.* Glenview, Ill.: Scott, Foresman, 1980.

Beres, M. E., and Musser, S. J. "Avenues and Impediments to Transformations: Lessons from a Case of Bottom-Up Change." In R. H. Kilmann, T. J. Covin, and Associates. *Corporate Transformation: Revitalizing Organizations for a Competitive World.* San Francisco: Jossey-Bass, 1987.

Blake, R. R., and Mouton, J. S. "Comparing Strategies for Incremental and Transformational Change." In R. H. Kilmann, T. J. Covin, and Associates. *Corporate Transformation: Revitalizing Organizations for a Competitive World.* San Francisco: Jossey-Bass, 1987.

Bowen, D. E., and Schneider, B. "Services Marketing and Management: Implications for Organizational Behavior." In B. M. Staw and L. L. Cummings (eds.), *Research in Organizational Behavior.* Vol. 10. Greenwich, Conn.: JAI Press, 1988.

Bowen, D. E., Siehl, C., and Schneider, B. "A Framework for Analyzing Customer Service Orientations in Manufacturing." *Academy of Management Review*, 1989, *14*, 75–95.

Brown, K. A., and Mitchell, T. R. "Employee Performance Obstacles in Retail Banking: Attitudes and Outcomes." Unpublished paper, Seattle University School of Business, 1988.

Eiglier, P., and Langeard, E. *Servuction.* Paris: Wiley, 1987.

Forum Corporation. *Customer Focus Research.* Boston: Forum Corporation, 1988.

French, W. L., and Bell, C. H., Jr. *Organization Development: Behavioral Science Interventions for Organization Improvement.* (3rd ed.) Englewood Cliffs, N.J.: Prentice-Hall, 1984.

Gronroos, C. *Service Management and Marketing: Managing the Moment of Truth in Service Competition.* Lexington, Mass.: Lexington Books, 1990.

Hage, J. *Theories of Organization.* New York: Wiley, 1980.

Hall, D. T. "Human Resource Development and Organizational Effectiveness." In C. J. Fombrun, N. M. Tichey, and M. A. DeVanna (eds.), *Strategic Human Resource Management.* New York: Wiley, 1984.

Hall, D. T. "Dilemmas in Linking Succession Planning to Individual Executive Learning." *Human Resource Management,* 1986, *25,* 235–265.

Kanter, R. M. *The Changemasters.* New York: Simon & Schuster, 1983.

Katz, D., and Kahn, R. L. *The Social Psychology of Organizations.* (2nd ed.) New York: Wiley, 1978.

Kilmann, R. H., Covin, T. J., and Associates. *Corporate Transformation: Revitalizing Organizations for a Competitive World.* San Francisco: Jossey-Bass, 1987.

Konz, A. M. "A Comparison of Dimension Ratings and Exercise Ratings in Assessment Centers." Unpublished doctoral dissertation, Department of Psychology, University of Maryland, 1988.

Lawler, E. E., III. *High-Involvement Management: Participative Strategies for Improving Organizational Performance.* San Francisco: Jossey-Bass, 1986.

Louis, M. R. "Surprise and Sense-Making: What Newcomers Experience in Entering Unfamiliar Organizational Settings." *Administrative Science Quarterly,* 1980, *25,* 226–251.

Lovelock, C. H. "Classifying Services to Gain Strategic Marketing Insights." *Journal of Marketing,* 1983, *47,* 9–20.

Lovelock, C. H. *Managing Services: Marketing, Operations, and Human Resources.* Englewood Cliffs, N.J.: Prentice-Hall, 1988.

Mirvis, P. H., and Berg, D. N. (eds.). *Failures in Organization Development and Change.* New York: Wiley-Interscience, 1977.

Moeller, A., Schneider, B., Schoorman, F. D., and Berney, E. "Development of the Work Facilitation Diagnostic." In F. D. Schoorman and B. Schneider (eds.), *Facilitating Work Effectiveness.* Lexington, Mass.: Lexington Books, 1988.

Nadler, D. A. "Organizational Frame Bending: Types of Change in the Complex Organization." In R. H. Kilmann, T. J. Covin, and Associates. *Corporate Transformation: Revitalizing Organizations for a Competitive World.* San Francisco: Jossey-Bass, 1987.

Parasuraman, A., Zeithaml, V. A., and Berry, L. L. "A Conceptual Model of Service Quality and Its Implications for Future Research." *Journal of Marketing*, 1985, *49*, 41–50.

Pennings, J. M., and Associates. *Organizational Strategy and Change: New Views on Formulating and Implementing Strategic Decisions*. San Francisco: Jossey-Bass, 1985.

Porter, L. W., and Steers, R. M. "Organizational, Work, and Personal Factors in Employee Turnover and Absenteeism." *Psychological Bulletin*, 1973, *80*, 151–176.

Roitman, D. B., Liker, J. K., and Roskies, E. "Birthing a Factory of the Future: When Is 'All at Once' Too Much?" In R. H. Kilmann, T. J. Covin, and Associates. *Corporate Transformation: Revitalizing Organizations for a Competitive World*. San Francisco: Jossey-Bass, 1987.

Schneider, B. "Notes on Climate and Culture." In C. Marshall, D. Schmalansee, and V. Venkatesan (eds.), *Creativity in Services Marketing*. Chicago: American Marketing Association, 1986.

Schneider, B. "Imperatives for the Design of Service Organizations." In C. F. Surprenant (ed.), *Add Value to Your Service*. Chicago: American Marketing Association, 1987a.

Schneider, B. "The People Make the Place." *Personnel Psychology*, 1987b, *40*, 437–453.

Schneider, B., and Bowen, D. E. "Employee and Customer Perceptions of Service in Banks: Replication and Extension." *Journal of Applied Psychology*, 1985, *70*, 423–433.

Schneider, B., and Gunnarson, S. "Organizational Climate and Culture: The Psychology of the Workplace." In J. Jones, B. Steffy, and D. Bray (eds.), *Applied Psychology in Business: The Manager's Handbook*. Lexington, Mass.: Lexington Books, forthcoming.

Schneider, B., and Konz, A. M. "Strategic Job Analysis." *Human Resource Management*, 1989, *28*, 51–63.

Schneider, B., Parkington, J. J., and Buxton, V. M. "Employee and Customer Perceptions of Service in Banks." *Administrative Science Quarterly*, 1980, *25*, 252–267.

Schneider, B., and Schechter, D. "Selecting the Service-Oriented Employee." In S. Brown, E. Gummesson, B. Edvardsson, and

B. Gustavsson (eds.), *Service Quality*. Lexington, Mass.: Lexington Books, 1990.

Schneider, B., and Schmitt, N. *Staffing Organizations*. (2nd ed.) Glenview, Ill.: Scott, Foresman, 1986.

Schuler, R. S., and Jackson, S. E. "Linking Competitive Strategies with Human Resource Management Policies." *Academy of Management Executive*, 1987, *1*, 207–219.

Tichy, N. M. "Foreword: Strategic Planning and Human Resource Management." *Human Resource Management*, 1983, *22*, 3–8.

Tushman, M. L., Newman, W. H., and Nadler, D. A. "Executive Leadership and Organizational Evolution: Managing Incremental and Discontinuous Change." In R. H. Kilmann, T. J. Covin, and Associates, *Corporate Transformation: Revitalizing Organizations for a Competitive World*. San Francisco: Jossey-Bass, 1987.

Weick, K. E. "Small Wins: Redefining the Scale of Social Problems." *American Psychologist*, 1984, *39*, 40–49.

Zemke, R., and Schaff, D. *The Service Edge: 101 Companies That Profit from Customer Care*. New York: New American Library, 1989.

7

Managing Human Resource Issues for High-Contact Service Personnel

David A. Tansik

Human resource, or personnel, management involves the processes by which an organization acquires employees, introduces them into jobs, trains them for their current jobs and develops them for subsequent ones, controls and evaluates their performance, compensates them, and manages their departure from the organization when that time arrives. Though as a "profession," human resource management in the United States dates back only to about the 1940s, problems involving special management attention to personnel issues have existed at least since the Industrial Revolution. In fact, it is on an industrial model that most human resource management practices have been developed. But, as noted in Chapter One, an industrial model is not always appropriate for the development of service management strategies and practices. This chapter, then, discusses human resource issues in the context of service organizations. The basic premise is that a service organization has two "cores": a high-customer-contact core and a low-customer-contact core. Further, these two cores have sufficiently unique employee requirements that different personnel practices and policies are appropriate for each of them. The focus of this chapter is on the high-contact core.

The chapter first presents a number of issues that illus-

152

trate the unique and important role of human resource management in service organizations. A key assumption is that human resource management issues for high-customer-contact service workers are different in many respects from those for low-customer-contact workers. Next, a number of factors concerning special knowledge, skills, and abilities (KSAs) of high-customer-contact workers are discussed. Finally, the implications of these factors for the performance of human resource management functions in the organization are considered.

Human Resource Issues for Services

Schneider and Bowen (1985) have found that several dimensions of service delivery (for example, courtesy and competency, adequate staffing, employee morale) are strongly related to customers' evaluations of the service they receive and their intentions to continue using the service. Further, they found significant agreement between employees' descriptions of an organization's service delivery process and customer evaluations of that service. Of special note is their finding that when employees favorably view the organization's human resource policies, customers tend to favorably view the quality of service provided. The implication is that an organization's human resource program can be a useful vehicle for managing both employees' needs and the quality of the organization's output. This relationship between employee and customer views of service underscores the fact that customers and employees are both physically and psychologically close during the service production and delivery process; indeed, service employees often identify with customers with whom they interact.

This issue is, of course, most applicable to the high-customer-contact employee. Chase and Tansik (1983) note that these employees are involved in a three-way interaction between themselves, customers, and the production process or technology (Figure 7.1). In contrast, low-customer-contact employees, such as manufacturing workers, are involved in a simpler, two-way interaction between themselves and the technology. This three-way interaction means that there is a need to manage

Figure 7.1. Employee-Customer-Technology Interrelationships.

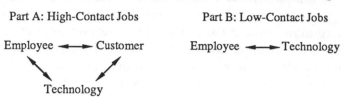

Part A: High-Contact Jobs   Part B: Low-Contact Jobs

Employee ←——→ Customer   Employee ←——→Technology

Technology

both the customer who is involved in the production process and the complex server-customer relationship.

Mills, Chase, and Margulies (1983) suggest that the cohesion between servers and customers can influence the productivity of the service organization. It is important to present to the customer employees who are perceived as competent. This perceived competence will serve to increase the employee's credibility with the customer, which in turn will generate greater trust by customers and will lead to an improved flow of information between the employee and the customer. This, then, will facilitate the production of the service. They likewise postulate that when the interpersonal attraction between customers and servers is high, the flow of information will also be improved.

The dyadic nature of the service encounter is evidenced in the above discussion. Solomon, Surprenant, Czepiel, and Gutman (1985) argue for greater attention to the encounter and propose that the "fusion of two people in a service setting is greater than the sum of its parts" (pp. 100–101). They go on to propose that these dyadic encounters should be viewed as role performances, which emphasizes the performance nature of the employee's job as well as the potential for developing scripts or repertoires. Solomon, Surprenant, Czepiel, and Gutman also propose that aspects of the dyadic encounter can be used to categorize service organization jobs. Thus, for example, a bank teller's job may be more closely related to that of an airline reservation clerk than to that of a bank loan officer. Various communications issues inherent in the encounter have been addressed by Nyquist, Bitner, and Booms (1985), who suggest that with proper selection and training of "front-line person-

nel," organizations can use the encounter as a valuable marketing tool.

Despite the role theory/repertoire nature of the service
encounter, a high-contact worker's job is often unique and not
easily classified with or compared to another's. For example,
uncertainty introduced by diverse customer demands (Chase
and Tansik, 1983; Tansik and Chase, 1988) often necessitates
behavioral adaptations and unique outputs by individual service workers. This, in turn, means that the designation of specific categories of functions to be performed by specific workers
may be difficult. Indeed, Crandall (1986) notes that it is difficult
to break down service work "into categories such as direct sales
or clerical because they may perform all these functions within
one job assignment" (p. 14). He goes on to argue that managers
should avoid "those techniques, such as job evaluation and work
measurement, which classify workers into groups rather than
recognize them as individuals" (p. 16).

Considering that the high-contact worker's job is a complex one and that the worker's performance and attitude can
strongly influence a customer's perceptions of the organization,
a particularly vexing issue is the fact that many of these jobs are
often lower-level positions, usually staffed by people who are in
their first job in the organization — for example, airline flight
attendants, bus drivers, fast-food counter attendants, receptionists, cashiers, retail store clerks, stockbrokers, bank tellers,
police officers, and hotel bellhops, among others. In many respects, the organization is trusting its reputation and cash flow
to the performance of these people. Few additional arguments
need to be made for the importance of an effective human
resource program in a service organization.

Special Skills for High-Contact Employees

Lovelock (1981) discusses a "service trinity" where the
(high-contact) service employee, at least in the mind of the
customer, (1) runs the organization, (2) sells the output, and (3) is
equated by the customer with the organization's output. Clearly,
customers expect a lot from the high-contact employee, and that

is why, as discussed above, these jobs tend to be complex. In Lovelock's conception, the employee must demonstrate both managerial and marketing abilities in addition to the technical (production) skills necessary to be "equated" with the output. While technical skills tend to be obvious and more easily articulated and evaluated (a broker should know how to buy stocks, a hair stylist how to cut hair, a bus driver how to drive), the other skills necessary for performing the managerial and marketing roles that are involved in interacting with customers prior to, during, and after performing the technical skill are more subjective, though no less important. Following are several knowledge, skill, and ability factors that, in addition to technical skills, are believed to be important for high-contact employees.

Interpersonal Skills. Bell (1973) describes work in an industrial society as primarily a "game against fabricated nature." In contrast, he describes work in the postindustrial services-dominated world as primarily a "game between persons" (pp. xvi–xvii). Games against fabricated nature tend to involve work where people become dwarfed by the machines they run as they produce "things" out of physical raw materials. In contrast, games between persons involve such service-related activities as patient-physician, teacher-student, or client-bureaucrat interactions. For these latter activities, a key raw material for the production of the product is information, which must usually be obtained from the customer. Clearly, interpersonal skills are important here as they relate to the communications process involved in obtaining this information.

Referring back to Figure 7.1, we can note how high-contact workers must deal with two interactions not required of workers in jobs dealing only with materials or things and not with people. First, the high-contact worker must manage the customer-technology interaction (this will be covered in more detail below). Second, he or she must interact directly with customers. These two additional interactions lie at the heart of the game between persons posited by Bell. To adequately manage all three of the high-contact interactions described in Figure 7.1, workers must possess both relevant technical and interpersonal skills. Both technical and interpersonal skills are *necessary*, but neither alone is *sufficient* for optimal job performance. Thus, for example, we expect airline flight attendants to be technically competent concerning the safety and passenger service aspects of their jobs, but we also expect them to be interpersonally pleasant and attractive (see Hochschild, 1983) as they instruct (that is, "train") passengers in the use of safety equipment and provide in-flight services.

The degree to which interpersonal or technical skills may be dominant in a given job, for a given service transaction, would seem to vary with the nature of the interactions between employee, customer, and technology. To the extent that the service can be rendered with little customer-employee or with minimal customer-technology interactions, technical skills for a given transaction may well be relatively more important. Likewise, high levels of these interactions will lead to a greater emphasis on interpersonal skills. Thus, there is no reason to expect that the importance of these skills will be *generally* equal across all types of high-contact jobs; for example, a convenience store clerk, versus a restaurant waiter, versus a physician. However, latent interpersonal abilities may well be necessary for special transactions. For example, while a convenience store clerk would in general exhibit only a moderate level of interpersonal skills during the typically brief (one- to three-minute) periods when customers are in the store, if an elderly, confused customer needed special help, these latent skills would have to become manifest. Similarly, there are times when physicians can operate as technocrats with little attention to interpersonal interactions (for example, when dealing with acute illnesses or emergencies), and other times when a good bedside manner is required to elicit information or cater to patients' special needs or requests.

The situational nature of the importance of interpersonal skills was empirically noted by Sutton and Rafaeli (1988) in their study of convenience store clerks. Here they found that interpersonal skills (the display of pleasant emotions to customers) were positively related to sales only in slow-paced stores; where the stores were busy, the relationship was not found. Their interpretation is that customers primarily want to receive the (technical) output of the store (here, convenience). If the store is busy, customers want prompt service and do not want clerks to "waste time" being pleasant and friendly. However, if the store is not busy, customers expect both convenience and pleasant behavior.

Given personality and other behavioral differences among people, it is obvious that some individuals possess better or at least more adaptable interpersonal skills than others. Without trying to dichotomize the world, suffice it to say that there are "people people" and "things people." In high-contact jobs where interpersonal skills are important, efforts should be made to ensure that "people people" occupy them. "Things people" are no less valuable to an organization; however, they should be utilized in jobs that emphasize their technical skills and do not require significant amounts of interpersonal interaction with customers.

Appearance. As mentioned earlier, Schneider and Bowen (1985) note that the climate of an organization is a key factor in customers' decisions to continue using its services. Climate is evidenced not only by employees' actions but by other, more physical factors. Danet (1981) discusses how factors such as furniture arrangements and the use of space as well as the physical appearance of servers (and customers!) impinge on the server-customer relationship. Evidence of the perceived importance of the high-contact worker's appearance can be seen in the time spent on this factor during the training of airline flight attendants (Hochschild, 1983). Appearance of the service employee, along with factors such as layout, cleanliness, furniture placement, and the like, is a part of the "atmospherics" (Kotler, 1973–74) of a service situation or encounter. As such, it is another variable to be considered in the selection and training of these workers.

Clearly, there are legal and moral limits to the use of appearance as a personnel selection and retention factor. Within these parameters, however, management often has considerable discretion. For example, dress codes or uniforms are often used to create an image. Note how Southwest Airlines uses shorts and T-shirts for flight attendants' uniform to convey the message of informality and friendliness. A teaching hospital with which I am familiar had no dress code for nurses when it first opened several years ago. Soon the "average" dress for nurses (most of whom were in their twenties) was jeans, sweat shirt, tennis shoes, and a stethoscope. Patients (most of whom were in their fifties or older) began to complain about the "unprofessional" conduct of the nurses. Management then in-stituted a dress code for all patient-contact staff. With virtually no changes in staff or, as nearly as could be determined, their technical performance, the complaints of unprofessional con-duct disappeared. Appearances do indeed seem to make a difference.

Hochschild (1983) discusses the appearance issue from a slightly different perspective, emphasizing the role or character that the high-contact worker must play in order to convey an image to the customer. Hochschild's focus is on such behaviors as the (often) "artificial" smile that airline flight attendants must use when greeting passengers and how these workers must manage their emotions so as to convey a proper (as defined by management) impression to the customer.

Coproduction Skills. Mills and Morris (1986) and Bowen (1986) have noted that customers are often treated as "partial employees" in service organizations. That is, customers often take part in the production of the output by doing something themselves or helping the service worker. Common examples of coproduction are carrying items to a cashier in a department store, filling out a deposit slip in a bank, and clearing one's own table in a fast-food restaurant. Beyond these rather basic exam-ples is the issue that organizations expect customers to possess certain knowledge or skills in order to efficiently obtain the service. Lituchy (1988) has noted how many of these behaviors are learned by children watching parents or others as part of the general process of socialization (for instance, how to use a grocery store or fast-food restaurant). For example, note how many experienced travelers know how to check in at an airport, obtain a boarding pass, go through security, board the plane, find their seat, get ready for takeoff, and so on. Imagine a flight made up entirely of first-time fliers, people who have never been to an airport before. Clearly, a different set of demands would be placed on the service personnel. Being able to work *with* a customer, possibly even "training" new customers, is important for high-contact workers in these situations. Such traits as tolerance of ambiguity (customers are not always homogeneous), patience (customers may learn slowly), and a "thick skin" (customers may blame the server for their own mistakes) would seem particularly useful.

In professional service organizations, the coproduction skills would seem to be especially important. Lawyers, financial consultants, architects, and others must often work closely with customers to determine what service is desired and to help customers provide necessary information. Coproduction skills, especially those concerned with helping customers articulate needs, define the desired service, and provide informational inputs, would seem to be crucial for such employees as paralegals or physician's assistants. Here the expectation is that less skilled (less costly) employees can "develop" or define the service production situation so that the professional need spend less time in producing and delivering the output. Mistakes made at the initial encounter level would be costly and detrimental to service production.

Sales. Chase (1981) and Chase and Tansik (1983) have argued that to promote operating efficiency, service organizations ought to separate those parts of the organization that do not require customer contact from those that do by decoupling them and placing them in back-office or off-site locations. Not all components can or should be decoupled, however, as some customer contact is often necessary to produce and deliver the service, or some contact may even be an integral part of the service. Chase (1988) has noted that where there is customer contact, the organization should use it as an opportunity to market more of its services or products. Thus, high-customer-contact workers should have sales skills. This rather directly follows from Lovelock's (1981) service trinity noted earlier.

Often called "cross-selling," this behavior by high-contact workers can be seen in many banks ("While I cash your check, wouldn't you like to look at our brochure on high-rate CDs?") or even at McDonald's (the counter attendant will usually suggest *one* additional item — watch for this the next time you go there).

Nonverbal and Self-Monitoring Skills. General communication skills, especially verbal ones, are implied in the interpersonal domain discussed above. In a study of outside sales representatives, Tansik (1985) found that sales personnel who were skilled at interpreting nonverbal communications had higher levels of sales than did those not so skilled. Additionally, those persons who were high self-monitors (Snyder, 1974) — that is, people who adjust their behavior in the context of a social situation — as well as good nonverbal perceivers showed the highest levels of sales. These latter individuals seemed not only to pick up nonverbal cues from customers but also to adjust their own behaviors (smiling, laughing, frowning, and so on at the "right times") in response to these cues. Weitz (1981) likewise found that the ability of salespeople to empathize with customers and the ability to adapt behaviors to specific settings were related to sales performance. And Caldwell and O'Reilly (1982) found that field representatives of a franchise organization who were high self-monitors received the highest performance evaluation scores. Thus, it appears that nonverbal communication abilities and the use of self-monitoring to adjust behavior in response to nonverbal as well as other cues facilitated performance in high-contact jobs.

Implications for Human Resource Activities

Given the nature of high-contact jobs and some of the KSAs particular to them, there are a number of special considerations that should be given to human resource activities involving workers in these jobs.

Recruitment and Selection. Berry (1981) discusses the use of marketing tools to attract and retain employees. This approach tends to view employees as "internal customers" of the organization. Advertising can be used not only to attract customers but also to shape attitudes and expectations of actual and prospective employees concerning the policies and climate of the organization.

Since recruiting efforts are generally job-specific, most organizations tend to use job descriptions based on job analysis to delineate the qualifications (KSAs) that applicants should possess. However, high-contact jobs, as noted by Crandall (1986), often do not fit into neat categories and are thus far less amenable to rigorous job analysis than are back-office or manufacturing jobs. Bowen (1983) likewise discusses the difficulty of writing job descriptions for services in comparison to manufacturing. Bowen does note, however, that the more a service job is scripted, the easier it is to analyze and describe.

For high-contact jobs, the analysis of technical abilities, while important, does not seem to be the crucial issue; rather, the stumbling block is the recruitment and selection of individuals whose interpersonal skills are more difficult to quantify. Schneider (1976) has noted, however, that predictors of behavior or performance in organizational psychology have tended to focus mainly on cognitive and motor aptitudes rather than interpersonal skills. The use of various instruments to measure behavioral skills and abilities that appear to be associated with good performance in high-contact jobs will be limited by various legal guidelines. While a complete exposition of the legal issues is beyond the scope of this chapter, suffice it to say that beginning with the *Griggs v. Duke Power Company* U.S. Supreme Court ruling in 1964 and through current Equal Employment Opportunity Commission (EEOC) rulings, the use of any test for hiring or promotion is restricted to those cases where the organization can show a statistically significant relationship between test scores and demonstrated job performance.

Given the above caveat, a number of instruments are available that might be validated for use in selecting high-contact employees. For example, "behavioral flexibility" may be predicted by a person's tolerance for ambiguity and low authoritarianism, which can be measured via the Central Life Interest instrument (Dubin, Champoux, and Porter, 1975). Snyder (1974) has developed the Self-Monitoring Scale to measure self-monitoring predispositions. And Rosenthal and others (1979) have developed the Profile of Nonverbal Sensitivities (PONS) test to measure nonverbal abilities.

More directly related to services is the Service Orientation Scale developed by Hogan, Hogan, and Busch (1984), which measures the predisposition to be helpful, thoughtful, considerate, and cooperative. This scale does not measure technical competence but is thought to measure behaviors necessary to maintain good relationships between customers and an organization. It is based on personality measures and identifies people who have "good adjustment, likability, social skill and willingness to follow rules" (p. 173). Each organization should determine which, if any, of these behavioral skills and abilities are relevant to its high-contact jobs. Then the selection process should involve identifying people with the appropriate attributes. Those without those attributes but with otherwise sound technical skills need not be rejected; opportunities for good performance may well exist for them in back-office or low-contact positions.

Some organizations have developed innovative testing procedures that do not rely on specific psychometric tests but do identify behavioral predispositions that are related to success on the job. One of the more innovative tests was developed by Seattle Metro, the bus system in Seattle, Washington. This is a two-hour videotape that simulates some sixty different situations that a driver may experience. At selected points, the simulation stops and the applicant is asked to choose an appropriate response for the driver from a list of alternatives. The choices do not require knowledge of organizational policies and practices but do require the use of good judgment, tact, and general customer relations skills.

Training. Training in service organizations is unfortunately often equated with programs such as McDonald's Hamburger University, Kentucky Fried Chicken's University, and Holiday Inn's Learning Center. While quite relevant for their own restaurants or hotels, much of the training here involves organizational policies and practices and technical skills for managers. The focus in this chapter is on training for high-contact workers such as might work in these organizations but who are not currently the managers.

To the extent that a high-contact job is repetitive, scripting may well be used. Ashforth and Ravid (1986) caution us about situations where workers in overly scripted jobs make errors caused by mindlessness; the script becomes routine and the worker so robotlike that special situations are not recognized. Lord and Kernan (1987), however, indicate that scripts can be used very effectively as learning devices, especially for the training of new employees. They state that as workers become more experienced, the scripts can be modified to accommodate unique or changing inputs. Their argument is that the scripts need not be so static that workers become lost and mindless within them and so exhibit the behaviors noted by Ashforth and Ravid; as workers gain experience, the scripts can be expanded to accommodate greater flexibility.

Training of new workers around well-developed scripts is a widely practiced procedure. With the process applicable to a wide variety of organizations, some of the aspects of McDonald's script-based training of new workers are illuminating. The training includes a process of specific steps for the counter attendant to take in serving a customer. Workers are taught how to (1) greet customers and (2) ask for their order (including a script for suggesting additional items). There is then a set procedure for (3) assembling the order (for example, cold drinks first, then hot ones), (4) placing various items on the tray, and (5) placing the tray where the customers need not reach for it. Next, (6) there are a script and procedure for collecting money and giving change. Finally, (7) there is a script for saying thank-you and asking the customer to come again. This script gives the organization significant control over and uniformity of the customer-server interaction and is easily enough learned that new workers can be quickly trained and put to work.

Similar script-based training may be done for jobs such as hotel desk clerks, clerks at airline ticket counters, police officers (for example, approaching a citizen for a traffic violation), supermarket cashiers, and many others. In most cases, for entry-level high-contact work, the script encompasses all or most of the technical aspects of the job. Given the low-level nature of these jobs, technical training, while important, is usually not a difficult issue. The more difficult training involves the development of many of the behavioral skills and abilities discussed above. Chase, Northcraft, and Wolf (1984) note the need for "contact training" of high-contact employees *after* they receive their technical training. For example, they describe a process where brokers would first receive technical training in portfolio analysis and only then would receive training in interpersonal issues involved in dealing with customers.

While many methods typically used for interpersonal training, such as sensitivity training, role playing, and behavioral modeling, have traditionally been used for supervisory and managerial training, there seems little reason that they could not be adapted for entry-level high-contact jobs. For example, a technique used by several retailers when opening a new department store is to have several "mock sales" before the grand opening. Local clubs or groups are given the opportunity to "shop" in the store using play money. The objective is to expose employees (sales, stockroom, and so on) to as many "real" situations as possible, all under the watchful eye of managers and trainers. Mejia (1984) reports on an approach where new bus drivers for a city transit system are assigned to the system's phone information service during their indoctrination program. Since this is where most passenger complaints are initially lodged, these new drivers develop a good understanding of the service expectations of their customers before they begin the job. Overall, the message is that behavioral skills and abilities training should not be overlooked and that this training should logically come after the technical training for a particular job.

Control and Evaluation. Berry's (1981) notion of the use of advertising to shape employees' perceptions of their jobs is a novel high-contact-employee control approach. The reasoning is that if employees understand what customers are being told to expect from the organization, they will be prepared to deliver that service.

Much of the literature on services management stresses the need for high-contact employees to have significant control over their own operations; that is, they should be empowered to act within certain defined constraints. Bateson (1985) urges that, in general, high-contact service employees be given more control over their jobs so as to better deliver the service output to the customer; customers are served best by employees with few controls over them. Mills and Posner (1982) argue for self-supervision by the service worker in professional organizations because of the need for a personal interface between customer and service producer. And Trevino (1986) contends that the low-level service worker will tend to be autonomous because of the need to obtain customer inputs for the service production process.

A key consideration here would seem to be both the degree of customer uncertainty and the cause-effect relationship between employee actions and the service output produced. For example, Ouchi and Maguire (1975) posit that, where uncertainty is high and the cause-effect relationships not clear, an organization should use output controls. That is, the focus of the control system should be on *what* the employee accomplishes rather than on the process or behaviors utilized to do it. They further contend that control based on employees following a specified process or exhibiting certain behaviors should be used when uncertainty is low or where the cause-effect relationship is well understood.

Ouchi (1977) also describes "ritualized control"; that is, control based on the degree to which a ritual was followed rather than on specific outcomes or behaviors. In such cases, management supervision is aimed at the degree to which the employee follows a ritualized pattern of behavior rather than at direct measures of what the employee produced. If employees are expected to follow a ritual, the organization must take steps to ensure that the employees know how and when to behave under the predicted circumstances. In addition, the organization must be sure that following the ritual will result in the desired outcomes. In these cases, sound training programs, often with periodic refreshers, are usually necessary to educate and so-cialize workers so that they internalize and adhere to the ritual. Thus, airline pilots with a "ritualized" procedure for preflight checks (among other job functions) can be expected to perform in known and predictable ways if the ritual is followed (for example, to delay a takeoff under certain conditions). Likewise, counter attendants in fast-food restaurants who follow a ritual can be expected to perform in predictable ways even without high levels of direct supervision.

Even with ritual control, some degree of self-discretion must often be left to high-customer-contact workers. For exam-ple, some amount of self-discretion could be given to bus drivers in, say, dealing with a case of a regular rider known to the driver who on a particular day has forgotten her weekly pass or in accommodating an elderly passenger who seems confused and does not have the exact change. Self-discretion will be especially necessary in cases where the employee is physically removed from the supervisor or there is a wide span of control and supervisors are not readily available for consultation.

Where a high-contact worker exercises large amounts of self-control over the work process, evaluation criteria may well have to have a significant qualitative bias. Since there is a high degree of customer-induced uncertainty concerning the desired output in such jobs (the output will vary between customers), there is a significant problem in establishing rigorous, quantifi-able goals for that output. This is not to suggest that quantifiable factors should not be utilized at all; what is at issue is the degree to which these are direct measures of service outputs—that is, *things customers want*—versus measures of system efficiency or factors that are only distantly related to the service received by the customer. These latter factors need not be only behavior or process measures; they can be (quantitatively described) surro-gates for the actual output received by customers. For example, Jan Carlzon (1987) notes how on-time departures and arrivals were a key component of SAS Airlines service (an "output" desired by customers) and how he imposed rigorous *direct* mea-sures of this on the system. Contrast this with measures of the performance of gate attendants, such as the number of passengers processed per hour, that might also yield a (surrogate) measure of on-time performance — if the "right" number of passengers is processed, the plane should be loaded and ready to go on time. Likewise, instead of qualitative measures of how well airline reservations clerks answer callers' questions and book reservations, a quantitative measure of number of phone calls answered per hour could be substituted. Employees in high-contact jobs who are evaluated on measures that are only indirectly related to the service output often complain that close attention to the numbers results in their not delivering the desired service to customers. Thus, the workers meet the imposed goals and get a good evaluation, but the organization may lose customers because of the nature of the product delivered. Mills, Chase, and Margulies (1983) argue that to counter this type of dysfunctional behavior, management should increase goal-setting behavior as overall goal specificity decreases. Note that the key in using qualitative measures is to realize that employees need not be totally free of measures of their behavior; rather, the measures used should be based on desired consequences and not simply on employee inputs into the system. This is closely related to Odiorne's (1979) work on management by objectives, in which he calls for measures of *what* employees do rather than of *how* they do it; that is, for output rather than process or behavioral controls.

Specifying output measures would seem to be an especially difficult task for services where the end output is not a product or a process (for example, a haircut, airline transportation) but is rather a behavioral outcome (for example, learning to dance). Where this behavioral outcome is mostly or totally dependent on the customer, the problem is exacerbated by the reduction in the employee's control over (and hence responsibility for) the service encounter. One approach to this issue has been posed by Chase and Tansik (1983): Where there is substantial self-control by the high-contact worker and few quantifiable measures of service output, evaluation criteria should be based on system effectiveness rather than efficiency measures. That is, the evaluation effort should concentrate not on specific work performance measures but rather on such factors as customer satisfaction with the organization, repeat sales, and overall organizational profitability.

Rewarding. In organizations, management tends to get the behavior from employees that it rewards. Thus, the message is that management should reward the behaviors that it wants. While seemingly an obvious admonition, its implementation is often problematic. Clearly, in service as well as other types of organizations, compensation and reward systems should be logically tied to the organization's evaluation system. Various wage and salary administration procedures to develop compensation programs that ensure equity across various job classifications in the organization are discussed in standard personnel texts. Service organizations do, however, have unique compensation problems when there are jobs for which customers substantially determine the employees' income, such as through tipping. Shamir (1983, 1984) notes that employees, such as restaurant waiters, who are dependent on tips for their income and who are high-volume tip receivers tend to identify more with customers' viewpoints than with management's. While this is somewhat understandable and not surprising, it does raise important issues for management. For example, as employees adopt customers' viewpoints, will they make decisions detrimental to the organization? Or will the identification with customers make the employees even more valuable as a source of information about customers' wants and expectations? An obvious approach when employees' compensation is too closely tied to customers is to sever the link and impose organization-based rewards. Many private clubs forbid tipping and instead pay workers a salary. This approach is intended to make employees loyal to the organization and not to individual customers or members.

The problem of customer versus organization loyalty is not limited to tip recipients. Any time management uses customer feedback about employees as an input to the evaluation-compensation decision, there may be a tendency for employees to adopt the same behaviors as tip recipients. With professional employees, such as teachers and physicians, such an approach could lead to delivering products for which the customer will rate the worker highly rather than products that are more professionally desirable. Thus, there are teachers who trade easy work loads (and decreased learning?) for good student evaluations. And there are physicians (many with rather large practices) who prescribe drugs "desired" by patients rather than dealing with underlying symptoms and diseases.

Development. Development differs from training in that it is concerned with preparing workers for high-level jobs rather than improving skills for the current one. A dilemma is that the next higher job for many high-contact workers is one that moves them into a role with decreased or no customer contact. Thus, a bank teller can be promoted to operations manager and deal with other tellers rather than customers, or a teacher can be promoted to principal and deal with other teachers. The danger is that the organization loses a good high-contact worker and may gain a not-so-good back-office worker.

Though it is more easily said than done, organizations should consider the creation of dual career tracks—one for high-contact and one for low-contact employees. This may well require the establishment of additional grades for current jobs (for example, assistant teller, teller, senior teller, and so on). The purpose is to provide promotional recognition and advancement for good high-contact workers without moving them out of a high-contact role. These jobs need not be different in name only but can also involve varied levels of responsibility and authority. Thus, senior tellers should have responsibility for training new tellers, in addition to other duties. Acquisition of these other duties by senior tellers may free branch managers from some tasks, and this time could be spent on customer contact activities designed to draw more funds into the organization.

Conclusion

There are important differences between work that is done in manufacturing or in back-office locations and the work done by high-customer-contact workers in the presence of the customer. Lovelock's (1981) discussion of the service trilogy portraying the high-contact worker as the manager, seller, and, indeed, the product itself in the eye of the customer captures the essence of this difference. Not only must these high-contact workers have the technical skills necessary to perform their jobs; they must also have the behavioral skills necessary to function in a job and an environment where they must produce and sell an output in the presence of the customer.

Thus, the skill and ability to communicate with customers, play roles and engage in behaviors desired by customers, and train customers to be coproducers of the product are uniquely required of high-contact workers. The dyadic nature of the service worker–customer encounter emphasizes these skills and abilities and requires the high-contact worker to possess more interpersonal skills than are normally required of manufacturing or back-office employees. Therefore, a sound human resource program in a service organization will structure the recruitment, selection, training, control, evaluation, compensation, and development activities in ways designed to ensure that the proper mix of technical and behavioral knowledge, skills, and abilities is maintained.

Several areas stand out as needing special attention by human resource managers, areas where theories of service design and management posit special issues but where practical applications have yet to be widely used. First is the area of high-contact-employee empowerment. It was pointed out above that customer uncertainty should lead to forms of employee self-control and to evaluation criteria that are output based. This leads to the notion that these employees must be empowered to make decisions (within constraints, of course) on issues germane to their jobs that affect customers. This ensures that customers' problems and requests will or should be dealt with expediently. It requires that substantial decision making be decentralized and that employees be given the skills, resources, and support necessary to deal with problems at their level. There are numerous anecdotes about employees being empowered to act and how this has led to increased attention to outputs and customer satisfaction. For example, Carlzon (1987) notes the SAS purser who decided on her own to compensate customers for a flight delay caused by bad weather by offering free coffee and biscuits, even though these were normally sold on flights. When a middle manager (the catering supervisor) turned down her order for these supplies, she used petty cash to purchase the items from another airline. Her attention to customers' needs and her ingenuity were admired by upper management (Carlzon, 1987, p. 67).

When high-contact employees are given substantial leeway in making decisions about their jobs or are not subject to close controls, management must ensure that decisions made and actions taken are indeed ones that are desired. While ex post facto reviews can be used to evaluate what happened, it would seem more important to develop sound training programs that socialize and indoctrinate employees into thinking and acting in ways desired by management. Indeed, the best control system for high-contact, empowered employees may well be the training program that management uses to let them know what is expected in the organization. Training, then, rather than control, becomes the watchword.

And, prior to training, selection of employees is crucial. The literature contains several suggestions and recommendations regarding high-contact employees' skills. For example, nonverbal and self-monitoring skills were seen as important in certain sales jobs, and a tolerance of ambiguity was predicted to be important for jobs involving high customer uncertainty. Still, there is little empirical evidence to support these recommendations. Given current regulations regarding employment testing, efforts by human resource managers to delineate desired skills and attributes in their own organizations and to begin to validate testing by relating these factors to actual job performance seem highly desirable.

Lastly, the development of career tracks that keep good high-contact employees in high-contact positions should be strongly considered. This may well necessitate substantial changes in job design and organizational structure. However, if attention to customers' needs is an important part of an organization's mission, then ensuring that the right people are on the firing line is crucial.

Human resource managers must realize that in many cases the person who represents the organization to the rest of the world, who collects the money, and who can easily cause customers to go elsewhere is the low-level entry employee at the bottom of the organization chart. These are crucial jobs that must receive the organization's most careful attention. They are not jobs to which management should pay attention only when all the other important work is completed.

References

Ashforth, B. E., and Ravid, G. "Poor Service from the Service Bureaucracy: The Role of Mindlessness." *Academy of Management Proceedings*, 1986, pp. 166–169.

Bateson, J.E.G. "Perceived Control and the Service Encounter." In J. A. Czepiel, M. R. Solomon, and C. F. Surprenant (eds.), *The Service Encounter: Managing Employee/Customer Interaction in Service Businesses*. Lexington, Mass.: Lexington Books, 1985.

Bell, D. *The Coming of Post-Industrial Society: A Venture in Social Forecasting*. New York: Basic Books, 1973.

Berry, L. L. "The Employee as Customer." *Journal of Retail Banking*, 1981, *3* (3), 33–40.

Bowen, D. E. "Integrating Organizational Behavior and Marketing in the Study of Service." Unpublished working paper, University of Southern California, 1983.

Bowen, D. E. "Managing Customers as Human Resources in Service Organizations." *Human Resource Management*, 1986, *25*, 371–383.

Caldwell, D. F., and O'Reilly, C. A., III. "Boundary Spanning and Individual Performance: The Impact of Self-Monitoring." *Journal of Applied Psychology*, 1982, *67*, 124–127.

Carlzon, J. *Moments of Truth: New Strategies for Today's Customer-Driven Economy*. New York: Harper & Row, 1987.

Chase, R. B. "The Customer Contact Approach to Services: Theoretical Bases and Practical Extensions." *Operations Research*, 1981, *29* (4), 698–706.

Chase, R. B. "Service System Productivity Requires More Than a Stopwatch." Working Paper, Graduate School of Business Administration, University of Southern California, 1988.

Chase, R. B., Northcraft, G. B., and Wolf, G. "Designing High-Contact Service Systems: Application to Branches of a Savings and Loan." *Decision Sciences*, 1984, *15*, 542–556.

Chase, R. B., and Tansik, D. A. "The Customer Contact Model for Organization Design." *Management Science*, 1983, *29*, 1037–1050.

Crandall, R. E. "Applying Industrial Engineering Techniques in Service Industries." *Industrial Management*, May–June 1986, pp. 13–16.

Danet, B. "Client-Organization Relationships." In P. C. Nystrom and W. H. Starbuck (eds.), *Handbook of Organizational Design*. Vol. 2. New York: Oxford University Press, 1981.

Dubin, R., Champoux, I., and Porter, L. "Central Life Interests and Organizational Commitment of Blue-Collar and Clerical Workers." *Administrative Science Quarterly*, 1975, *20*, 411–421.

Hochschild, A. R. *The Managed Heart: Commercialization of Human Feeling*. Berkeley: University of California Press, 1983.

Hogan, J., Hogan, R., and Busch, C. M. "How to Measure Service Orientation." *Journal of Applied Psychology*, 1984, *69*, 167–173.

Kotler, P. "Atmospherics as a Marketing Tool." *Journal of Retailing*, 1973–74, *49*, 48–64.

Lituchy, T. "The Socialization of Customers as Partial Employees: Generic Skills, and When They Are Learned." Paper presented at the national meeting of the Academy of Management, Anaheim, Calif., Aug. 8, 1988.

Lord, R. G., and Kernan, M. C. "Scripts as Determinants of Purposeful Behavior in Organizations." *Academy of Management Review*, 1987, *12*, 265–277.

Lovelock, C. H. "Why Marketing Management Needs to Be Different for Services." In J. H. Donnelly and W. R. George (eds.), *Marketing of Services*. Chicago: American Marketing Association, 1981.

Mejia, S. B. "Employee Motivation: Developing a Customer Orientation Among Transit Drivers." Unpublished paper, Department of Management, University of Arizona, 1984.

Mills, P. K., Chase, R. B., and Margulies, N. "Motivating the Client/Employee System as a Service Production Strategy." *Academy of Management Review*, 1983, *8*, 301–310.

Mills, P. K., and Morris, J. H. "Clients as 'Partial' Employees of Service Organizations: Role Development in Client Participation." *Academy of Management Journal*, 1986, *11*, 726–735.

Mills, P. K., and Posner, B. Z. "The Relationships Among Self-Supervision, Structure, and Technology in Professional Service Organizations." *Academy of Management Review*, 1982, *25*, 437–443.

Nyquist, J. D., Bitner, M. J., and Booms, B. H. "Identifying Communication Difficulties in the Service Encounter: A Critical Incident Approach." In J. A. Czepiel, M. R. Solomon, and C. F. Surprenant (eds.), *The Service Encounter: Managing Employee/Customer Interaction in Service Businesses*. Lexington, Mass.: Lexington Books, 1985.

Odiorne, G. S. *MBO II*. Belmont, Calif.: Fearon, Pittman, 1979.

Ouchi, W. G. "The Relationship Between Organizational Structure and Organizational Control." *Administrative Science Quarterly*, 1977, *22*, 95–113.

Ouchi, W. G., and Maguire, M. "Organizational Control: Two Functions." *Administrative Science Quarterly*, 1975, *20*, 559–569.

Rosenthal, R., and others. *Sensitivity to Nonverbal Communication*. Baltimore, Md.: Johns Hopkins University Press, 1979.

Schneider, B. *Staffing Organizations*. Santa Monica, Calif.: Goodyear, 1976.

Schneider, B., and Bowen, D. E. "Employee and Customer Perceptions of Service in Banks: Replication and Extension." *Journal of Applied Psychology*, 1985, *70*, 323–433.

Shamir, B. "A Note on Tipping and Employee Perceptions and Attitudes." *Journal of Occupational Psychology*, 1983, *56*, 255–259.

Shamir, B. "Between Gratitude and Gratuity." *Annals of Tourism Research*, 1984, *11*, 59–78.

Snyder, M. "The Self-Monitoring of Expressive Behavior." *Journal of Personality and Social Psychology*, 1974, *30*, 526–537.

Solomon, M. R., Surprenant, C. F., Czepiel, J. A., and Gutman,

E. G. "A Role Theory Perspective on Dyadic Interactions: The Service Encounter." *Journal of Marketing*, 1985, *49* (4), 99–111.

Sutton, R. I., and Rafaeli, A. "Untangling the Relationship Between Displayed Emotions and Organizational Sales: The Case of Convenience Stores." *Academy of Management Journal*, 1988, *31*, 461–487.

Tansik, D. A. "Nonverbal Communication and High Contact Employees." In J. A. Czepiel, M. R. Solomon, and C. F. Surprenant (eds.), *The Service Encounter: Managing Employee/Customer Interaction in Service Businesses*. Lexington, Mass.: Lexington Books, 1985.

Tansik, D. A., and Chase, R. B. "The Effects of Customer Induced Uncertainty on the Design of Service Systems." Paper presented at the national meeting of the Academy of Management, Anaheim, Calif., Aug. 8, 1988.

Trevino, L. K. "The Technology/Control Relationship in Service Organizations." Paper presented at the national meeting of the Academy of Management, Chicago, 1986.

Weitz, B. A. "Effectiveness in Sales Interactions: A Contingency Framework." *Journal of Marketing*, 1981, *45*, 85–103.

8

Applying Behavioral Management Techniques in Service Organizations

Fred Luthans
Tim R. V. Davis

As the other chapters of the book repeatedly point out, the major challenge facing service-sector organizations is to become more productive. Although the measurement problems are inherently difficult and controversial, few would argue with the statement that the status of service productivity is pretty bleak (Chipello, 1988; Clark, 1986). This is especially true when the service sector is compared to the manufacturing sector. American manufacturers finally seem both to be improving the quality of goods that they produce and to be winning the battle to lower costs and raise output (Nasar, 1988; Skinner, 1985). Service firms, on the other hand, have not yet solved their problems and face a significant challenge in terms of both the quality and quantity of service delivery.

The labor-intensive nature of most service organizations makes them harder to manage, from a human resource management perspective, than manufacturing businesses. It is important to note that the productivity gains made by manufacturing have come largely through technological innovations (Heskett, 1986; Quinn and Gagnon, 1986), not through improved human resource management. Also, the "downsizing" strategy used recently by many manufacturers in essence admits that they can-

177

not deal with the human resource side and can become more efficient only by getting rid of employees. These technological and downsizing solutions to enhancing productivity are not as readily available to service organizations. Instead, a major solution for increasing service-sector productivity lies in more effective human resource management, not replacing human resources with robots or simply getting rid of them.

It is often possible to improve quantity by spending lavishly and sacrificing quality, or vice versa — spending a great deal to improve quality while sacrificing quantity. But how can both be accomplished? The results of the well-known profit impact of market strategy (PIMS) study conducted by the Strategic Management Institute (Buzzell and Gale, 1987) confirm that the most profitable companies combine an emphasis on quality with high output or high market share. In strategic terms, these approaches to competing have often been viewed as opposite (Porter, 1985). In other words, firms compete either on price (high volume/low cost and standard products) or on differentiation (low volume/high cost and quality products). The intensity of domestic and foreign competition is making it necessary to constantly upgrade quality, lower costs, and compete on both quality and low cost/quantity.

Many service firms in the airline, financial, and health care industries are finding this competition strategy particularly hard to implement. Airlines and financial institutions are faced with deregulation, while hospitals must withstand increasingly stringent rules and procedures. Several factors make it difficult to improve the quality of service and at the same time lower cost and increase the amount of service delivered. Services are less easy to break down and discuss in precise, operational terms than is manufacturing, which can measure quantity, and cost of manufactured goods. Management tends to talk about service delivery in vague generalities or slogans and to assume that employees know what to do. Second, the actions of employees in the delivery of service tend to be variable, inconsistent, and difficult to control. Internal or external customers experience varied levels of service on different occasions when interacting with the same or different employees. Third, the front-line employees who provide the service often have the lowest levels of skills and are the least motivated members of the service organization. Yet the organization's reputation and the perceived level of service overwhelmingly depend on the relationship and interaction of the front-line employee with the customer (Luthans, 1988). The purpose of this chapter is to report the results of the application of behavioral management aimed at improving the delivery of quality service by front-line employees and in some cases also reducing costs and increasing service output at the same time.

The Behavioral Management Approach

The behavioral approach to managing service employees examines the cues that precede and the consequences that follow the occurrence of specific, observable service performance behaviors. Very briefly, cues set the occasion for the delivery of service behavior on the part of front-line employees, and consequences determine whether this behavior will be repeated. In other words, service behavior is a function of its consequences. Service behavior followed by reinforcing consequences tends to be strengthened and to increase in frequency. Service behavior followed by punishing consequences tends to be suppressed and weakened and to decrease in frequency. If no consequences follow the service behavior, it is extinguished (that is, it ceases to be performed).

The background and specific steps of behavioral management are described in detail by Luthans and Kreitner (1985) and Luthans (1989). For service applications, the general steps of behavioral management can be summarized as follows: (1) identifying service performance in specific, operational behavioral terms; (2) measuring the base-line or current frequency of the service behavior; (3) analyzing the cues and consequences supporting the service behavior; (4) developing an intervention strategy to cue and reinforce improved service behavior; and (5) evaluating for improved quality and/or quantity of service delivery. The data-collection method used with this approach to managing service delivery most often requires direct observation of behavior. Applied behavioral research designs such as reversals and multiple base lines (Komaki, 1977; Luthans and Davis, 1982) are generally used to establish causal conclusions on the impact of behavioral management interventions on service behaviors.

A growing number of studies have clearly demonstrated how behavioral management can be used to effectively manage front-line service employees and support personnel to deliver improved service. This chapter reviews a sampling of these studies, which have been conducted in a variety of service applications, including retailing, banking, fast-food restaurants, real estate sales, and hospitals. From detailed descriptions of the procedures and results of these studies, a clear picture emerges of how behavioral management of front-line service employees can lead to improvement of both the quantity and the quality of service delivery to internal and external customers.

Applications of Behavioral Management

Managing the Service Behaviors of Grocery Store Clerks. A major problem in the service delivery of many retailers, such as grocery stores and department stores, is that frequently the front-line service people are nowhere to be found, the shelves are not adequately stocked with merchandise, and the customer may have to endure a prolonged wait before receiving necessary service or assistance. Komaki, Waddell, and Pearce (1977) investigated these problems in a grocery store that was having difficulty controlling these important areas of customer service.

During the base-line measurement period, the clerks were often observed to be socializing in the storeroom instead of working out on the store floor. When the owner-manager caught them talking in the stock room, he would reprimand and nag at them. Consequently, when clerks reentered the store floor and started stocking the shelves and helping customers, these behaviors were being negatively reinforced by threats made by the boss. The owner often complained about having to constantly keep after his employees. However, when asked whether he had ever specifically outlined what he wanted the employees to do, he replied that "they ought to know, since that was what they were getting paid to do" (Komaki, Waddell, and Pearce, 1977, p. 341).

After further discussions between the researchers and the owner-manager of the store, they decided that it might be wise to set some performance goals with employees so that they would understand what was expected of them. First, it was agreed that at least one worker should be in the store within three feet of a display shelf, a meat or produce counter, or the meat refrigerator whenever the store was open for business. Second, customers should be assisted when they first entered the store and within five seconds of requesting assistance for weighing produce or asking for items. Third, the merchandise display shelves, produce counter, and meat counter should be kept filled to at least 50 percent of capacity when inventories were available.

The observed frequencies of these targeted service behaviors were assessed by the research team during the base-line period. Observations were conducted at random intervals, four times each day. The presence or absence of at least one clerk in the store was noted, along with the presence of any customers, the occurrence or nonoccurrence of any customer assistance within the specified time period, and the number of shelves and counters that were filled to at least 50 percent of capacity. Inter-rater reliability checks were performed by an independent observer at seven-day intervals. Correlations between these observations were very high ($r = .98$ and $.99$). A behavioral analysis of antecedents and consequences of desired and undesired on-the-job performance revealed few antecedents that cued the appropriate service behaviors or consequences that supported the desired service behaviors.

Each of the targeted service behaviors that needed to be improved was introduced separately to the employees at staggered intervals as part of a multiple-base-line research design. To encourage employees to exhibit these behaviors, some potentially reinforcing consequences were also introduced. The consequences consisted of time off with pay, feedback on performance, and praise and recognition from the owner-manager. The owner-manager agreed to give the clerks time off with pay each time they attained at least 90 percent of the desired behaviors. During the intervention with the first and second service behaviors, the clerks had the opportunity to obtain one and two hours off with pay. With the intervention with the third behavior, the clerks were told that if they met the 90 percent criterion for all three desired service behaviors, they would be given a half day off weekly with pay.

When the first application of the staggered interventions in the multiple-base-line design began, the employees' incidence of being on the store floor, as opposed to the stock room socializing, gradually improved from a base-line mean of approximately 53 percent to 86 percent. Feedback on this desired service behavior was displayed in the stock room. Performance on the other two targeted service behaviors—customer assistance and shelf stocking (on which feedback had not yet been given)—remained at low base-line levels of 35 percent and 57 percent, respectively. When the intervention was introduced on the second service behavior, customer assistance improved from 35 percent to 87 percent. At the same time, the first service behavior, being on the floor, continued at the postintervention level, while the third behavior, shelf stocking, remained at the low base-line level (feedback was provided only on the first two behaviors). When the intervention was introduced to the third service behavior, shelf stocking also improved, from a base-line mean of 57 percent to 86 percent. Feedback was being provided on all three service behaviors throughout this third phase of the multiple-base-line design.

The use of the multiple-base-line design provides strong causal support that the combination of goal clarification, feedback, and recognition and praise was responsible for the improvements in the delivery of service quality and quantity. While the reactions of the customers were not formally measured, a number of customers indicated that they had noticed the improvements and commented on the improvement in the service that they had received. Giving employees a half day off each week for doing their jobs properly may seem like an excessively generous reward, but the cost of lost wages was more than made up in increased business and greater customer satisfaction.

These types of rewards seem very desirable and needed for many of the low-paid front-line service jobs in the retail industry.

Improving the Selling and Service Behaviors of Sales Clerks in Department Stores. In another application of behavioral management in the retail industry, Luthans, Paul, and Baker (1981) examined the effects of positive reinforcement (paid time off or equivalent cash and a chance to win a week-long paid vacation) on targeted service behaviors of eighty-two retail sales clerks in a large department store. Sixteen departments were randomly assigned to an experimental group and a control group, with eight departments in each group. A reversal design and a field experiment comparing the experimental group with the control group were used to analyze the effects of the behavioral management approach. The service behaviors of the front-line employees targeted for this study consisted of the following:

1. *Selling:* conversing with customers, showing merchandise, assisting with fitting and selection, ringing up sales, and filling out charge slips
2. *Stock work:* arranging and displaying merchandise, folding and straightening merchandise stocks or racks, tagging, replenishing stocks or racks, and packing and unpacking merchandise
3. *Miscellaneous:* all other duties of the sales clerks, such as directing customers to other departments, checking credit ratings, handling returns, receiving instructions, and formal communications with supervisors or co-workers
4. *Dysfunctional idle time:* non-work-related dysfunctional service behavior, such as socializing or just standing or sitting around
5. *Absence from the work station:* absence of the sales clerk from the assigned work area for no legitimate reasons

During the base-line phase (the first four weeks), subjects were told that a customer survey was under way and that observers would be in their departments from time to time. Base-line measurements were established for the five categories of service behavior. No significant differences were found between the experimental group and the control group during this preintervention phase of the experiment. A functional analysis of these behaviors was also performed to determine what cues and consequences supported the targeted behaviors. The typical pattern found was that the salespeople were reprimanded by their supervisor when they did not perform their tasks, were slow in aiding customers, or did not stock the merchandise racks adequately; when they did do these things, nothing was said. In other words, the sales clerks were punished for undesired service behaviors and received no consequences or reinforcement for desired behaviors.

At the start of the intervention phase of the study (weeks five through eight), both the experimental and control groups received clarification of performance standards for the target behaviors. They had been constantly told in vague terms about the importance of waiting on customers immediately and the necessity to keep the shelves stocked, but more specific operational definitions of these expectations were needed so that the reinforcement intervention could be administered contingently. These standards were similar to those used in the grocery store study described earlier. The salespeople were told that they should be present in the department (within three feet of displayed merchandise) during assigned working hours, that customers should be helped within five seconds of requesting assistance, and that display shelves and racks should be kept at least 70 percent filled. Subjects in both groups were also told that observers would be gathering data on their performance.

Members of the experimental group only were then told that they would receive time off with pay or equivalent cash and an opportunity to compete in a drawing for a one-week, company-paid vacation for two if they met the performance standards. The number of hours off with pay or equivalent cash could be obtained in increments so that, as more of the desired service behaviors were performed, subjects were compensated accordingly. This contingent reinforcement intervention was then put into effect for four weeks. The specific selling, stock work, and miscellaneous behavioral categories were collapsed into a single category termed "aggregate retailing behavior," while absence from the work station and idle time were collapsed into a composite measure of dysfunctional behavior. The experimental group had a dramatic increase in aggregate retailing behavior ($X = 433.2$) compared to the control group ($X = 362.2$). The behavioral management approach had a similar impact on decreasing the dysfunctional service behaviors of the experimental group ($X = 225.4$), while the control group remained at the same level of frequency ($X = 293.8$). In both cases, these differences were statistically significant.

During the final phase of the study (weeks nine through twelve), the reinforcement intervention was withdrawn from the experimental group (the reversal, or return to base line). Observation measures were continued in both the experimental and control groups for another four-week period. The improvements in the experimental group in both aggregate retailing behavior and dysfunctional behavior continued at the intervention levels. Natural reinforcers such as the supervisor's praise, positive customer reactions, and such self-reinforcing contingencies as the feeling of a job well done may have been responsible for maintaining the service behaviors at high performance levels. A subsequent replication study (Luthans, Paul, and Taylor, 1985) using tighter controls in the field setting found similar results during the intervention but a reversal during the postintervention phase.

In another department store application, Brown, Mallott, Dillon, and Keeps (1980) studied the service behavior of three full-time salespeople in the men's furnishings department of a store. They compared the effects of training versus a behavioral management intervention of performance feedback on service behaviors. The research design was a combination multiple-base-line design across subjects with reversal. The following service behaviors were targeted for analysis:

1. *Approach:* The salesperson should approach the prospective customer, wait on the customer if the customer approaches the salesperson, or assure the customer that he or she will be taken care of if the salesperson is helping someone else.

2. *Greeting:* The salesperson should greet the customer with a warm "Hello," "Good morning," and so on.
3. *Courtesy:* The salesperson should talk to the customer and make him or her feel welcome and comfortable.
4. *Closing:* The salesperson should thank the customer and make sure that the customer is satisfied.

The subjects were told that some observation work would be done on their service behavior, but they were not told precisely what that would be. One of the researchers observed occurrences or nonoccurrences of the above behaviors twice per week for approximately three hours per session. A second observer recorded approximately 25 percent of these sessions as a reliability check. The agreement between the two observers was 88.5 percent, well within the acceptable range. Base-line observations were done for four days. Performance on the four service behaviors occurred at a fairly low level ($X = 49.7$ percent).

Following the base line, all the salespeople attended customer service training given by the store's training manager, receiving instruction in courtesy standards, listening skills, handling customer complaints, and the relationship between customer service and the performance appraisal. The observers collected data for four weeks following the training to assess how this affected the four customer service behaviors noted earlier. The training program produced a small increase in the four customer service behaviors ($X = 59.3$ percent). This was followed by a feedback period in which the salespeople were given graphed information each day their performance was observed on the occurrence or nonoccurrence of the four targeted service behaviors. The average level of performance of these behaviors immediately shot up to high levels and remained at a high level ($X = 84.7$ percent).

A second base-line period then followed, in which the salespeople's behavior was recorded but not fed back. Performance declined to 70 percent during this period. Finally, another intervention was introduced, in which the salespeople were told that management would receive feedback from customers on their behavior and that a contest was to be held in which the salesperson who received the highest ratings from customers would be awarded a $25 gift certificate. All salespeople were instructed to give a specially prepared questionnaire to all the customers that they waited on. The questionnaire contained items related to the four customer service behaviors. Performance of the salespeople on the four customer service dimensions rose again to approximately the same levels as during the feedback period. In the end, the feedback of the customer responses was never provided and the contest money was never awarded because not one of the more than 500 questionnaires that were handed out was returned by the customers.

Of the four customer service behaviors, the salespeople performed the "approach" or "closing" behaviors much more frequently than the "greeting" and "courtesy" behaviors, with which they seemed less comfortable. The possession of certain social skills seemed to be a determinant of whether the salespeople got positive reactions from customers on these behaviors. For example, some salespeople were comfortable initiating casual conversation with customers and got good reactions from them, while others were somewhat awkward and received negative reactions from customers. The researchers observed on numerous occasions that the four service behaviors were not consistently reinforced by customers. In fact, customers did not respond at all to most of the service behaviors. Whether training is effective seems to depend on the consequences of the newly learned behaviors in the work environment.

The researchers concluded from their study that, because performance improved dramatically at the beginning of the feedback period and again when the customer feedback was announced, service behavior was under antecedent control. Another interpretation of the dramatic improvement that occurred at the beginning of the first feedback intervention would be that the feedback served to clarify performance goals or behaviors for the salespeople, as did Komaki, Waddell, and Pearce's (1977) intervention in the grocery store. The dismal failure of the customer questionnaire part of this study points up the need to reward the customer when attempting to solicit feedback of this type.

These studies demonstrate the value of a behavioral management approach to defining job responsibilities, setting standards, and rewarding the service performance behaviors of sales clerks in retail settings. Prior to these interventions, management was punishing the sales clerks for poor performance without clarifying what the clerks were really responsible for. Not only did the punishment fail to get the desired results, but, of course, the clerks resented the harsh treatment, and it had a dysfunctional impact on their service performance. Behavioral management programs such as those described above can have a positive impact on the critical employee behaviors that lead to improved delivery of service to retail store customers.

Increasing the Accuracy of Cashiers in a Drugstore. An indirect but nevertheless important aspect of the delivery of service in retail stores is the cashier's accuracy and dependability in handling cash. Problems occur when the total recorded by the cash register does not coincide with the money turned in by the cashier. In an early behavioral study of a small restaurant, a group response cost was used to combat this problem (Marholin and Gray, 1976). Cash shortages were subtracted from the paychecks of employees cashiering on the days that shortages were reported. During base-line conditions in that restaurant study, as much as 9 percent of the daily sales take was unaccounted for. When the intervention was implemented, the cash shortage was greatly reduced. The problem with this approach is that it is a form of group punishment. The fact that the innocent get punished along with the guilty is probably not going to improve the delivery of service in the long run. The front-line service employees may find other ways to express their discontent, and this may, in turn, have a negative effect on the relationship with the customer.

Newby and Robinson (1983) decided to test alternative ways of improving cashier service behavior. They examined the effects of different types of feedback on cashier precision, punctuality, and money checkout proficiency in a retail drugstore.

They focused on cashier precision or accuracy (reducing short-ages), employee punctuality in starting work, and compliance with checkout procedures when turning in cash at the end of a shift. Each of these aspects of cashier performance was defined in precise behavioral terms. Cashier precision was measured by totaling the gross amount of transactions and comparing it with the amount recorded by the cash register. The gross transaction figure included all cash, checks, and bank card totals plus all refunds paid to customers, all credits for coupons and special discounts, and any overcharge corrections made by the cashier.

The drugstore management had a goal of no more than a 0.5 percent (approximately $11.00) discrepancy in the daily take. This figure was known only to management. Punctuality was measured by employees' punch-in time on a time clock. If an employee was more than one minute tardy, he or she was considered late. Compliance with checkout proficiency requirements when turning in cash was defined in terms of six procedures:

1. All bills should face in the same direction.
2. All bills should be arranged in order of their denomination.
3. All checks should face in the same direction.
4. All checks should be stamped with the store's deposit number.
5. The checkout slips for all refunds, credits, and corrections should show the employee's name, date, and register number.
6. All receipts from bank cards, refunds, and so on should be clipped to the checkout slip.

A checkout proficiency of 100 percent required a cashier to complete all six steps before placing the money in an envelope and depositing it in the safe.

A modified reversal design (AB_1B_2AC, where A represents the base-line condition, B reinforcement, and C reinforcement plus feedback) was used to test the effects of group feedback (B_1), individual feedback (B_2), and reinforcement plus individual feedback on the behaviors of precision, punctuality, and proficient checkout procedures. The first intervention consisted of group feedback on all three behavioral measures. The performance of all cashiers on each measure was pooled and publicly posted above the time clock in the stock room. During this phase, the mean shortage of money actually increased from 1.5 percent during the base-line period to 2.3 percent. Punctuality also dropped during this period, from an average of 65 percent to 62.5 percent. Checkout proficiency improved slightly, from 69 percent correct completion to 71.4 percent. When individualized feedback (each cashier received feedback on his or her own performance on the three variables) replaced group feedback in the stock room, dramatic improvements were realized. Cash shortages dropped to an average of 0.55 percent, punctuality improved to an average of 86 percent, and checkout proficiency improved to 92 percent.

The third intervention included reinforcement along with individualized feedback. If any employee was within 0.4 percent of the register total, that employee could receive a free movie pass. If an employee also came to work on time and followed the six checkout procedures on any single day, that cashier could receive a coupon for a free soft drink and free candy bar. (These rewards were chosen by the cashiers themselves.) The reward program combined with individual feedback resulted in daily cash discrepancies falling to an average of 0.23 percent, punctuality rising to 90 percent, and correct checkout procedures reaching the 95 percent level.

The ineffectiveness of the group feedback condition may be explained by a number of underlying factors. First, pooling performance feedback obscures individual results and may reduce individual accountability. Some employees may feel that there is no point in trying harder because they cannot control their own results. Other employees may feel that they can slack off because poor individual performance is buried in the group's overall results. Another consideration is that when there is no interdependency between individuals, group performances becomes irrelevant. The absence of any group goals or payoffs in this situation made group feedback ineffective.

The success of individual feedback may also be due to a number of factors. First, the cashiers became clearly aware of their own performance for the first time. Each cashier would enjoy the highly reinforcing consequence of seeing his or her performance improve on the feedback chart each day. Also, because the performance of all cashiers was publicly displayed for everyone to see, competition may have played a part in the improvements. Another interpretation of these results, however, may be that the behavior was being not positively but instead negatively reinforced — that is, cashiers improved their performance to avoid being viewed as poorer performers by management and co-workers.

The third behavioral management intervention, individual feedback plus reinforcement, produced the best results. Here the presence of the rewards (movie tickets, drinks, candy bars) created a positive consequence that led to the cashiers increasing desired behaviors. In this case, the cost of the rewards was less than the money saved by more accurate cashier totals. Also, the cost of implementing the intervention was less than the savings in time resulting from gains in punctuality and the improvement in how employees turned in their cashiered receipts. The long-run, indirect, but most important impact, however, was that the service delivered to customers was definitely improved. In summary, this study shows the value of applying a behavioral management approach to cashiers whose speed, accuracy, and courtesy are critical to the quality and quantity of service delivery.

Improving Productivity and Service of Front-Line and Back-Room Bank Employees. The behavioral management approach has also been applied to banks. For example, a new reward system was recently introduced at Union National Bank in Little Rock, Arkansas (Dierks and McNally, 1987). In this application of behavioral management, both front-line service employees and "back-room" personnel serving internal customers were involved. Unlike the other applications discussed so far, which concentrated primarily on improving the quality of service delivery, this bank application shows a behavioral management approach to have a direct effect on lowering costs and increasing output of both front-line and back-room service employees.

The approach was first used in the bank's proof department, where employees encode machine-readable numbers on the bottoms of checks so that they can be processed by the computer. Rapid processing and accuracy are needed so that the checks can be credited to the bank's account with a minimum of delay. A base-line period of five weeks was used to track the number of checks each operator processed. The average number processed during this period was 1,065 checks per hour.

During several interventions that were equivalent to a multiple-base-line design, management provided graphed feedback, praise and recognition, and contingent reward bonuses. Average performance in the proof department rose from the base-line figure of 1,065 checks per hour to an average of 3,500 checks per hour. The contingent reward bonuses have been kept in effect for six years, and proof operators now earn the equivalent of 50 to 70 percent of their base salary from these bonuses. From being one of the biggest problem areas, the proofing department became one of the most smoothly running operations in the bank. Other benefits were also realized from this approach. Employee turnover fell from 110 percent per year to zero, absenteeism was cut nearly in half, the head count was reduced from eleven full-time and three part-time employees to three full-time and six part-time employees, overtime hours were reduced from 475 a year to 13, and the savings from faster processing time amounted to $100,000 a year.

A second reward program focused on the behavior of front-line service employees, the tellers. In this application of behavioral management, point values were assigned for the number of new customer accounts, increases in transactions, reductions in absenteeism, and improved daily differences or cash outages. Points were tallied each day and summarized into weekly averages from which extra pay was determined. During a base-line period, tellers averaged thirty-two points. This figure increased dramatically to an average of seventy-one points when the contingent rewards were introduced. For instance, during the base-line period, tellers obtained 102 new accounts per year, whereas during the intervention, this figure rose to 4,300 new accounts. Daily differences improved from an outage of $15,961 to $13,772 per year, and the average yearly transaction count increased from 17.9 to 29.5. Overall, customer volume increased 67 percent, while teller staffing levels were actually reduced. Tellers have a stake in keeping the head count down, because with more people, the reward opportunities for each teller tend to decline. The main advantages of this approach with the tellers, besides the significantly increased earnings, have been clear, unambiguous work goals and individual recognition for outstanding work.

In designing these and other reward systems with the bank, management set a goal of a 5:1 ratio of revenues to costs. The bank also increased the ratio of bonuses to base salary by freezing base salaries when the bonuses were introduced. The base salary was set just below the market rate, but the combination of base pay and bonuses was above the market average.

Another advantage to the bank has been the elimination of subjectivity in performance appraisal. Employees now know exactly how they are performing, how much is expected, and how they compare to their peers. The main disadvantage of the program has been the difficulty in administering and budgeting salaries. Giving everyone the same salary increases is clearly much simpler but far less effective in ensuring the quality and quantity of service delivered to internal and external customers than basing pay on performance.

Developing Customer Friendliness in Fast-Food Restaurant Workers. In many service organizations, especially in fast-food restaurants, the front-line service personnel that interact with the customer are the most junior, inexperienced, and low paid. Yet they have the biggest impact on the delivery of service to customers. As we have discussed so far, the main challenge for behavioral management is how to get these employees to provide quantity and quality service to customers. Other approaches have had little success. For example, Cooper and Oddie (1972) implemented a social skills training course for cafeteria workers in two motorway restaurants in the United Kingdom. Most of this consisted of cognitive awareness and interpersonal skills training. The training was evaluated by the use of questionnaires asking customers and trainees to rate improvements. The problem with this cognitive training approach was that the general nature of the training and evaluation process gave little indication of how the trainees' service behavior had actually changed and improved.

In contrast, Komaki, Blood, and Holder (1980) used a behavioral management approach in a fast-food restaurant. They chose to examine one aspect of front-line employee service behavior—friendliness to customers. This was one in a three-step sequence: First, they defined friendliness in behavioral terms; second, they conducted an on-site observation of the occurrence of customer friendliness; and, third, they carried out an analysis of the antecedents and consequences that encourage employees to engage in more friendly behavior toward customers.

The first step, defining customer friendliness, was accomplished with the help of the restaurant's management. It was jointly agreed that two observable behaviors—smiling at customers and talking to customers—were good indicators of the quality of service delivery by front-line employees. These behaviors were observed by "mystery customers"—observers who entered the restaurant posing as customers, ordered a meal or refreshment, sat down, and recorded instances of employee friendliness at the counter or in the eating area on wallet-sized data sheets. Interrater reliability checks were carried out by comparing the scores of the primary observer with those of a second, independent observer at random intervals. The agreement between the two observers averaged between 91 and 97 percent.

An analysis of antecedents and consequences was carried out during a base-line period to determine what cued and supported customer friendliness. Although in-store training emphasized the importance of customer service, no on-the-job cues and payoffs had been identified to encourage friendliness toward customers. To correct this problem, specific cues and consequences were designed into the typical interaction with the customer. For example, four cues were designated for smiling: when greeting the customer, when taking the order, when telling the customer about the dessert special, and when giving the customer change. Employees were encouraged to observe whether customers smiled back—a natural reinforcer for smiling. A second consequence was provided by supervisors in the form of praise and recognition. Supervisors were encouraged to recognize each employee's smiling behavior at least once a day and to keep a record of their own recognition behavior on a checklist.

In addition to the behavioral analysis of smiling, an analysis was carried out of the cues and consequences affecting talking or conversing with customers. The store manager pointed out to employees that beginning a conversation is a valuable social skill. Employees were taught "opening lines" ranging from information about food to inquiries about customer preferences. Cues were identified for initiating talk, and consequences were created for employees—self-recording their own behavior and recognition by supervisors.

Each regimen of behavioral change was gradually added in a multiple-base-line research design. During a three-week base-line period, front-line employees in the cash register area smiled less than half (41.2 percent) of the time. Following the intervention focusing on smiling, employees smiled on average two-thirds (67.3 percent) of the time. This was maintained for a ten-week intervention period. Talking with customers, which was less of a problem, also improved, from a base-line average of 88.1 percent to an intervention level of 90.0 percent. Other behavioral interventions were implemented in the dining room area. Employees were generally surprised by how often their own smiles were reciprocated with smiles from customers.

This study shows that a relatively vague quality service concept such as customer friendliness can be defined in behavioral terms and that a behavioral management approach can have a definite causal impact on improving the quality of service delivery by relatively inexperienced, low-paid front-line service employees. There seem to be definite advantages to identifying these service behaviors and making them specific so that service employees know how to behave and supervisors know what to reward. In other words, friendliness is a skill that service employees can be taught and that can be improved on the job. The behavioral management approach seems to be a definite improvement over trying to define personality traits or to train people in vague aspects of interpersonal dynamics or simply hoping that they will follow the company slogan for customer service.

Increasing Customer Calls by Real Estate Sales Agents. Service applications in the real estate industry involve sales agents contacting new buyers and sellers of homes and following up with existing customers. Similar to the bank application discussed earlier, this application concentrates on the quantity of service behaviors. In real estate, the quantity of service behaviors could be measured in terms of the number of client contacts made by agents. It is generally recognized in this service industry that the more client contacts made, the more house listings and sales will result.

One study (Anderson and others, 1982) examined the effects of a token reinforcement program on the service behaviors (client contacting) of sixteen salespeople in a real estate firm. The company was not performing well and had too many agents in the field who barely generated enough sales to cover the resources spent on them. This company had tried a number of training programs to increase the productivity of the sales agents, including seminars, "pep talks," and cassette tapes that created momentary enthusiasm but did little to change agents' service behaviors. Discussions with the owner-broker of the business revealed that no clear directions were provided to agents as to what they should do every day to sell homes or get house listings (their two most important functions), no measurement system was used to track the agents' activities and to link them to sales-related outcomes, and no feedback was provided to agents concerning their performance.

After extensive discussions with the broker, it was decided that the two behaviors most critical to closing sales were calls on prospective clients ("initials") and return visits ("follow-ups"). Information on these calls needed to be collected and tracked with sales performance. A behavioral management intervention was developed with the assistance of the broker that combined feedback and reinforcement as a means of encouraging sales agents to make more client contacts, both "initials" and "follow-ups." A reversal design (*ABAB*) was used to test the effectiveness of the approach.

During a twenty-week base-line period, sales agents recorded the names, addresses, and phone numbers of all clients that they contacted, along with the actions they took during these meetings. They recorded the information on specially provided forms and turned it in to management every week. Frequencies of the two different types of client contact behaviors were broken out for each sales agent and displayed in the sales office. Charts also provided weekly information, by agent, on four relevant performance indices: numbers of pending sales, actual sales, pending listings, and actual listings obtained. In addition, monthly sales volume was collected, but not posted, for each agent. Random reliability checks were carried out on the contact reports turned in by the salespeople. Clients were contacted by telephone or mail under the guise of a "courtesy call" to confirm that a sales contact had actually been made. One hundred independent reliability checks revealed no instances of inaccurate or falsified contact reports.

At the end of the base-line period, a token reinforcement procedure was introduced that required a minimum of fifteen follow-up calls and six initial calls within a contracted period before credits could be earned for each additional contact. A contract period was set at one week, at the end of which the record of each agent was reset to zero. Credits were awarded during biweekly sales meetings and could be accumulated and/or traded in for any of sixty items. These items ranged from ten gallons of gas (11 points) to a registered slate pool table (1,000 points). The actual cost to the company for each point was about thirty-five cents.

Both service behaviors, "initials" and "follow-ups," increased upon introduction of the token system and leveled off at a higher level than the base line. Performance decreased during a two-week return-to-base-line period (no contingent reinforcement) and then again showed a pronounced increase during a second intervention (token reinforcement) period, which was maintained for six weeks. While the use of self-recording and feedback of results throughout the study may have increased the number of calls made by the agents, the feedback and reinforcement condition produced the most client contacts. The use of the reversal design provides strong support that feedback alone was insufficient to sustain high levels of client-contacting service behavior, as performance dropped off during the second base-line period. A comparison of call frequencies with ongoing sales results supported a close relationship between these two variables. Correlation coefficients between initial contacts and sales, between initial contacts and listings, between personal follow-ups and sales, and between personal follow-ups and listings all exceeded .61. Thus, as customer contacts increased, sales and listings increased as well.

An interesting issue with this study is the influence of feedback of performance information. It would have been interesting to know what the client-contact levels were prior to the base-line period when performance data were collected by the sales agents. Unfortunately, self-recording by sales agents was essential to collecting performance data. There were no performance data on sales agents' contact behavior before the agents started recording themselves, so it was not possible to compare performance before and after self-recording. The only comparison that could have been made was between the information that the agents self-recorded and the information that was compiled and displayed by management. Would agent self-recording have been as effective without management feedback of the data? The management feedback served notice that the broker was aware of each agent's contact performance. Also, displaying individual contact, sales, and listing data side by side set up a competitive condition that could have increased the quantity of the agents' service behavior.

Improving the Productivity and Service of Hospital Staff. Although the applications presented so far have been in private-sector service firms, it is important to recognize that behavioral management can also be successfully applied to not-for-profit service organizations. For example, behavioral management has been used to improve the quantity and quality of service behaviors of hospital personnel (Snyder and Luthans, 1982). The behavioral management intervention in this case consisted of performance feedback and recognition and praise (positive reinforcement) to increase the quantity and improve the quality of targeted service behaviors in a large health care facility. As shown in Table 8.1, the service behaviors were operationalized as patient throughput, billings, time and cost of completing different jobs, errors, complaints, backlogs, and reprocessing of work.

Unlike the other studies discussed here, which used multiple-base-line or reversal designs, this hospital study had to use a simple *AB* design. For each targeted service behavior, the results during a base-line and an intervention period were recorded. Stronger causal support for the behavioral changes would have been achieved if a reversal design could have been used. However, in this study, as in many real-world applications, the hospital management was unwilling to withdraw the intervention and return to base-line conditions just to demonstrate the effectiveness of the approach. Nevertheless, the fact that the service behaviors improved in every case (see Table 8.1) provides strong support that the behavioral management approach can have a positive impact on the delivery of service in a health care organization.

In another health care study, reported by Connellan (1978, pp. 178–179), behavioral management was used to improve the quality of performance of the housekeeping department in a 550-bed urban hospital. Prior to the behavioral management approach, several quality improvement programs had been implemented but had failed to produce discernible changes. In this case, the housekeeping supervisors who carried out inspections of the cleaning work were taught to give clear performance feedback with the use of graphs and check sheets and to provide recognition and praise when the job was done right. An extinction strategy (that is, absence of feedback), rather than punishment, was used when the job was done poorly. At the outset of the behavioral management approach, clean-

Table 8.1. The Impact of Behavioral Management on the Service Behaviors of Hospital Personnel.

Hospital Unit	Service Behavior	Preintervention Measure	Postintervention Measure	Percentage Change
Emergency room clerks	Registration errors (per day)	19.16	4.580	76.10
Hardware engineer group	Average time to repair (minutes)	92.53	33.250	61.40
Medical records file clerks	Errors in filing (per person per audit)	2.87	.078	97.30
Medical records	Complaints	8.00	1.000	875.00
Transcriptionists	Average errors	2.07	1.400	33.00
	Average output	2,258.00	2,303.330	2.00
Heart station	Average EKG procedures accomplished	1,263.00	1,398.970	11.00
	Overdue procedures	7.00[a]	4.000	42.80
Eye clinic	Daily patient throughput	19.00	23.000	21.00
	Daily patient teaching documentation	1.00	2.800	180.00
	Protocols produced	0.00	2.000	200.00
Pharmacy technicians	Drug output (doses)	348.80	422.100	21.00
	Posting errors	3.67	1.480	59.70
	Product waste (percentage)	5.80	4.350	25.00
Radiology technicians	Average patient throughput (procedural)	3,849.50	4,049.000	5.00
	Retake rate (percentage)	11.20	9.950	11.20
Patient accounting	Average monthly billings	2,561.00	3,424.500	33.70
Admitting office	Time to admit (minutes)	43.73	13.570	68.97
	Average cost	$15.05	$11.730	22.00
Data center operations	Systems log-on (time)	1:54	1:43	13.40

Note: All averages are arithmetic means.

[a] Estimate.

Source: Adapted from Snyder and Luthans, 1982, p. 72.

liness levels were reported to be averaging only 33 percent of fully clean. Within two months of using behavioral management, the quality reached 86 percent. Clearly, the quality of service had been dramatically improved.

Still another study (Stephens and Burroughs, 1978) tested the impact that behavioral management had on reducing absenteeism in six nursing units of a large hospital. Although absenteeism is not a direct service behavior, few would argue that absenteeism does not at least indirectly affect the quantity and quality of service. Absent employees overburden employees on the job who must take up the slack or require replacements or substitutes who do not do as good a job. In either case, absenteeism has a definite impact on how much and how well service is delivered.

Each nursing unit in this application contained four different types of front-line service employees: registered nurses, licensed practical nurses, ward clerks, and nursing assistants. The six units, which were composed of an even mix of these employees, were randomly assigned to two treatment groups. Members of group A were told that they would be eligible to participate in a lottery for cash prizes if they were not absent over a three-week period. Members of group B were told that they would become eligible to participate in a cash lottery if they were not absent during eight randomly selected days over the same three-week period. Each lottery allowed for the chance to win a cash prize of $20.

Absenteeism levels were monitored through three separate periods: base-line, intervention, and postintervention. A three-week base-line period was used to assess existing absenteeism levels in the different units. Subjects were unaware that absenteeism was being monitored during this period. Several days before the behavioral management intervention began, the subjects were informed that a reward program would be introduced to reduce absenteeism. The intervention was followed by a final two-week postintervention period in which the reward program was withdrawn.

Both treatment groups had similar levels of absenteeism during the base-line period, and both showed decreased absenteeism when the intervention was put into effect. Treatment group *B*, whose goal was no absenteeism during eight randomly selected days, had a slightly greater decrease in absenteeism than did treatment group *A*, whose goal was no absenteeism at all. The researchers had surmised that treatment *B* might be more effective than treatment *A* because it did not require a perfect attendance record. They felt that some employees might not even try if they had to have a perfect attendance record. However, the difference between absenteeism in the two groups was not significant. More than 40 percent of all subjects in each group had some absenteeism during the base-line period, whereas approximately 30 percent were absent during the intervention period.

The total amount of cash prizes paid out as rewards to discourage absenteeism was very small compared to the improved delivery of service as well as actual dollar savings realized from increased attendance. In this hospital, as in many other service organizations, employees could build up sick leave and receive full pay while taking days off for reasons other than illness. This policy actually encourages employees to be absent. While some absenteeism for legitimate reasons is inevitable, over the long term the reward program could lower overall absenteeism, increase the quality and quantity of service delivery to patients and internal customers, and even produce direct savings in health care costs.

These studies demonstrate the tangible positive impact that the behavioral management approach can have on the complex and heretofore assumed "unmanageable" health care industry. With the increasing pressure to lower costs, raise productivity, and improve the quality of service to patients and internal and external customers, it would seem that hospitals could greatly benefit from this approach.

Considerations for the Use of Behavioral Management

Having described a sampling of successful applications of behavioral management in service organizations, we should briefly note when the approach is best used and air some potential problems and popular misconceptions about behavioral management. Both practical experience and research to date indicate that behavioral management is best applied in, though certainly not limited to, standardized service operations in which customer needs can be predicted in advance and employee performance can be broken down into specific behaviors. The approach is less applicable to customized professional services (legal, accounting, consulting) in which customer or client needs are not known in advance and employees must adapt or tailor services to fit each customer's unique requirements. Even so, in these latter applications, behavioral management may still have a dramatic impact on the routine, backroom clerical, accounting, and mail-room operations.

Behavioral management may require a somewhat different application in service organizations than in manufacturing organizations. For instance, problems may arise when the service behaviors are defined in terms of internally derived standards that may differ from external customer needs and expectations. In such cases, employees may be trained and rewarded to provide services that customers do not really value. For example, hearing a long-distance operator drone the statement "Thank you for using AT&T" may be irritating to a hurried business executive who had no choice of the long-distance carrier that he or she was using. The same is true for many of the insincere, "have-a-nice-day" attempts at using behavioral management. Such phony, obviously manipulative approaches may even backfire with customers.

The extent to which service delivery fits customer needs may depend partly on the quantity and quality of feedback obtained from the customer. Effective service organizations obtain customer feedback through multiple sources, such as customer reply cards, customer surveys, mystery shoppers, and customer compliments and complaints (Davis and Horney, 1988). This input is then used to adapt services to fit customer perceptions and expectations. Generally, customer input has not been solicited in the design of behavior management programs. Management has relied mainly on its own judgment along with the input of lower-level employees and external consultants. Greater attention needs to be given to ways of incorporating customer feedback in service organization development interventions (Davis and Luthans, 1988).

Care needs to be taken to ensure not only that the employee performance behaviors targeted for improvement under behavioral management cover the most important aspects of customer service but that other important behaviors are rewarded as well. Otherwise, employees may perform to look good on those few behaviors that are targeted for change and ignore other aspects of customer service. However, it is important to remember that only the most critical, highest-impact behaviors are targeted in a behavioral management approach. These could be called the "20–80" behaviors — the 20 percent of behaviors that affect 80 percent of the quantity and quality of service, as opposed to the 80 percent of behaviors that affect only 20 percent of the quantity and quality of service (see Luthans and Kreitner, 1985, and Luthans, 1989, for other such details on behavioral management).

In most behavioral management programs, individual incentives are offered so that each employee has the opportunity to receive attractive rewards contingent strictly on his or her own performance. This system works well in areas of performance where individual employees work independently of others, so that the employee competes with him- or herself to receive valued rewards. In cases where employees' jobs are interdependent, the reward system should encourage cooperation and teamwork or else there may be destructive competition between members. Here group incentives would be preferable to individual rewards or some combination of both.

Several misconceptions about the application of behavioral management programs also merit discussion. A typical concern is that employees may resist having aspects of their jobs defined in behavioral terms, either because they fear that this will limit their freedom of action or because they fear that they will be punished if they fail to perform well on targeted behaviors. Neither of these fears has any real foundation when behavioral management is implemented correctly. First, in most behavioral management interventions, employees are consulted for their suggestions on how performance can be improved, which are then used in designing the intervention; behaviors are not imposed on employees without their consultation and consent. Second, most behavioral management programs do not attempt to manage all aspects of a person's job but only the key performance behaviors that need to be improved for effective delivery of service. There is plenty of room for freedom of action. Third, behavioral management works well only under conditions of positive reinforcement, not negative reinforcement or punishment. It generally will not succeed if management tries to enforce behavioral compliance through punitive means. These issues need to be cleared up before an organization implements a successful behavioral management program for service delivery.

Conclusion

The various applications discussed in this chapter demonstrate the positive impact that a behavioral management approach can have on the quantity and quality of service delivery. This approach requires focusing on observable service employee behavior. The observational methods used in most of the study designs forced a live investigation of what really happens at the point of customer contact. There is minimal opportunity for inaccurate recall and response bias, which have been frequent problems with traditional questionnaire-based research on customer service.

Behavioral management is a relatively simple and inexpensive way to improve the quantity and quality of service delivered to internal and external customers. It takes a positive rather than a negative approach. Behavioral management attempts to find ways of rewarding service employees for doing things right. Too often, there is a tendency to dream up simple slogans or to pressure employees to improve without telling them what to do. In some instances, not only has management failed to define appropriate service performance behavior, but there is also little understanding of what behaviors produce what results. The process of recording service behaviors and tracking results can help management understand these relationships.

As most of the studies showed, the feedback of service performance information to employees can be a powerful intervention strategy for behavioral management. In a surprisingly large number of cases, service employees have little idea of how they are doing. Regularly displayed feedback can keep employees aware of their performance and, as shown in the studies reviewed, lead them to increase desirable service behaviors. Where feedback alone is insufficient, monetary rewards and time off can also be used to reinforce desired service behaviors. Some of the "contrived rewards" (those that cost money, such as bonuses) may decline in potency over time, but these can usually be changed to maintain interest. "Natural rewards" (rewards that do not cost money, such as supervisory attention and recognition) usually do not become dull or decline in importance over time. Employees generally can never receive enough attention and recognition. Importantly, however, phony, "sugar-coated" praise is not suggested. It does not last and can even backfire as a reinforcer for desired service behaviors. More longitudinal research, such as the Union National Bank study, is needed to test the long-term impact of different types of reinforcers.

According to the behavioral management approach, training programs for front-line service delivery need to deal with specific behavior. Vague attempts at improving the interpersonal relations skills of front-line employees are unlikely to have very much effect. In order for new behaviors to transfer from the training situation to the workplace, they must not only be defined and practiced in precise detail but also be cued and reinforced in the actual work setting. Only then will they become a part of the service employee's day-to-day behavior pattern.

Behavioral management is certainly not the panacea for the productivity problems facing service organizations. However, as clearly shown in the applications discussed in this chapter, a behavioral approach may be a step in the right direction in meeting the significant challenges facing human resource management in service organizations in the 1990s.

References

Anderson, D. C., and others. "Behavior Management of Client Contacts in a Real Estate Brokerage: Getting Agents to Sell More." *Journal of Organizational Behavior Management*, 1982, *4* (1), 67–95.

Brown, M. G., Mallott, R. W., Dillon, M. J., and Keeps, E. J. "Improving Customer Service in a Large Department Store Through the Use of Training and Feedback." *Journal of Organizational Behavior Management*, 1980, *2* (4), 251–264.

Buzzell, R. D., and Gale, B. T. *The PIMS Principles: Linking Strategy to Performance*. New York: Free Press, 1987.

Chipello, C. J. "Foreign Rivals Imperil U.S. Firms' Leadership in the Service Sector." *Wall Street Journal*, Mar. 21, 1988, pp. 1, 10.

Clark, L. H. "Manufacturers Grow Much More Efficient, but Employment Lags." *Wall Street Journal*, Dec. 4, 1986, p. 1.

Connellan, T. K. *How to Improve Human Performance: Behaviorism in Business and Industry*. New York: Harper & Row, 1978.

Cooper, C. L., and Oddie, H. "Group Training in a Service Industry: Improving Social Skills in Motorway Service Area Restaurant." *Interpersonal Development*, 1972, *3*, 13–39.

Davis, T.R.V., and Horney, N. "Guest Feedback and Complaint Handling in the Hospitality Industry." In *Proceedings of the International Conference on Service Marketing*. Vol. 5. Cleveland, Ohio: Academy of Marketing Science and Cleveland State University, 1988.

Davis, T.R.V., and Luthans, F. "Service OD: Techniques for Improving the Delivery of Quality Service." *Organizational Development Journal*, 1988, *6* (4), 76–80.

Dierks, W., and McNally, K. A. "Incentives You Can Bank On." *Personnel Administrator*, Mar. 1987, pp. 60–65.

Heskett, J. L. *Managing in the Service Economy*. Boston: Harvard Business School Press, 1986.

Komaki, J. "Alternative Evaluation Strategies in Work Settings: Reversal and Multiple-Baseline Designs." *Journal of Organizational Behavior Management*, 1977, *1*, 53–77.

Komaki, J., Blood, M. R., and Holder, D. "Fostering Friendliness in a Fast Food Franchise." *Journal of Organizational Behavior Management*, 1980, *2* (3), 151–164.

Komaki, J., Waddell, W. M., and Pearce, M. G. "The Applied Behavior Analysis Approach and Individual Employees." *Organizational Behavior and Human Performance*, 1977, *19*, 337–352.

Luthans, F. "The Exploding Service Sector: Meeting the Challenge Through Behavioral Management." *Journal of Organizational Change Management*, 1988, *1* (1), 18–28.

Luthans, F. *Organizational Behavior*. (5th ed.) New York: McGraw-Hill, 1989.

Luthans, F., and Davis, T.R.V. "An Idiographic Approach to Organizational Behavior Research: The Use of Single Case Experimental Designs and Direct Measures." *Academy of Management Review*, 1982, *7* (3), 380–391.

Luthans, F., and Kreitner, R. *Organizational Behavior Modification and Beyond*. Glenview, Ill.: Scott, Foresman, 1985.

Luthans, F., Paul, R., and Baker, D. "An Experimental Analysis of the Impact of Contingent Reinforcement on Salespersons' Performance Behavior." *Journal of Applied Psychology*, 1981, *66* (3), 314–323.

Luthans, F., Paul, R., and Taylor, L. "The Impact of Contingent Reinforcement on Retail Salespersons' Performance Behaviors: A Replicated Field Experiment." *Journal of Organizational Behavior Management*, 1985, *7* (1/2), 25–35.

Marholin, D., and Gray, D. "Effects of Group Response–Cost Procedures on Cash Shortages in Small Businesses." *Journal of Applied Behavior Analysis*, 1976, *9*, 25–30.

Nasar, S. "America's Competitive Revival." *Fortune*, Jan. 4, 1988, p. 48.

Newby, T. J., and Robinson, P. W. "Effects of Grouped and Individual Feedback and Reinforcement on Retail Employees' Performances." *Journal of Organizational Behavior Management*, 1983, *5* (2), 51–68.

Porter, M. E. *Competitive Advantage: Creating and Sustaining Superior Performance*. New York: Free Press, 1985.

Quinn, J. B., and Gagnon, C. E. "Will Services Follow Manufacturing into Decline?" *Harvard Business Review*, 1986, *64*, 95–105.

Skinner, W. *Manufacturing: The Formidable Competitive Weapon.* New York: Wiley, 1985.

Snyder, C. A., and Luthans, F. "Using OB Mod to Increase Hospital Productivity." *Personnel Administrator*, Aug. 1982, pp. 67–73.

Stephens, T. A., and Burroughs, W. A. "An Application of Operant Conditioning to Absenteeism in a Hospital Setting." *Journal of Applied Psychology*, 1978, *63* (4), 518–521.

Part Three

Operations Management
in Service Firms

9

Creating Personalized
Service Delivery Systems

W. Earl Sasser
William E. Fulmer

When *Time* magazine decided to examine the state of customer service in the United States in the late 1980s, it did not pull any punches. "Why Is Service So Bad?" was the bold headline on the magazine's February 2, 1987, cover. The accompanying article reported in depth on the abysmal state of customer service in America: "Personal service," *Time* observed, "has become a maddeningly rare commodity in the American marketplace." Millions of American consumers seem to agree. From coast to coast, public sentiment suggests that customer service is lousy and continuing to deteriorate. Ask any consumer about his or her experiences in the service marketplace and you are likely to hear a litany of horror stories indicting car repair shops, hotels, hospitals, airlines, rental-car agencies, and scores of other service businesses. Why, at a time when service industries have been growing more robustly than most other sectors of the American economy, does it seem that service quality has been declining? Is it inevitable that this decline will continue?

Why Service Has Declined

Several factors contribute to the widely perceived decline in customer service. First, service companies across the country are struggling to cope with a changing work ethic. Second, ours is an increasingly impersonal and fast-paced society. Perhaps most significantly, many U.S. service firms are suffering from regional labor shortages that drive up local wage scales and compel companies to offer expensive employee perquisites in order to attract and retain personnel. Higher labor rates create unrelenting pressure to increase labor productivity; productivity programs have overshadowed efforts to improve the level and quality of service.

Of course, external, or environmental, factors explain only part of the problem. Much of the trouble can be attributed to internal, or structural, causes. Specifically, we believe that many firms have suffered deteriorating customer service because they have pursued a vision of operational excellence that was modeled after manufacturing companies. In short, many service firms view themselves from a manufacturing perspective. Consequently, they have adopted service delivery systems and operational and quality-control techniques that are based on manufacturing models. Though these models are often useful for organizing production facilities, they have their limitations when applied to service organizations that create, market, and sell highly intangible products.

Consider the traditional manufacturing design continuum, as described by Hayes and Wheelwright (1984, pp. 197–228). At one end of the continuum are flexible job shops. At the other extreme are assembly lines. As one moves from job shops toward assembly line facilities, one typically must make a trade-off between customization and low cost. It is a fundamental strategic choice of whether to pursue a cost leadership or a differentiation strategy (Porter, 1980). A key task of management is to match the process type to a set of product characteristics. Figure 9.1 presents this design choice as it relates to service industries. The job shops of the service world are businesses, such as printshops and French restaurants, that are staffed with highly skilled, knowledgeable employees who deliver differentiated services tailored specifically to fit the individual customer's needs. As one moves along the diagonal line in Figure 9.1, one encounters service "production lines" such as those developed at

Figure 9.1. Matching Major Process and Service Characteristics.

Service Characteristics

Process Types	I Low volume, low standard- ization, one of a kind	II Multiple services, low volume	III Few major services, higher volume	IV High volume, high standard- ization
I Job Shop	French Restaurant			
II Batch Process				
III Assembly Line				McDonald's

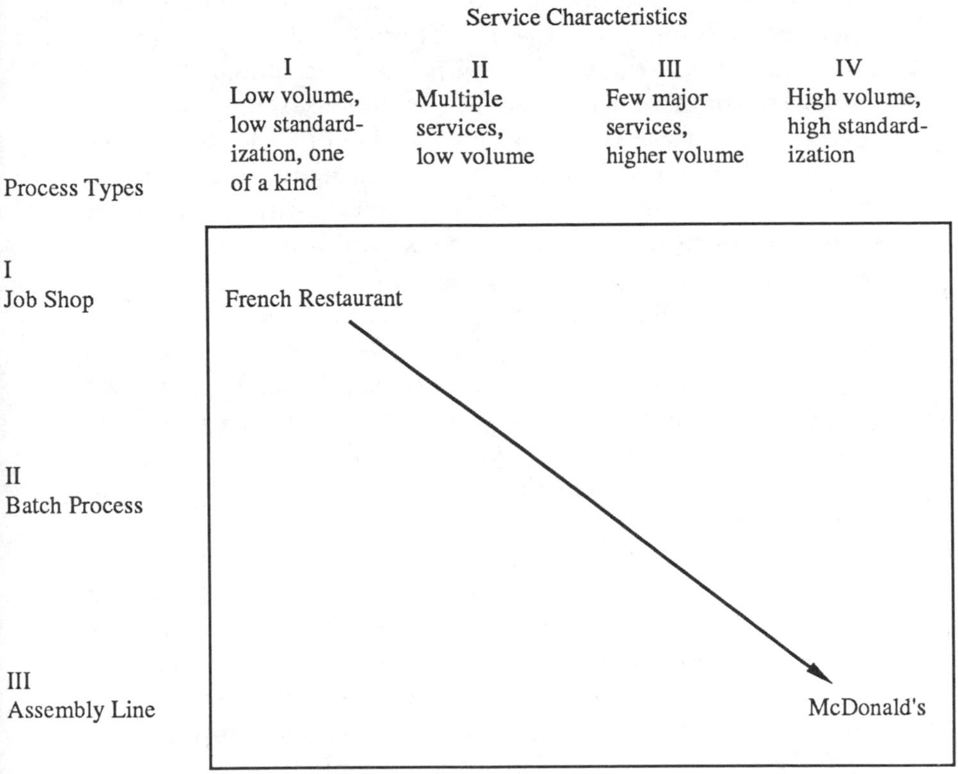

Source: Adapted from Hayes and Wheelwright, 1984, and Chase and Bowen, 1988.

McDonald's and H&R Block (Levitt, 1972, 1976). These companies have embraced assembly-line production designs that use a relatively low-skilled labor force to provide a highly standardized service to large numbers of consumers at a relatively low cost.

The job-shop approach can produce a customized service with a great deal of personal interaction between the customer and service provider, but service job shops are often slow and inefficient. Moreover, they are difficult to replicate successfully in multiple sites. Consequently, most service businesses, as they have grown, have attempted to move along the manufacturing design continuum from a highly personal job shop to an often impersonal assembly-line operation that could be planted any-where in the country or the world. The assembly-line design was especially attractive to service companies that wanted to rapidly expand the number of their operations and also compete in low-margin industries. These companies sought to build "service factories" that applied assembly-line techniques to the delivery of services in a concerted effort to drive down direct labor costs. In industries such as fast food, this assembly-line approach to service has enjoyed considerable success.

The assembly-line approach offered quick, consistent, cost-efficient service. It brought manufacturing efficiencies to service firms. It reduced the number of people needed to deliver a service, increased the speed of delivery, boosted worker pro-ductivity, and improved the consistency of the service. In some exceptional companies that developed strong corporate cultures and offered extensive training to frontline staff, the standardized service was provided in a friendly manner. But there was a price to pay, and it was exacted in the form of reduced customization and personal contact. Unfortunately, the assembly line usually has little flexibility to tailor the service to individual customer needs. Indeed, we are convinced that the production-line approach to service has been inappropriately applied in many operations, resulting in many unhappy customers.

As service companies move along the manufacturing de-sign continuum from job shop to production line, they redefine "good service." Less and less does good service mean providing customers with what they want, when they want it, and where they want it, at a reasonable price. Instead, production-line service operations provide a standardized product at a low price (compared to that of job shops) in an impersonal atmosphere. If the company is exceptional, its employees try to compensate for the lack of "personalized service" by being "personable"—that is, they train their employees to smile, be friendly, and say things such as "Have a nice day." We certainly do not want to criticize those rare organizations that have friendly frontline people, but we do suggest that there is more to "personalized service." We believe that personalized customer service should encompass three major elements:

1. *Identification of true needs*: The service should identify the customer's true needs; when those needs are not clear to the customer, the service system should try to help identify and articulate those needs.
2. *Satisfaction of the customer's basic needs*: The service must satisfy each individual customer's needs. To do so requires that the service be delivered in a way that acknowledges the individuality of each customer (whether the customer is a person or a corporation); that is, the customer should be known and/or treated as an individual entity, not as a mass market or even a market segment.
3. *Satisfaction at the customer's convenience*: Ideally, the service should be provided when and where the customer wants it.

In general, good service is often personal, although personal service is not always personalized. Greeting customers by name but providing them with a standardized product that does not satisfy their specific needs should not be confused with personalized service.

The design of service delivery systems for the 1990s presents a basic challenge: how to use information technology to tailor services to individual customer specifications and then to deliver those services in an efficient but friendly, personalized manner at almost any time the customer desires and to almost any place the customer wishes. Clearly, this is a tall order, and prior to the revolution in information technology, it was difficult, if not impossible, to meet all three of our elements of personalization. *Personalized* had come to mean slow and inefficient, and fast, mass-produced services were seldom personal or personalized. With the dawning of new communication technologies, the parameters of what is possible have been greatly expanded.

Personalizing Service Delivery Systems

Advances in information and communication technologies are creating a brave new world for service companies. Not only are these new technologies revolutionizing the way in which companies deliver services; they are making it possible for service firms to leap into a dynamic new operating dimension where service can at once be both efficient and personalized. In fact, we contend that service companies no longer have to choose between service delivery systems that are inefficient but personalized and those that are efficient but impersonalized. Consequently, they do not have to choose between a strategic emphasis on low cost and one on differentiation.

We see emerging a dynamic new model of highly efficient, personalized service delivery systems that are empowered by information and communication technologies. These powerful new technologies, when harnessed and used with strategic purpose, will enable companies to mass produce cost-effective yet customized and convenient services—that is, they will make possible the "mass customization" of services. By investing in new information and communication technologies, service firms are discovering new opportunities to create new products, win new customers, and leapfrog competitors who cling to the old ways of doing business. In effect, these new technologies can invalidate the process and service characteristic matrix shown in Figure 9.1. In the years ahead, service firms will, we believe, apply these new communication and information technologies in three key ways:

1. *Diagnosis and identification of individual customer needs*: Service providers will develop powerful customer data bases containing detailed information about individual consumer needs, habits, and preferences.
2. *Individualized execution and improvement of customer encounters*: Service providers will monitor individual service encounters to ensure that customers receive high-quality, personalized service and that individual customers are satisfied with their service encounters.
3. *Customer convenience*: Service providers will ensure that customers can purchase or receive services when and where it is most convenient for them.

Using information technology in these ways, service companies can build more holistic — and consequently stronger — relationships with their customers.

Diagnosis and Identification of Individual Customer Needs. The advent of inexpensive but powerful computers now makes it possible for companies of all types and sizes to develop files on new customers and maintain comprehensive files on existing customers. This capability presents exciting possibilities for service organizations. For example, using this customer data base, frontline service providers will be able to know on the spot which customers are first-time clients and which are loyal repeat customers. Such information will enable service staff to acknowledge and personally reward the valued repeat customer and to solicit feedback and other important information from new customers. It also will help service organizations identify customer needs, often before the customer realizes that such needs exist. For example, Otis Elevator has created a special high-tech, highly personal customer-service system to help it respond more quickly and effectively to emergency service calls on its elevators. The system combines a sophisticated customer data base, called OTISLINE, with a central 800-number customer-service dispatch center that operates twenty-four hours a day. The OTISLINE data base enables customer-service representatives to retrieve comprehensive customer files in less than five seconds, and then to identify the precise location of the elevator needing servicing, even though the customer may be calling from thousands of miles away and may be able to provide only a telephone number or building name ("OTISLINE," 1986, p. 12). In another application of the new technology, Stratus Corporation, a manufacturer of computer parts, can identify and even service a customer's needs before the customer is aware of those needs. When a customer's mainframe computer malfunctions and a back-up part takes over, a Stratus factory automatically receives a signal from the computer that a new part is needed. The first time the customer knows that there is a problem is when the replacement part arrives by Federal Express the following morning (Davis, 1987, p. 14).

A firm can now actually attach a detailed personal transaction history to the names of its customers; this service history then becomes the cornerstone on which to build a much more personal relationship with the consumer. No longer will the customer's relationship with the company be so fragmented and departmentalized that there will be such unfortunate incidents as the rejection by a bank's credit card division of a loyal bank customer's VISA application because the division could not verify the customer's income, even though the customer directly deposited her paychecks at the bank. A financial services organization, whose different divisions handle a single customer's many different accounts—mortgage, auto loan, checking, savings, IRA, CDs, and so on—can now personalize that customer's service. One central ledger can reflect all of the customer's accounts; a customer need not receive a separate statement for each account. When a transaction occurs in one account area, the change can be reflected instantly in the customer's total record. Thus, the bank officer reviewing the customer's credit card application would immediately see that the customer always makes her auto and home loan payments on time, has a $15,000 certificate of deposit and $5000 in her checking account, and is credit worthy. The officer could then immediately approve the customer's credit card application and perhaps identify new services that might interest her.

Knowledge of a customer's sales and service history can provide a business edge. In the hands of frontline salespeople, such individual customer information presents a powerful selling tool. Service employees are able to call the repeat customer's attention to new products or services that the customer's past purchasing history indicates might be of special interest to him or her. Moreover, since the new information technology allows customer files to be called up at many different locations, the firm can direct customers to different company stores providing individual sales, products, or services of special customer interest; this in turn will help build a customer-company relationship that is stronger and more valuable than a simple customer-store or customer-employee relationship. With the new information technologies, a record of each service transaction can be easily and cheaply added to an existing customer file. These updates help sketch an increasingly detailed profile of each customer's preferences and predilections. The files can be used to diagnose problems, identify unarticulated needs, and sell additional products and services. Unlike most corporate assets, these customer files appreciate rather than depreciate in value.

Individualized Execution and Improvement of Customer Encounters. Not long ago, it was a clerical nightmare for even the smallest companies to monitor, record, and track every customer service encounter. All that has changed with the advent of new information technology in the 1980s. For example, in an ever-growing number of supermarkets and retail stores, electronic scanning devices instantly record and monitor sales at checkout, improving the speed of customer checkout, improving billing accuracy, and providing detailed customer receipts. Moreover, the scanner systems provide management with daily inventory updates and a detailed analysis of performance by product, by department, and by store. Indeed, many businesses are now finding it is well worth the cost and effort to set up customer-encounter tracking systems that help companies monitor and maintain performance standards. In addition to providing valuable operating information that serves as a yardstick to measure the ongoing quality of a firm's service system, customer-service encounter systems can help attentive firms preempt bad service encounters. OTISLINE, for example, allows Otis Elevator to produce "excess callback reports," which focus company attention on elevators receiving an unacceptably high number of service calls. This enables the company to effectively troubleshoot its elevators and then direct resources to fixing minor problems before they reach crisis proportions.

Tracking customer-service encounters will enable companies to tailor preprogrammed, real-time responses to individual customer inquiries. At the simplest level, firms can provide immediate information in response to frequently asked customer questions. General Electric provides an excellent example. The company has created a state-of-the-art, technologically driven customer-assistance service called the GE Answer Center. The Answer Center, which operates twenty-four hours a day and is built around a toll-free customer assistance telephone system, is equipped with a fast-response data base that offers more than 750,000 answers to common customer questions. The data base allows GE representatives to quickly find and provide the proper answer, as well as to identify the closest dealer, provide dealer operation hours, and even give specific directions for reaching the dealer's location.

Other companies are using information technology to revive and revamp their service delivery systems. Rental-car companies, for example, are using electronic sensors to help process their cars more quickly and accurately. The "AutoFuel" system uses sensors to gather information about cars and send it quickly to a computer. Budget Rent-a-Car, for example, has been installing AutoFuel sensors in its cars' rear bumpers. When a customer returns a vehicle, the sensors record the car's identification number, odometer reading, and fuel level and the time and date. The system transmits the information to the rental office computer, where charges are calculated and a bill prepared, often before the customer finishes parking the car. A similar AutoFuel system is envisioned for self-service gas stations. The system would entirely automate the service station system so that customers could use unstaffed gas stations twenty-four hours a day, with all gas charges automatically billed to the customers' accounts. "AutoFuel will become what 24-hour banking is today," predicts Marty Goldstein of Resource Network International, which markets the system for its developer, Israel's Tadiran, Ltd. ("Put a Sensor in Your Tank," 1988, p. 11).

The Geostar Corporation of Washington, D.C., and Omninet Corporation of Los Angeles have both developed satellite-supported location and communication services for long-haul truck lines. The systems, which are designed to assist transportation companies in locating individual trucks at any time of day or night, help the firms improve scheduling accuracy for customer pickups and deliveries, a point of major frustration for many consumers. The impact of such systems promises to be dramatic. Inefficient vehicle routing and scheduling are costly for customers and transportation companies alike. Customers shipping parts for "just-in-time" assembly lines, for instance, cannot tolerate late or missed deliveries. Using these satellite-locator services, companies can actually track the progress of their trucks on computer-display maps, pinpoint current positions, and forecast which truck in a large fleet will be first available to pick up a new load. Moreover, when a truck strays from its route, its course can be easily and quickly corrected. In case of trouble, drivers can punch a button to call for help (Cook, 1988, p. 64).

The new technologies have countless other potential applications among service firms for improving customer encounters. Imagine, for instance, how an airline, learning that one of its flights will be several hours late, could notify scheduled passengers of the delay before they leave their homes or offices for the airport. Given the information storage and retrieval capabilities of airline computer systems, such personalized service is certainly feasible, though seldom practiced. Of course, in business as in life, things sometimes will and do go wrong. The occasional foul-up is to be expected. The pressing issue then for service companies is how to recover from such a service breakdown. By linking customer files to service encounter files, companies can identify service problems and move quickly both to correct the problems and to apologize personally to the inconvenienced customers, regardless of whether the customers actually bothered to complain. For example, a colleague of ours recently was delayed at Chicago's O'Hare Airport because of a severe storm that affected all flights in and out of the airport. He later received a letter from his airline acknowledging that he had been delayed in Chicago and apologizing for the inconvenience it might have caused him. The airline indicated that it valued him as a loyal customer and offered him additional frequent-flyer account credits as a further gesture of apology.

Customer Convenience. From the consumer's vantage, the ultimate in service is to be served at any time and any place that suits his or her needs. The new technology offers the potential for many companies to do just this. "Any product (or service) that is information based, whether in the form of sound, image, words, or data, can probably be adapted to any time, any place delivery," observes Stanley M. Davis (1987, p. 49) in the book *Future Perfect*, which explores extensively the idea of any-time, any-place service.

As automated teller machines (ATMs) have demonstrated, a growing number of financial transactions can now be performed at times convenient to the customer rather than during banks' limited and inconvenient working hours. Operating twenty-four hours a day, ATMs help drive down transaction costs as well as providing more convenient service to customers. But ATMs are just the first step on the widening trail toward personalized service delivery systems. Some financial institutions and brokerage houses already allow customers to use personal computers in their homes to link up with their bank and stock accounts via telephone and modem. Indeed, Fidelity Investments, the Boston-based mutual-fund giant, has developed a system that allows customers to switch funds and check price quotations directly by telephone twenty-four hours a day. And Citicorp, in conjunction with Panasonic's Matsushita Electric, has developed a portable personal computer terminal that is the size of a calculator and plugs easily into a phone. Using this device, customers can link up with the bank's computer and perform nearly all the transactions available on the most sophisticated ATMs. Such technological innovations make it easy for customers to use the bank's various services without leaving their homes or offices.

The competitive advantage of Otis Elevator's OTISLINE is its ability to collapse both distance and time. The results from OTISLINE have been impressive. Faster response, a key customer criterion for judging the quality of service, gives the company an edge in winning and keeping lucrative elevator service contracts, and, by quickly identifying and repairing problem elevators, Otis can reduce overall service call-backs. Indeed, Otis has determined that by reducing service call-backs by one per year per installed elevator, the company would save $5 million annually.

A wide assortment of phone-linked monitoring and diagnostic systems are currently being developed to improve home health care service for pregnant women, high-risk infants, and adults with heart, sleep, and other ailments. Indeed, new technology has helped turn home health care service into a $14-billion-a-year industry. Primarily because of cost and customer comfort, the place of service delivery has shifted from the producer's to the consumer's domain. In short, medical care has come home again as new technology has helped create a cost-effective any-time, any-place customer service system.

In the retail goods industry, "electronic data pipelines" are being used to revolutionize the way companies conduct business. Seminole Manufacturing Company has developed a communications service and software product that serves as an electronic link connecting the computers of customers, producers, and suppliers. This information pipeline permits all three groups instantly to exchange sales data, new orders, shipment information, inventory receipts, and invoices. This dynamic data interchange enables each company in the link to use fewer data-entry employees, while also reducing the chance for human error and avoiding information-transfer delays of days or even weeks. In use at Wal-Mart stores, the electronic data pipeline helped the retail chain cut delivery time on polyester slacks by 50 percent and also raised pants sales by 31 percent over nine months ("An Electronic Pipeline. . . .," 1987, p. 80).

Another new technology—compact disk data storage—promises to bring whole libraries into the offices of doctors, lawyers, and countless other professionals. One small disk can record ten million addresses and telephone numbers and can be read through a personal computer. An entire legal library recorded on compact disks could fit conveniently on a lawyer's credenza (Slutsker, 1988, pp. 90–91). Average citizens are benefiting too from the new technology. Hyatt Legal Services, for instance, offers LawPlan, a prepaid legal advice and counsel program, to twenty million homes with access to the Cable Value Network ("Prepaid Legal Advice. . . ," 1988). Indeed, shop-at-home cable television systems allow consumers to purchase a wide range of goods and services at virtually any time and any place. In some large metropolitan areas, consumers can place grocery orders via a cable television or computer link and then have the goods delivered directly to their homes. "Shifting the determination of a product's final configuration downstream, into the space of the consumer, has very practical consequences," contends Davis (1987, p. 55). "Consumers who create and control the manufacture of their goods and services are likely to consume more than those who do not."

Automate or "Informate": The Decision Facing Service Providers

Information has become a valued new resource, an essential corporate asset. Unlike most tangible assets, information is dynamic and flexible. It is easily shared, easily transferred. It can be in many places at the same time. Information technology makes it possible to provide service that is personal, personalized, and convenient. Information transmitted instantaneously throughout an organization also can empower either the consumer or the service provider and in some cases both.

Empower the Consumer—Automate. For the consumer, technology-enhanced service systems are liberating. The information technology has *automated* the service process, empowering customers and providing them with personalized, sometimes even personal, convenient service. Consider, for instance, the twenty-four-hour automated teller machines. The more sophisticated ATM systems are personal in the sense that they greet customers by name on the display screens. They are personalized to the extent that individual consumers can choose from a broad range of transactions, customizing the amount of cash they withdraw, transferring funds back and forth between accounts, or requesting an updated personal account statement that is printed on the spot, and they make it possible for consumers to bank at any time of day in almost any place. If customers have any problem or questions, they just reach for a twenty-four-hour telephone hot line installed next to the ATM that connects them directly to the bank's customer-service department.

In another service arena, a Hartford, Connecticut, technology company has developed an $89.95 software-and-service product designed to let customers plot their own customized local weather forecasts whenever they desire. The "Accu-Weather Forecaster" enables users to tap into the Accu-Weather, Inc. data base, which compiles comprehensive weather information from the National Weather Service and other sources. The software allows transportation and insurance companies, pilots, farmers, fire departments, and other customers to manipulate the data on a personal computer, to help tailor their forecasts for local target areas ("Whither the Weather?" 1988, p. 11).

Empower the Service Provider—Informate. Other communication technologies empower customers in a different but equally exciting way. These technologies *informate* the service process, empowering frontline employees, who in turn empower the customer. In her book *In the Age of the Smart Machine*, Shoshana Zuboff (1984) observes how new technologies, when used creatively, provide service staff with superior information that can be retrieved instantaneously—that is, they "informate" the process. This information increases service providers' overall knowledge of the service process and makes them capable of critical judgments on matters that would previously have been handled by upper-level or mid-level managers. Thus, frontline employees are granted real authority that allows them to better help their customers at the point of initial customer contact. Customers receive direct, personal service that is more efficient, more convenient, and more easily personalized.

Northeast Utilities, for example, spends about $75 million a year on computers targeted at improving customer service. One sophisticated system pinpoints the location of a caller before a customer-service representative even picks up the phone. In this way, customer-service representatives can identify and resolve service problems much more quickly and efficiently than ever before. Consider a typical repair call from a homeowner complaining that he has lost power in his house. Northeast Utilities instantaneously pinpoints on a computer map where the service failure has occurred. Displaying the service network as a broad-reaching tree, the computer quickly pinpoints the failure's cause by identifying where on the network of connecting branches service remains unaffected and where it has stopped. Service crews can then concentrate their repair efforts in the needed areas. Equally important, Northeast Utilities' computers record customer service histories. While speaking to a client, a service representative can determine whether a home or particular service district is experiencing repeated service problems. This allows the service provider to use the computer to troubleshoot serious problems. Several calls reporting tree-limb outages might signal the company that a statistically high number of outages have occurred in this particular area; thus, the company knows that it should accelerate its tree-pruning program in this neighborhood in order to avoid future problems. Previously, says a company spokesperson, such probabilistic analysis was seldom done because it had to be computed manually, a nearly impossible task given the tens of thousands of customers the utility serves. Now the computer does it automatically for customer service representatives.

Whether to empower the consumer or to empower the service provider is a key strategic question for managers of service firms. We do not believe that one approach is necessarily superior to the other. Each path leads in a different direction and confronts different issues along the way. Management must choose the path that coincides most closely with its long-term goals and strategic operating plan.

Issues Raised by the New Technologies

The emergence of so many new technologies in the service sector raises a host of thorny issues for both service providers and their customers. For instance, does a new technology complement the organization's structure and its strategy? If it does not, what will be the operational consequences of introducing it? Consider the case of Shenandoah Life Insurance

Company of Roanoke, Virginia. Several years ago, the company discovered that even though it had installed a modern computer system, the firm still required twenty-seven working days and action by thirty-two employees to issue certain types of life-insurance policies. The problem was organizational, not technological. Despite the new computer systems, clerks continued to work as they always had, in assembly-line fashion: One specialized in processing the retirement of old policies, another issued new policies, a third transferred cash values from the old to the new, and so on. Once the organization identified this internal problem—organizational structure and technology were not complementing each other—the problem was resolved. Less specialized clerks now work in teams and use the computer system to its full advantage. Processing time has been cut to as little as two days, and over the past three years, transactions have risen by 28 percent, while the number of workers handling them has decreased by 15 percent (Wessel, 1988).

Other issues raised by the introduction of new technology can prove even more philosophically and ethically challenging. Among the more nettlesome commonly recurring questions are the following:

- Who owns the information in a customer data base?
- Who inside and outside the organization should have access to sensitive information in a customer data base?
- Does a consumer have any right to privacy that would prevent a service company from entering potentially sensitive demographic, psychographic, or historical data into a customer file? (How will consumers feel knowing that someone knows what magazines and periodicals they read, what foods and beverages they consume, what movies they watch, what investments they make, what telephone numbers they call, what organizations they support?)
- What is an organization's responsibility for staff members—both management and frontline employees—whose jobs become obsolete because of technological advancements?
- How can employees best be trained first to accept newly

introduced technology and then to achieve maximum results from it?

- How can customers be prepared and trained for the advent
  of new technology that may very well affect the way in which
  traditional products and services are delivered to them?

The last two of these issues are among the more troubling for
many organizations. From the start, there may be strong employee resistance to the new technologies and the rapidly changing workplace that they promote. Employee concern typically
centers around two primary questions: How will the new technologies be used, and will they jeopardize individual job security? When these concerns are not addressed, staff morale
may deteriorate, which may quickly lead to declines in productivity and product quality. For customers, too, new technology
can be misunderstood and thus rejected. Customers are likely to
resist new technology if they are exposed to it without adequate
explanation of why it has been installed or if their only exposure
to it is indirect, through service staff complaints about new-
fangled systems or through failing product quality resulting
from the new technology being poorly introduced. Few things
are more frustrating for a customer who has experienced faulty
or inferior service than to receive as explanation or excuse "It
must be a computer error."

When used creatively, new technology is a means for
organizations to provide higher-quality, lower-cost, more convenient personalized service, while reducing "busy work" for employees and consumers. Technology can and should be a liberating tool that frees service managers and employees, ultimately
allowing them to pay even closer attention to their customers.
Unfortunately, many organizations view technology as an end in
itself, as simply a way to cut costs, to reduce staff, or to police
employees and customers. Who can blame people for resisting
new technology if their primary exposure to it is through some
mysterious system that has been installed to monitor worker
productivity and performance, rather than to help workers to
become more productive and to provide better service? Technology used only as an impersonal "Big Brother" tool to police

employees and customers can do much more harm than good. Consider those companies that have seen a precipitous decline in customer satisfaction after installing productivity monitors on employee telephone lines. These well-intentioned but clumsy attempts to spur productivity have often inspired employees to become curt and to rush when dealing with customers so that they can complete more calls. Indeed, some customer service representatives have been known to hang up on customers pretending that the line had been disconnected rather than spending time to answer a difficult or time-consuming customer question.

As Zuboff (1984) points out, the new technologies can rob workers of important skills and job gratification, thus increasing the impersonality and remoteness of the work environment, or it can "informate" employees, empowering them with knowledge and authority that enables them to better serve their customers.

Conclusion

Today—not tomorrow—is the time for both large and small service firms to evaluate the strategic use of technology in their organizations. Improving and personalizing service delivery systems through technology is not a future concept. Indeed, 85 percent of all investment in high-tech equipment since 1970 has been by service industries (Nasar, 1987, p. 44).

The new information and communication technologies are not panaceas for all service problems. They do not represent a quick and easy solution to long-term operating issues. Productivity has been dropping, one might note, in the huge finance and insurance industry despite the fact that many of this sector's companies have invested heavily in new technology. Indeed, overall productivity among the nation's service industries is no higher now than it was in 1979, with the exception of such deregulated sectors as commercial banking, telecommunications, and railroads, which have all scored impressive annual productivity gains ranging between 4 and 10 percent for the past several years (Nasar, 1987). Yet when properly planned and managed, the new information and communication technologies hold out exciting opportunities for service organizations to personalize their delivery systems, offer a greater range of products, curb lagging productivity, and increase overall service quality and efficiency. Moreover, these new technologies, which typically increase the speed and reliability of service transactions, can reduce or eliminate many cumbersome, low-skill, labor-intensive tasks previously required to complete the most routine service transactions.

Those service companies that simply chase costs down the manufacturing design continuum, creating ever more intricate assembly-line service delivery systems without considering how technology can help them automate or informate their organizations, will be losers in the long run. Communication and information technologies are here to stay. They have changed forever the service economy in the United States. Every service company should take stock of this change; every service company should carefully evaluate what opportunities and challenges have been created by this change. In the 1990s, the winners in world services will be those companies that best use the technology to their customers' and their own strategic advantage.

References

Chase, R. B., and Bowen, D. E. "Integrating Operations and Human Resource Management in the Service Sector." In C. C. Snow (ed.), *Strategy, Organization Design, and Human Resource Management*. Greenwich, Conn.: JAI Press, 1988.

Cook, W. J. "Truck 54, Where Are You?" *U.S. News & World Report*, Mar. 21, 1988, p. 64.

Davis, S. M. *Future Perfect*. Reading, Mass.: Addison-Wesley, 1987.

"An Electronic Pipeline That's Changing the Way America Does Business." *Business Week*, Aug. 3, 1987, p. 80.

Hayes, R. H., and Wheelwright, S. C. *Restoring Our Competitive Edge*. New York: Wiley, 1984.

Levitt, T. "Production-Line Approach to Service." *Harvard Business Review*, 1972, *50* (5), 41–52.

Levitt, T. "The Industrialization of Service." *Harvard Business Review*, 1976, *54*, 63–74.

Nasar, S. "Productivity Puzzle." *Fortune*, June 8, 1987, p. 44.

"OTISLINE." Case no. 9-186-304, Harvard Business School Case Services, 1986.

Porter, M. E. *Competitive Strategy: Techniques for Analyzing Industries and Competitors*. New York: Free Press, 1980.

"Prepaid Legal Advice via Cable TV." *Business Week*, Aug. 8, 1988.

"Put a Sensor in Your Tank." *High Technology Business*, June 1988, p. 11.

Slutsker, G. "Search Me." *Forbes*, Jan. 25, 1988, p. 90–91.

Wessel, D. "Service Industries Find Computers Don't Always Raise Productivity." *Wall Street Journal*, Apr. 19, 1988, p. 37.

"Whither the Weather?" *High Technology Business*, June 1988, p. 11.

"Why Is Service So Bad?" *Time*, Feb. 2, 1987, p. 48.

Zuboff, S. *In the Age of the Smart Machine*. New York: Basic Books, 1984.

10

Measuring and Managing
Service Quality

David A. Collier

Airline flight attendants who serve food and beverages in a friendly and efficient manner; cashiers who take too long to ring up your groceries or to check you out of the hotel; nurses who respect your privacy and who are always around when you need them; mechanics who do not explain the technical reasons for replacing your automobile's ignition system; dentists who promise prompt, friendly service and technical competence and meet or exceed those promises; telephone customer-service representatives who "never really solve your problem"; clerks who provide service with a smile — service encounters (Czepiel, Solomon, and Surprenant, 1985), also called service transactions, episodes, or experiences, such as these have been the subject of much public debate over the past few years (Russell, Grant, and Szonskl, 1987; Peters and Waterman, 1982; Leonard and Sasser, 1982; Quinn and Gagnon, 1986). Is the service good or bad? How does the customer evaluate service? How can managers achieve excellent service quality?

This chapter examines how managers define, measure, establish standards for, monitor and control, and evaluate service quality. This overview gives the reader a sense of the complexity and interdisciplinary nature of service quality, introduces some service management terms and concepts, and enhances appreciation of the strategic importance of service quality in the marketplace. The list of references at the end of the chapter is a starting point for a deeper look at the topic of service quality.

One idea with which everyone seems to agree is that extraordinary service quality is where most organizations gain a competitive advantage in the marketplace. For example, one recent study (Roth and van der Velde, 1988, pp. xix–xx) made the following summary points about service quality in the U.S. financial service industry: "(a) service, service, and more service is seen as the most critical element of marketplace success to the 1990s, (b) bankers should place as much, or even more, emphasis upon maintaining good relationships with existing clients as they do in acquiring new ones, and (c) quality programs are a dominant factor in the operations strategic portfolio."

In many other service industries, such as wholesale and retail trade, telecommunications, transportation, food and restaurant services, hotels and lodging, leisure and entertainment, and medical, legal, and other professional services, the importance of competing on service quality is much the same. For example, one health care consultant (Sturm, 1988, p. 68) noted that "relationship management recognizes that a service company's business activities do not have a beginning and an end but constitute a series of experiences with the customer. These experiences build on each other and create a continuing economic relationship. The more you do to manage those experiences, the greater the return."

Moreover, the technical quality of a product is not always easy for the customer to evaluate. Therefore, customers may depend on complementary, peripheral, or supporting services that accompany the purchase of a product to evaluate the overall purchase. Recently, several executives from an international company that produces gasoline reinforced this point: "Most customers can't and don't evaluate the technical quality of the physical product but focus most of their attention on the facility, the people, and the service delivery process associated with buying gasoline. Service quality is where we gain a competitive advantage in the marketplace!" (Collier, 1988a).

There is some evidence that service quality performance is directly related to a firm's profitability. Using the profit impact of market strategy (PIMS) data base maintained by the Strategic Planning Institute, Thompson, DeSouza, and Gale (1985, pp. 20–25) found that "in only 15 percent of the markets is service 'irrelevant' in the customer perception of quality. In most markets, service plays a significant part in the purchase decision; and in many markets, service is actually more important than product." They conclude that "service quality is a key to profitability and growth — even for firms that are thought of as primarily manufacturers." Luchs (1986, pp. 12–17) arrives at similar conclusions from a product-quality perspective.

One final point must be addressed before we examine the management task of defining service quality. Managing service quality in the U.S. domestic market is difficult, but to introduce a service to international markets is even more challenging. How must the definition and delivery of a service be changed to adapt to a new set of cultural values? How do customers in different cultures perceive and evaluate service quality? Are Western or United States–based methods and models of service quality valid in other cultures? Current research and thinking on such questions are limited. As Riddle (1988, p. 20) concludes, "Cultural influences on service delivery and perceived service quality have been largely ignored and have only recently begun to receive attention. However, as competition increases, sensitivity to cultural issues as they affect customer expectations, customer evaluations, and employee performance will make the difference at the margin." Lehtinen (1988), who describes the Asian, American, European, and Soviet service styles, supports Riddle's conclusion.

Defining Service Quality

One common characteristic of the literature that attempts to define and model service quality is its interdisciplinary nature. Defining service quality requires knowledge from many disciplines, such as marketing, psychology, operations, human resource management, economics, and business strategy. Several basic concepts about how a service organization provides a service help explain why defining service quality is such a complex and difficult management task. The process is often the service, the delivery of the service involves the simultaneous execution of marketing and operations tasks, the service has tangible (high goods content) and intangible (low or no goods content) attributes, the customer often experiences the service in the place where it is produced, the service itself cannot be inventoried, the creation and delivery of a service often involve a high degree of interaction between the customer and high-contact employees, service quality can be measured according to marketing (external) and/or operations (internal) information, customers judge the service process at least as much as the service outcome, and true service quality is best measured by the customer's perception of it. Given these basic ideas and an appreciation of the complexity of a service encounter, we will examine the meaning of the terms *service* and *quality*.

As Sasser, Olsen, and Wyckoff (1978, pp. 10–11) first observed, a service can be defined as a package of explicit and implicit benefits performed with a supporting facility and facilitating goods. They also note that a service possesses tangible (high goods content) and intangible (little or no goods content) attributes.

A service can be an idea, entertainment, information, knowledge, change in the customer's appearance or health, social innovation, circumstance (being at the right place at the right time), convenience, food, security, or any of a number of other things. Service may also be defined as a deed, a performance, a social event, or an effort and output that is consumed where it is produced.

Quality has also been defined in many ways, such as conformance to specifications, the degree to which customer specifications are satisfied, a fair exchange of price and value, fitness for use, and doing it right the first time. In fact, Garvin (1988, pp. 40–41) describes five approaches to defining product quality, each with a different viewpoint.

Most of these ideas about quality are founded in goods-producing rather than service-producing industries. Basic ideas and premises about product or goods quality are not always directly transferable to service quality (Collier, 1985, pp. 1–15). Parasuraman, Zeithaml, and Berry (1985, p. 42) point out that service quality is more difficult for the consumer to evaluate than goods quality; perceptions of service quality result from a comparison of consumer expectations with actual service performance; quality evaluations are not made solely on the outcome of a service but also involve evaluations of the "process" of service delivery; and the customer has fewer tangible cues when purchasing a service than when purchasing goods. Definitions of service quality differ by industry and by the nature of the services provided. Although there seems to be no consensus on a definition of service quality applicable to all industries, services, and viewpoints, we can examine three generic views of service quality. The more ways we define and view service quality, the better we will understand it.

One general definition of service quality is that it is a comparison by the customer of his or her expectations prior to experiencing the service with service delivery system performance. Customer expectations can be established by advertising, previous personal experience, conversations with other users of the service, culture, and the like. The actual performance level of the service delivery system depends on many controllable factors, such as facility, process, equipment, job design, employee incentive and bonus programs, training programs, employee scheduling, strategic plans, and management decisions. In addition, uncontrollable factors, such as the behavior of other customers in the service delivery system, the weather, competitors' performance and influence, traffic congestion, and labor shortages can affect the performance level of the service delivery system.

A second view of service quality emphasizes defining the words *customer*, *service*, *quality*, and *levels*, each of which has a purpose if one is to truly understand service quality as applied to any organization (Collier, 1987a, p. 79):

> Excellent customer service and quality levels (CS&QLs) means consistently meeting customer

expectations (external service standards and cost) and service delivery system performance criteria (internal service standards, cost, and revenue).

Excellent customer service and quality levels are achieved by the consistent delivery to the customer of a clearly defined service package specified by many internal and external standards of performance.

- *Excellent* means achieving performance standards 100 percent of the time.
- *Customer* is the next entity (person/department/firm) that receives, pays for, or experiences the output of the service (or manufacturing) delivery system. The customer includes entities within as well as outside your primary organizational identity.
- *Service* is any primary or complementary activity that does not directly produce a physical product—that, is the nongoods part of the transaction between buyer (customer) and seller (provider).
- *Quality* is the distinctive tangible and intangible properties of a product and/or service that is perceived by the customer as being better than the competition.
- *Levels* implies that a measurement system is in place to quantify, monitor, and evaluate CS&QLs.
- *Consistent* means daily conformance (low or no variability) to all standards of performance.
- *Delivery* means getting the right service in the right way to the right customer at the right time. The service delivery system provides the service.
- *Service package* is a clearly defined set of tangible and intangible attributes the customer recognizes, pays for, uses, and/or experiences. The package can be a service or group of services.

- *Specified* means by management.
- *Internal* standards of performance focus on in-house or backroom operating and marketing criteria that are hidden or decoupled from the customer. Measurement can be more objective against numerical specifications.
- *External* standards of performance focus on out-in-the-field or frontroom operating and marketing criteria that the customer expects/perceives while using or experiencing the product and/or service. Measurement is usually more dependent on human judgment.

A third view of service quality, and possibly the most sophisticated, recognizes that there are several ways to misspecify and mismanage the definition and delivery of excellent service quality. Parasuraman, Zeithaml, and Berry (1985, pp. 41–50) call these *gaps* and identify five of them in their service quality model (see Figure 10.1). The first gap is the discrepancy between consumer expectations and management perceptions of those expectations. Managers may think that they understand why the customer buys their service and define service quality specifications according to this perception. But what if management's perception is wrong? The second gap is the discrepancy between management perceptions of what features constitute a target level of service quality and the task of translating these perceptions into executable specifications. Even if these areas are congruent and well managed, the service delivery system must execute these service quality specifications. The third gap, then, is the discrepancy between service quality specifications documented in operating and training manuals and their implementation. The fourth gap is the discrepancy between actual service delivery system performance and external communications to the customers: The customer should not be promised a certain type and level of service quality unless the service delivery system can achieve or exceed that level. Finally, the service quality perceived by the customer is a function of the magnitude and direction of the fifth gap, that between expected service and

Figure 10.1. A Service Quality Model.

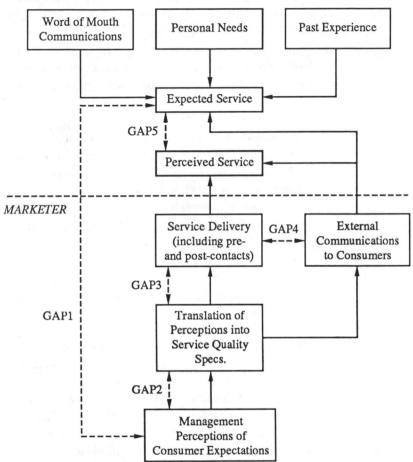

Source: A. Parasuraman, V. A. Zeithaml, and L. L. Berry. Reprinted from *Journal of Marketing*, Fall 1985, Vol. 49, p. 44, published by the American Marketing Association. Reproduced with permission.

perceived service. This fifth gap is a function of the other four. Parasuraman, Zeithaml, and Berry (1985) make an important contribution to the service quality literature by proposing this model of service quality.

Measuring Service Quality

A service-providing organization cannot evaluate service quality without reliable measures. Once the organization knows its relative competitive position with regard to service quality, it can refine its service quality standards, design the service delivery system to monitor and control service quality, and begin to use excellent service quality as a competitive weapon in the marketplace.

However, as Williams and Zigli (1987, p. 14) point out, "Progress is being made in defining service and service quality parameters, but imprecision and manufacturing mentality make the task difficult." As we have previously discussed, the concepts and models for measuring product quality are not always comprehensive enough for service quality. One must be able to understand the intricate details of a service encounter, to identify and quantify the attributes of a service encounter, and to correctly measure customer expectations.

Service firm managers must be able to quantify not only the tangible but also the intangible attributes of the service package. Intangible attributes include security, convenience, ambience, privacy, respect, friendliness, competence, safety, empathy, reliability, responsiveness, politeness, and honesty. It is an exciting challenge for management to quantify and measure these intangible attributes and integrate these intangible measures with the tangible attributes of the service package and service encounter. As Crosby (1979, p. 16) states, "Anything can be measured if you have to do it." The attribute may have to be evaluated on a binary scale (such as yes or no) or an ordinal scale (such as 1 to 5), but a ratio scale (such as from zero to two minutes processing time) is usually the best. Probabilities, proportions, and revenue-cost-service trade-offs are other ways to quantify service quality attributes. In one study ("Making Service a Potent Marketing Tool," 1984), managers were surprised to find that the value in revenues from each loyal customer, adjusted for inflation, since 1979 was $142,000 over the lifetime of a satisfied automobile buyer. For supermarkets, the value was $22,000 over a five-year period, and for appliance manufacturers it was $2,840 over twenty years. Once "the dollar value of a loyal customer" is quantified, managers pay more attention to service quality.

According to Crosby (1979, p. 1), "quality is free. It is not a gift, but it is free." Crosby advocates quantifying the cost of poor quality because correcting errors is expensive. It involves the cost of additional facility, labor, and equipment capacity and the loss of repeat business and associated revenue. It costs three to five times as much to attract a new customer as to keep an old customer happy. Crosby (1981) also notes that "the only way to measure quality from a management standpoint is by calculating the price of nonconformance—How much does it cost you to make and overcome errors? In manufacturing companies, it runs about 23 percent of sales; in service companies it is more than that."

Once the general concepts discussed in this chapter are applied to an actual service package and service delivery system, the service quality attributes become much more specific, detailed, and numerous. Rosander (1985, pp. 117–125) provides as an example the attributes of the major subsystems of a large hotel: reservations, room, food, bar, checkout, and eighteen other supporting services. This example demonstrates how complex and data-oriented a service quality measurement system can be.

American Airlines (Lewis and Booms, 1983) provides another example. It defines and measures service quality for two of its many airline subsystems as follows: (1) the last bag from a flight should be available in the baggage claim area within fifteen minutes after the arrival of the flight, and (2) airline reservations by telephone should be answered within twenty seconds at least 80 percent of the time. These measures are internal standards of performance. External measures of service quality might be made by using customer surveys to solicit customers' perceptions of baggage claim or telephone reservation service. Customer surveys usually use ordinal scales to measure such attributes.

According to Collier (1987a, p. 85), internal and external service quality standards of performance must, over time, become congruent. In the short term, though the service delivery system may be meeting its internal standards of performance, it may not be performing well in the eyes of the customer (or vice versa). These situations can lead to excess operating costs, inappropriate advertising messages and target markets, over- or undertraining of employees, allocation of resources to the wrong areas of the service delivery system, and so on. This is confusing to the customer, not to mention the employees. Over the long term, good managers try to explain and correct this gap between internal and external measures of service quality.

In practice, companies seldom have matching sets of internal and external measures of service quality (Collier, 1988b, 1988c). In fact, many companies rely solely on either internal or external measures of service quality. Even when both sets of service quality information are available, the marketing and operations functions seldom cooperate and coordinate their service quality measurement systems.

An even more disturbing finding was documented in a 1987 Gallup survey (Reip, 1988, pp. 24–25): "Of 698 upper-level executives of American industrial and service firms, 64 percent indicated that customer complaints were their leading indicator of quality. Quality reports, which only 19 percent considered important, was the second choice. These findings suggest that they would rather get their information from strangers than from their own family, so to speak." Another study (LaLonde, 1985, p. 186) found that "the majority of firms studied do not have specific policy or a means for operationally defining and measuring customer service performance."

While many companies, such as American Airlines, American Express, Citicorp, Disney Productions, Frito-Lay, IBM, Marriott, McDonald's, Minnesota Mining & Manufacturing, and Wal-Mart, do excel at service quality (Hostage, 1975; Peters and Waterman, 1982; Lewis and Booms, 1983; Donnelly, Berry, and Thompson, 1985; Peters and Austin, 1985), much more needs to be done by academics and practitioners alike to define and measure service quality. We have only just begun.

Establishing Service Quality Standards

Once a service quality measurement system is in place, management must set a multitude of standards for performance, such as detailed plans and procedure manuals specifying how to greet the customer, how to process the application, how to lay out and design the service facility, how to set the dinner table, how to handle customer complaints, how to dress, how frequently to clean the facility, how to staff each shift, and the like. In general, service quality standards must be established for all the resources, such as facilities, equipment, procedures, people, and knowledge, necessary to create and deliver the service.

Setting service quality standards is a challenging job. Some companies and managers simply give up on trying to define, measure, and set standards for service quality. But excellent companies that employ service quality as a key part of their competitive strategy do define, measure, and set standards for service quality performance. There are many models of successful implementation. Service-providing organizations can learn and have learned much from the work-measurement literature (Krajewski and Ritzman, 1987, pp. 209–247) founded in goods-producing industries.

Why are service quality standards of performance so important? One reason is that they provide benchmarks on which all subsequent management decisions are based, as shown in Figure 10.2. Service quality standards are key parameters in designing the facility layout; making facility, equipment, process, and staff capacity decisions; devising detailed schedules for the use of these resources; justifying automation; designing training programs; and the like. All of these management decisions affect revenues, cost, and service levels and the firm's competitive position.

As Collier (1987b, pp. 45–46) notes, "For service firms, setting standards for service quality is often an overlooked but key step in the disaggregation process. Only then does the service firm have a definitive and negotiable basis for changing

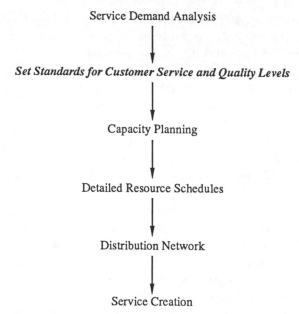

Figure 10.2. The Overlooked Step in the Service Capacity
Scheduling Decision.

Service Demand Analysis

Set Standards for Customer Service and Quality Levels

Capacity Planning

Detailed Resource Schedules

Distribution Network

Service Creation

Source: Collier, 1987b. Reproduced by permission.

plans and schedules." He concludes that "Approaches to the service capacity–scheduling decision vary widely. For example, many fast food restaurants, based on detailed analyses, set standards for service by decision rules such as allowing 24 worker-hours for the first $300 in daily sales and one additional worker-hour for each additional $30 in sales. Banks often use standard customer service times in queuing models to set capacity levels for bank tellers. Airline service delivery systems use many service capacity-scheduling methods such as mathematical programming to schedule crew members. But in all cases, service quality standards should be the fulcrum upon which the total service capacity-scheduling process hinges" (p. 47).

Monitoring and Controlling Service Quality

At the point of service creation and delivery, all the resources and knowledge of the provider of the service must come together in exactly the right way to ensure an excellent service encounter for the customer. It is at this point that the customers compare their expectations with actual service delivery system performance and ultimately arrive at their perceptions of service quality. Jan Carlzon, the managing director of Scandinavian Airlines Systems, was the first to call this instant in time "the moment of truth" (Peters and Austin, 1985, pp. 59, 78). He defines a moment of truth as an episode in which a customer comes in contact with any aspect of the company, however remote, and thereby has an opportunity to form an impression. Monitoring and controlling millions of moments of truth for most firms is the supreme challenge. But by managing these moments of truth well, we manage the customer's perception of service quality (Collier, 1989a).

How do organizations monitor and control service quality? Although far from a comprehensive list of ways to monitor and control service quality, the outline below presents four general approaches often used by service firm managers:

I. Service facility, process, equipment, and job design approach
    - Design the service facility layout and process to control customer movement.
    - Standardize the service facility, process, and job designs.
    - Use more automation (and less employee discretion).
    - Use electronic monitoring of equipment and employee performance.
II. Quality-through-people approach
    A. Routine service providers
        - Institute intensive training and retraining programs.
        - Institute employee economic incentive, bonus, and profit-sharing programs.
        - Institute employee recognition and motivation programs.
        - Keep employees informed about the importance of service quality to their company's competitive

position via newsletters, meetings with management, and so on.

B. Professional and managerial service providers
- Provide educational programs on managing service quality.
- Add extra layers of management to supervise one another.
- Couple managers' performance appraisal to service quality performance.
- Monitor standards through professional associations, licensing agencies, and peer review.
- Provide top-level management motivation and encouragement by wandering around.
- Use the judicial system to protect service concepts and facility, equipment, job, and process designs.

III. Systems and procedures approach
- Set up service quality audit and inspection teams.
- Provide detailed procedural manuals and job checklists.
- Institute quality-control techniques such as statistical process control, fishbone diagrams, quality circles, zero-defects programs, acceptance sampling, and unannounced audits and inspections.
- Develop and implement staff and equipment schedules that maximize service levels and minimize costs.
- Use value of a loyal customer and cost of poor quality in economic analysis.
- Maintain safety capacity in the form of extra service channels, standby labor pools, and "stock-out" backup or recovery plans.
- Develop a comprehensive service quality management system.

IV. External communications approach
- Influence customer expectations through target service levels and service package offerings.
- Influence employee performance through external advertising so that employees must live up to or exceed what the ads promise.

- Measure, monitor, and evaluate the customer's perception of service quality via external measurement techniques such as customer surveys, focus-group interviews, and customer-service comment cards.

The first approach emphasizes service facility, process, equipment, and job design. All these features of the service delivery system help customers form an impression about what type of service quality to expect if they enter the system. As a service business grows to have hundreds or even thousands of service facilities scattered over a wide geographical area, it is imperative that the service facility, process, equipment, and job designs are standardized if one wants to consistently monitor and control service quality. Sasser, Olsen, and Wyckoff (1978, pp. 534–566) discuss the importance of a "standard or dominant facility design" prior to growth and examine how nonstandardized facilities, processes, and jobs can lead to greater managerial complexity. Sherowski (1983) also describes how facility design helps create an image and set of expectations in the customer's mind.

Automation can also have a role in monitoring and controlling service quality. Examples of the automation of services (Collier, 1985, p. 22) include automated teller machines, optical mail scanners, automated sales or billing systems, electronic ambulance-dispatching systems, electronic office systems, hotel electronic key systems, rental-car electronic reservation systems, automated security systems, automated french-fryer machines, electronic speak-and-spell learning aids, automated trust portfolio analysis, and entertainment by robotic characters such as those at Disney World. Automation provides consistent services that may not require the customer to interact with a human service provider. The customer usually benefits by more convenient and faster service, while the service-providing organization may be able to provide more services over a wider geographical area at a lower total cost than without automation. On the negative side, electronic monitoring of workers such as telephone customer-service representatives, reservations and credit card operators, and data-entry and word-processing operators creates mental and physical stress and reduces the workers' control over their own jobs. The computer is always monitoring and never needs a coffee break! Job performance evaluations can be based on numbers, such as keystrokes per minute and time away from the electronic work station. Furthermore, greater skill levels are necessary to repair and maintain automation.

A second approach (Peters and Waterman, 1982, pp. 233–278) can best be characterized as "quality through people." In its simplest form, a charismatic leader, by constantly communicating and motivating his or her employees, can influence them to excel at providing the service. These highly motivated employees can then monitor themselves on the "millions of moments of truth" executed daily by the service delivery system. As Peters and Austin (1985, p. 277) conclude, "The excellent companies have a deeply ingrained philosophy that says, in effect, 'respect the individual,' 'make people winners,' ' let them stand out,' and 'treat people like adults.'" They note that most excellent companies upgrade the status of individual employees by giving them titles such as crew member (McDonald's), cast member (Disney), and associate (Wal-Mart).

The quality-through-people approach has been divided into routine service providers and professional and managerial service providers to highlight the degree of discretion that people have in their jobs. For routine service providers, such as clerks and cashiers, they may find that facility, process, equipment, and job design and company systems and procedures provide little opportunity to conduct their job any way other than the prescribed company way.

As professional judgment replaces routine systems and procedures, the employee or service provider has much more discretion about how to perform the job and handle the service encounter. Professional service organizations rely more on professional managers or service workers, such as vice-presidents of marketing or operations or medical doctors or lawyers, to monitor and control service quality themselves than on the organization's systems and procedures. Haywood-Farmer and others (1985, p. 66) observe that "[professional] employees are hired based largely on their background, education, intelligence, and interpersonal skills. Judgment and discretion are the essence of professionalism."

Chase (1978, 1983) introduces the concept of high- and low-customer-contact employees and service delivery systems. With high customer contact, production efficiency is assumed to be inherently limited because of the uncertainty that the customers introduce into the service creation process. Service delivery systems characterized by low customer contact are seen as being essentially free of this type of uncertainty and therefore capable of high levels of production efficiency. As Chase (1978, p. 138) comments, "From this conceptualization, it follows that service systems with high customer contact are more difficult to control and more difficult to rationalize than those with low customer contact."

How one motivates, trains, and rewards people to monitor and control service quality, therefore, differs markedly between routine and professional service providers and between high- and low-customer-contact employees. Likewise, the definition and measurement of service quality is more difficult and subjective in professional service organizations such as Coopers and Lybrand consulting services and law offices than in routine service organizations such as McDonald's and Marriott Hotels.

The third approach focuses on the systems and procedures of service creation and delivery. Haywood-Farmer and others (1985, p. 66) observe that with this approach, "People are trained thoroughly in the only allowed way to produce and deliver the service. Jobs tend to be small and repetitive. In short, we take a manufacturing view and quality control is similar to that in a manufacturing plant." They cite Levitt's (1972) description of McDonald's service delivery process as an example. With this third approach, managers may observe actual service encounters and record their observations in the form of written comments or numbers. For example, managers at major telephone operator centers routinely listen in on their customer-service representatives (CSRs) as they interact with customers, compare the conversations with standard script dialogues, and record comments about the tone and attitude of the CSRs.

Similarly, a regional audit team of a fast-food chain might use a stopwatch to measure average customer waiting time before placing an order and compare it with a target service quality standard to determine whether corrective action is necessary.

The fourth approach emphasizes influencing customer expectations and employee commitment through external communications. Promotion, advertising, and world-of-mouth communications with the customer all attempt to build up and enhance an image of the service delivery system and the service encounter. What is promised to the customer by these external communications must be provided by the service delivery system (closing the fourth and fifth gaps in Figure 10.1).

These external communications not only help set customer expectations but also affect employee commitment to providing excellent service. Many excellent service companies target as much as a third of their external advertising at their employees, not their customers; employees must meet or exceed the level of service promised in the advertisements. This fourth way to monitor and control service quality also enables measurement of service quality from the customer's (external) perspective. The marketing function usually evaluates the customer's perception of service quality by means of external measurement techniques, such as customer surveys, customer interviews, focus groups, and comment cards.

The Service Quality Map

In most organizations, evaluating marketing and operations service quality performance is a data-oriented management task that involves a large number of variables and observations for many different types of services. Because the marketing and operations functions define and evaluate service quality differently — marketing uses external measurement techniques to evaluate customers' perceptions, and operations measures performance according to internal standards (average processing time, number of units processed in a given period of time, error rates, conformance to script dialogues, and so on) — the different sets of performance-measuring data that they produce are seldom comparable. When management attempts to interpret these differing data to arrive at an overall evaluation of service quality, the result is often extra meetings, unnecessary disagreements within and between functional areas, and poor decision making, all affecting the quality and timing of decisions and ultimately the organization's profitability and market share.

Recognizing that the process is often the service for service-providing organizations, recent work by Collier (1988b, 1989b, forthcoming) attempts to quantitatively define service quality for both marketing and operations. Collier explains the relationships between marketing and operations through a "service quality map," which combines insights gained through flow charting the service delivery process and evaluating customer perceptions of service quality with the power of multivariate data-analysis techniques. A service quality map can describe many independent subsystems and relationships, one highly interrelated network of relationships, or a single subset of a more comprehensive network.

Joreskog and Sorbom (1986) have devised a comprehensive computer program, called LISREL, that can model a wide variety of relationships using techniques such as factor analysis, path analysis, panel analysis, structural equation models, multiple regression, simultaneous equation systems, econometric models, and many other multivariate data-analysis techniques. These techniques can be used to decompose and interpret linear relationships among a set of directly observed (measured) variables as well as hypothetical (unmeasured) variables by assuming certain causal relationships. They can be combined in many ways to produce one comprehensive model, often called a covariance structure model. The cause and effect among variables can be modeled with more or less complex relationships between variables, errors in variables, and errors in equations. Reciprocal causation (that is, X_1 affects X_2, and X_2 affects X_1) is one of many features that can make covariance structure models quite powerful. LISREL was used to estimate all coefficients and evaluate all models discussed in the remainder of this section.

Figure 10.3, a flow chart depicting the general process for

creating and delivering credit card services, illustrates how a service quality map can be used to quantitatively tie together the service quality data from marketing and operations. It captures the major relationships between the internal service quality performance measures used by operations (denoted with the suffix o) and the results of surveys to evaluate customer perceptions of service quality conducted by marketing (denoted with the suffix m). The process illustrated here can be decomposed into one recurative path model defined by the variables Lo, Do, Ro, So, Po, Co, and Cm (subsystem one), one multiple regression model defined by Lo, To, Bo, and Am, and five independent and simple regression models for the relationships between Lo and Lm, Ro and Rm, Do and Dm, So and Sm, and Po and Pm. Each of these seven models is related to one of the seven customer survey service quality criteria.

Figure 10.3 shows simply a flow chart of the process and how management thinks the process is related to customers' perceptions of service quality; it is not itself a service quality map. The simplest service quality map is the correlation coefficient between specific pairs of marketing and operations service quality criteria. For example, in the process illustrated in Figure 10.3, the operations area measured on-line availability (Lo) as the percentage of total prime-time hours the system was available for customer use and inquiries, and the customer-service department administered a survey to determine customers' satisfaction with on-line availability (Lm). The customers' reaction to the degree of on-line service was captured by a positive 0.715 correlation factor between Lo and Lm. Even this simple statistic took much of the human interpretation of the data out of the service quality evaluation process and eliminated some management disagreements.

Unfortunately, direct relationships among independent paired variables are the exception, not the rule, and that is where the power of covariance structure modeling helps model more complex networks. An examination of subsystem one of the process illustrated in Figure 10.3 will demonstrate how service quality maps can be used in this way (Collier, forthcoming, contains a more complete discussion, including statistical

Figure 10.3. Marketing and Operations Service Quality Relationships for Credit Card Processing.

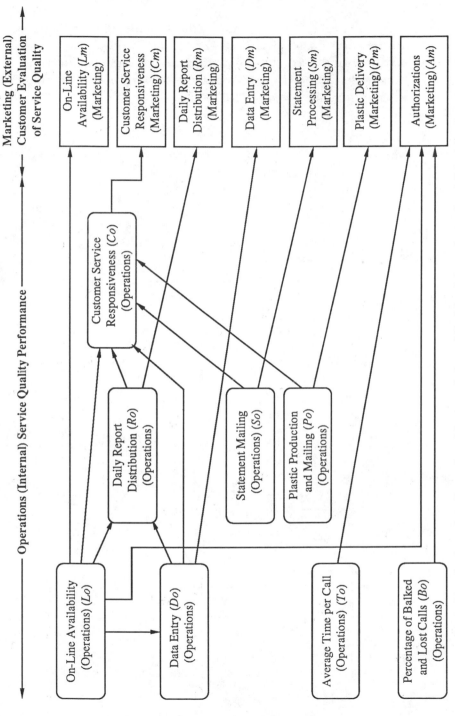

Source: Collier, forthcoming. Reproduced by permission of *Decision Sciences* journal published by the Decision Sciences Institute at Georgia State University, Atlanta, GA.

details). The relationships among the variables of subsystem one are reproduced in Figure 10.4, with the appropriate LISREL notation for the structural equation model. The structural equation model defined by Joreskog and Sorbom (1986, p. I.6) can be written in general form as follows:

$$y = \beta y + \Gamma x + \zeta \tag{1}$$

where: y = a vector of observed dependent variables measured without error

β = a matrix of coefficients relating dependent variables to one another

Γ = a matrix of coefficients relating the independent variables to the dependent variables

x = a vector of observed independent variables measured without error

ζ = a vector of errors in equations

The four structural equations based on equation 1 that characterize the relationships shown in Figure 10.4 are as follows:

Figure 10.4. Path Analysis Model of Subsystem One.

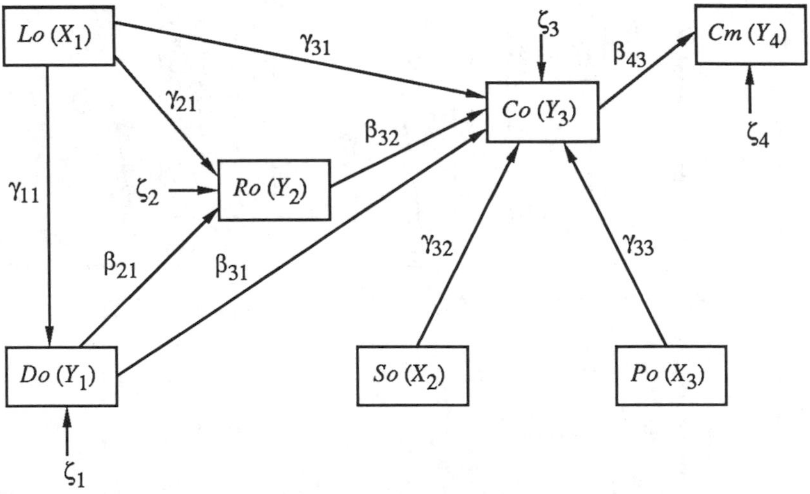

Source: Collier, forthcoming. Reproduced by permission.

**Table 10.1. Parameter Estimates for Management's Model of
Customer-Service Responsiveness.**

Model Parameter	Estimates for Model 1
β_{21}	0.161
β_{31}	0.376
β_{32}	0.006
β_{43}	0.832
γ_{11}	0.585
γ_{21}	0.373
γ_{31}	0.381
γ_{32}	-0.301
γ_{33}	0.264
ζ_1	0.658
ζ_2	0.765
ζ_3	0.371
ζ_4	0.309

Source: Collier, forthcoming. Reproduced by permission.

$$y_1 = \qquad\qquad + \gamma_{11}x_1 \qquad\qquad + \zeta_1 \qquad (2)$$

$$y_2 = \beta_{21}y_1 \qquad + \gamma_{21}x_1 \qquad\qquad + \zeta_2 \qquad (3)$$

$$y_3 = \beta_{31}y_1 + \beta_{32}y_2 + \gamma_{31}x_1 + \gamma_{32}x_2 + \gamma_{33}x_3 + \zeta_3 \qquad (4)$$

$$y_4 = \qquad \beta_{43}y_3 + \qquad\qquad\qquad + \zeta_4 \qquad (5)$$

Careful examination of these relationships reveals how equations 2 through 5 were formulated. That is, these four equations describe the causal relationships shown in Figure 10.4. These causal relationships were hypothesized by management prior to any multivariate data analysis; that is, this was how management thought that the service quality variables were related. The question now is whether the service quality data support management's hypothesized causal structure model.

The LISREL parameter estimates for the relationships documented in Figure 10.4 and equations 2 through 5 are summarized in Table 10.1. Since the original data were standardized, the relative magnitude of the beta (β) and gamma (γ) parameter estimates and their associated operational activities indicate their relative importance in determining the customer's perception of customer service responsiveness (Cm). For example, the timeliness of data entry (Do) was very important for customer-service responsiveness (Co): $\beta_{31} = 0.376$. Thus, equations 2 through 5 quantitatively relate the customer's perception of service quality to the actual performance of the credit card delivery process. This is the essence of a service delivery map.

Once these equations and parameter estimates have been developed, they can be used to answer many interesting questions, such as the following:

- Where in the operations process can we get the most improvement in perceived service quality for the least cost?
- What will happen to the customer's evaluation of service quality if operations' performance on criterion X deteriorates by a given percentage?
- Where in the service delivery process is overachievement of service quality unnecessary?
- Can we tie a manager's performance appraisal into downstream departments' performance?
- Can we use the insights gained from service quality maps to improve customer survey design?
- What standards of service quality performance make the most sense?
- What is the relative importance of key operational activities from the customer's viewpoint?

By providing answers to questions such as these, service quality maps can help managers to gain a competitive advantage in the marketplace.

Consider, for example, managers of a bank's credit card delivery process trying to decide between two projects (Collier, 1989b, forthcoming). Project A would provide their main computers with a more reliable backup electrical power supply and more backup computer systems and procedures. The managers estimate that project A would cost $50,000 and increase on-line availability (Lo) by 1 percent. Project B would improve the systems, procedures, and training of personnel responsible for plastic production and mailing (Po). Project B is also expected to cost $50,000, and they estimate that it would improve plastic

Table 10.2. Service Quality Map for Customer-Service Responsiveness.

Project	Cost	Projected Operational Improvement	Predicted Increase in Cm
A	$50,000	1% increase in on-line availability (Lo)	5.5 points
B	$50,000	3% improvement in plastic production and mailings (Po)	1.5 points

production and mailing by 3 percent. Which project would improve the customer's perception of customer-service responsiveness (Cm) the most? Use of a service quality map (see Table 10.2) shows that the $50,000 would best be spent on improving on-line availability (Lo). Equations 2 through 5 and the path analysis model shown in Figure 10.4 predict that this project would increase the customer's perception of customer-service responsiveness (Cm), as measured by a 100-point customer survey scale, from a current base of 92.4 to 97.9, or an increase of 5.5 points. The same amount of money spent on plastic card production, turnaround, and mailing would increase Cm only to 93.9, or an increase of 1.5 points.

Service quality maps do have some disadvantages. For example, they assume that customer surveys provide an accurate measure of service quality from the customer's perspective and that in-house service quality statistics accurately measure how well the service delivery process performs; they are myopic models based on historical relationships and may ignore new customer variables that emerge as conditions change; available marketing and operations service quality performance data may not lend themselves well to sound statistical analyses; and, since the use of service quality maps represents change, it can trigger new personal and organizational relationships between the marketing and operations functions of the service-providing organization.

Still, service quality maps provide the manager with a road map of how excellent service quality is created and delivered as seen through the eyes of the customer. Formulating all the equations and parameter estimates necessary to develop service quality maps forces managers to better understand their service delivery processes and the customer's perception of service quality. Service quality maps tie the marketing and operations functions together and force managers to "think service management."

Implications for Future Research

Any research on service quality requires at least a minimal understanding of business strategy, marketing, operations, and human resource management and familiarity with the many different types of service industries. Unfortunately, universities usually reward faculty who specialize in one very narrow part of a discipline; historically, there has been little incentive for doctoral candidates or young faculty members to do research on service quality. It is our hope that books such as this will encourage more research on service quality and enlighten faculty about the need for an interdisciplinary approach to research on issues concerning service management. The term *service management* itself suggests an interdisciplinary approach to managing service organizations; it is a term that fortunately is growing in popularity.

As to what the subject of such research should be, the possibilities are numerous. There are very few service quality concepts, paradigms, or techniques to help practicing managers or to provide a basis for a theory of service quality. The field could greatly benefit from efforts such as the following:

- More integrative and collaborative research efforts among the traditional disciplines of engineering, operations, marketing, human resource management, psychology, and business strategy.
- More research on how to quantify the cost of poor service quality and the value of a loyal customer and to incorporate these dollar values into traditional capital budgeting, profit-and-loss, and control systems of the organization.
- More research on how best to organize, motivate, train, and

reward employees to achieve excellent service quality. For example, do the traditional models of functional organizational structure support or hinder excellent service encounters?

- More research on the impact of culture on service quality concepts and models, with a focus on international markets.
- More research on coordinating and evaluating marketing and operations service quality information.
- Better teaching materials to train students and practicing managers about service quality.

Implications for Practicing Managers

Most practicing managers work hard to define, measure, set standards for, monitor, control, and evaluate service quality. To be successful, this effort takes people who simultaneously think about marketing, operations, and human relations—that is, think "service management." It takes commitment and leadership from top-level management. It takes managers who become "service quality champions." It takes the allocation of company resources frequently with little immediate and tangible evidence of economic benefit. It takes courage and perseverance. But, as some companies have already demonstrated in the marketplace, over the long term, it means more profitability and greater market share than ever before. As noted elsewhere (Collier, 1987a, p. 90), "For most service organizations with hundreds of facilities, thousands of employees, hundreds of service packages, and millions of microactivities that result in good service, a permanent service quality management system is needed. A permanent, efficient, and effective service quality management system is a long-term commitment to the customer."

Practicing managers need better models and techniques to help them manage service quality. The following suggestions can help managers enhance their understanding of and knowledge about service quality:

- Rotate managers in and out of key functional areas such as marketing and operations so that they gain the service management perspective from their experiences.
- Support research on service quality by providing funds, company data, and access to practicing managers.
- Read and study service quality literature from functional areas and viewpoints different from your own. Visit customers, employees, and salespeople. See service quality from as many vantage points as possible.
- Work with university faculty to develop courses on service management and service quality. Create job opportunities in the area of service quality in your company and encourage students to major in this field of study.

In the long term, more interest from researchers, students, and practicing managers in how to define, measure, set standards for, monitor and control, evaluate, and manage service quality will enhance the service encounter for millions of customers worldwide. Managers must plan for service quality just as they plan for sales, budgets, capacity expansion, advertising campaigns, acquisitions, and the like. Excellent service encounters occur because of dedicated people who care about and listen to the customer.

References

Chase, R. B. "Where Does the Customer Fit in a Service Operation?" *Harvard Business Review*, 1978, *56* (6), 137–142.

Chase, R. B. "The Customer Contact Model for Organization Design." *Management Science*, 1983, *29* (9), 1037–1050.

Collier, D. A. *Service Management: The Automation of Services*. Englewood Cliffs, N.J.: Prentice-Hall, 1985.

Collier, D. A. "The Customer Service and Quality Challenge." *Service Industries Journal*, 1987a, 7 (1), 77–90.

Collier, D. A. *Service Management: Operating Decisions*. Englewood Cliffs, N.J.: Prentice-Hall, 1987b.

Collier, D. A. The Ohio State University Executive Development Program, Columbus, July 31–Aug. 12, 1988a.

Collier, D. A. "Evaluating Marketing and Operations Service Quality Information." Paper presented at the Quality in Services Symposium, University of Karlstad, Sweden, Aug. 14–17, 1988b.

Collier, D. A. "Process Moments of Trust: Analysis and Strategy." *Service Industries Journal*, 1989a, *9* (2), 205–221.

Collier, D. A. "Service Quality Maps: The Power of Sensitivity Process." Paper presented at the national meeting of the Decision Science Institute, New Orleans, Nov. 22–23, 1989b.

Collier, D. A. "A Service Quality Process Map for Credit Card Processing." *Decision Sciences*, forthcoming.

Crosby, P. B. *Quality Is Free.* New York: McGraw-Hill, 1979.

Crosby, P. B. *Quality Newsletter #6.* Winter Park, Fla.: Quality College, 1981.

Czepiel, J. A., Solomon, M. R., and Surprenant, C. F. (eds.). *The Service Encounter: Managing Employee/Customer Interaction in Service Businesses.* Lexington, Mass.: Lexington Books, 1985.

Donnelly, J. H., Berry, L. L., and Thompson, T. W. *Marketing Financial Services.* Homewood Ill.: Dow Jones–Irwin, 1985.

Garvin, D. A. *Managing Quality.* New York: Free Press, 1988.

Haywood-Farmer, J., and others. "Controlling Service Quality." *Business Quarterly*, 1985, *50* (4), 62–67.

Hostage, G. M. "Quality Control in a Service Business." *Harvard Business Review*, 1975, *53*, 98–106.

Joreskog, K. G., and Sorbom, D. "LISREL." (4th ed.) Mooseville, Ind.: Scientific Software, 1986.

Krajewski, L. J., and Ritzman, L. P. *Operations Management: Strategy and Analysis.* Reading, Mass.: Addison-Wesley, 1987.

LaLonde, B. J. "Customer Service." In J. F. Robeson and R. G. House (eds.), *Distribution Handbook.* New York: Free Press, 1985.

Lehtinen, J. R. "Global Customer Service Style." Paper presented at the Quality in Services Symposium, University of Karlstad, Sweden, Aug. 14–17, 1988.

Leonard, F. S., and Sasser, W. E. "The Incline of Quality." *Harvard Business Review*, 1982, *60*, 163–171.

Levitt, T. "Production-Line Approach to Service." *Harvard Business Review*, 1972, *50* (5), 41–52.

Lewis, R. C., and Booms, B. H. "The Marketing Aspects of Service Quality." In L. L. Berry, G. L. Shostack, and G. D. Upah (eds.), *Emerging Perspectives on Service Marketing.* Chicago: American Marketing Association, 1983.

Luchs, R. "Successful Businesses Compete on Quality—Not Costs." *Long Range Planning,* 1986, *19* (1), 12–17.

"Making Service a Potent Marketing Tool." *Business Week,* June 11, 1984, pp. 164–170.

Parasuraman, A., Zeithaml, V. A., and Berry, L. L. "A Conceptual Model of Service Quality and Its Implications for Future Research." *Journal of Marketing,* 1985, *49,* 41–50.

Peters, T., and Austin, N. *A Passion for Excellence.* New York: Random House, 1985.

Peters, T., and Waterman, R. H. *In Search of Excellence: Lessons from America's Best-Run Companies.* New York: Harper & Row, 1982.

Quinn, J. B., and Gagnon, C. E. "Will Services Follow Manufacturing into Decline?" *Harvard Business Review,* 1986, *64,* 95–105.

Reip, R. W. "Make the Most of Customer Complaints." *Quality Progress,* Mar. 1988, pp. 24–25.

Riddle, D. I. "Culturally Determined Aspects of Service Quality." Paper presented at the Quality in Services Symposium, University of Karlstad, Sweden, Aug. 14–17, 1988.

Rosander, A. C. *Applications of Quality Control in the Service Industries.* New York: Marcel Dekker, 1985.

Roth, A. V., and van der Velde, M. *The Future of Retail Banking Delivery Systems.* Rolling Meadows, Ill.: Bank Administration Institute, 1988.

Russell, G., Grant, M., and Szonskl, W. "Pul-eeze! Will Somebody Help Me?" *Time,* Feb. 2, 1987, pp. 48–57.

Sasser, W. E., Olsen, R. P., and Wyckoff, D. D. *Management of Service Operations: Text, Cases, and Readings.* Boston: Allyn & Bacon, 1978.

Sherowski, H. "Marketing Through Facilities Design." In L. L. Berry (ed.), *Emerging Perspectives on Service Marketing.* Chicago: American Marketing Association, 1983.

Sturm, A. C. "Hospitals Must Learn to Keep Customers." *Modern Healthcare,* Feb. 26, 1988, p. 68.

Thompson, P., DeSouza, G., and Gale, B. T. "The Strategic Management of Service Quality." *Quality Progress*, June 1985, pp. 20–25.

Williams, R. H., and Zigli, R. M. "Ambiguity Impedes Quality in the Service Industries." *Quality Progress*, July 1987, pp. 14–17.

11

The Impact of Information
Technologies on Operations
of Service Sector Firms

Albert H. Rubenstein
Eliezer Geisler

This chapter examines the role of information technology in the operations of the service-sector firm and its impacts on the effectiveness of the firm's operations and competitive posture. What does the information system (IS) or information technology (IT) activity or group really contribute to a company and its strategic objectives? Our research involves the exercise of caution and a careful testing of existing measures in some of the leading service firms, such as banks, insurance companies, professional services, communication, transportation, and retail sales firms, in trying to answer this question. Most service companies do not venture into direct measurement of the *strategic* impacts of information systems and technology. They understand the problems of imputation and attempt to measure only some of the impacts of the IS or IT activity on the operating units. Thus, they regard IS or IT primarily as a *support* function, with well-defined and relatively easily measurable contributions to the internal efficiency of the operating units.

The key characteristic that distinguishes between companies that regard IT mainly as a support function and those that assign it a more strategic role is the organizational status of the chief information officer, or CIO (in most service companies the manager or director of the IS unit). In companies that assign a strategic role to IT, the CIO is often a member of the select group of top executives who run the company. Thus, in these companies, the CIO has access to the chief executive officer informally as well as through formal channels, and his or her inputs to strategic decisions are sought and respected. In most service companies, where IT is regarded as merely a support function, with almost no strategic role, the CIO (if there is one) functions primarily as the head of the IS unit, reporting to the chief financial officer or another top executive. In these cases the CIO has very little access to the chief executive officer and very little input to strategic decisions.

For a service firm to change its view of IT as primarily a support function, measured by near-term *efficiency* criteria rather than longer-term *effectiveness* criteria, both management and professional IT personnel have to view IT from a strategic perspective. This requires the use of criteria, indicators, and measures specifically developed to assess the strategic contributions of IT to that particular firm rather than general or vague output and impact criteria that may not apply to the firm's specific circumstances and needs. In the following sections, we introduce and discuss a methodology that can help accomplish this in a cost–effective manner. First, we briefly describe how our research group at Northwestern University entered into research on indicators of effectiveness, first for science and technology or R&D and more recently for information technology in the service industries. Next, we discuss some particular indicators of the effectiveness of information technology in the firm. Then, drawing on the preliminary results of our field surveys, we describe different approaches to IT used by various service-industry firms. Finally, we offer some recommendations for developing or improving the strategic view of IT in the service firm.

Background: Research on Measuring Effectiveness

This chapter reflects the research and practical interests of the authors over many years (Rubenstein, 1953, 1957, 1960,

1966, 1968, 1971, 1976, 1979, 1988; Rubenstein and others, 1973; Geisler and Rubenstein, 1980, 1986, 1988). A major issue that has driven this continuing interest has been a comparison of the immediate with the longer-term and the direct with the indirect outputs and impacts of service operations. Until about 1986, when the Center for Information Technology was formed at Northwestern University, our research focused primarily on technology-related service activities and functions inside the firm, such as R&D, engineering, product development, strategic technology planning, operations research and management sciences (OR/MS), technical intelligence, scientific and technical information, and the impact of a given organization (firm, government agency, research institute) on other organizations and sectors (for example, agriculture, environment, energy, space, health care, industry, defense). In other words, we have been interested in what an organization contributes to its environment, both directly and indirectly.

In our earliest research (Rubenstein, 1953, 1957), we tried to distinguish between the direct, immediate outputs of a given service activity and the less easily identified and measured indirect or long-term outputs and impacts. In addition to the long time periods involved in such activities as new product development, the difficult economic accounting and political problem of imputation of costs and returns to a contributory service activity makes a straightforward "credit and blame" accounting system very difficult if not impossible for most service activities. The question always arises: What did this group, function, activity, or department *really* contribute to an ultimate outcome or impact, such as changes in maintenance of sales, profit, and growth levels and reputation and survival of the organization? Most responses to this kind of question are based on arbitrary assumptions and models (production functions) for a given activity. For example, the purchasing function can either be viewed as a necessary component of a firm's activities and assigned an arbitrary "amount" of credit for obtaining the right goods and services at the right price at the right time and place or be ignored in the attempt to "cost out" all the major contributing functions. Attempts to do the former systematically lead to many of the ambiguities and conflict-ridden processes of setting transfer prices within the firm. The purpose of such exercises is not trivial, however, since credible pricing, make-or-buy, cost-reduction, and reward-punishment decisions require such information.

In our current research on the role of information technology in the whole service firm, we are not yet trying to tackle the imputation problem head on. We are heavily engaged in a necessary prior step—identifying and attempting to measure, where feasible, levels of outputs or impacts of the information components of service firms in terms of their immediacy and directness and their potential effects on other operations, the firm's products (services), and the service firm itself. This chapter, then, reports our progress to date and our plans for the future in researching the role of information technology in the management of operations within the service firm and its impacts on the performance of the firm in the marketplace and in its financial environment. In the next section, we introduce a procedure for developing indicators for the outputs and impacts of information technology at various stages.

Indicators of Effectiveness

A starting point for exploring the role of information technology in the management of service-sector firms and the service operations of other firms is to ask the simple-minded question "What is information technology (the aggregate of computers, telecommunication systems, paper handling systems, software, and so on) expected to do for the firm, in both the short term and the longer term?" The obvious answer is "make sure that the proper information gets to the right people at the right time, in the right form, at a reasonable cost." That is helpful as a starting place for research and improved practice, but only as a very first step. Our work and that of other researchers and the managers responsible for information technology must go far beyond that and address the question of how one identifies and, where feasible, measures the right level of information (amount, timing, place, quality, cost, and so on). A key to going beyond the platitudinous and the unmeasurable is to use the indicators approach, which has been the basis of our research for several decades. Indicators are descriptors that enable the manager, the researcher, or the employee to express or recognize in operational terms the actual, the intended, and the potential outputs and impacts of an information technology activity.

In this section, we present some initial indicators that are capable of operational definition and, in many cases, measurement along some scale or according to a set of agreed-on attributes for various levels of the information functions in the firm. While there is a great deal of generalizability at various levels of abstraction between the service firm as an organizational and economic entity and the service operation within a manufacturing firm or other type of organization, emphasis in this chapter is on the role of information technology in the service firm. In both cases, the information technology operation serves clients or customers with needs and constraints, including limited resources to pay for the information technology or the information components of goods and services, and personal preferences for the form and method by which information is provided to them.

Certainly the routine information flows in banks, insurance companies, and other service firms (and the information components of nonservice firms) have been in place for a long time and are constantly undergoing change to make them faster or cheaper or to meet some other efficiency or productivity requirement. Seldom, however, are the information flows systematically examined to determine who needs them, what they are doing for the firm, whether they can be done in an entirely different manner, how their outputs and impacts can be measured, or how they relate to the main activities and purposes of the firm. Improvements in information systems through the introduction of electronics and other technology have often, though not always, followed an incremental path in which productivity of a given operation or substitution of technology for labor is the main driver. A few firms have taken a basic, all-encompassing look, with potentially remarkable results. But most service firms have only nibbled along the edge of this major opportunity for radical improvements in production and delivery of information services, both as part of internal operations and as key components of the services that they provide to their clients or customers.

In this section, we explore some specific indicators that can be useful both in analyzing the outputs and impacts of information systems and in providing managers of such functions and their superiors and clients or customers with tools for monitoring and evaluating impacts and outputs. Some of these indicators can be converted into direct measures such as scales, attributes, or binary scores, since their operational definitions contain implicit measurement possibilities. Others will require careful application of experience and insight as well as negotiation to establish what are "reasonable" descriptors (indicators and surrogate measures) of performance ("we can't put a dollar value on it, but we agree that they are doing okay on this indicator").

Internal Direct Indicators. These are illustrative indicators of the actual performance of the information functions — what they actually do and produce. These indicators may or may not have any intrinsic value or longer-term or significant impacts on the overall performance of the firm. That remains to be seen as the imputation process and the "path of impact" for each indicator are explored. At the most trivial level, for example, one of the things that information people (as well as most other people in the firm) do is "go for coffee." A case could be made that "without coffee, people will not be alert or do their work properly." However, to preserve our sanity, such activities will have to be subsumed in an "other factor or factors" global indicator in which it is probably hopeless to trace their impacts in a credible and significant way. This, by the way, is not a new idea. More than thirty-five years ago, when one of us was involved with the Institute for Reduction of Industrial Absenteeism (an early entry into the field of productivity studies in industry), one of the consultants identified "Coke machines" as the key to productivity! Before and since then, the effects of music, wall color, and other amenities to productivity have been seriously studied. All of these factors probably do contribute to productivity or, ultimately, effectiveness of the function and the firm, but they are part of the measurement "noise" in attempts to identify a limited number of significant indicators.

A more significant example of an internal direct indicator is the cost of "producing" and delivering the information, including the costs of acquiring, maintaining, and upgrading (through training) the human resources in the information areas of the firm and the costs of capital and other equipment and systems, including software, much of which are expensed currently. While these may seem to be input indicators, they are included among direct output measures because they help to determine the potential costs and value of the information outputs to the clients or customers. A category, batch, or piece of information that costs too much to be economically justifiable as part of the firm's products (that is, services to customers or clients) is not adequately meeting the needs for information. Other direct internal indicators include the speed and timeliness of response to specific flows (whether standard reports and expected software are received when needed by internal clients) and the quality of the information produced—accuracy, legibility, clarity of presentation, supporting evidence where needed, relation to other information that will support or use it downstream.

Internal Indirect Indicators. One such indicator is the unit's track record in anticipating and reacting to changes in needs for information and means of delivering it—whether the information activity is up to date on the changing state of the art and the potential for improvements through technology. Another is the downstream costs of further processing and delivering the information that other activities in the firm have to use or contribute to. For example, the focal information unit may produce information or information products quickly and at a seemingly low cost, but downstream functions may have to undo a lot of its work, spending time and resources clarifying it, refining it, and correcting mistakes (for example, in software). A third internal indirect indicator is the unit's contribution to new product (service) development by providing new ideas, improved technology-based features, and greater reliability, quality, and sales appeal.

Indicators Specific to Clients. There are a great many possible indicators of client or customer satisfaction and comfort with the information provided as part of the products (services) of the service firm. Market researchers have many ways of testing such satisfaction, including such direct indicators as complaints and such indirect but significant indicators as brand loyalty, repeat orders, and contract renewals. Many of the products of information technology for the service firm involve embedded information, software, and aids to use (for example, instruction manuals and brochures, such as the often-maligned booklets accompanying insurance policies). Some illustrative indicators are perception of awareness, follow-up, and caring for the needs and desires of the clients or customers; maintenance and upgrading of embedded and accompanying software and information aids; cost saving from product improvements and applications of information technology being passed on to the client or customer — (for example, is the time saved by a partner in a law firm being reflected in the charges for the firm's professional services?); and the accessibility and ease of use of the information and the service in which it is embedded (is it difficult for the customer to use the product or service, or is consideration for the customer evident in its design and delivered form — for example, telephone access to people who can credibly answer questions about a mortgage, a bank account, a lost or late order?). Many more potentially useful and measurable indicators can be found in the marketing and market research literature.

General Indicators of Long-Term Impacts on the Firm. Here is where we recycle to the earlier questions of how information technology is affecting the firm's costs and benefits and why money is being invested in acquiring, further developing, and maintaining information technology — especially expensive and exotic new equipment, products, software, and systems. Ideally, one would like to be able to detect and impute the impacts of information technology on global measures such as growth, profitability, survival, and market share. In some cases, such as during the short period of proprietary advantage provided by a new service, it is possible to assign credit in some fashion to the individuals or groups that invented, developed, refined, or commercialized the service embedding a new information technology or application. Imputing contributions of information technology to longer-term survival, growth, and market share is more difficult—in most cases, impossible. However, some indicators of contributions to the fortunes of the firm may be identified and measured. Examples of these include overall quality of service to customers; warranty and legal costs associated with given products or services; effective use of capital funds, particularly working capital; and the ability of the firm to recover from mistakes, bad market reactions, or threats from competitors—having new features and even new products ready for quick commercialization when needed to counter a competitor's threat or changes in the environment.

Approaches to Information Technology by Service Firms

As a starting point for our research on indicators of effectiveness of information technology in service firms, we initiated an extensive survey to examine the actual practices of service firms in measuring the outputs and impacts of their information technology. We have surveyed more than fifty service industry companies in four sectors: financial companies (banks, insurance companies, and investment brokerage houses); transportation; food distribution; and professional services (engineering and advertising). Our survey identified three broad approaches that service companies take to their information technology. These approaches, which primarily reflect the attitudes of top management toward information systems in general and new information technology in particular, are (1) an expressed desire to *lead* in the sector or the industry,

(2) an implicit or explicit desire to *follow* other firms in the sector, and (3) lack of a declared or inferable strategy.

Leading the Sector or Industry. This approach to information technology is manifested in top management's declared desire to lead the sector or the industry in installing unproven, perhaps risky hardware, software, and general information systems in various aspects of the firm's operations. Such an approach tends to be passed along to the information systems function in the form of a policy explaining the company's reliance on information technology as a strategic variable, as well as in the form of support to the information systems function. One company using this approach is a very large bank headquartered in the Midwest. The bank assigned its vice-president in charge of information to sit in on meetings of the top echelons of the bank. A comprehensive plan for utilization of information technology was developed, with inputs from IS and with the assistance of external consultants. One outcome of this plan was the generation of an early version of combined periodical account reports to depositors. This was a major innovation in reporting to clients, which involved a certain degree of risk, since clients' dissatisfaction with the revised format might have caused some market share losses.

Many of the companies that indicate that they espouse the leadership approach are identified by other companies in the sector and the industry as leaders—as the companies that tend to be the first out with new technology in the information area. These companies also tend to utilize some of the effectiveness indicators mentioned earlier in this chapter to evaluate their information technology. They are apt to include in the analysis and evaluation of their information systems and technology some indicators specific to clients as well as general indicators of long-term impacts on the company.

Following the Sector or Industry. The majority of service companies that we have surveyed declare themselves to be followers in their sector or industry. This approach is usually evident in the indifference on the part of top management to the potential strategic value of information and information technology and weak financial and moral support to the IS unit. These companies tend to adopt only proven systems and to avoid radical IT approaches and the introduction of untested hardware and software. In evaluating their information systems and technology, they tend to concentrate primarily on internal indicators of actual performance of the systems, using them to assess the operational efficiency of the systems and the contributions of the technology to improvements in the productivity of operating units. Emphasis is thus placed on indicators of timeliness, accessibility, quality, cost, and the like. Some companies with this approach also utilize internal indirect indicators, such as downstream costs and contributions to new products and services, principally improved reliability and added features of a product or a service. An example of this approach is a major food retailer in the metropolitan Chicago area that delayed the installation of scanning equipment at its checkout counters, although these have already been used in other regions of the country. "We'll wait till Safeway starts, then we'll try it here," the company's executive in charge of information systems told our interviewers. He clearly stated that the policy of the company is to take minimum risk and to implement technological innovations in the information-processing field only after they have been proved by others to be effective and relatively risk-free.

Lack of Declared Strategy. Some 20 percent of the service companies we interviewed have no declared strategic approach to information systems and technology. They tend to make decisions about their information needs and technology on a case-by-case basis, without an overall guiding strategy. These companies tend to provide little support to their IS units, and their evaluation of information technology tends to concentrate almost entirely on the use of internal direct (cost-saving and efficiency) indicators. Another characteristic of these companies is the reliance of top management on the IS manager primarily for inputs to the technical, internal aspects rather than the strategic aspects of decisions about information technology. A good example in this category is a transportation company whose major line of business is small-package delivery. This company lacks a coherent approach to or policy regarding information technology and tends to lag substantially behind other companies in the industry in implementing new technologies, primarily because of the inability of its management to decide on the economic viability of a given technology. The company's IS unit is relatively small and powerless, even by the standards of its industry.

Integrating Information Technology into Management Functions

Most service companies have developed modes of integrating their information systems and information technology into the key management functions, such as marketing, inventory control, purchasing, finance and accounting, and human resources. As in the manufacturing industries, most service companies tend to install information technology in a decentralized manner for different functions of the firm, without a comprehensive and coordinated plan of action. This leads to a situation in which "islands of automation" are formed. A marketing function of a major service firm may purchase and install an information system to accomplish well-defined goals of the function (for example, sales forecasts, market segmentation) while another function installs a different information system to attain its own specific goals, with little coordination between systems and technologies.

Service companies that have assigned a strategic role to their IT function are more likely to channel efforts toward coordination of their information technologies among the various management functions. Notable examples of successful applications of information technologies in service firms have helped to create a popular belief that these companies, and perhaps the service industries in general, have managed to attain significant competitive advantages through these applications. Airlines reservation systems, automated teller machines, some package and delivery companies' tracking systems, and some proprietary software used by insurance companies have intensified the public image of highly proficient companies with a well-developed strategic use of information technology. Such an image is somewhat exaggerated. However, our survey of service firms did identify several large companies with well-publicized proprietary information technologies and systems. One insurance company, for example, has a state-of-the-art information system in its marketing division. The system contains information on potential customers, their demographic, social, and economic attributes, and other variables of interest to insurance marketers. The company also has a centralized information system that provides its salespeople with instantaneous pricing for complex insurance policies and a sophisticated system for its premium collections and investments. Although all these systems enhance the productivity of the specific functions they serve, most are inadequately coordinated and do not usually allow for satisfactory exchanges of information. Thus, when top management needs a cross-functional report, the report is prepared by a special staff that has to analyze various functional areas and translate and assemble individual reports into one comprehensive overview of strategic value to the chief executive officer.

Another area affected by information technology is human resources. With the emphasis on technologies that improve accessibility, speed, accuracy, timeliness, and other such attributes of information, workers feel the need to keep up with the technology as well as with the advances in their functional areas. Training and professional development are not always effective in bringing about rapid adaptation to the new technology, so many service companies find it difficult to implement new technologies and have them working smoothly as soon as they had planned. Shortcuts and compromises abound, leading to lengthy trial periods, "debugging" of human errors, and the overall feeling of a need to learn to live with untested systems, imperfect yet innovative technologies, and a variety of behavioral problems in implementing state-of-the-art information technologies. An illustrative example emerges in our study. Several large banks and two insurance companies have made large-scale investments in revised software for internal reporting. In one case, after a whole year of introducing the "new system," a bank's top management was told that employee training and "debugging" and adaptation costs would almost double the cost of the system. In another case, the performance of an insurance company's system was much lower than had been expected. In both cases, top management had to reduce their expectations, take shortcuts, and compromise on what they expected the system to do, given its high cost.

Managerial Implications

To date, information technologies have contributed to the success of service companies primarily by improving efficiency of the operating functions and units, and this is the criterion that most service companies have used to measure their benefits. Yet these evaluation frameworks and the measures that they utilize generally fail to provide credible answers to the more strategic questions that top management usually pose and other stakeholders of the companies tend to ask: How does information technology help the company to achieve its overall objectives of growth, profitability, and competitive stance? Are we better serving a given segment of our clientele? If so, how? How can or should information technology contribute to such improved service?

Managers of most of the service companies we surveyed seem to be concerned mainly with routine problems and demands, to the extent that many tend to prefer short-term showings of dramatic improvements in productivity and outcomes of individual functions (sales, inventory control, investment portfolio, purchasing) as direct and measurable results of the introduction and the implementation of information technology. Such showings are usually at the expense of improved coordination and strategic utilization of the technologies. The key question is whether service companies that do not limit their use of information technology to improving unit productivity and efficiency but try to integrate it into their longer-term strategic perspective are more successful overall and more resilient than others.

Our survey indicates that some companies that do go beyond mere improvements in productivity to a strategic mode of utilizing IT are perceived by their competitors as more successful than others. We were not able to test such perceptions with statistical data of these firms' performance measures. However, firms in our sample tend to list as the most successful companies in their sector those that we categorized as making a more significant effort to implement information technology from a strategic perspective, as well as giving the IS managers much more influence and power in executive decisions of the company. Managers can increase the success of their efforts by doing the following:

1. Develop a policy regarding information systems and technology for both the short and the long term; it may be simply a few statements pointing out the basic direction in which the firm should go. Make the policy known to all management levels.
2. Involve the manager in charge of information in decisions that require changes in hardware or software; he or she may already have a solution.
3. Tie the information technology issue directly into your strategic planning. Keep asking how information technology fits into the strategic scheme and whether it can provide solutions to particular problems, trends, or situations.
4. Assign a top manager to have overall charge of information systems and technology. Make sure that this area is enjoying "clout" in the organization.

Information technology in service companies may be too important to the long-term welfare of the firm to be left to the sole discretion of IS managers or the part-time attention of top managers. Although it may be difficult to credibly measure the benefits and impacts of IT for individual functions and the company as a whole, service companies are discovering that sooner or later they have to implement strategically focused IT if they are to stay competitive or even in business.

Conclusions and Recommendations

The ideas in this chapter suggest three areas of action for service industry firms interested in enhancing the value of their total investment in information technology. First, refocus, where necessary, the entire set of information technology resources in the firm to meet the company's strategic goals as well as its current tactical ones, such as unit productivity, short-term cost savings, and efficiency of specific operations. These less global targets should, indeed, remain important, but they should be placed in the larger perspective of the firm's competitive posture, its longer-term strategies, and the threats, needs, and opportunities that it is likely to face as the environment changes and competition for the consumer's attention and loyalty increases. Second, examine the resources, organization, and assigned missions for information systems and technology throughout the firm—across divisional, functional, and staff lines. The goal here is to eventually achieve integration and synergy of the existing and planned information systems and technology in the firm with a dual focus on internal operations and externally oriented technology and business strategy. This means more than simply the kinds of routine or obvious efforts at integration that involve standardization of software and equipment and the ability of information systems in different parts of the organization to communicate with and augment each other. It means true integration that ties information systems and technology into the strategic plans of the company, including strategic technology planning, business planning, human resource planning, marketing planning, and financial planning. Third, make a serious effort to apply some of the ideas and approaches discussed in order to provide a better decision base for information technology in the company.

The indicators approach presented here can be used in selecting technology and R&D or systems projects throughout the firm; making make-or-buy decisions—determining the ultimate costs and benefits of a given acquisition or internal development by considering the life cycle of the system or application of information technology; monitoring the operations of information systems throughout the firm to make sure that they are performing according to expectations and in support of the mission of the unit that is using them (operations, marketing, R&D, pricing, billing, inventory, customer service, and so on); and making long-term evaluations of whether the information technology or system has been accomplishing or contributing significantly to the longer-term goals assigned to it. Given the ever-increasing cost of information technology and its crucial role in the service industries firm, such analytical approaches are likely to yield high payoffs.

References

Geisler, E., and Rubenstein, A. H. "A Methodology for Monitoring and Evaluating the Outputs of a Federal Research Laboratory." Paper presented at the ninth annual Department of Defense/Federal Acquisition Institute Acquisition Research Symposium, Annapolis, Md., June 9–11, 1980.

Geisler, E., and Rubenstein, A. H. "Key Measures of Effective Utilization of Application Software in New Production Systems: A Life-Cycle Approach." In Society of Manufacturing Engineers, *Proceedings: Manufacturing Processes, Machines and Systems*. Dearborn, Mich.: Society of Manufacturing Engineers, 1986.

Geisler, E., and Rubenstein, A. H. "How Banks Evaluate Their Information Technology." *Bank Administration*, Nov. 1988, pp. 14–16.

Rubenstein, A. H. "Information Flow: A New Approach for Cornering Trouble Spots in Management." *Columbia Engineering Quarterly*, Nov. 1953.

Rubenstein, A. H. "Setting Criteria for R&D." *Harvard Business Review*, 1957, *35* (1), 95–104.

Rubenstein, A. H. "Integration of Operations Research into the Firm." *Journal of Industrial Engineering*, 1960, *11* (5), 421–428.

Rubenstein, A. H. "Economic Evaluation of Research and Development: A Brief Survey of Theory and Practice." *Journal of Industrial Engineering*, 1966, *17* (11), 615–620.

Rubenstein, A. H. "Some Comments on Training for the Future

of the Management Sciences." *Management Science*, 1968, *14* (11), 727–730.

Rubenstein, A. H. "A Longitudinal Study of the Development of Information Style." In E. Grochla and N. Szyperski (eds.), *Management-Information-Systeme*. Wiesbaden, Germany: Betriebswirtschaflicher Verlag, 1971.

Rubenstein, A. H. "Technical Information, Technical Assistance, and Technology Transfer—The Need for a Synthesis." *R&D Management*, 1976, *6*, 145–150.

Rubenstein, A. H. "R&D Flow Charts Provide Innovation Output Measures." *Industrial Research/Development*, Apr. 1979, pp. 49–52.

Rubenstein, A. H. "In-House R&D on Information Systems and Telecommunication in the Service Industry Firm." Paper presented at the Symposium on Management of the R&D-Marketing Interface, University of Southern California, Feb. 1988.

Rubenstein, A. H, and others. "Behavioral Factors Influencing the Adoption of an Experimental Information System." *Hospital Administration*, 1973, *18* (4), 27–43.

12

Making Continual Improvement a Competitive Strategy for Service Firms

James A. Fitzsimmons

In an article exploring growth strategies for service firms, Carman and Langeard (1980, p. 11) state that "The effect of learning and experience on total unit cost has never been demonstrated in a service situation." On first reading this statement, I was appalled at the implications for management, customers, employees, and the national economy if services once in place could not be improved on. In a nation described as a service economy, the standard of living is in jeopardy if productivity in service firms is not continually enhanced.

The history of economic development is a history of learning from experience and applying this knowledge to improving productivity. For example, Henry Ford has been credited with discovering the revolutionary concept of the moving assembly line in which material is moved past work stations in a factory. However, this idea could have originated from agriculture, where equipment is moved through stationary fields for planting and harvesting. This analogy could be extended to service firms, where customers are moved to or through a process at a fixed facility. Thus, it is possible for lessons about improving productivity learned in one sector of the economy to be applied, with proper translation, in another.

Because economic development generally proceeds from agriculture to manufacturing and then to services (the Clark-Fisher hypothesis [Clark, 1957]), we should be looking at new manufacturing developments for productivity ideas that can be translated by analogy for use by service firms. Since the Carman and Langeard article was published, such a revolutionary manufacturing concept has been discovered.

For the past several years, we have all been students of the Japanese manufacturing philosophy. First, we observed the use of the Kanban system and concluded that the secret must be this novel method of shop-floor control. Further study revealed the emphasis on inventory reduction, and we coined the phrase *just-in-time* (JIT) to describe the process of production with zero inventories. Our understanding of JIT led to an appreciation of its effect on quality improvement. To our surprise, we discovered a method of organizing production that yields high-quality products at low cost. This realization shattered our long-held assumption that quality and cost were a trade-off. The production function itself now becomes a strategic competitive weapon. The success of Japanese penetration into foreign markets is witness to the effectiveness of this competitive strategy.

I believe that a further lesson can be learned from our study of Japanese manufacturing. Identifying inventory as undesirable because it hides mistakes and decouples workers allows us to see its most serious fault. Management and, more importantly, workers are not motivated to engage in problem solving. When inventory is reduced, problems can no longer be buried or sent to a rework area but must be faced immediately by the workers themselves.

The focused factory of Skinner (1974) is automatically achieved with daily attention to incremental improvement in quality and cost reduction. A manufacturing culture is established where everyone is responsible for process and quality improvement. It is not necessary to rely on a staff of industrial and manufacturing engineers to provide ideas for process improvements; instead, the workers dealing with the process every day are asked to use their minds as well as their hands. The competitive implications of the experience curve are well known, and the leading Japanese manufacturing firms have institutionalized the concept in their organizations through the use of JIT.

The concept of making continual improvements in the production process is central to a firm's competitive strength and a nation's productive growth. Since approximately 70 percent of the GNP of the world's leading economic nations is generated by the service sector, a productivity improvement ethic for services is needed to ensure future prosperity.

JIT Benefits in Manufacturing

Our discussion begins with a review of the ancillary benefits that result in a manufacturing environment when a JIT inventory system is introduced. In a work about Japanese manufacturing techniques, Schonberger (1982) revealed the hidden lessons to be found in just-in-time production. As a first step, lot sizes are reduced by making improvements that reduce the setup times. The smaller lot sizes begin a chain of effects that represent significant benefits that go well beyond reduced costs of carrying inventory.

One of the benefits of reduced lot sizes is increased worker motivation. When lot sizes are small, defects are discovered quickly and their causes can easily be traced. This becomes obvious at the lower limit—with a batch size of one, each worker passes parts to the next worker as they are completed. Operations become closely linked and workers dependent on each other. This ensures fast feedback when quality problems arise because work cannot progress by picking out the good parts from a large batch. Thus, quality problems and process imbalance become visible instead of being hidden by inventory that decouples stages in the production process. This heightened awareness results in problem-solving behavior by the affected workers. Ideas for cutting lot sizes, improving delivery performance, and controlling defects originate with those close to the problem source. Workers become dependent on each other, and a team approach to the job is fostered. When a problem occurs, everyone is affected, and the focus of attention is on the problem that has caused a disruption in the flow of production. Problems are viewed as opportunities to improve the manufacturing process or the consistency of product quality. All the benefits that follow from JIT production, such as less inventory in the system, fewer indirect costs, fewer rework hours, less material waste, and smoother output rates, are the result of a structural change in the manufacturing process that automatically encourages workers to become problem solvers. A previously untapped creative resource, workers' minds, is released to improve the production process. The need to avoid errors becomes apparent, so that workers take responsibility for their own production and become committed to doing a good job because of peer expectations.

A powerful feature of JIT production is the intervention of management to stress the system to expose hidden problems and thus to start the improvement cycle again. A deliberate reduction of buffer inventory levels is accomplished by removing Kanban cards from the system. With smaller buffer stocks between work stations, quality and output irregularities become more readily apparent. Thus, management has the ability to continually promote the search for process improvements. Complacency does not drive the experience curve. Thus, unit cost reduction from the learning curve is accelerated, resulting in a competitive strategy based on simultaneously improving quality levels and reducing cost. Previously, a product's cost and quality were considered a trade-off—low quality was associated with low cost. Now the unthinkable—high quality at low cost—is possible. No wonder the Japanese are such formidable competitors.

The Inventory and Waiting Line Analogy

In manufacturing, the focus of our attention is on material resources. JIT views idle material resources or inventory as an "evil" to be eliminated or at least reduced. In services, the focus of our attention is on human resources. The "evils" to be eliminated or reduced are customer waiting lines and idle staff.

Table 12.1. The Inventory and Waiting-Line Analogy.

Feature	Inventory	Waiting Line
Costs	Opportunity cost of capital	Opportunity cost of time
Space	Warehouse	Waiting area
Quality	Poor quality hidden	Negative impression
Decoupling	Promotes independence between production stages	Allows division of labor and specialization
Utilization	Machines kept busy by work-in-process inventory	Servers kept busy by waiting customers
Coordination	Detailed scheduling unnecessary	Avoids matching supply and demand

As Table 12.1 shows, inventory and waiting lines share some common features.

Costs. The cost of a customer waiting in line, like the cost of capital tied up in inventory, is an opportunity cost. Of course, unlike investment in inventory that can be quantified in financial terms, the cost of keeping customers waiting for service is subjective and difficult to quantify. However, as illustrated by the case of a business executive who successfully sued his doctor for time he lost as a result of being kept waiting in the doctor's office, real costs can be associated with customer waiting. The most important of these costs is loss of future business.

Space. Storing inventory requires space and the associated investment in a protective facility. Waiting lines also create the need for unproductive space that must be attractively furnished. Banks have been known to devote half of their expensive real estate to drive-in banking facilities, with most of the area being a driveway.

Quality. As inventory is an excellent place to hide poor quality, the intangibility of service makes quality judgment difficult for customers. Thus, customers use time kept waiting in line and other surrogate measures to evaluate service performance.

As Maister (1985) notes, because excessive waiting is viewed as psychological punishment, it creates a significant negative impression of the service that is difficult to overcome.

Decoupling. Waiting lines also perform some of the same functions in the management of services that inventory did for manufacturing before the advent of JIT. The decoupling function of inventory has been used for years to simplify the management of production operations. Work-in-process inventory allows management to divide the production process into independent departments or stages that can be managed in a decentralized fashion with supervisors and foremen having centralized production control. Waiting lines serve a similar decoupling function by permitting division of labor and specialization. For example, lines forming before a commercial teller at a bank cannot be served by idle retail tellers or, heaven forbid, by a loan officer. Thus, management is able to create different job classifications and pay according to skill requirements, with high-customer-contact tellers paid at entry-level wages. This division of labor has its price in loss of flexibility in responding to customer demands.

Utilization. In manufacturing, work-in-process inventory has traditionally been used to avoid machine or operator starvation. Keeping an inventory of inputs before an operation would ensure high labor and equipment utilization. Waiting customers are used in a similar role to keep service personnel busy and pressured to work at a productive rate. The post office is notorious for employing this strategy as a cost-saving measure, but physicians also keep their waiting rooms full to avoid being idle themselves.

Coordination. Job shops keep high levels of inventory because of the complexity of coordinating the operation. Detailed scheduling of the operation as a whole is impossible, and inventory is used to decentralize the scheduling and allow individual machine centers to focus on selecting jobs from their queue. For service managers, waiting lines are used to store excess demand when it is impossible to adjust service capacity. Restaurants have traditionally used the bar as a staging area for customers who walk in without reservations.

Excessive inventory in a factory or long waiting lines at a service are reflective of poor management. This excessive use of idle resources to create a smooth operation reveals a lazy management unwilling to assume the responsibility of continual process and quality improvement. Such organizations will thus be handicapped in the marketplace without a competitive operations strategy.

Continual Improvement as Part of Organizational Culture

How can continual improvement in process and quality be made a part of the service firm's organizational culture? What is needed is a clear and visible signal that problem solving is required. Excessively long waiting lines of customers or idle servers are obvious indications that the service is not being provided effectively. An effective approach to such problems is redeploying personnel to better serve the customer while maintaining effective utilization of human resources. When the problem is an excessively long waiting line, back-office personnel could assist in performing the service — for example, platform personnel at a bank could open additional teller windows or stockers could help checkout clerks bag groceries in a supermarket. When the problem is front-office idleness, customer-contact personnel could help in the back office — tellers could help prepare the mailing of customer account statements or checkout clerks could help stock shelves.

What can be learned from these experiences to improve the service process in the future? If queues of customers develop at the same time each day, redeployment can be instituted before the lines form instead of in reaction to them. Other ideas could be developed, such as use of an express lane during busy periods or preapproval of checks. Ideas should flow naturally, because service employees are themselves service customers and know instinctively what solutions should guarantee reasonable results. In a bank, for example, rather than opening extra teller windows, it might be more efficient to staff special desks for such time-consuming services as selling travelers' checks and certificates of deposit. A bank employee or even a sign could direct arriving customers to the appropriate server. With this type of approach, the many short transactions are expedited and the congestion eliminated quickly. Customers with minor requests, who are generally in a hurry, will be served promptly. Customers with more demanding requirements are usually more willing to wait, because the ratio of service time to wait time meets their expectations. These examples illustrate the need for improved real-time communication among service personnel. In the JIT environment, this is accomplished by Kanbans and other simple devices. Service firm employees should certainly also be able to create innovative methods to alert their co-workers to changing levels of customer demands and, thus, initiate the necessary redeployment of resources. The resulting interconnectedness will promote a team approach to customer service.

A major distinction between the traditional manufacturing organization and JIT is the source (direction) of production control. In the traditional organization, work is released to the first stage of the production process and pushed through the plant from one station to the next. In the JIT system, production orders originate at final assembly and work is pulled from upstream stages as needed. Thus, the entire production system becomes interconnected, and work is focused on meeting the needs of final demand. Each work station is both a customer for upstream stations and server for downstream stations. The result is a chain of workers acting as one team. With services, the process flow is seldom as well defined as that in manufacturing, and there is thus a need for innovative communication linkage between servers. In JIT manufacturing organizations, work is pulled by final assembly from upstream stations. With services, in contrast, upstream stations, such as the receptionist, are the first to experience customer demand. Thus, these stations will be in a position to provide advance warning to downstream stations to prepare for arriving customers. Ideally, when a customer enters a service system, a "greeter" identifies the customer's particular needs and uses an internal communication system (Kanban) to alert downstream service providers. As in the JIT manufacturing system, the customer "pulls" resources into play as needed.

Some service organizations already use this approach. At McDonald's, for instance, when long lines develop, a service person walks up the line taking orders to speed the transaction time at the counter and possibly to deter customer reneging. At a motor vehicle license and registration office, a greeter is stationed just inside the entry to provide the customers with forms and directions to the appropriate service counter. The most comprehensive example of the service-pull philosophy is found at the Limited retail clothing stores. The stores use electronic cash registers that immediately transmit the details of each sale directly to the company's huge Columbus, Ohio, warehouse. There sales trends are analyzed and orders are placed with factories around the world to meet the demand indicated by the sales figures.

As these examples illustrate, the customer automatically becomes the focus of attention when service employees redeploy their efforts to reduce waiting lines. Peters and Waterman (1982) rediscovered what we always knew—that in a competitive environment, the customer comes first. Thus, even if new ways to improve service are not immediately discovered, at least the customer is aware that special efforts are being made on his or her behalf.

Management Implications

Allowing service employees the discretion to react to customer needs creatively requires changes in organizational structure. Table 12.2 presents some features of the work environment as they are found in the traditional organizational structure and as they would be in a proposed new organizational structure for service organizations. Our proposal begins with the assumption that a service organization operates as an open system in its environment. This does not suggest that some backroom activities cannot be treated as a buffered core. How-

Table 12.2. Organizational Structure and the Work Environment.

Dimension	Traditional Structure	Proposed Structure
System assumption	Closed system	Open system
Job-design premise	Division of labor	Flexibility
Structure	Rigid	Fluid
Relation to others	Individual	Teamwork
Employee orientation	Task	Customer
Management role	Supervisor	Coach
Technology role	Replacing human effort	Assisting service delivery
Information	Efficiency	Effectiveness
Work scheduling	Push	Pull

ever, for customer-contact personnel, we premise job design on the need for flexibility. Adam Smith's concept of "division of labor," although appropriate for the closed systems found in manufacturing, is counterproductive in an open service environment. Flexibility in service jobs means cross-training employees to be able to perform or facilitate each other's activities. Cross-training implies an increased organizational commitment to personnel and, thus, a change in attitude from emphasizing high turnover and use of minimum-wage labor to treating workers with the same respect due customers.

The organizational structure must be fluid to permit the redeployment of personnel to meet fluctuations in customer demand. Back-office personnel must occasionally share the task of serving customers directly. If applied to services, the restrictive union work rules found in manufacturing would nullify the competitive advantage of this operations strategy. Working as a team becomes the norm, with attention focused on the customer instead of mere task completion. The role of management changes from that of the traditional supervisor or checker to that of coach and team builder.

Technology becomes more important as a method to assist in service delivery than as a method to replace human contact. An exception to this approach is the promotion of self-service via devices such as automated tellers and airline ticket-dispensing machines. For example, Southwest Airlines offers a free cocktail to customers using their credit cards to purchase tickets at the self-service machine. This role of the customer as a participant in the service process to increase productivity has been addressed by Lovelock and Young (1979). Computerized information processing will play a central role in this high-tech/high-touch service delivery system. The creative use of information is central to the effective delivery of service and acts as the Kanban to permit the prepositioning of service delivery activities in a "pull" work-scheduling environment.

It is interesting to note the implications of a service "pull" philosophy based on corporate flexibility and real-time information processing as opposed to the traditional mass-marketing "push" philosophy practiced by most manufacturers. In a service pull environment, the operations function becomes critical instead of being taken for granted as it is in the push environment, where marketing is critical. With the exception of some group services, such as lectures, sporting events, and theater, services are not batched but are instead directed at the individual. Without the setup involved in manufacturing, a service pull system can be easily implemented. Customer experience with service pull systems will provide incentive for manufacturers to adopt a more service-oriented approach. Eventually we will witness the transformation from a "push" economy to a "pull" economy.

Conclusion

We began this chapter with the premise that service productivity could be enhanced through application of experience gained in manufacturing. We discussed the competitive success of the Japanese concept of JIT, which provides an environment of continual improvement in manufacturing by focusing on inventory reduction, and its application to waiting lines in services. We found that focusing service personnel on waiting-line reduction creates a problem-solving environment that fosters continual improvement in process and quality. We also found that such a focus requires a new management style and organizational structure. Thus, we are faced with a potential revolution in the way we view work in a service economy. We now have the opportunity to fully engage the entire range of human talents in the delivery of services. No longer must employees be expected to spend their day at a repetitive, boring task with limited human interaction, as they often must do in manufacturing. Instead, work could become an enjoyable experience providing a sense of accomplishment in the most rewarding human endeavor, serving others.

References

Carman, J. M., and Langeard, E. "Growth Strategies for Service Firms." *Strategic Management Journal*, 1980, *1*, 7–22.

Clark, C. *The Conditions of Economic Progress.* (3rd ed.) London: Macmillan, 1957.

Lovelock, C. H., and Young, R. F. "Look to Consumers to Increase Productivity." *Harvard Business Review*, 1979, *57* (3), 168–178.

Maister, D. H. "The Psychology of Waiting Lines." In J. A. Czepiel, M. R. Solomon, and C. F. Surprenant (eds.), *The Service Encounter: Managing Employee/Customer Interaction in Service Businesses.* Lexington, Mass.: Lexington Books, 1985.

Peters, T. J., and Waterman, R. H., Jr. *In Search of Excellence: Lessons from America's Best-Run Companies.* New York: Harper & Row, 1982.

Schonberger, R. J. *Japanese Manufacturing Techniques.* New York: Free Press, 1982.

Skinner, W. "The Focused Factory." *Harvard Business Review*, 1974, *52* (3), 113–121.

Part Four

Marketing in Service Firms

13

Managing Relationships with Customers: A Differentiating Philosophy of Marketing

John A. Czepiel

The marketing of services is especially sensitive to the relationship between customer and suppliers. Statements such as "Service encounters are first and foremost social encounters" (McCallum and Harrison, 1985, p. 35) reflect the kind of thinking that services marketers must adopt if they are to truly understand the underlying bases of their businesses. The idea that the unit of analysis in marketing should be the *relationship*, the mutual recognition of some special status between exchange partners that is the result of a successful series of service encounters, is representative of the major shift in analytical orientation required. The time-honored focus on the transaction is an insufficient conceptual framework for the issues facing services marketers.

Marketers have much to gain by thinking about their customers in relational terms. Since few businesses are built on the basis of one-time-only customers, it pays to think in a longer time frame about how the firm's actions either support or inhibit the development of a relationship with a customer. Service firms, since they are often in direct contact with their customers, have the ability to build parallel economic and personal ties with their customer base. Such strong ties enable the firm to

299

both better serve its customers and deter competitive efforts to win those customers away.

It is the goal of this chapter to explore the meaning of a relationship in the context of economic exchange and its importance in services marketing. The first section examines the evolution of the thinking that has expanded the concepts of marketing to allow a relational approach. Next, we explore the idea of a market-based relationship and then analyze the appropriateness of the concept in the context of services. Subsequent sections discuss how power affects the shape of relationships, the impact of business strategy on power and the firm's philosophy regarding its customer relationships, and how those ideas could be used in services marketing. The chapter closes with an exploration of the research issues raised by a relational approach.

Expanding the Concepts of Marketing

At one time, the realm of marketing study was limited to the business world and its scope restricted to the transaction. The idea that other types of organizations needed to manage their exchanges with their client constituencies or even that they could use marketplace-like techniques to attract clients was a major departure for the discipline. An article entitled "Broadening the Concept of Marketing" (Kotler and Levy, 1969) explored the use of marketing concepts in a wide range of organizations in which the concepts of sales or the transaction were inappropriate. Several years later the same authors proposed that marketing expand its domain to include the marketing-like behaviors that buyers used in attracting sellers in an article entitled "Buying Is Marketing, Too!" (Kotler and Levy, 1973). These ideas suggested that existing marketing concepts were inadequate to capture the reality of marketplace behavior.

With this as a background, Bagozzi's work on "Marketing as Exchange" (1975, 1979) was a logical development. The notion of an exchange of values (money, goods, services, or other currency) as the core of marketplace behavior was not unique. After all, economics is based on the idea that exchange *creates value* since both parties are better off after the exchange than before. What was new was that it could prove useful for marketers to view customers not as a fisherman views fish but as full-fledged exchange partners: people with whom the seller had exchange *relationships*. The prior concept of marketing as a stimulus-response function where marketers "poke" and consumers respond was found wanting in comparison.

At about the same time, outside of the marketing discipline, there were those who were challenging the dominant concept of the transaction that was enshrined in contract law and economics as the unit of analysis. The legal concept of a discrete transaction consists of two anonymous parties exchanging clearly identified things of value under a set of agreed-upon conditions at a given time and place. In this view, the transaction is the only association or relationship contemplated by the parties. Macneil (1980) and Williamson (1975, 1981) both have made basic contributions to developing the concept of *relational exchange* using such ideas as the social contract and transaction costs. The "there's a sucker born every minute" orientation implied by the focus on the transaction as the unit of analysis has been giving way to the idea that real marketplace behavior more often consists of a continuing series of exchanges between *exchange partners*. This echoed Levitt's (1981) idea that the role of marketing is to get and *keep* customers.

Further, these ideas opened up the concept of the exchange *process* itself. The definition of an exchange as a discrete legal contract between strangers was enlarged to encompass extended noncontractual exchanges, in which the relationship itself replaces the contract as the governing mechanism. Since the simple discrete contract formed but the smallest minority of economic exchange behavior, the new approach was a better conceptual approximation of reality.

The Concept of Exchange Relationships

All exchanges, by definition, involve a relationship. The relationship may be short and simple and have no future (as with those between tourists and souvenir sellers), or it may be involving, complicated, and long-term (as are those between large computer systems users and their suppliers). The former type of exchange is seldom thought of as a relationship, although it meets the technical requirements: an association or connection between two parties. More commonly, we think of an exchange relationship as one that encompasses an extended series of interactions and transactions over time. More importantly, an exchange relationship involves some recognition of a special status between the exchange partners.

Issues of interest in exploring exchange relationships include questions about the desirability of a relationship, the choice of relationship partners, and the development of the relationship. Two such issues are discussed in this section: the relative weighting of the economic and social content in exchange relationships and the function that relationships have in economic exchange.

The Content of Exchange Relationships. Exchange relationships differ from purely social relationships in that they have both economic and social aspects. A major issue is the relative weighting of and the interplay between the core of the relationship—the exchange of economic values—and the supporting interactional framework within which exchange occurs—the social or relational aspect. Economic anthropologists have long been concerned with the balance and interplay between the two. In her review of the literature, Marks (1988) notes that exchange relationships have long been seen as a mixture of the symbolic and the economic, the social and the functional, and the transaction and the relationship. While anthropologists who study exchange do so to see "how social exchange is played out against a background of economic exchange" (Marks, 1988, p. 64), of equal interest here is the reverse—how economic exchange occurs against a background of social exchange.

The content of a relationship can be broken down into two elements: the content of the core exchange and the content of the relational interaction. While the economic predominates, it would be wrong to assume that social exchange does not occur in parallel with economic exchange, just as one would not expect the interaction that accompanies a purchase to be purely

Figure 13.1. The Content of Exchange Relationships.

	20% Task	80% Nontask
80% Economic	16%	64%
20% Social	4%	16%

Content of Core Exchange (left axis)

Content of Relational Interaction (bottom axis)

task oriented (relating directly to the completion of the exchange). Some economic exchange may even result purely from a desire for social exchange. One can imagine someone making purchases in order to meet an attractive sales clerk, for example, or simply out of the need to avoid loneliness.

Figure 13.1 shows a hypothetical exchange relationship in which there is an eighty-twenty split in both the content and interactional elements. This is probably a pretty close depiction of many exchange relationships. As expected, the relationship would not exist if the economics did not work, since 80 percent of the total exchange is concerned with economics; but only 16 percent of the relationship's content is directly concerned with the execution of exchanges. How the interplay between the two contents works to further the goals of each party to the relationship is the next issue to be discussed.

The Function of Relational Content. The first function of relational content is to provide the exchange partners with an alternative to the discrete legal contract—a framework for exchange within which each is relatively assured that the exchange partner is honest and trustworthy. "The notion of profit historically has been considered to be inimical to morality, honesty, and trust," notes Marks (1988, p. 48). Anthropologists hypothesize that honesty in exchange relationships is inversely related to social distance. The exchange relationships with close kin are different from those with whom has but tribal ties. Exchanges involving more distant partners with whom there are but weak village or tribal ties are "fair," while trades with those who are nonkin and nontribal can be the most opportunistic. In fact, the aim in these latter trades "is the unearned increment" (Sahlins, 1965, p. 148). As Marks (1988, p. 55) sums it up, "In societies where one does not trade with kin, then one need not act morally."

While prior experience with an exchange partner is a good hard indicator of future performance, closing the social distance between the exchange partners *ensures* the fairness of future exchanges. Social distance is reduced not only by the conscious acts of the partners but also by the simple associations and interactions that necessarily occur as the core exchanges take place. Harrison (1977), for example, has demonstrated that "mere exposure" to another can cause an increase in affect. But mere exposure to an exchange partner is a small effect compared to the conscious actions taken by buyers and suppliers to extend their professional associations into the social arena. The three-martini lunch does have a real purpose. Gaining a buyer's trust is a critical task in many marketplace settings (Schurr and Ozanne, 1985; Swan, Trawick, and Silva, 1985), and establishing a social relationship parallel to the professional is a more "natural" approach than a legal contract.

Another function is that the framework of a relationship offers the potential for more effective and more efficient exchange. Dwyer, Schurr, and Oh (1987) suggest that a relationship can yield "significant gains in the joint—and consequently individual—payoffs as a result of effective communication and collaboration to attain goals" (p. 14). Many markets require that suppliers be intimately involved with customers' operations and goals in order to be able to recommend products and services that solve customers' real problems. This requires an openness that comes more easily within a relationship than with unknown suppliers. Peters and Waterman (1982) term it being "close to the customer." They quote an IBM financial executive who makes customer calls and who insists that his subordinates do so too: "How's someone going to design a receivables policy if he doesn't know the customer?" (Peters and Waterman, 1982, p. 161).

The simplification of the exchange process that occurs when it takes place within a relationship offers the potential for major improvements in efficiency. Williamson's (1981) work on transaction costs highlights some of the unique investments that buyers and sellers make in initiating and completing exchanges that relational exchanges can spread out or eliminate. As one simple example, suppliers in many business-to-business markets frequently begin production and even ship orders on the basis of phone calls from regular customers who need supplies but cannot process the formal paperwork for a purchase order quickly enough. Such shortcuts between exchange partners can do much to improve the efficiency of the process ("OEM-Supplier Accords. . . ," 1985). "Just-in-time" manufacturing requires extremely close relationships between supplier and customer to achieve its efficiencies.

Finally, an exchange relationship fills the very real social and psychological needs of the exchange partners. "Relational exchange participants can be expected to derive complex, personal, non economic satisfactions and engage in *social* exchange" (Dwyer, Schurr, and Oh, 1987, p. 12). Marketplace behavior has always been motivated by more than strict economic functionality. Klaus (1985) notes that satisfaction with exchange interaction is a function of performance in both task-related behaviors and what he terms "ceremonial" behaviors. These latter he defines as behaviors meeting the psychological needs of both partners.

As noted in the opening words of this chapter, service encounters are first and foremost social encounters. As these encounters cumulate into a relationship, stable patterns of behavior and shared experiences evolve with the repeated interactions, perhaps as much because of as in spite of the variability and complexity of social life (Weick, 1979). This need for a certain amount of stability in exchange partners and in the interactions with them may be a function of the need to suppress one's own feelings in commercial interactions, as Hochschild (1983) contends. The ultimate expression of this need for stability is psychological loyalty—the combination of trust and liking that results in a commitment to an exchange partner (Gilmore and Czepiel, 1987).

Whatever the cause, the social element in exchange relationships is neither frivolous nor a leftover appendage from an earlier evolutionary era. It works for individuals as individuals. It works for those who interact in the marketplace as representatives of their organizations. It works, too, for the organizations themselves. And it works not only for its own sake (a worthy one) but in the service of effectiveness, efficiency, and the protection of both partners.

Exchange Relationships in Service Settings

Exchange relationships are especially prevalent and relevant in the service setting (Czepiel, Solomon, and Surprenant, 1985). At the highest conceptual level, this is because services are customer-involving. The inability to insulate the core production function from the customer and the need for active customer participation in service design and delivery are such that traditional concepts of organizational boundaries are inadequate. "A typical feature of service companies is that one of their outputs is *new social relationships* and that they have to extend their organizing capability well outside their own company" (Normann, 1984, p. 16). Customer relationships are important in such settings.

Services have to deal with the customer not only at the abstract, organizational level but also at the practical, people-to-people level. As Bowen and Schneider (1988) have pointed out, Bell's (1973) metaphor describing work in postindustrial society as a "game between persons" is an especially fitting description of services. The term *service encounter* was coined specifically to describe the interactions that occur between participants in service exchanges who are nominally strangers (Czepiel, 1980;

Czepiel, Solomon, Surprenant, and Gutman, 1985). Continued "neutral" or impersonal exchanges between real human beings are satisfying neither to the client nor to the service provider. As interactions between individuals or between an individual and a firm are repeated over time, the motivation for the development of a social aspect to the relationship necessarily increases (Czepiel, Solomon, Surprenant, and Gutman, 1985). Hollander (1985) notes that the appropriate level of recognition and personal attention given to the regular customer (or to the regular service provider) is an issue of long standing in the literature.

At a more mundane level, large categories of services are purchased only within the framework of a formal and sometimes even mechanical relationship between client and supplier (Lovelock, 1983). Examples include telephone service, schooling, financial services, and insurance. An equal number do not require a formal association but involve regular and continued (if not continual) exchanges. Many public services, as well as for-profit economic free goods, such as broadcast communications, fall into this category. Retailers are another type of major service organization with which customers develop long-term exchange relationships, even if only because of their geographical convenience or monopolies. Lovelock (1983), in fact, sees the kind of relationship that exists between customer and service organization as a key criterion in understanding a service.

The concept of an exchange relationship is especially relevant to service situations. Whether its importance is defined in organizational or interpersonal terms or simply in terms of the realities of membership or geography, some form of relationship is the reality for service firms. The next section examines how power affects the philosophy that each partner has toward its relationships.

Power and the Relationship Philosophy

At the heart of any relationship is the question of power. It is power that determines the equality of the exchange partners and, inevitably, how each will act toward the other — the philosophy that each has about the relationship. In some relationships—international political ones, for example—the use of power is obvious and blatant. In more personal and familial relationships, its use is more often subtle, if not disguised. Marketplace exchange relationships tend to lie someplace in between the two, perhaps closer to the political end of the spectrum.

Dwyer, Schurr, and Oh (1987) use the terms *buyer-maintained relation, seller-maintained relation*, and *bilateral relationship maintenance* to distinguish among the different types of relative motivational interest (in other words, power) in a relationship. They base their approach on Thibaut and Kelley's (1959) exchange theory, which posits that relationships are based on each party's assessment of the rewards to be gained from the association in contrast with those available outside the association. This approach was generalized and termed *interdependence theory* in later work by Kelley and Thibaut (1978), in which they analyze the patterns of interdependence within a relationship and define power as the ability to control one's own and the other's outcomes and behaviors.

The source of power in economic exchange relationships is direct—it is the ability of each party to choose whether to enter into or to withhold its participation from an exchange. Since value is created in exchanges—both parties must be better off after the exchange than before if it is to occur—there is frequently competition for exchange partners. The balance of power is determined by the relationship of supply to demand, corrected for the risks of finding and the costs of switching exchange partners (Porter, 1980). An excess of supply relative to demand provides buyers with many alternative suppliers, each of which is seeking exchange partners—the classic buyer's market. The opposite situation creates a seller's market. In neither of these situations does the partner most in demand have any motivation for a relationship. Discrete transactions are the best alternative. In such a situation, the only possible inducement for a relationship would be for the partner in excess supply to accept complete subservience to the other by promising to match or exceed any alternative partner's offer. This is often the case in highly oversupplied industrial commodity markets.

Relationships are of interest only when supply and demand are closer to being balanced. Since in most markets there is seldom perfect knowledge of the true state of supply and demand, this leaves large areas in which relationships are possible and desirable to the partners. It is in these settings that the partners each find that the additional benefits that accrue from an exchange relationship outweigh the benefits to be gained from a transactions approach, especially after correcting for the risks and costs incurred. It is in such settings that seller-maintained, bilateral, and buyer-maintained relationships are found. It is the relative power balance between the participants that determines the firm's (and the buyer's) philosophy about the relationship.

Key to any business strategy is the ability to avoid or mitigate the effects of competition. In Porter's (1980) terms, a firm that has a strategic advantage in its ability to deliver unique benefits to the marketplace (a differentiated product strategy) is able to avoid direct competition—no other firm can provide those benefits. Such a firm possesses more power than its customers and can dominate relationships with them. If the customer demands the core service, there is no alternative to the one supplier.

Citibank has long been able to provide levels of the key core service elements in retail banking that its competitors have not been able to match. Its widespread branch network and leadership in the number and performance of its ATMs made it the overwhelming choice in the New York City market. There was a time when this functional advantage was so strong that Citibank appeared to pay relatively less attention to the relational aspects of its relationship with its customers (an attitude it has since decisively changed for the better). For example, on one occasion during that period it attempted to require customers with small balances to perform all of their transactions with ATMs—they could no longer interact with the teller force. While it pulled back after a widespread public outcry, it was clearly surprised by the response. Its overwhelming power was such that it was not able to conceive that its actions would be opposed. The point is that none of its competitors would have been able even to seriously consider such an action. Their lack of power would not have enabled them that luxury.

However, the strategic advantages that underlie business strategies seldom retain their potency. Patents expire, competitors work hard to match performance advantages, customers seek alternative sources for the monopolized benefits, and substitutes demonstrate their economic attractiveness. The high-handed approach to customers economically possible in a monopolist's strategy becomes a liability when competition emerges. Not only do customers not immediately forget the years of their ill treatment, but the organization itself finds that it is difficult to eliminate the arrogant attitude that its members exhibited during the "fat years." Monopoly power allows dominance but does not condone arrogance.

However, few service firms are able to command such power. The reality is that a differentiated product remains a differentiated product only until the emergence of the first follower. After that, it begins to behave as a commodity. And, as Thomas (1978) and Bhide (1986) have pointed out, most service businesses are unable to protect their offerings sufficiently to prevent rapid imitation by competitors. Therefore, since it is impossible to avoid competition, most must pursue strategies designed to mitigate competition's effects. Porter's (1980) classic strategy to mitigate the effects of competition, achieving a position of low-cost producer, does little, however, to redress the relative balance of power between buyer and seller. By definition, firms pursuing low-cost strategies are delivering parity benefits (at best) to the marketplace. Therefore, if the firm chooses to use its strategic advantage (low operations costs) in the marketplace rather than to bolster its profits, its only possible move is to lower price. Such a move has two implications for customer relationships. First, since the offering is a parity offering, the only reason for a customer to choose it is its low price. In the parlance of the streets, you are loved not for what you are but because you are a cheap date. Second, any apparent relationship that may seem to form under such conditions is likely to be more illusory than real. The basis for choice and the apparent relationship is the low price. The relationship, therefore, will last only as long as the price is kept low. Give the customer a lower price from another supplier and the relationship will end. Only the differentiated product strategy works to favor the seller in a relational context.

Clearly, when all suppliers have approximately equal ability to provide the core service desired, customers can afford to exchange only with those they "like." The best that most service firms can do (since they cannot affect the power balance) is to work on the noncore elements of the exchange—the relational aspects and switching costs. This is the situation for most service businesses. They focus on developing the relationships that they hope will differentiate them from among the host of suppliers who are able to deliver parity performance on the core elements of value in the exchange.

Levitt (1981) discusses this issue in some detail. His criticism is that most service businesses are good in the courtship phase but frequently do poorly in the marriage. One of the reasons for this, perhaps, is that insufficient thought and resources are devoted to the customer-keeping function in comparison to the customer-attracting function (Rosenberg and Czepiel, 1984). Keeping customers requires a philosophical reorientation with respect to customer relationships. It requires that the firm invest in relationship maintenance in substantive ways. For a customer to exit a relationship once having been attracted to it is a sign that the initial promises have not been fulfilled.

Jackson (1985) treats the issue of switching costs at length. The idea is that a firm should try to lower the costs for potential customers who wish to switch to them while increasing the cost of switching for existing customers. Clearly, customers appreciate the former and resist the latter. While there are some advantages to be gained in maintaining relationships by the skillful manipulation of switching costs, it is not an easy concept to implement. More important, customers understandably chafe at policies designed to restrict their ability to choose other exchange partners unless there is a clear value benefit to be gained.

Strategically, it seems that only those few service businesses that are able to produce unique benefits for their customers can dominate their customer relationships. And even in that monopoly position, the firm must temper its use of that power lest it spoil its long-term position in the market. For, as has been demonstrated, few monopoly positions in service businesses are as long-lasting as a market's remembrances of past ill treatment by a supplier. Most services are parity offerings and depend on building relationships as a strategy to offset the effects of competition. Many, however, seem better at attraction than maintenance. They forget that customers want substance in a relationship.

Managing from a Relational Perspective

There are four questions that a firm seeking to make the best use of the relational aspects of its service offering needs to address: (1) What should be the firm's philosophy toward customer relationships, given its market strategy? (2) What is the desired and actual distribution of customers by the strength of their relationship with the firm? (3) What are the key elements of style and substance that customers use to judge relational performance? (4) What is the best way to organize the firm to develop the attitudes and behaviors necessary to deliver the valued relational behaviors?

Relational Philosophy. A firm's philosophy about customers and the customer relationships permeates the organization. The highly competitive company president who goes all out to win on every point in negotiations with customers should not be surprised to find that employees are doing the same. While the firm's market position dictates to some extent the feasible range of relational stances available to it, there is considerable leeway within all but the most subordinate relationship roles with customers to fine tune that relational stance into a philosophy that fits the unique needs of the firm and its customers.

Customers are sensitive to the status of their relationships with suppliers. After all, the cues that they receive from their suppliers' words and actions are not very different in kind from those that they use to interpret the status of their personal and familial relationships. To assume that customers interpret their suppliers' actions only in terms of their functional content and not their symbolic content is unrealistic. Firms, therefore, need to be as sensitive to developing the nuances of relational language as they are to the language they use in advertising and public relations.

It would seem that, as a beginning, a firm could position itself in a two-dimensional space, with attitude toward the exchange partner as one dimension and dominant relational mode as the other dimension (see Figure 13.2). The firm can choose how it relates to its customers. It can choose relationship managers who are adept at building close personal ties to clients via attendance at the theater or sporting events, lunches, dinners, and the like. Or it can build the relationship through more professionally substantive actions, such as sponsorship of joint technical seminars, affairs at which management experts speak, and plant visits, all of which provide the opportunity to build professionally based personal contacts between two firms. Similarly, it can examine its attitude toward customers by examining how it treats them. A business that always resolves billing disputes in its own favor, takes advantage of every opportunity to renegotiate contracts, or seldom seems able to respond to special requests is telling its customers that it views business as a "zero-sum game" in which every gain by the customer is a loss to the firm, that the customer is not very important. A cooperative attitude, however, need not be demonstrated by giving away the store. It simply says that the firm views its actions in a longer time frame, that short-term gains are frequently less valuable than they appear.

Where do the firm's relationships seem to fall in these terms? How would customers with whom the firm has the most positive relationships position it on the map? How do competitors position themselves? How do the requirements of the different positions on the map compare to the skills of the key managers of the firm? How do they compare to those who must initiate and maintain relationships? Which position on the map is best for the firm?

Figure 13.2. Mapping the Firm's Relational Philosophy.

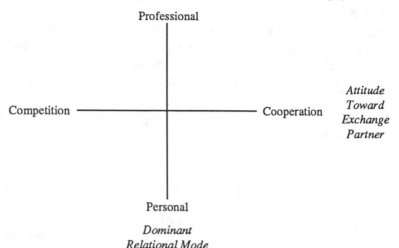

Relationship Distribution. A business is ultimately based on the portfolio of its customer relationships. Some very successful businesses have portfolios composed of only opportunistic transactions; others exchange only with those with whom there are long-standing relationships. The firm needs to determine the shape of its preferred distribution of customer relationships.

It is not a difficult task to array customers on a scale representing the strength of the relationship with the firm. How many one-time-only customers are there in the business's base? What percentage of the business comes from those with whom there is a very close relationship? What is the relative profitability of each category? What is the desirable mix from a profit standpoint? A risk-minimization standpoint? At what point on that scale does the firm risk losing customers to competitors? What is the average tenure of a customer? Only by beginning to monitor and measure the relationships a firm has with its customers can it begin to take charge of them. There are few guidelines available for determining whether any particular portfolio is more or less appropriate for a firm. However, experienced members of the sales function usually have strong experience bases by which to guide the examination and understand the processes by which the portfolio can be changed.

Key Relational Elements. The key task of the marketing function is to know what is necessary to satisfy customers better than competitors can. Marketers are well versed in researching customer needs. What customers need and want and what they are willing to pay for it are the substantive bases of customer relationships and are issues that marketers tackle regularly. But customer relationships can founder on issues of style as well as substance. While it is true that no amount of style can overcome a lack of substance (Crosby and Stephens, 1987), there are generally many firms able to deliver the same level of substance—in which case, style reigns as the deciding factor. How many firms, however, have data-based knowledge of customers' preferences for relational elements? This is a key issue about which few firms have as much knowledge as they do about the more concrete elements of the offering. Yet my review of a few proprietary studies across business and consumer services makes it clear that customers base a large proportion of their evaluations of substantive performance on the skills of the individual managing the relationship for the supplier firm.

It is doubtful whether the key elements of successful relationships vary much from setting to setting at the conceptual level. The elements of perceived service quality detailed by Parasuraman, Zeithaml, and Berry (1985) are basic to both the substantive and relational elements of offerings. The five dimensions that their research found important in affecting customers' perceptions of the quality of service—reliability, responsiveness, tangibles, assurance, and empathy—are cued as much by how an act is performed as the reality of the act itself. Some, such as assurance (the knowledge and courtesy of employees and their ability to convey trust and confidence) and empathy (caring, individualized attention to the customer), are clearly relational. An important issue that the theory doesn't address is the exact form that the theoretical constructs take from industry to industry. What specific acts embody the concept? Salespeople, account managers, service providers all need concrete guidance about how to treat customers, as Bowen and Schneider (1988) have pointed out. Research is needed to provide that input.

Organizational Requirements. The importance of organizational form, culture, and climate to the performance of service providers in meeting customers' needs has been well documented. Whether it is the relationship between marketing and operations functions (Czepiel, 1980) or the role of the individual in serving the customer (Schneider, 1973, 1980), the effects of the firm's organization on both the individual service transaction and the relationship are real and measurable.

Many services are produced by large organizations in which the provider is seldom the beneficiary of his or her own success in managing customers. In fact, in many large service organizations, such as the large commercial banks and computer firms (IBM's business is as much a service business as product business), the relationship between supplier and client firms is likely to involve multiple contracts spread among a number of different functional groups. Managing and linking together the many different connections are important tasks if the relationship is to be successful (Crane and Eccles, 1987).

Bowen and Schneider (1988) provide an excellent overview of the organizational behavior issues raised by services. There are, however, few hard and fast rules about how to best organize the firm to develop and maintain mutually satisfying relationships with customers. As Bowen and Schneider (1988) point out, task complexity and interdependence (because of customer involvement) "make it difficult to specify a priori how employees are to behave in the generally unpredictable range of circumstances that may arise during service provision. Consequently, core cultural values are particularly important sources for guiding and perhaps thereby controlling service employee behavior" (p. 63). A clearly articulated philosophy about the firm's attitude towards customers and relationships with customers is the most positive organizational principle there is.

Research Issues

The four questions listed above could just as easily have been put in the form of research issues. The fact is that there have been but a few research studies published that have adopted a relational stance to understanding marketplace behavior. This section suggests some potentially profitable or particularly intriguing directions for research.

Questions at the concept level abound in relationships. Many researchers will likely find the yes-no approach to whether a relationship exists too conceptually simplistic to mirror actual observed behavior. One possible direction would be to seek to define a relationship in terms of the interaction content and then to develop measures of association strength and longevity. Gilmore and Czepiel (1987) suggest that some method of capturing the history of a relationship would be useful, because the present state of a relationship is more a function of the timing and sequencing of prior events than of their mere occurrence. Understanding the relational aspects of marketplace behavior may be more important than confirming its existence.

Relationships between individuals and organizations present some difficult conceptual issues surrounding the "existence" of those organizations and the ability of an individual to have a relationship with an organization per se. How do the employees who represent the organization fit into the relational net, and what is the balance between the personal and the professional in the performance of the relational duties on behalf of the organization? How can a client trust an abstract entity such as an organization? How do such concepts as image and reputation (Weigelt and Camerer, 1988) work to help consumers establish relationships with organizations or their offerings? The use of relational concepts will require much conceptual development if anthropomorphism is to be avoided.

The use of relational constructs seems obvious in situations where buyer and seller have equal power — in business-to-business settings, for example. Both parties are frequently conscious of a relationship's existence and may even take care to develop and maintain it. But many relationships may be unconscious or asymmetrical. Consumers are not always conscious of their marketplace behavior but may, nonetheless, have unconscious expectations about appropriate behavior on the part of those with whom they have unconsciously established marketplace relationships. What behavioral expectations does a consumer have about the firm and broker from whom he or she has bought automobile insurance for five or ten years? What if that consumer has never had a traffic ticket or accident claim in that period? How does that affect the relationship? Some relationships may be asymmetrical, where one party is conscious of its relational behavior while the other either is unconscious of, is unaware of, or denies its existence?

Loyalty is a concept used to describe the ultimate outcome of a relationship—it is what binds one to another when such constancy seems contrary to self-interest (Gilmore and Czepiel, 1987). Marketers have long researched what has been termed *brand loyalty*, although most of that work has been focused on choice behavior and preference models rather than on the psychological state of loyalty or the social processes by which relational ties are established between buyer and seller. Much work is necessary to explore the validity of the application of this important social and political construct to marketplace relationships. Trust and commitment seem central in its composition, but much work remains to be done on how loyalty actually develops (Czepiel and Gilmore, 1987).

Finally, marketers are ultimately concerned with initiating and maintaining exchanges. Measures of the effect of the relational aspects of exchange need to be developed. What percentage of the variance in marketplace behavior can be explained by relational constructs? How do relational effects vary across differing market settings? While, for many, the development of knowledge about marketplace relationships is worthy for its own sake, for others, such knowledge is worthwhile only if it can be shown to have practical application.

Summary

Relationships are an integral part of social and political life. The development of relational concepts that can be used to understand and analyze marketplace behavior is especially relevant to the marketing of services. The intangible nature of services, the extent to which they involve the customer in the producing organization, and the long-term formal and informal ties that they establish with their customers are some of the reasons for this.

This chapter has presented the core ideas relating to relationships as they affect services, concentrating on how the firm's market strategy sets its philosophy toward its customer relationships. The chapter has raised four managerial questions: what the firm's philosophy regarding customer relationships should be; how the firm's customer portfolio can be evaluated according to different relationship types; how the elements of style and substance that customers use to judge relational performance can be identified; and what kind of organization is needed to elicit and support the valued behaviors. The research questions raised included how to measure relational strength; how to identify the role of the individual in linking organizations; how relational constructs work in situations where little conscious thought is given to the purchase act (such as in many consumer markets); and whether the concept of loyalty is applicable. It is hoped that the practical and scholarly gains to be achieved by a greater attention to relational constructs have been sufficiently demonstrated that the reader will be motivated to explore and apply them.

References

Bagozzi, R. P. "Marketing as Exchange." *Journal of Marketing*, 1975, *39*, 32–39.

Bagozzi, R. P. "Toward a Formal Theory of Marketing Exchanges." In O. C. Ferrell, S. W. Brown, and C. W. Lamb (eds.), *Conceptual and Theoretical Developments in Marketing*. Chicago: American Marketing Association, 1979.

Bell, D. *The Coming of Post-Industrial Society: A Venture in Social Forecasting*. New York: Basic Books, 1973.

Bhide, A. "Hustle as Strategy." *Harvard Business Review*, 1986, *64*, 59–65.

Bowen, D. E., and Schneider, B. "Services Marketing and Management: Implications for Organizational Behavior." In B. M. Staw and L. L. Cummings (eds.), *Research in Organizational Behavior*. Vol. 10. Greenwich, Conn.: JAI Press, 1988.

Crane, D. B., and Eccles, R. G. "Commercial Banks: Taking Shape for Turbulent Times." *Harvard Business Review*, 1987, *65*, 94–100.

Crosby, L. A., and Stephens, N. "Effects of Relationship Marketing on Satisfaction, Retention, and Prices in the Life Insurance Industry." *Journal of Marketing Research*, 1987, *24*, 404–411.

Czepiel, J. A. *Managing Customer Satisfaction in Consumer Services Businesses*. Report no. 80-109. Cambridge, Mass.: Marketing Science Institute, 1980.

Czepiel, J. A., and Gilmore, R. "Exploring the Concept of Loyalty in Services." In J. A. Czepiel, C. Congram, and J. Shanahan (eds.), *The Services Challenge: Integrating for Competitive Advantage*. Chicago: American Marketing Association, 1987.

Czepiel, J. A., Solomon, M. R., and Surprenant, C. F. (eds.). *The Service Encounter: Managing Employee/Customer Interaction in Service Businesses*. Lexington, Mass.: Lexington Books, 1985.

Czepiel, J. A., Solomon, M. R., Surprenant, C., and Gutman, E. G. "Service Encounters: An Overview." In J. A. Czepiel, M. R. Solomon, and C. F. Surprenant (eds.), *The Service Encounter: Managing Employee/Customer Interaction in Service Businesses*. Lexington, Mass.: Lexington Books, 1985.

Dwyer, F. R., Schurr, P. H., and Oh, S. "Developing Buyer-Seller Relationships." *Journal of Marketing*, 1987, *51* (2), 11–27.

Gilmore, R., and Czepiel, J. A. "Reconceptualizing Loyalty in Economic Exchange Relationships: Are Marketers People?" Unpublished working paper, Graduate School of Business Administration, New York University, 1987.

Harrison, A. A. "Mere Exposure." In L. Berkowitz (ed.), *Advances in Experimental Social Psychology*. Vol. 10. New York: Academic Press, 1977.

Hochschild, A. R. *The Managed Heart: Commercialization of Human Feeling*. Berkeley: University of California Press, 1983.

Hollander, S. C. "A Historical Perspective on the Service Encounter." In J. A. Czepiel, M. R. Solomon, and C. F. Surprenant (eds.), *The Service Encounter: Managing Employee/Customer Interaction in Service Businesses.* Lexington, Mass.: Lexington Books, 1985.

Jackson, B. B. *Winning and Keeping Industrial Customers: The Dynamics of Customer Relationships.* Lexington, Mass.: Lexington Books, 1985.

Kelley, H. H., and Thibaut, J. W. *Interpersonal Relations: A Theory of Interdependence.* New York: Wiley, 1978.

Klaus, P. G. "Quality Epiphenomenon: The Conceptual Understanding of Quality in Face-to-Face Service Encounters." In J. A. Czepiel, M. R. Solomon, and C. F. Surprenant (eds.), *The Service Encounter: Managing Employee/Customer Interaction in Service Businesses.* Lexington, Mass.: Lexington Books, 1985.

Kotler, P., and Levy, S. J. "Broadening the Concept of Marketing." *Journal of Marketing,* 1969, *33,* 10–15.

Kotler, P., and Levy, S. J. "Buying Is Marketing, Too!" *Journal of Marketing,* 1973, *37,* 54–59.

Levitt, T. "Marketing Intangible Products and Product Intangibles." *Harvard Business Review,* 1981, *59,* 94–102.

Lovelock, C. H. "Classifying Services to Gain Strategic Marketing Insights." *Journal of Marketing,* 1983, *47,* 9–20.

McCallum, J. R., and Harrison, W. "Interdependence in the Service Encounter." In J. A. Czepiel, M. R. Solomon, and C. F. Surprenant (eds.), *The Service Encounter: Managing Employee/Customer Interaction in Service Businesses.* Lexington, Mass.: Lexington Books, 1985.

Macneil, I. R. *The New Social Contract: An Inquiry into Modern Contractual Relations.* New Haven, Conn.: Yale University Press, 1980.

Marks, J. R. "Disguise and Display: Balancing Profit and Morality in the Pit of a Commodities Exchange." Unpublished doctoral dissertation, Department of Anthropology, Graduate School of Arts and Sciences, New York University, 1988.

Normann, R. *Service Management: Strategy and Leadership in Service Businesses.* New York: Wiley, 1984.

"OEM-Supplier Accords Yield Productivity Improvements." *Marketing News,* Oct. 25, 1985, p. 20.

Parasuraman, A., Zeithaml, V. A., and Berry, L. L. "A Conceptual

Model of Service Quality and Its Implications for Future Research." *Journal of Marketing*, 1985, *49*, 41–50.

Peters, T. J., and Waterman, R. H., Jr. *In Search of Excellence: Lessons from America's Best-Run Companies*. New York: Harper & Row, 1982.

Porter, M. E. *Competitive Strategy: Techniques for Analyzing Industries and Competitors*. New York: Free Press, 1980.

Rosenberg, L. J., and Czepiel, J. A. "A Marketing Approach for Customer Retention." *Journal of Consumer Marketing*, 1984, *1*, 45–51.

Sahlins, M. "On the Sociology of Primitive Exchange." In M. Banton (ed.), *The Relevance of Models for Social Anthropology*. ASA Monograph 1. London: Tavistock, 1965.

Schneider, B. "The Perception of Organizational Climate: The Customer's View." *Journal of Applied Psychology*, 1973, *57*, 248–256.

Schneider, B. "The Service Organization: Climate Is Crucial." *Organizational Dynamics*, 1980, *9* (2), 52–65.

Schurr, P. H., and Ozanne, J. L. "Influences on Exchange Processes: Buyers' Preconceptions of a Seller's Trustworthiness and Bargaining Toughness." *Journal of Consumer Research*, 1985, *11*, 939–953.

Solomon, M. R., Surprenant, C. F., Czepiel, J. A., and Gutman, E. G. "A Role Theory Perspective on Dyadic Interactions: The Service Encounter." *Journal of Marketing*, 1985, *49* (4), 99–111.

Swan, J. E., Trawick, I. F., and Silva, D. W. "How Industrial Salespeople Gain Customer Trust." *Industrial Marketing Management*, 1985, *14*, 203–211.

Thibaut, J. W., and Kelley, H. H. *The Social Psychology of Groups*. New York: Wiley, 1959.

Thomas, D.R.E. "Strategy Is Different in Service Businesses." *Harvard Business Review*, 1978, *56*, 158–165.

Weick, K. E. *The Social Psychology of Organizing*. Reading, Mass.: Addison-Wesley, 1979.

Weigelt, K., and Camerer, C. "Reputation and Corporate Strategy." *Strategic Management Journal*, 1988, *9*, 443–454.

Williamson, O. *Markets and Hierarchies: Analysis and Antitrust Implications*. New York: Free Press, 1975.

Williamson, O. "The Economics of Organization: The Transaction Cost Approach." *American Journal of Sociology*, 1981, *87*, 548–576.

14

Evaluating the Role and Place of Marketing in Service Firms

John E. G. Bateson

The environment is changing and redefining what it takes to be successful for many service firms. At one time, a successful, efficient operation was enough to generate success. The emergence of more and better competitors in the marketplace has changed all that. Now other people can guarantee delivery of a parcel before noon or provide a clean, attractive bedroom. Now it is necessary to better understand customer needs and to find new ways to compete. A typical reaction of top management to these problems is to institute marketing. Unfortunately, in many cases, a firm's first experience with marketing is less than successful. Marketing departments may be ineffective, or open warfare may break out between the marketing and operations groups. The problem is usually that marketing has been placed in the wrong place in the organization and has been given the wrong role to play.

The purpose of this chapter is to discuss the role and place of the marketing department in a service firm. Although the application of marketing to services is becoming increasingly accepted, very little has been written about the appropriate place and role for the marketing department. It is, perhaps, assumed that all that is necessary is to copy the manufacturing company's organizational structure (George and

Barksdale, 1974). The limited literature on the subject (Gronroos, 1980, 1985) actually suggests something very different: the dismantling of the marketing department. This chapter develops a framework in which to consider these issues. The first section discusses some of the basic operational dilemmas created by the nature of services, particularly the high degree of interrelatedness between marketing and operations decisions. The next section suggests a contingency model that posits that the place of the marketing department is a function of the underlying technology, the competitive environment, and the objectives set by senior management. This model is used to examine whether the marketing function should be embodied in a marketing department and where in the organization the department should be located. Finally, the role of the marketing department as a short-term change agent is discussed.

The Nature of the Service Product

It is now generally accepted that one of the key differences between goods and services is the experiential nature of services. When consumers purchase a service, they purchase an experience (Bateson, 1977, 1979). Langeard, Bateson, Lovelock, and Eiglier (1981) suggest that the experience can be thought of as an interactive process in which the consumer interacts with all visible components of the service firm and with other consumers if they are present in the service setting. The visible components of the service organization can in turn be broken down into the physical artifacts and the service personnel.

Such a perspective highlights the problems faced by operations personnel within service organizations. To polarize and simplify the argument, operations management theorists suggest that a theoretically ideal operation can be created if the operation can assume that raw materials arrive at a predetermined time and at a perfect quality level and that the market can accept its output at a constant rate. With such assumptions, the uncertainty is removed from the operation. This is known in the literature as "isolating the technical core" (Thompson, 1967). In the absence of uncertainty, procedures can be systematized, labor replaced with capital, and capacity levels set accurately to ensure optimal utilization. Moreover, the management task is considerably simplified and the need for supervisory labor correspondingly reduced.

With this simplified perspective, the problems faced by operations managers in services become apparent. Raw material for the service operation consists of the components of the experience: the physical environment, the contact personnel, the other customers, and the consumer. Only the physical environment can be predictably controlled by management; the other components are human beings who will approach any service experience with a set of expectations and moods that can vary hour by hour and are influenced by factors outside the control of the service firm. In addition, consumers tend to arrive in the service organization in peaks and troughs, making successful capacity management very difficult. Capacity set for peaks implies long idle time for staff, who may become disgruntled by it. Capacity set for less than the peaks can generate periods of hyperactivity. To compound all of this, while some of the peaks will be predictable, others will be totally unpredictable. Although approaches are available to solve some of these operational problems, the nature of the service product means that life is more complex for service operations managers than for managers of manufacturing organizations.

The Operations-Dominated Organization. In an organization dominated by operations and the efficiency ethic, managers can implement a number of strategies to increase efficiency. The operations manager may try to isolate the core (Thompson, 1967), to reproduce the ideal process. As much as possible of the organization will be removed from the main source of uncertainty—the customers. This can lead to the removal of personal or telephone contact and the introduction of a mail-only system. From an operations manager's perspective, the mail system is ideal, since it allows buffering on both the input and the output sides of the process. Chase (1978) advocates the clear separation of service operations into the parts that deal with consumers and those that do not. The latter are suitable for production technology; the former are not.

If it is not possible to isolate the system from the customer, the impact of the customer can at least be minimized. Inventories of customers can be created on the input side to ensure that the system can be run flat out. By not trying to cope with the peaks, the organization can improve capacity utilization. Both of these require long queues by customers wishing to use the service. The customers can be "production-lined" themselves (Levitt 1972): Choice or customization from within the process can be minimized and consumers trained to introduce the minimum uncertainty into the system. Customers of McDonald's do not ask for rare hamburgers or things that are not on the menu, and they bus their own tables, improving operational efficiency by doing part of the work themselves.

The Operations Efficiency–Marketing Effectiveness Trade-Off. The very real danger for the firm employing such approaches is that it starts to lose its marketing orientation. To use Schneider's (1980) terminology, the organization becomes bureaucratically oriented. It reverts to an orientation of "using and protecting existing production facilities or raw materials" (p. 54). The reason for this is that there is almost invariably a trade-off between operations efficiency and marketing effectiveness. Each of the operational changes described earlier may improve efficiency but may also change the very nature of the service experience or product. Removing part of the organization from customer contact may remove quality clues used by consumers. Queues may be operationally efficient, but they tend to be viewed negatively by consumers. Consumers can be production-lined only with their consent. Using the consumer as a worker may be intrinsically attractive to consumers (Bateson, 1985a, 1985b), but it may also require incentives in the form of convenience or money.

Moving toward marketing effectiveness is just as traumatic for operations as moving away from it is for marketing. Most of the added features in services that marketing wants to build into the system will cause disruption and uncertainty and hence increase cost. For example, marketing logic can dictate longer open hours, which may mean split-shift working. The need to broaden the range of services offered at each outlet can add undue complexity. Retail banks in the United Kingdom now offer more than 250 different products through their outlets. Although justifiable from a marketing point of view, the operational impact has been dramatic. Staff training time has escalated. The operation of the teller windows has also changed because of the diversity of the requests received from customers. All these operational problems are solvable, but probably at the expense of the old, simple, highly efficient process. The operations department ideally wants to operate in a "people processing mode" (Klaus, 1985). It wants to minimize the uncertainty introduced into the system by the customers, but many marketing strategies involve giving discretion to the customers and hence increase uncertainty. In an organization dominated by the operations function, the trade-off between operations efficiency and marketing effectiveness will always favor operations.

For service businesses, the operation is the product. What the customer is buying is the interaction with the environment and service personnel. These are the visible components of service operation. Even the invisible parts of the service operation can directly influence the experience of the customer. The routine maintenance in a car-rental company, which the customer never sees, directly influences the reliability of the car and the driving experience. Without a working operation, the firm has nothing to sell. The economics of the operation are the economics of the firm. In the absence of competition, an efficient operation is all that is necessary. Such was the state of many service firms when they were formed, especially if demand exceeded supply.

Of course, if competition creates the need for marketing effectiveness, then a trade-off has to be made between the two opposing demands. The decisions made by either of the functions depend very much on the other. For example, an operational decision to isolate the technical core means that part of the visible components of the service firm will become invisible.

It is crucial from the marketing point of view to understand what the removal of these visual clues will do to customers' evaluation of the services. It may be that the components that are removed are the key parts of the service purchased by the consumer. At McDonald's, for example, the reduction in customization and the production-lining of the whole process hinges on the availability of a large market. If insufficient customers are available, the process will be highly efficient but, from a marketing point of view, totally ineffective, and the firm will fail. The McDonald's strategy is a volume strategy.

Who Should Make the Marketing Effectiveness–Operations Efficiency Trade-Off? Manufacturing companies are often organized along functional lines: manufacturing is dealt with in one department and marketing in another (see Figure 14.1). Such an approach has the advantage of allowing each group to develop its own expertise, organization, and culture according to the task that it faces. Other approaches clearly exist; firms can be organized along market or product lines. The functional structure, however, provides the best framework for understanding the problems likely to arise when the marketing function is first introduced into an organization.

Differentiation and integration are the basic concepts for understanding organizational structure (Lawrence and Lorsch, 1967a). Differentiation describes the extent to which an organization divides decision-making authority into units with different goals, time horizons, reward structures, and task specializations. Integration refers to the emphasis placed on integrating and controlling the units in an organization. Mechanisms used to provide integration can be divided into conventional and nonconventional (Galbraith, 1973). Conventional methods are the familiar coordinating and controlling techniques of plans, rules, policies, standard operating procedures, meetings, and referral of problems to superiors. These integrating mechanisms are usually sufficient for organizations that are not highly differentiated. Coordination of highly differentiated organizations usually requires the use of more costly, nonconventional integrating mechanisms, such as designation of individuals to

Figure 14.1. Organizational Structures of Typical Manufacturing
and Service Firms.

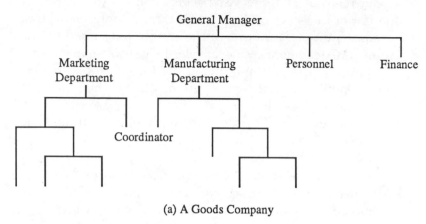

(a) A Goods Company

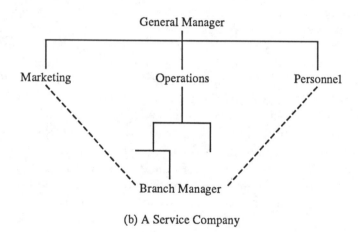

(b) A Service Company

perform the integrating role (Lawrence and Lorsch, 1967b),
temporary teams, matrix organizations (Sayles, 1976), and the
creation of organizational culture.

Integration between manufacturing and marketing can
often be a problem. Culturally, a marketing and a manufacturing department can be very different. The original work by
Lawrence and Lorsch (1967c) suggested that marketing had
longer time horizons than manufacturing, was less rigidly and

hierarchically organized, and tended to reward innovativeness and creativity, which were less valued in manufacturing. These findings were reviewed in the study by Langeard, Bateson, Lovelock, and Eigler (1981), which found differences in revenue versus cost orientation, time horizons, and motivations for change between service operations and marketing departments. Fortunately, in manufacturing companies, the availability of inventory allows the two to operate semiautonomously, at least in the short term. Manufacturing needs to know the likely demand that marketing will create and the particular products that are needed, but once these targets are agreed on, the two can operate separately. Production can be scheduled to create sufficient inventory to be available when it is needed. Marketing does not need to know when or how production is performed. Once inventory is available, it can be formally transferred—indeed, it is often "sold"—by manufacturing to marketing. Coordination is often achieved by a planning manager or coordinator; conflicts between functions are resolved by the general manager. The emergence of just-in-time systems is clearly changing this, since it forces the two departments to be much more closely integrated.

In a service firm, the technology is very different. There is very little opportunity to inventory anything, and the system itself contains no inventories; it is a real-time experience. The impact of this is that the coordination of the different functions takes place at two points in the organization—at the very top and the very bottom. At the bottom, the site manager is often called on to make trade-offs between marketing, operations, and personnel. While the site manager may frequently receive conflicting orders from different functional groups at the head office, he or she does have day-to-day control of the service operation, which provides the experience that the consumer buys. Marketing cannot take possession of the "product," as it can with goods, since it must be created in real time in the field. For example, in an accounting firm, it is usually the individual accountant that has to make the trade-off between the cost effectiveness of doing an audit and the needs of the client, to decide how much to reduce operational efficiency in order to spend time with the client offering general business advice.

Faced with such a problem and the need to tip the balance in favor of marketing effectiveness, the organization must decide whether to create a marketing department and, if so, where in the organization to place that department. Should it be a centralized head-office function? Should it be decentralized as individuals or small departments based at the sites? Gronroos (1980, 1985) suggests that the marketing role should be decentralized and, indeed, that there should be few formally titled marketing people. He draws the important distinction between marketing orientation, the marketing function, and the marketing department. According to Gronroos, "Marketing orientation means that a firm or organization plans its operations according to market needs. The objectives of the firm should be to satisfy customer needs rather than merely to use existing production facilities or raw materials" (Gronroos, 1985, p. 16). A marketing orientation is clearly a philosophy that puts the customers' needs first in any trade-off. It does not require a formally designated marketing department.

The functions of marketing include product design, pricing, and promotion. While these functions must be carried out if an organization is to operate, they need not necessarily be carried out by a formal marketing department. Gronroos suggests that all that is necessary is to create a marketing orientation and that the various marketing functions should be carried out by people throughout the organization. Indeed, he argues that the creation of any form of marketing department may be counterproductive in that it could lead to an attitude that worrying about the consumers is the marketing department's job and others in the organization need not be concerned with it. Thus, the creation of the department, particularly a centralized one, can destroy the orientation that it was created to produce. Unfortunately, Gronroos's suggestion is more complex than it at first appears. The field of organizational behavior has long since abandoned the idea that there is one best way to structure and manage an organization. Instead, research has shown that certain organizational features work in some environments and not in others. This has become known as the contingency approach (Ashby, 1968; Miles, Snow, and Pfeffer, 1974).

A Contingency Model of Marketing Organization

According to contingency theory, what is the most appropriate organizational structure depends on the environment faced by the organization and the production technology that it employs (Burns and Stalker, 1971; Lawrence and Lorsch, 1967b; Lorsch and Morse, 1974). Because organizations operate in constantly changing environments, they must adapt to fit the circumstances that they face at any given time. Thus, there is no uniquely successful organizational place for the marketing department; different environments imply different organizational solutions. And a design that is appropriate at one time may become outmoded if the environment evolves.

Organizations should not be simply reactive; rather, management should continuously develop growth plans and attempt to improve profit performance by whatever means possible. The appropriate marketing organization is therefore the outcome of a dynamic tension between the external environment, particularly competition; the objectives of management; and the underlying technology of the firm, which is partly at management's discretion (see Figure 14.2).

The Competitive Environment. Organizations do not exist in isolation but must be responsive to their competitive environments. In a service firm with no competitors, it would be possible to subjugate the need for marketing effectiveness to operational efficiency. This is a rare situation, however. For most firms, there are few barriers to competition other than location. Service marketing, then, is a response to competitive pressures. An increasingly competitive environment may require stronger coordination of marketing decisions, which may mean the creation of a marketing function, either at the site level or centralized, to collect relevant information and generally improve the quality of marketing decision making. Unfortunately, efforts to adopt a marketing orientation often encounter conflict with

Figure 14.2. Marketing Organization as the Outcome of a
Three-Way Tension.

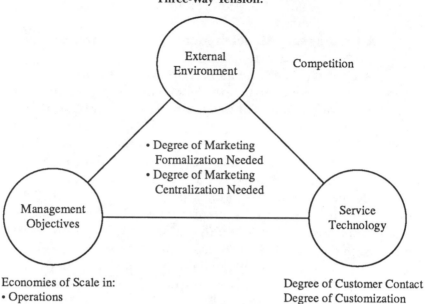

Economies of Scale in:
- Operations
- Marketing
- Personnel and Management

the goal of operational efficiency. Particularly if the organization has been operations-dominated in the past, a strong marketing department may be necessary to prevent the very natural search for operational efficiency from predominating.

Management Objectives. Contingency theory posits that the effectiveness of an organization can be judged only in terms of the objectives set for it. At the heart of those objectives for many managements is the search for growth — not necessarily growth for its own sake but rather to enable economies of scale so that reduced costs can create a competitive advantage (Porter, 1980). The three key areas where such economies can be obtained are operations, marketing, and personnel and management, particularly site management.

A large-scale operation is more amenable to the kinds of

operational tactics described earlier and more capable of generating the excess resources needed to invest in research and development to create economies of scale. Clearly, however, an organization that invests in new technology, either hard or soft, should implement that technology in as many sites as possible. Economies of scale within operations, then, are more easily created in a centralized organization than in a decentralized one.

Within marketing, perhaps one of the key ways to realize economies is the creation of a brand name, which can permit higher prices than charged by unbranded competition. Brands appear to work by offering consumers a guarantee of quality. Such quality guarantees, of course, require the "product" to be consistent. Here, again, centralization creates an advantage. In a decentralized system, the trade-off between operations and marketing is made at the site level and in the context of local markets, so that it is extremely unlikely that the service offered at the different sites will be the same. It should be noted that contingency theory reveals that the creation of a brand itself involves a trade-off. If local markets differ, logic would imply the creation of "local products" to fit them. Branding trades off that local market fit against the economic benefits of the brand.

Economies of scale can also be beneficial in employee recruitment and training if these tasks are carried out by a centralized operation or personnel function rather than individual operating managers. Perhaps more important, scale can yield economies of management. A completely decentralized management system requires a high caliber of manager, as each manager has to be capable of running a business successfully. In a more centralized system, the skill of the individual manager can be replaced with procedures and systems. Each of the key sources of economies of scale therefore implies centralization of the operations department. The creation of a brand implies a centralized advertising function, at the very least. Such a function would be responsible for maintaining the brand identity and creating suitable advertising. However, such centralization of the operations department also poses the risk that the organization will become completely operations-dominated, particularly if marketing is not centralized but is a site-level responsibility. Therefore, where operations are centralized, a strong marketing department is necessary to countervail the dominance of the operations group.

The Technology Matrix for Services. Figure 14.3 shows a matrix suggested by Maister and Lovelock (1982). One axis of the matrix represents the organization's degree of customer contact. According to Chase's (1978) concept of an interactive system in which consumers participate, the higher the level of customer contact, the higher the inefficiency produced by the uncertainty that customers introduce in the system. The second axis of the matrix represents the amount of customization of the service available to the consumers. Here, the less customization, the greater the system's ability to operate in ideal "production-line" fashion. A number of sample systems have been introduced into the cells to illustrate how the matrix is used. For example, a travel agency can operate in a number of cells simultaneously. Booking a plane ticket by telephone for a business traveler fits into the low-low cell. But when the agency is operating as a shop—that is, dealing with customers on site—the degree of customization can vary according to the service being performed; for instance, providing an airline ticket for a business traveler or designing a multistop European trip for a holidaymaker.

From an operations perspective, the ideal cell is the one that is low on both axes: Customer contact is minimized, so that large parts of the organization can be isolated and run like a manufacturing plant (Chase, 1978), and customization is also minimized, so that the operating system can be focused on a limited range of output and hence its efficiency increased (Skinner, 1974). However, a move to this cell may have major implications for marketing. Customers who seek contact and customization may be willing to pay a premium for them. For a top-quality French restaurant, for example, the loss of efficiency resulting from providing greater contact and customization than would be provided by, say, McDonald's is compensated for by the price that can be charged (although interestingly, the two restaurants may target the same people on different occasions).

Figure 14.3. The Customization–Customer Contact Matrix.

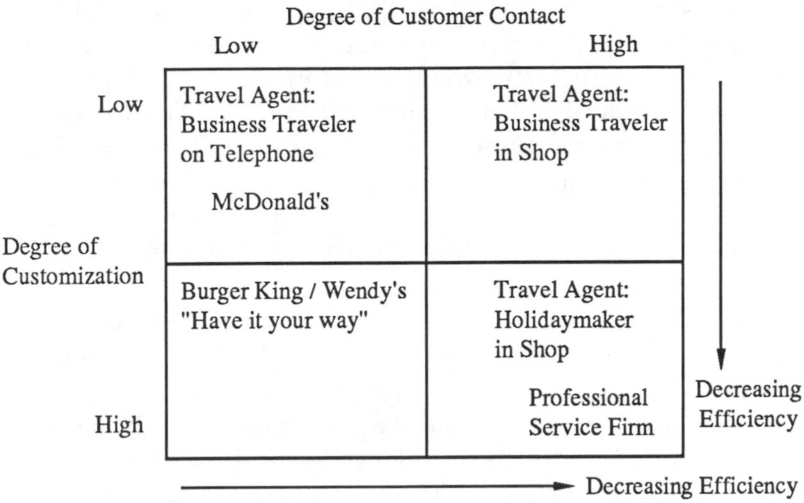

Degree of Customer Contact

	Low	High	
Low	Travel Agent: Business Traveler on Telephone McDonald's	Travel Agent: Business Traveler in Shop	
Degree of Customization			
High	Burger King / Wendy's "Have it your way"	Travel Agent: Holidaymaker in Shop Professional Service Firm	Decreasing Efficiency

Decreasing Efficiency

Source: Adapted from Maister and Lovelock, 1982.

The different cells suggest different roles for the marketing departments of different firms. Consider, for example, the provision of legal services by a traditional law firm and by Hyatt Legal Services. The traditional law firm will fit into the high-high cell in the matrix, with lawyers in close contact with clients and customizing the service client by client. Except for routine cases, there will be little scope for economies of scale. In addition, since the product is often created in clients' offices rather than in those of the firm and is sold by the individual consultant-professionals themselves, it is clear that a central marketing department could have little influence over the product and that most of the marketing function will be carried out at the individual level. Hyatt Legal Services, in contrast, falls into the high-low cell in the matrix. While employees are in close contact with clients, they have little discretion to customize the product. Because the firm's practice is restricted to routine types of cases, operations can be simplified and economies of scale generated. The resulting savings can be passed on to the consumer in the form of lower fees. In this type of operation, the service is

branded to add value to the consumer in a market that traditionally is not heavily branded. This implies a centralized marketing role; in addition, the systematization of operations implies centralization. One would therefore expect such firms to
have strong, centralized marketing departments. Another example of high customer contact but little discretion to customize
the product is found in the airline industry. Airline cabin personnel must adhere to closely defined rules and the systems
designed counteract the drive for operational efficiency that
might jeopardize customer safety.

Many firms with high customer contact use "mystery shoppers" to check on the behavior of their staff. The score card for
one fast-food chain's mystery shopper covers everything from
the cleanliness of the rest rooms and the tidiness of the store to
the temperature of the food and a script for service staff to use
when greeting customers and taking orders. Can such a system
engender a marketing orientation in customer-contact staff
members? Many firms are recognizing that such an approach
can turn their staff into "brainwashed robots" and, indeed,
produce the opposite of the effect desired. Rather than falling
victim to the "have a nice day" syndrome, firms should establish
educational and promotional programs for staff members so
that they can respond to the needs of customers within the limits
set by the system. A recent experience of a colleague of mine
demonstrated how such an orientation can work to tremendous
effect. On a flight on Scandinavian Airlines, he asked for a copy
of the London *Times* but was told that they had all been taken, so
he took a copy of another newspaper instead. A few moments
later the stewardess returned with a slightly crumpled copy of
the *Times:* She had noticed that the captain was carrying a *Times*
when he came on board, and she had borrowed it for the
passenger!

The Marketing Department as a Change Agent

As mentioned earlier, the use of a marketing department
to change an organization's orientation by creating an advocate
for the consumer within the organization poses the risk that

operations personnel will come to feel that they no longer have to be concerned about customers' needs, since that is the role of the marketing department (Gronroos, 1985). Such a situation might even result in open warfare between the two departments (Lovelock, Langeard, Bateson, and Eiglier, 1981). These risks can be minimized by the use of the complex integration approaches suggested by organizational behavior theorists. According to these theorists, such conflicts result from differences in orientation between the marketing and operations departments. Operations departments, by their very nature, tend to be cost-driven; their focus is on evaluating the operation to find ways to cut costs and simplify procedures. This approach tends to have a short time horizon. Marketing, by comparison, is looking for ways to enhance the "product" to create a competitive advantage, which is not likely to be achieved in the short term. Coordination of such highly differentiated functions with such competing perspectives usually requires the use of nonconventional integrating mechanisms. Organizational behavior theory suggests a number of useful strategies.

Interfunctional task forces provide a classic way of forcing disparate individuals to work together and, in so doing, to gain a better understanding of each other's perspectives. Similarly, interfunctional transfers can create informal networks of employees from different departments who come to understand and trust each other. For example, the transfer of a manager whose orientation is toward operations to a role that requires a marketing perspective can produce a general manager who has the experience to make rational and clear trade-offs between operations and marketing and the direct contacts with both groups that make it possible to overcome many of the traditional barriers to change.

Conclusion

The emergence of competition means that a marketing orientation is increasingly necessary in service firms. But creating such an orientation is no easy task. Simplistic solutions such as introducing a marketing department modeled after those found in firms that manufacture consumer packaged goods or integrating the marketing function throughout the firm with no formal marketing department do not take into account the complexity of the problem. The contingency approach developed by organizational behavior theorists suggests that appropriate solutions will vary organization by organization and market by market and will change over time and must always take into account management's need to generate economies of scale, the competitive environment, and the underlying technology of the firm.

Such a dynamic view of organizations raises the question of how much it matters whether a firm initially makes the wrong decision about the place of marketing in the organization. There is limited evidence (Langeard, Bateson, Lovelock, and Eiglier, 1981) that an unsuccessful marketing department can damage the effectiveness of the function for a long time. A deeper question is whether the centralization demanded by the search for economies of scale is compatible with a marketing orientation. If the result is always a strong, central marketing department at war with a strong, central operations department, the price of the disharmonies that ensue may be greater than the cost savings achieved.

References

Ashby, W. R. "Variety, Constraint, and the Law of Requisite Variety." In W. Buckley (ed.), *Modern Systems Research for the Behavioral Scientist: A Source Book*. Chicago: Aldine, 1968.

Bateson, J.E.G. "Do We Need Service Marketing?" In *Marketing Consumer Services: New Insights*. Report no. 77-115. Cambridge, Mass. Marketing Science Institute, 1977.

Bateson, J.E.G. "Why We Need Service Marketing." In O. C. Ferrell, S. W. Brown, and C. W. Lamb, Jr. (eds.), *Conceptual and Theoretical Developments in Marketing*. Chicago: American Marketing Association, 1979.

Bateson, J.E.G. "Perceived Control and the Service Encounter." In J. A. Czepiel, M. R. Solomon, and C. F. Surprenant (eds.),

The Service Encounter: Managing Employee/Customer Interaction in Service Businesses. Lexington, Mass.: Lexington Books, 1985a.

Bateson, J.E.G. "Self-Service Consumer: An Exploratory Study." *Journal of Retailing*, 1985b, *61* (3), 49–76.

Burns, T., and Stalker, G. H. *The Management of Innovation*. London: Tavistock, 1971.

Chase, R. B. "Where Does the Customer Fit in a Service Operation?" *Harvard Business Review*, 1978, *56* (6), 137–142.

Galbraith, J. R. *Designing Complex Organizations*. Reading, Mass.: Addison-Wesley, 1973.

George, W. R., and Barksdale, H. C. "Marketing Activities in the Service Industries." *Journal of Marketing*, 1974, *38* (Oct.), 65–69.

Gronroos, C. "Designing a Long Range Marketing Strategy for Services." *Long Range Planning*, 1980, *13* (Apr.), 36.

Gronroos, C. "Innovative Marketing Strategies and Organizational Structures for Service Firms." In L. L. Berry, G. L. Shostack, and G. D. Upah (eds.), *Emerging Perspectives on Services Marketing*. Chicago: American Marketing Association, 1985.

Klaus, P. G. "Quality Epiphenomenon: The Conceptual Understanding of Quality in Face-to-Face Service Encounters." In J. A. Czepiel, M. R. Solomon, and C. F. Surprenant (eds.), *The Service Encounter: Managing Employee/Customer Interaction in Service Businesses*. Lexington, Mass.: Lexington Books, 1985.

Langeard, E., Bateson, J.E.G., Lovelock, C. H., and Eiglier, P. *Services Marketing: New Insights from Consumers and Managers*. Report no. 81-104. Cambridge, Mass.: Marketing Science Institute, 1981.

Lawrence, P. R., and Lorsch, J. "Differentiation and Integration in Complex Organizations." *Administration Science Quarterly*, 1967a, *12*, 1–47.

Lawrence, P. R., and Lorsch, J. "New Management Job: The Integrator." *Harvard Business Review*, 1967b, *45*, 142.

Lawrence, P. R., and Lorsch, J. *Organization and Environment: Managing Differentiation and Integration*. Homewood, Ill.: Irwin, 1967c.

Levitt, T. "Production-Line Approach to Service." *Harvard Business Review*, 1972, *50* (5), 41–52.

Lorsch, J. R., and Morse, J. J. *Organizations and Their Members: A Contingency Approach*. New York: Harper & Row, 1974.

Lovelock, C. H., Langeard, E., Bateson, J.E.G., and Eiglier, P. "Some Organizational Problems Facing Marketing in the Service Sector." In J. H. Donnelly and W. R. George (eds.), *Marketing of Services*. Chicago: American Marketing Association, 1981.

Maister, D. H., and Lovelock, C. H. "Managing Facilitator Services." *Sloan Management Review*, 1982, *23* (4), 19–31.

Miles, R. E., Snow, C. C., and Pfeffer, J. "Organizational Environments: Concepts and Issues." *Industrial Relations*, Oct. 1974, pp. 244–264.

Porter, M. E. *Competitive Strategy: Techniques for Analyzing Industries and Competitors*. New York: Free Press, 1980.

Sayles, L. R. "Matrix Management: The Structure with a Future." *Organizational Dynamics*, 1976, *5* (Autumn), 2–17.

Schneider, B. "The Service Organization: Climate Is Crucial." *Organizational Dynamics*, 1980, *9* (2), 52–65.

Skinner, W. "The Focused Factory." *Harvard Business Review*, 1974, *52* (3), 113–121.

Thompson, J. D. *Organizations in Action*. New York: McGraw-Hill, 1967.

15

Managing Interactions Between Operations and Marketing and Their Impact on Customers

Christopher H. Lovelock

Customers often complain that service organizations are unresponsive and bureaucratic. They describe confusing facilities in which they have had to run from pillar to post in order to complete a transaction, lengthy lines, personnel who decline to serve them because "that's not my job" or "I'm not allowed to do that," inconvenient service locations and hours, replacement of service people by machines that customers are expected to operate themselves, and seemingly unnecessary rules and regulations. These experiences are but a few of the many tedious impacts of operations on customers. However, an operations manager would be entirely justified in claiming that each of these situations also reflects a businesslike trade-off between customer satisfaction and efficient management of operations. Marketers who seek to respond to customer preferences must understand operations strategy—and the concepts that underlie it—before rushing to advocate new service features and changes in delivery systems.

Figure 15.1. The Search for Compatibility.

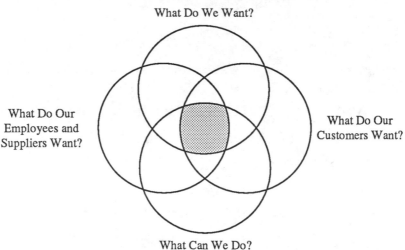

Conflict and Compromise in Service Businesses

Managing any type of organization entails conflict between differing goals and agendas. This is particularly true in businesses with a high degree of customer contact (Chase, 1978, 1981), which brings customers much closer to the operation than is the case when they deal with the service firm at arm's length. The challenge for service managers is to search for compatibility between four basic forces in a service business: what the organization's management wants, what its employees and suppliers want, what customers want, and what the organization is actually capable of doing. These forces are represented as four circles in Figure 15.1 (an extension of a simpler, three-element schematic by Longman, 1987). Top managers need to consider the intersection of each of six pairs of circles:

- Is what we (management) want something that we (the firm) can do? If not, our goals are meaningless.
- Is what we want what our employees and suppliers want? If not, many prospective employees may choose not to work

for our organization, and neither employees nor suppliers will try very hard to help us achieve our corporate goals.

- Is what we want what our customers want? If not, we may gain a reputation as a tightfisted, uncaring, even unethical organization unwilling to emphasize responsiveness to customers and interested only in its own goals and agenda.
- Is what employees and suppliers want what customers want? If not, customers will quickly detect a lack of interest among service personnel in meeting users' priorities and perhaps a lack of enthusiasm for providing customers with a quality service experience.
- Is what employees and suppliers want what we can do? If not, the firm may not be able to pay competitive wages and fees, provide satisfactory working conditions, and offer either the training or technological leverage that many service workers require to perform at top efficiency.
- Is what we can do what our customers want? If not, both parties are barking up the wrong tree. Either we must look for different market segments, ones that value what our firm has to offer, or we must change what we can do to bring it into line with what our customers want.

The goal of effective management, of course, is to bring these four circles into the closest possible convergence so as to maximize the shaded area in the middle—the win-win area where all parties enjoy a mutually rewarding relationship. The focus of this chapter is on enhancing the convergence between what the firm can do, which is largely determined by its operational capabilities, and what the customers want—which it is marketing's responsibility to determine and shape.

Operations and Marketing

No management function is unimportant in service businesses, but two functions, operations and marketing, drive management strategy in today's marketplace. Unfortunately, managers responsible for these two functions are sometimes at odds with each other in their conceptions of how to meet the organization's goals. Successful service firms work to integrate operations and marketing (Heskett, 1986).

The operations function is at the core of the business, since it creates and assembles the service product, often as it is delivered. Historically, operations concerns (discussed in more detail later) have dominated service management. With increasing competition in service industries, many firms have sought to develop an effective marketing function to act as a bridge between the organization and the environment within which it operates. Marketing is concerned with identifying needs and trends within the marketplace and developing a strategy for targeting specific market segments. Marketers' responsibilities include creating new product concepts and distribution and pricing strategies, developing communication programs, and monitoring the activities of the competition. But the introduction of a marketing orientation into service businesses has sometimes met with resistance from operations executives, who often see marketing as just an add-on function that should be confined to consumer research and communication efforts (Lovelock, 1984). Consequently, when marketers seek to get involved in product design and service delivery, their efforts may be resented by operations managers as an intrusion into the operating domain.

The issue is not merely a matter of turf: It reflects the operations focus on delivering a smoothly running and cost-efficient service. Langeard, Bateson, Lovelock, and Eiglier (1981) note how a seemingly attractive product innovation championed by marketing management in a quick-service restaurant chain led to serious operational difficulties. The product in question was a new menu item. As a senior operations executive recalled, "It was a big mistake. Our stores are small. They didn't have space for the new equipment that was needed. It [the menu item] was really popular with our customers, but started to mess up the rest of our operation. . . . Marketing people are often very creative but should concentrate more on being total businessmen. Operations people tend to rate the marketing folks on how well they understand the operation" (p. 89).

Key Operational Issues and Concepts. Despite interfirm and interindustry differences, there are a number of key operations issues and concepts with which all marketers of high-contact services ought to be familiar. This chapter discusses eleven operational issues that are as relevant to marketers as to operations personnel: productivity improvement, make-versus-buy decisions, facilities location, standardization versus customization, batch versus unit processing, facilities layout and design, job design, learning curves, management of capacity, quality control, and management of queues. All are concepts commonly discussed in operations management textbooks (see, for instance, Chase and Aquilano, 1989; Fitzsimmons and Sullivan, 1982; Hendrick and Moore, 1985; Sasser, Olsen, and Wyckoff, 1978). Marketers need to understand why these issues are of concern to operations managers and how they affect both operations and marketing strategy. But learning is not a one-way street. It is most important that operations personnel recognize the implications of their strategies for the customers they serve.

Interrelationships Between Issues. Many of these issues are, of course, interrelated. For instance, effective management of capacity is very important for improving productivity. Establishing appropriate queuing systems helps to ensure that capacity is used to the best advantage. The design of facilities should reflect the need to handle queues that might be anticipated. And consideration should be given to processing customers or objects in batches rather than one by one.

Certainly, most of the previously noted issues also apply to low-contact services, such as mail order, credit cards, insurance, and telecommunications—especially to their back-office operations. However, when the customer is virtually excluded from the factory and deals with the service supplier at arm's length, the nature of the operation obviously has relatively less impact on the customer (and vice versa). Issues such as facilities location, layout, and design and batch versus unit processing have little bearing on customers whose only interactions with the organization are by mail, telephone, facsimile machine, or interactive computer. Hence, this chapter focuses on those service industries — such as passenger transportation, hospitality, health care, professional services, traditional forms of retail banking, participatory entertainment, education, and personal care — that tend to have a high degree of contact with their customers.

Marketing Implications

Our review of the eleven operational issues listed above begins with issues involving decisions that reflect the broad operational strategy of the organization and then deals with issues involving day-to-day operational activities. For each issue, we examine how operational decisions affect customers and consider the appropriate role for marketing.

Productivity Improvement. At the heart of most operational strategies is the search for productivity improvements, which are achieved when the volume or value of output increases in relation to the volume or value of inputs. Operational approaches to achieving this goal include working employees harder, recruiting and training more productive employees, reducing employee turnover, investing in more efficient equipment, automating labor tasks, eliminating bottlenecks that lead to unproductive downtime in the operational processes, standardizing both the process and the resulting service output, and instituting tighter controls on all fronts (Heskett, 1986). At issue for marketers is whether these approaches are positively or negatively received by customers. Among the potential marketing problems are that overworked employees may deliver lower-quality service, customers may perceive automated service delivery as inferior to human interaction, and they may be turned off by too much standardization. Certainly, such approaches are likely to fail if not planned and managed with customer needs and preferences in mind.

In a high-contact service, where customers are involved in the production process, there may be opportunities to make customers themselves more productive. Mills (1986) emphasizes the importance of socializing the customer to behave as a "partial employee." Bowen (1986) argues for managing customers as human resources in service organizations. Goodwin (1988) states that four steps are necessary to socialize customers to behave in desired ways: learning new skills, developing a new self-image, developing new relationships with providers and even fellow customers, and acquiring new values. Lovelock and Young (1979) suggest three broad strategies for changing customer behavior in ways that will increase the productivity of the operation:

- Change the timing of customer demand to encourage use of the service during periods when demand is low and productive capacity is underutilized.
- Involve customers more in the production process, encouraging them through self-service or interactions with machines to take over tasks formerly performed by service personnel.
- Get customers to use intermediaries for the delivery of certain service elements.

What we see here is the use of marketing to help solve operational problems. However, incentives such as time and cost savings may be needed, especially when customers are asked to change established habits (Langeard, Bateson, Lovelock, and Eiglier, 1981; Bateson, 1985).

Make-Versus-Buy Decisions. Make-or-buy choices by a service company are simply vertical integration decisions and usually reflect such criteria as costs, quality control, and availability of capacity. Examples of common buy decisions in services include subcontracting recruitment and training of employees to temporary help firms, using contract food services, and entering into agreements with intermediaries such as travel agencies, 800-number operators, and brokers to supply information, accept reservations, and make sales. In some instances, these decisions are made because the firm lacks the capability to do the work itself. But often management concludes that outside suppliers can perform the task more cheaply or better (or both).

Another reason for subcontracting tasks is that this decision frees up scarce capital and labor resources that can be better deployed on the core business.

From a marketing perspective, using outside suppliers results in loss of control to a third party, who may place a higher priority on serving other clients. It may make it harder for the firm to be responsive to customers and to resolve complaints. Further, customers will tend to blame shortcomings on the supplier of the core service, rather than the subcontractor. But there may be important benefits, too, from buying rather than making. Subcontractors who specialize in delivering a particular service can generally do it better than the firm itself could. Tapping into national networks and employing agency representation allow a firm to increase its geographical coverage and thus enhance its sales potential. Finally, the use of subcontractors at peak periods allows the firm to be responsive to surges in demand.

Work can also be delegated to customers through the medium of self-service. Gas stations, for instance, often provide a choice between full-service and self-service pumps, offering a substantial discount for self-service to compensate customers for their efforts. But, at a broader level, do-it-yourself decisions by customers may actually represent competition for service businesses. Current or prospective customers may decide to employ their own labor and expertise rather than going to a service firm, to purchase their own equipment instead of retaining a service supplier, or to self-insure rather than buying insurance. Understanding customers' needs, motivations, and resources is central to the development of effective marketing strategies.

Facilities Location. Operations and marketing personnel are often at odds about where service facilities should be located. Operations concerns usually revolve around issues such as cost per square foot, convenient access for delivery trucks and other suppliers, simplified maintenance, good security, and easy access for employees. Marketers, by contrast, seek a pleasant and safe location that will help to define the image of the service organization, often arguing for proximity to other services that the customer may need—especially when their own service is not one that customers would ordinarily make special trips to obtain. They tend to want a site that customers will find easy to reach from their homes or workplaces by car, by public transportation, or on foot.

Marketers who feel that the present location is suboptimal have a variety of opportunities for improvement. One approach is to make the most of the present site by promoting access to it through means such as better maps and signing, creation of new parking areas, or institution of shuttle-bus service. Perhaps the appeal of the location can be enhanced by developing cooperative efforts with complementary service providers. If the present location is having a negative effect on sales and there seems to be little chance of improving it, marketing's best course of action may be to conduct studies documenting the potential for increasing revenue by relocating.

Standardization Versus Customization in Delivery System Design. Standardization involves limiting service options and achieving consistency in output by adopting a production-line approach to service creation and delivery—"manufacturing in the field," as Levitt (1972) described it. This approach entails division of labor, limited discretion for workers, substitution of technology for people, and management of customer behavior to achieve conformance with the operating system. In search of greater productivity and the ability to compete on price, many service firms are moving away from customization and high client contact toward a less labor-intensive "service factory" environment (Maister and Lovelock, 1982; Schmenner, 1986).

Led by franchisers, more and more service firms are standardizing their operating procedures. Costs are reduced as a result of economies of scale, and bottlenecks become easier to identify and eliminate. Quality control is aided by increased conformance to clear specifications. And standardization of job tasks allows the organization to recruit relatively unskilled, inexpensive workers who require only limited training to perform highly routinized tasks. However, standardization has its disadvantages when seen from a marketing perspective: Variations in needs tend to be ignored, and customers may tire of a uniform, homogenized service output. Further, service may start to deteriorate as employees performing highly repetitive tasks become bored and robotlike in their dealings with customers.

Marketers should understand the forces that drive the search for standardization. Instead of resisting the concept, they should look for opportunities to customize peripheral elements — for example, letting customers choose garnishes, dressings, and salad bar items in a fast-food restaurant — or to personalize the service through use of the customer's name in person or in print. Marketers should work with operations personnel to identify the relative appeal of alternative service formulations to different market segments and should promote such advantages as predictability and consistency of quality.

Batch Versus Unit Processing. Batch processing means dealing with multiple customers or items simultaneously instead of singly. This may yield economies of scale as well as making the most efficient use of capacity. Examples include transporting a group of people in a bus rather than sending each individual separately by taxi, teaching a large class of students rather than giving individual tutorials, and waiting for a large group to form before giving a tour of a museum or historic site; the restaurant chain Benihana of Tokyo seats and serves customers in groups of eight (Sasser and Klug, 1972).

Among the marketing drawbacks of batch processing is that it makes a customer feel that he or she is just one of a crowd. Further, the behavior and demeanor of other customers become part of the service experience, service scheduling tends to be less flexible, and sometimes customers have to wait until a large enough group has been assembled to constitute an economically viable batch. Marketing benefits include the possibility of lower prices for consumers and the fact that other customers may contribute positively to the experience ("meet interesting people"). Not all batch processing requires customers to interact with one another directly (airline flights, movies, and sports events, for example, do not). However, when people are thrust together in ways that require interaction—such as an extended group tour—it is generally a good strategy for the marketer to facilitate introductions, such as holding a get-acquainted cocktail party at the beginning of a tour.

Facilities Layout and Design. A fundamental choice facing all service providers is how to arrange the layout of the work flow to promote both efficiency and customer satisfaction. Operations experts identify several alternatives for laying out departments within a service facility (see, for example, Chase and Aquilano, 1989, p. 359).

With a process or job-shop layout, similar equipment or functions are grouped together in one area, requiring customers to travel from area to area according to the established (or desired) sequence of operations. Hotels, colleges, and many hospital facilities are designed this way. Such facilities are not always laid out with customer convenience in mind, sometimes requiring users to travel around the facility and even to double back in their tracks. In a flow-shop or assembly-line layout, equipment or work processes are arranged linearly according to the progressive steps by which the service is created or assembled. Examples include cafeteria service in a restaurant and well-organized registration lines in colleges or motor vehicle license departments. One of the marketing challenges here is to ensure that operations provides sufficient capacity at each step in the process to keep the line moving and also allows customers to skip steps in the process that they may not need—otherwise, they may waste time waiting at several points in the process and become frustrated. Another problem emerges in self-service situations when a customer inadvertently forgets to take a particular step (such as picking up a dessert in the cafeteria line) and has to go through the entire process again in order to attend to just one item. Advance instructions for the entire process, proper use of signs for each step in the process, sequencing that reflects customers' logic (desserts after main dishes), and roving customer service personnel who are available to answer questions will help to minimize difficulties. Finally, in a fixed position layout, customers remain at one location and service comes to them. Examples include table service in a restaurant, cable TV subscriptions, home shopping services, and in-flight airline services.

Many service organizations offer a bundle of services, comprising a combination of different processes. Airline service is a prime example, since it involves reservations, arrival at the airport, check-in, boarding, in-flight service, disembarking, baggage retrieval, and departure from the airport. The problem for customers is that switching from one process to another is likely to cause confusion and even, for novice users, disorientation. Such problems are likely to be compounded by poor use of signs, absence of instructions, and failure of customer-service agents to provide guidance.

A final issue in facilities design is physical appearance and imagery. Kotler (1974) has argued that retailers (and, by inference, other service delivery sites) should be designed with "atmospherics" in mind in order to create a desired mood, image, and ambience for the service organization. Many hotels, for instance, make elaborate attempts to create a dramatic atmosphere in their lobbies and atriums. The operational mind-set may see such efforts as poor space utilization, requiring extra expenditures on climate control and wasteful investment of scarce capital resources in unproductive assets such as sculptures and artwork. But marketers have their eyes focused on the revenue side of the ledger. They will argue for a landscaped exterior with ample parking and an attractive interior design geared to customer comfort, convenience, and even excitement. They want their customers to feel that they are being *served*, rather than being *processed* like some inanimate object in a factory. They want customers to return in the future and to spread the word to friends and acquaintances. To the greatest extent possible, marketers seek to disguise the factory.

Job Design. Although progress has been made in automation, many service delivery systems still involve interactions between customers and service personnel. Even automated services usually have to be backed up by customer-service agents who can intervene, in person or by phone, to help customers who have run into problems. The goal of job design is to study the requirements of the operation, the nature of customer desires, the needs and capabilities of employees, and the characteristics of operational equipment in order to develop jobs that strike the best balance between sometimes conflicting demands.

Marketers often worry that operations-oriented employees may be unresponsive to customer needs. They may argue that customer satisfaction should be paramount in designing and filling customer contact positions, but operations managers are likely to have other agendas—to develop the most efficient combination of labor and technology, to reduce the potential for human error, to minimize the risk of fraud and waste, and—in certain situations—to create teams of employees working on complementary tasks who will collectively be more productive than if they worked independently (even assuming that they possessed the full array of necessary skills). In many instances, operations managers seek inputs from human resource managers on designing jobs that reflect the capabilities of the available work force, generate reasonable job satisfaction, and provide a stepping stone to positions requiring greater skill or responsibility.

As competition in service industries has increased, there has been more pressure on operations (and human resource) managers to design customer-contact jobs with customer needs in mind. This has sometimes forced a change in recruitment criteria (it may be necessary to appraise personality characteristics as well as technical skills). Similarly, training may have to be revamped to reflect marketing considerations. Increasingly, job evaluation measures reflect performance on marketing-related criteria as well as operational ones (Langeard, Bateson, Lovelock, and Eiglier, 1981). In some instances, customer-contact personnel may need to be given greater discretion and authority to deal with customer requests or emergencies, since there may not be time to pass the request "through channels."

Learning Curves. Formally defined, a learning curve is a line (usually sloping downward from left to right) that displays improvement in the relationship between the time or financial costs per unit of production and the number of consecutive units produced. As noted by Chase and Aquilano (1989), such curves can be applied to both individual and organizational learning: "Individual learning is improvement that results from a person repeating a process and gaining skill and efficiency. . . . That is, 'practice makes perfect.' Organizational learning is improvement that results from practice as well but also comes from changes in administration, equipment and product design" (p. 516).

An operational strategy predicated on driving the service production process down the learning curve poses both problems and opportunities for marketers. The most important challenge for marketing is to increase demand for the service, since without increased usage, it will take longer for the firm to move down the learning curve. Advertising, sales and promotional efforts, and lower prices may all have a role to play in demand stimulation. As the process of service delivery speeds up as a result of greater experience, customers can expect to be served faster, and the cost savings may be passed along to them in the form of lower prices, thus stimulating further demand (unless the firm decides to keep the benefits for itself in the form of higher profits).

Faster service with fewer errors may yield a competitive advantage, especially for time-sensitive consumers. On the other hand, if the service firm uses faster service as an excuse to cut the number of service delivery channels, customers are likely to find the wait for service just as long, even though transaction time itself is now shorter. Moreover, faster service may not be what customers want: They may feel that the quality of personal interactions with service providers has declined. Another risk in having service providers concentrating on (and being measured on) speed of service is that they may not take the time to determine customers' needs and problems carefully, thereby losing opportunities for both cross-selling and effective problem resolution.

Where customers are actively involved in the production process, either through self-service or by working cooperatively with service personnel, learning curve theory may apply to the customers themselves. As they become more proficient with machines such as automatic ticket dispensers or teller machines, they can complete transactions faster. Not only do these customers save themselves time and hassle, they also make the machines more productive and reduce waiting times for others. Marketers can contribute to efficiency by pointing out to operations managers that when new services are being introduced (or new customers are being attracted to existing services), there is a learning curve for consumers, too. Providing extra assistance and advice to these customers when they first make use of the service may lead to faster and smoother interactions later, to the benefit of all parties.

Management of Capacity. The capacity of an organization can be defined as the highest quantity of output possible in a given time period with a predefined level of staffing, facilities, and equipment. In short, there is an upper limit to the number of customers that the operation can handle. Some firms pursue a strategy of level capacity, with fixed hours of operation. Others use a more flexible approach, varying schedules and available capacity in a "chase-demand" approach. Capacity planning is vital for service firms that seek to match productive resources to fluctuating demand levels. It helps to keep costs down by avoiding wasteful underutilization of people, buildings, and machines when demand is low, minimizes loss of revenues from customers seeking service during peak periods, and it reduces the risk that staff and employees will become bored and sloppy as a result of having too little to do or burn out as a result of being overworked and under excessive pressure.

Possible approaches to managing capacity include using part-time employees, sharing capacity with other firms, and focusing employee efforts on key tasks during peak hours (Sasser, Olsen, and Wykoff, 1978). Although such procedures may enable the firm to increase its capacity to serve more customers (which is a marketing plus), the downside is that regular customers may perceive service quality as compromised by such measures. Creative marketing solutions to resolving imbalances between demand and capacity include managing demand through pricing and promotional strategies, searching for countercyclical services in periods of low demand for the original service, and identifying countercyclical locations where movable assets (such as rental cars or highly mobile employees) can be more profitably redeployed (Lovelock, 1984).

Quality Control. Quality control is concerned with ensuring that service execution consistently conforms to predefined standards. The marketer's task is to ensure that these standards reflect the needs and preferences of target market segments. Budgetary pressures on operations may lead to nonconformance with specifications as a result of understaffing, use of inferior labor or materials, lack of inspections, failure to invest in needed improvements or even in basic cleaning and maintenance, and poor execution by employees who feel overworked, underpaid, frustrated by unsatisfactory working conditions, or otherwise put upon.

Quality problems are often perceptual: What an operator may consider to be quality work may not be so perceived by the customer. Sometimes this results from unrealistic expectations on the customer's part (perhaps stimulated by salesperson claims or advertising messages that imply unrealistically high standards of performance). On other occasions, customers may not realize just how good service execution actually was, since the operations personnel failed to point out the quality of work performed.

Marketing opportunities in the area of quality start with continual monitoring of customer needs, preferences, and evaluations. The findings should then be fed back to operations personnel, who may find them useful for future redesign of the service or of quality-control standards, as well as current control of quality to conform to existing service standards. One useful way for marketers to work with customer-contact personnel is to get employee feedback on customer reactions to service; research by Schneider, Parkington, and Buxton (1980) shows that employees and customers tend to have similar perceptions of service quality. Another is encouraging employees to draw customers' attention to features of performance execution that are not immediately obvious, in order to emphasize the quality of service delivered.

Management of Queues. Waiting for service is an almost universal phenomenon: Virtually every organization faces the problem of waiting-line systems (or queues) somewhere in its operation (Maister, 1979). People line up for tickets, they wait for seats in a theater, they wait for their bills after a restaurant meal. Things as well as people wait for processing, of course: Letters pile up on an executive's desk, shoes sit on racks waiting to be repaired at the shoemaker's, checks wait to be cleared at a bank, an incoming phone call waits to be switched to a customer-service representative by the automatic call distributor. In each instance, a customer may be waiting for the outcome of that work — an answer to a letter, a pair of shoes ready to be picked up, a check credited to the customer's balance, contact made with the customer-service representative in place of listening to recorded Muzak while on hold.

Waiting lines occur whenever the number of arrivals at a facility exceeds the capacity of the system to process them. The first task in queue management is to determine the rate of arrivals over time so that serving capacity may be planned accordingly. A reasonable operational strategy is to optimize the use of labor and equipment by planning for average throughput. So long as the people or things to be processed arrive at the average rate, there will be no delays. However, fluctuations in arrivals (often random in nature) will lead to delays at certain times as the line backs up following a clump of arrivals.

Any one of a variety of queuing systems can be selected to suit the nature of the operation. It may use single- or multiple-stage systems (in the latter instance, the customer goes through several sequential queues, receiving a different service element at each stage). Multiple channels may be offered to increase processing capacity. Management must decide whether each line should be allowed to form separately (as in supermarket checkouts) or whether new arrivals should form a single line (the "snakes" in bank lobbies and airport terminals) before being directed to the next available channel when they reach the head of the line. Another issue is whether to segregate customer lines according to the nature of the transaction—such as separate check-ins for first class, business class, and coach in an airline terminal or express lines in supermarkets and banks for customers with simple transactions that can be made quickly.

An operational mind-set could be swayed by considerations of space utilization, allocation of work between servers, and pressures on servers to speedily process customers in their lines. Marketers, however, would probably be more concerned about choosing the system that customers are likely to find fairest and least confusing. They should use insights from segmentation research to identify situations in which it would be appropriate to establish priority lines for certain customers—those who are valued and frequent users or whose business is either more profitable (first-class passengers) or faster to process (eight grocery items or fewer at a supermarket checkout).

Customers dislike being kept waiting for service, especially when it involves uncertainty or when the waiting process seems inequitable (Maister, 1985). Effective marketers try to anticipate the degree of patience in new arrivals: For any given size of line (or length of wait), how many prospective customers will simply balk at the apparent delay and walk away? Similarly, what proportion of those waiting for service will give up (or "renege") after a certain amount of time and leave the line? Further, as everyone knows, reservation systems are fallible. Hence, there is a risk that "overflow" customers may decide to try a competitor and never return.

Marketers should look for ways to make waiting more palatable. There may be opportunities to take information, cross-sell other services, and entertain the customers while they wait. The Disney Corporation is a master at designing waiting areas that make the wait look shorter than it is, give the customer the impression of constant progress, and make the wait seem to pass more quickly because customers are being amused or diverted as they wait.

Strategic Implications

Coming to terms with the differing and sometimes conflicting perspectives of marketing and operations personnel poses a challenge for managers in both of these functional areas. Marketers need to understand operational concepts and strategies, both in general terms and as these apply to specific situations. They must recognize how pursuit of a particular operational strategy will contribute to the efficiency of the organization and result in cost savings, faster service, or other benefits. In addition to determining how a given operational strategy may affect customers and thereby affect marketing strategy, marketing managers should also ask themselves how a proposed marketing activity may affect operations.

Operations managers should recognize that an operational strategy designed to reduce costs may actually be counterproductive by turning off customers and thereby eroding revenues and net profits. Above all, when working in high-contact service environments, operations personnel should recognize that processing human beings is much more complex than processing inanimate objects.

Table 15.1 summarizes the eleven operational issues presented earlier and the prototypical orientation of operations and marketing managers toward each of them. The challenge, of course, lies in finding the optimal balance between these sometimes conflicting concerns. A starting point is an evaluation of these concerns in the context of the firm's current business strategy. Porter (1980, 1985) identifies three generic competitive strategies: overall cost leadership, differentiation, and focus. We briefly consider the implications of each below.

Cost Leadership Strategies. Achieving industrywide cost leadership requires that all functional policies be oriented toward this objective. In operations, this means emphasizing efficient facilities, aggressively pursuing cost reductions through tight cost control and avoidance of marginal customer accounts,

Table 15.1. Operations and Marketing Perspectives on Operational Issues.

Operational Issues	Typical Operations Goals	Common Marketing Concerns
Productivity improvement	Reduce unit cost of production	Strategies may cause decline in service quality
Make-versus-buy decisions	Trade off control against comparative advantage and cost savings	"Make" decisions may result in lower quality and lack of market coverage; "buy" decisions may transfer control to unresponsive suppliers and hurt the firm's image
Facilities location	Reduce costs; provide convenient access for suppliers and employees	Customers may find location unattractive and inaccessible
Standardization	Keep costs low and quality consistent; simplify operations tasks; recruit low-cost employees	Consumers may seek variety, prefer customization to match segmented needs
Batch versus unit processing	Seek economies of scale, consistency, efficient use of capacity	Customers may be forced to wait, feel "one of a crowd," be turned off by other customers
Facilities layout and design	Control costs; improve efficiency by ensuring proximity of operationally related tasks; enhance safety and security	Customers may be confused, shunted around unnecessarily, find facility unattractive and inconvenient
Job design	Minimize error, waste, and fraud; make efficient use of technology; simplify tasks for standardization	Operationally oriented employees with narrow roles may be unresponsive to customer needs
Learning curves	Apply experience to reduce time and costs per unit of output	Faster service is not necessarily better service; cost saving may not be passed on as lower prices
Management of capacity	Keep costs down by avoiding wasteful underutilization of resources	Service may be unavailable when needed; quality may be compromised during high-demand periods
Quality control	Ensure that service execution conforms to predefined standards	Operational definitions of quality may not reflect customer needs, preferences
Management of queues	Optimize use of available capacity by planning for average throughput; maintain customer order, discipline	Customers may be bored and frustrated during wait, see firm as unresponsive

and minimizing costs in such functional areas as customer service, personal selling, and advertising.

These policies will tend to favor the operations perspective toward each of the eleven operational issues. Marketing's most effective role here will be to assist operations in achieving its objectives by (1) targeting communication efforts at customers who will be most likely to accept a somewhat stripped-down level of service; (2) encouraging customers to use the service in ways that will contribute to increased productivity; (3) educating customers to use the service effectively without much assistance from sales or customer-service staff; and (4) insisting on the lowest possible price consistent with profitability objectives in order to compensate customers for the no-frills nature of the service and for such inconveniences as low-rent locations, bare-bones facilities, lack of personal assistance, and queuing or crowding.

Differentiation Strategies. The generic strategy of differentiation involves creating an offering that is perceived as unique in the industry. Distinctive service will usually support a higher price and will tend to generate significant brand loyalty from customers willing to pay more in return for benefits unavailable elsewhere. Firms adopting this posture should evaluate each of the eleven operational issues in the light of their implications for customer satisfaction. Marketers will need sufficient clout to deal with operations on equal terms. Where disputes occur, top management may need to mediate. Here, the objective can be described as employing those operational concepts that will provide meaningful competitive differentiation without allowing costs to balloon out of control or the operation to grind to a halt for lack of needed resources.

Focus Strategies. A focus strategy differs from the previous two strategies in that it rests on selection of a narrow competitive arena within an industry. It is an intelligent choice for a small organization. This strategy begins with selection of a particular buyer group or geographical area to target or a limited product line to offer. Some focus strategies seek to combine each of these elements, targeting a certain type of customer in a particular geographical area with a specific service. Within the target segment, focus strategies can be divided into cost focus and differentiation focus. In both instances, marketing input is critical in selecting the nature of the focus and ensuring that operations can deliver an appropriate configuration for the target segment (if not, another segment must be sought).

If the target segment is highly price-sensitive, operational strategies must emphasize cost control. But if marketers have adequately researched segment needs, they will be able to argue against cost-cutting measures that will result in delivery of a service that is insensitive to the needs of the chosen customers. For instance, the elderly are a growing market segment. The great majority of older consumers have limited resources and so are quite price-sensitive. However, physical infirmities, a reluctance to travel very far, and concerns about personal safety may make many such customers unwilling to use self-service options, patronize distant facilities, or learn to use new high-tech delivery systems. On the other hand, since many of them are retired, they may be less pressed by time constraints and thus willing to wait longer for service and to patronize service facilities at off-peak times during daylight hours.

If the target segment is willing to pay a premium for service features unavailable elsewhere — such as customized service where attention to customer preferences and convenience is a key objective — marketers should be in the driver's seat, much as they are with a differentiation strategy. A key task here is to discourage operations from seeking false efficiencies that will reduce customer satisfaction.

Areas for Future Research

Where can researchers make a contribution toward improving the interface between operations and marketing in high-contact service businesses? Several broad areas are appropriate for further study: organizational structure, technology, human resources, new approaches to market segmentation, and customer education. Below are suggested questions for re-searchers to address in each area.

Organizational Structure. What is the most effective way of organizing the marketing and operations functions so that the two work well together? Under what circumstances should marketing personnel report to managers in the operations chain of command and vice versa? Do matrix organizational structures work well in service businesses where managers from different functions must work together on a project or product basis or within branches serving specific geographical areas? To what extent can the general management function be "pushed down" the organization so that line managers are responsible for managing both the operations and marketing functions jointly?

Technology. What roles have been played by marketing and operations in developing and introducing new technologies for creating and delivering services? Langeard, Bateson, Lovelock, and Eiglier (1981) provide good insights from their study of automated teller machines; studies of other new technologies would be helpful as well. What are the costs and payoffs of building greater "user friendliness" into new technological systems that customers are asked to use themselves?

Human Resources. Should human resources be subservient to the operations and marketing functions or carry equal authority in strategic planning and execution? How does one select and train employees who are expected to be good at both operational execution and marketing-oriented tasks such as referral selling? How does one motivate, measure, and evaluate the performance of people in such dual-responsibility jobs?

New Approaches to Segmentation. Two broad approaches to segmentation are user characteristics (such as demographics, psychographics, location, and benefits sought) and user responses (such as product-related behavior and sensitivity to marketing variables). Important research opportunities exist in services to observe differences in responses among consumers to alternative service configurations based on different operational concepts and then to correlate these with differences in user characteristics. An example is provided by Bateson (1985), who reported on consumers' disposition to use various types of self-service options in several different industries.

Customer Education and Motivation. Changes in operational procedures or introduction of new services often require customers to interact with the service organization in new ways, not only during service delivery but also in performing such tasks as placing orders and making payments. What forms of education are most effective in helping customers to understand and accept new procedures and services: advance distribution of printed literature, on-site written instructions, graphic displays, videotapes, recorded voice instruction, touch-sensitive video screens, personal demonstrations, telephone hot lines, or other media? Merely providing information may not suffice to change behavior. What incentives are most effective in bringing about trial and ongoing use of innovative procedures and services: cash payments, discounts, sweepstakes, gifts, personal recognition, or other approaches?

Conclusion

Historically, operations has been the dominant management function in most service businesses, reflecting its central role in creating and delivering the service. In today's highly competitive service markets, good marketing management is also becoming essential to success. Unfortunately, marketers and operations personnel may tend to pull in different directions, the former advocating improved service features that will appeal to customers and the latter emphasizing efficiency and cost control.

In practice, both groups of managers should be looking for ways to work together: Marketers may be able to develop customer-oriented strategies designed to make the operation run more efficiently, while operations concepts can be employed to provide better service to customers. Since the marketing function is relatively new to many service firms, it is incumbent upon marketing managers to develop a good understanding of key operational concepts so that they can learn how the business works and then develop marketing strategies that mesh with operations.

References

Bateson, J.E.G. "Self-Service Consumer: An Exploratory Study." *Journal of Retailing*, 1985, *61* (Fall), 49–76.

Bowen, D. E. "Managing Customers as Human Resources in Service Organizations." *Human Resource Management*, 1986, *25*, 371–384.

Chase, R. B. "Where Does the Customer Fit in a Service Operation?" *Harvard Business Review*, 1978, *56* (6), 137–142.

Chase, R. B. "The Customer Contact Approach to Services: Theoretical Bases and Practical Extensions." *Operations Research*, 1981, *29* (4), 698–706.

Chase, R. B., and Aquilano, N. J. *Production and Operations Management: A Life-Cycle Approach.* (5th ed.) Homewood, Ill.: Irwin, 1989.

Fitzsimmons, J. A., and Sullivan, R. S. *Service Operations Management.* New York: McGraw-Hill, 1982.

Goodwin, C. "Training the Service Consumer to Contribute to Service Productivity." *Journal of Services Marketing*, Fall 1988, pp. 71–78.

Hendrick, T. E., and Moore, F. G. *Production/Operations Management.* (9th ed.) Homewood, Ill.: Irwin, 1985.

Heskett, J. L. *Managing in the Service Economy.* Boston: Harvard Business School Press, 1986.

Kotler, P. "Atmospherics as a Marketing Tool." *Journal of Retailing*, Winter 1974, pp. 48–64.

Langeard, E., Bateson, J.E.G., Lovelock, C. H., and Eiglier, P. *Services Marketing: New Insights from Consumers and Managers.* Report no. 81-104. Cambridge, Mass.: Marketing Science Institute, 1981.

Levitt, T. "Production-Line Approach to Service." *Harvard Business Review*, 1972, *50* (5), 41–52.

Longman, R. "The W3 Diagram." Unpublished paper, 1987.

Lovelock, C. H. *Services Marketing.* Englewood Cliffs, N.J.: Prentice-Hall, 1984.

Lovelock, C. H., and Young, R. F. "Look to Consumers to Increase Productivity." *Harvard Business Review,* 1979, *57* (3), 168–178.

Maister, D. H. *Note on the Management of Queues.* No. 9-680-053. Boston: Harvard Business School Press, 1979.

Maister, D. H. "The Psychology of Waiting Lines." In J. A. Czepiel, M. R. Solomon, and C. F. Surprenant (eds.), *The Service Encounter: Managing Employee/Customer Interaction in Service Businesses.* Lexington, Mass.: Lexington Books, 1985.

Maister, D. H., and Lovelock, C. H. "Managing Facilitator Services." *Sloan Management Review,* 1982, *23* (4), 19–31.

Mills, P. *Managing Service Industries: Organizational Practices in a Post-Industrial Economy.* Cambridge, Mass.: Ballinger, 1986.

Porter, M. E. *Competitive Strategy: Techniques for Analyzing Industries and Competitors.* New York: Free Press, 1980.

Porter, M. E. *Competitive Advantage: Creating and Sustaining Superior Performance.* New York: Free Press, 1985.

Sasser, W. E., and Klug, J. *Benihana of Tokyo.* No. 9-673-057. Boston: Harvard Business School Press, 1972.

Sasser, W. E., Olsen, R. P., and Wyckoff, D. D. *Management of Service Operations: Text, Cases, and Readings.* Boston: Allyn & Bacon, 1978.

Schmenner, R. W. "How Can Service Businesses Survive and Prosper?" *Sloan Management Review,* Spring 1986, pp. 21–32.

Schneider, B., Parkington, J. J., and Buxton, V. M. "Employee and Customer Perceptions of Service in Banks." *Administrative Science Quarterly,* 1980, *25* (June), 252–267.

16

Communicating with Customers About Service Quality

Valarie A. Zeithaml

As firms and researchers are beginning to understand the nature of perceived service quality, they are recognizing that a major cause of dissatisfaction is the gap between what a firm promises about a service and what it actually delivers (Parasuraman, Zeithaml, and Berry, 1985). Accurate and appropriate communication—advertising, personal selling, and publicity that do not overpromise or misrepresent—is essential to delivering services that customers perceive as high in quality.

Literature on the advertising of services in general is scarce (notable exceptions are George and Berry, 1981; Legg and Baker, 1987; Wolfinbarger and Gilly, 1988), and research on communicating service quality in particular is virtually nonexistent. A key reason for the scarcity of literature in this area is that the process of meeting customer expectations in services involves issues that cross disciplinary boundaries. Because service advertising promises what *people* do—and because what people do cannot be controlled in the way that machines that produce physical goods can be controlled—this type of communication involves functions other than the marketing department. In goods firms, the marketing and operations functions can (in theory) be totally separate, because goods can be fully designed and produced by the operations function and then turned over to marketing for promotion and sale. While there is usually interaction between operations and marketing in a goods firm, technically it is not necessary, because each department could perform its job separately. In services, however, marketing and operations can rarely be separated. Therefore, successful services advertising becomes the responsibility of both marketing and operations: Marketing must accurately but beguilingly reflect what happens in actual service encounters, and operations must deliver what is promised in advertising. If advertising or personal selling sets up unrealistic expectations for customers, the actual encounter will disappoint the customer. In a similar way, operations must cooperate with advertising to carry out themes of courtesy, responsiveness, and reliability that are presented in advertising. Interdependence exists, making cooperation and communication between these two functions critical.

The second disciplinary boundary that must be crossed is the one between human resources and marketing. To deliver excellent customer service, firms must treat their employees as customers (Berry, 1981; Gronroos, 1985). How the human resource function serves employees through training, motivation, compensation, and recognition has a powerful impact on the quality of service that employees deliver.

Breaking down the walls between functions is difficult and time consuming, but high-quality service delivery requires understanding and cooperation across different departments. Good research on communicating service quality also requires that researchers span several disciplines: marketing, organizational behavior, and operations. This chapter considers the issues that are involved in (1) researching communications about service quality and (2) developing appropriate and effective communications about service quality. The first section describes a research instrument that could be used to research and measure service quality. Then a number of interdisciplinary propositions are offered to provide a starting point for exploration in this area. These propositions deal with marketing and organizational issues that affect the accuracy and effectiveness of communication. The propositions are testable; verification or refutation through later research could suggest strategies for improving communication efforts.

SERVQUAL: A Multiple-Item Scale
for Measuring Service Quality

The literature on service quality in general and on communications about service quality in particular has been largely conceptual. Ideas and strategies suggested in these conceptual articles are intriguing and intuitive, yet empirical confirmation remains to be accomplished. To empirically test assumptions about the relationship between service quality and company communication, a valid and reliable instrument measuring service quality is necessary. A potentially useful instrument for providing this empirical verification is SERVQUAL, a multiple-item scale for determining consumer perceptions of service quality (Parasuraman, Zeithaml, and Berry, 1988).

SERVQUAL is a generic instrument that has desirable psychometric properties and that captures the most important aspects of consumer perceptions of service quality. Its development involved several phases (described in detail in Parasuraman, Zeithaml, and Berry, 1988), beginning with an exploratory study to delineate the conceptual domain and then entailing several data-collection phases that refined the instrument. The resulting SERVQUAL scale consists of twenty-two items representing consumer expectations and twenty-two matching items representing consumer perceptions of the service delivered by a specific company. These items are used to measure five abstract dimensions that capture the construct of perceived service quality:

1. Reliability—ability to perform the promised service dependably and accurately
2. Responsiveness—willingness to help customers and to provide prompt service
3. Assurance—knowledge and courtesy of employees and their ability to inspire trust and confidence

4. Empathy—caring, individualized attention to customers
5. Tangibles—physical facilities, equipment, and appearance of personnel

These measures are then used to compute perceived service quality by subtracting expectations from perceptions ($SQ = P - E$). The five dimensions and the dual measures (expectations plus perceptions) provide flexibility and diagnostic capability. In the sections that follow, suggestions will be offered about possible uses of SERVQUAL in testing the propositions. In addition to the SERVQUAL scale, Parasuraman, Zeithaml, and Berry (1985, 1988) have developed measures to capture four areas of discrepancy, or "gaps," in a firm's delivery of service, as well as the variables that explain each of the four gaps (see Chapter Ten).

Interdisciplinary Propositions

This section presents a number of propositions, most of which span departments and disciplines, that deal with key ideas or issues in communicating service quality. The development of many of these key ideas was based on three seminal conceptual papers in the area (George and Berry, 1981; Legg and Baker, 1987; Wolfinbarger and Gilly, 1988). The discussion below describes the interdisciplinary aspects of each proposition and offers suggestions for further research.

Focus of Advertising Theme. Communicating service quality begins with an understanding of the importance to customers of the various aspects of service quality. Isolating quality dimensions that are most important to customers provides a focus for advertising efforts.

Proposition 1:   Focusing on the most important dimension of service quality will result in more effective communications than focusing on other dimensions.

Using SERVQUAL and techniques for measuring direct or indirect importance weights (described in Parasuraman, Zeithaml, and Berry, 1988, 1989), researchers can evaluate the salience of the five service quality dimensions for any service industry. Despite expectations to the contrary, previous research by the developers of SERVQUAL (Parasuraman, Zeithaml, and Berry, 1988, 1989) has provided surprisingly consistent rankings of the dimensions across service industries. In virtually all the empirical work accomplished thus far, reliability stands above all others in importance, regardless of the specific service: Customers consistently rank reliability as the most important of the five dimensions.

Proposition 2: Advertising that emphasizes reliability will be more effective than advertising that focuses on any other service quality dimension.

Several explanations can be offered for the salience of reliability. First, it may be ranked as most important because customers truly believe that outcome, rather than process of delivery (which is captured in the other four dimensions), is the most vital aspect of a service. If this is the case, reliability would continue to be rated most important over time, and companies would be best served by focusing on this dimension in advertising. However, reliability may now be pivotal, because customers are conditioned to low levels of service performance (as witnessed by the spate of articles in the popular press bemoaning the declining state of service in the United States) and long for the days when reliable service was possible. If this explanation is true, improved service levels in an industry would lead to perceptions that all competitors meet expectations for reliability, and responsiveness, which has been the second most important dimension, would emerge as most important.

Objections to an emphasis on reliability in advertising are frequently heard in discussions with executives. Bank executives question, for example, "We're reliable, our competitors are reliable — why focus on something that everyone has?" If, in fact, all competitors in industry are reliable, this dimension would not differentiate among firms, and companies would obtain the biggest impact by stressing another dimension. However, this response often results from a misperception that customers believe a service to be reliable. It is worthwhile to obtain evidence from the customer that all banks are perceived as reliable. SERVQUAL could be used to obtain a comparison between expectations and perceptions (including perceptions of competitors) that would confirm or refute executives' projections about customer beliefs.

Proposition 2 suggests that, lacking other evidence, reliability should be a central focus of advertising. American Airlines' "The On-Time Machine" campaign is an example of this approach. Before accepting this general finding as valid for any particular industry at any given time, companies would be well advised to collect data on the importance of the dimensions and focus on ones that are most critical to the customer base.

Using Communication to Manage Customer Expectations. According to Parasuraman, Zeithaml, and Berry (1985), service quality is by definition the amount of congruence between customer expectations and perceptions of the actual service. The expectations that customers bring to the service affect their evaluations of its quality. This suggests that the higher the expectation, the better the delivered service must be to be perceived as high in quality. Therefore, promising reliability in advertising is appropriate only when reliability is actually delivered. Promising no surprises at a hotel, as Holiday Inn once did, is disastrous if what actually happens in the delivery process is many surprises. It is essential for the marketing department to understand the levels of service delivery (for example, percentage of times the service is provided correctly, percentage and number of problems that arise) before making these promises. Before making its claims about on-time arrival, American Airlines knew that it had the best on-time-arrival record in the industry. The airline also planned systems to be responsive to problems encountered when a flight was late.

If advertising shows a smiling young woman at the counter in a McDonald's commercial, the customer expects that—at least most of the time — there will be a smiling young woman in the local McDonald's. If advertising claims that a customer's wake-up call will always be on time at a Ramada Inn, the customer expects no mistakes. Raising expectations to unrealistic levels may lead to more initial business but invariably fosters customer disappointment and discourages repeat business.

> Proposition 3:   Holding service level constant, customers with higher expectations will evaluate quality more negatively than will those with lower expectations.

How can service providers lower expectations without losing business? No research has yet been done to answer this question, but several strategies offer potential and could be tested empirically. One strategy would be to explain in communications those aspects of service that create problems in the industry as a whole, rather than just in the focal company. When deregulation and intense competition led to poor on-time performance in the airline industry, American Airlines ran an advertisement entitled "Why Are Airlines Always Late?" It described conditions in the industry as a whole — overcrowded airports, poor scheduling, peaks and valleys in demand — that caused delays and then described company actions under way to alleviate this problem. The company simultaneously lowered expectations of airlines in general and raised perceptions of American Airlines' efforts to improve customer service. The advertisement was immensely successful and led to the broader "On-Time Machine" campaign. Another way to manage expectations is to describe the service delivery process and provide the customer a choice between quicker, lower-quality provision and slower, higher-quality provision. In advertising or consulting, for example, speed is often essential but interferes with performance. If customers understand this trade-off, they can make informed choices.

   In both these strategies, marketing reflects a full and accurate understanding of the operations function — how long it takes to accomplish a project, how successfully the company delivers, how often mistakes occur. In order to have this understanding, the marketing and operations functions must interact at some level. This communication bridge between marketing and operations is essential in managing expectations. We propose, therefore, that:

> Proposition 4:   When marketing and operations interact to create external communications, customer expectations are more realistic than when these functions do not interact.

The more realistic customer expectations are, the smaller is the gap between expectations and perceptions of delivered service quality. The impact of level of expectation on perceived service quality can be tested empirically by inducing different levels of customer expectations in experimental settings. SERVQUAL or similar instruments could calibrate the impact of levels of expectations on evaluations of quality.

Focus on the Evidence. The importance of tangibles in communicating about services is well documented (Shostack, 1977; Berry and Clark, 1986; Zeithaml, 1981; Zeithaml, Parasuraman, and Berry, 1985). Legg and Baker (1987) provide a theoretical justification for the importance of tangibles. According to their reasoning, tangibles provide *vivid information* — information that creates a strong or clear impression on the senses and produces a distinct mental image. The use of vivid information is particularly desirable in advertising services that are intangible and complex. Among the specific strategies for effective use of vividness are (1) featuring the tangibles, such as by showing the bank's marble columns or gold credit card; (2) representing the service with related tangibles, such as Qantas Airlines' use of the koala bear (Berry and Clark, 1986); (3) explaining the service in concrete rather than abstract terms; (4) evoking strong emotion, such as with AT&T's successful "Reach Out and Touch Someone" campaign; and (5) encouraging customer identification, such as by using popular local celebrities in promotion.

Because services are performances that cannot be seen,

touched, or otherwise sensed, tangibles associated with the service provide clues about its nature and quality. Planning and
communicating the tangible and intangible elements of the
service so that they are mutually reinforcing and vivid can help a
service company improve its quality image. Legg and Baker
(1987) provide a series of useful and testable propositions about
aspects of vividness in advertising, the most important of which
is restated below.

> Proposition 5:   The more vivid the advertisement, the
> stronger the effect in influencing consumer expecta-
> tions about quality.

One type of vividness involves what Alesandri (1983) calls
interactive imagery. Imagery, defined as a mental event that involves the visualization of a concept or relationship (Lutz and
Lutz, 1978), can enhance recall of names and facts about products. Interactive imagery integrates two or more items in some
mutual or reciprocal action (Alesandri, 1983), resulting in improved recall. Research in advertising confirms that interactive
images facilitate recall of company or brand names, and inducing these visualizations can be an effective way to communicate
about quality. Legg and Baker (1987) suggest that this type of
imagery is useful in conveying messages about services such
that:

> Proposition 6:   Interactive imagery is more effective
> than noninteractive imagery in enhancing service
> quality perceptions.

To be effective, advertising that is vivid and that uses
interactive imagery requires coordination and communication
among functions. The tangibles associated with a service are
often developed in the operations function, particularly when
they involve the physical place where the service is provided.
Marketing is in many cases limited to using the same theme or
ambience in its advertising that is expressed in its physical
environment. If the operations and marketing functions inter-

act effectively, the representation in external communications will be influenced positively.

Employees as a Target of Advertising. George and Berry (1981) emphasize that customer-contact personnel are an important second audience for services advertising. Featuring actual employees doing their jobs or explaining their service in advertising is one way to communicate to employees that they are important. The featured employee also becomes a standard for other employees in the company by modeling high performance.

> Proposition 7:   Advertising that features actual employees doing their jobs is more effective in communicating excellence than advertising that uses professional talent. The effect will be present in both the primary audience (customers) and the secondary audience (employees).

One possible explanation for this effect is that in featuring employees, the marketing department must interact with at least some of the people in operations. Therefore, the communication and coordination needed to create the advertising close the gap between external communications and delivery. This proposition would be relatively easy to test in a laboratory experiment using both customers and employees as respondents. Several versions of a commercial could be prepared (the technology currently exists to produce low-cost but professional "rough cuts" of commercials) and shown to respondents. Their perceptions on the five dimensions of quality as well as on other concepts (such as job satisfaction, credibility, confidence) could be explored with SERVQUAL.

Similar benefits can be achieved through the use of other forms of advertising if customer-contact employees can be involved in the advertising process itself. A common complaint of contact employees is that companies run advertisements promising customers certain services or benefits before employees are told about the advertisements and often before they are even told about the services. When customers come to them asking for the services, they feel uninformed, left out, and helpless (Berry, Zeithaml, and Parasuraman, 1985). This problem can be avoided by involving operations employees in the advertising process by interviewing them about service or watching actual service encounters. Employees can be shown advertisements before they are run so that they feel prepared for the service they will be expected to perform for the customer.

Proposition 8: The gap between external communications and delivery will be smaller if employees are involved in the process of advertising preparation than if they are not involved.

Proposition 9: The gap between external communications and delivery will be smaller if employees are shown commercials before they appear than if they are not.

Proposition 10: The more positive employees feel about the advertising that the company runs, the more willing they will be to provide service.

Using Price to Set Quality Expectations. The link between price and quality is intuitively obvious. More than ninety research studies in the past thirty years have been designed to test the general wisdom that price and quality are positively related. The body of literature summarized by Olson (1977) is based on the assumption that there is a general relationship between price and perceived quality. Despite the expectation of a positive relationship, results of these studies have provided mixed evidence. The positive price–perceived quality relationship has not surfaced clearly except in situations where methodological concerns such as demand artifacts (Sawyer, 1975) could offer alternative explanations for the result (Monroe and Krishnan, 1985; Olson, 1977). Peterson and Wilson (1985) argue that the relationship between price and perceived quality is not universal and that the direction of the relationship may not always be positive. Both Peterson and Wilson (1985) and Olshavsky (1985) argue that price-quality studies should not emphasize documenting the general price–perceived quality relationship but should instead emphasize delineating the conditions under which price information is likely to lead to an inference about quality. In examining the conditions under which price and quality have been positively related, Zeithaml (1988) proposed that the use of price as an indicator of quality depends on (1) availability of other cues to quality, (2) price variation within a class of products, (3) product quality variation within a category of products, (4) level of price awareness of consumers, and (5) consumers' ability to detect quality variation in a group of products.

A major factor believed to affect the price–perceived quality relationship is the other information available to the consumer. When intrinsic cues to quality are readily accessible, when brand names provide evidence of a company's reputation, or when the level of advertising communicates the company's belief in the brand, the consumer may prefer to use those cues instead of price. However, in other situations—such as when quality is hard to detect or when quality or price varies a great deal in the category—consumers may believe that price is the best indicator of quality. Price is likely to be used as a quality indicator under these conditions, many of which describe situations that face many consumers when purchasing services (Zeithaml, 1982).

> Proposition 11:   Price sets expectations for quality of service, particularly when other cues to quality are not available, price varies within a class of services, service quality varies within a category, or consumers feel unable to detect quality variation in a group of products.

> Proposition 12:   When the customer lacks information about the quality of a service, customers will use price as a surrogate for quality.

Studies to investigate propositions 11 and 12 could be designed experimentally, manipulating price in between-subjects designs to avoid demand artifacts. The use of a dual measure of expectations and perceptions could provide insight into the mechanism by which price influences service quality perceptions. It is conceivable that price affects both expectations and perceptions.

Implications for Researchers and Practitioners

Each of the propositions presented in this chapter could be tested either experimentally or in the field through the use of existing measures of service quality. Many of them have not been examined in empirical research, largely because they require concepts that span the disciplines of operations, marketing, and human resources. Only by extending the field of investigation beyond a single discipline can we fully understand and test these service quality issues.

For practitioners, each of the propositions suggests strategies to improve service quality delivery and communication about delivery by improving coordination among departments in a service firm. Coordination between marketing and operations can result in communication that accurately reflects service delivery, thus reducing the gap between customer expectations and actual service delivery. Coordination between marketing and human resources can enhance the ability of each employee to become a better marketer. Coordination between finance and marketing can result in prices that accurately reflect the customer's evaluation of a service. In service firms, these functions need to be integrated to produce consistent messages and to narrow the service quality gaps.

References

Alesandri, K. L. "Strategies That Influence Memory for Advertising Communications." In R. J. Harris (ed.), *Information Processing Research in Advertising*. Hillsdale, N.J.: Erlbaum, 1983.

Berry, L. L. "The Employee as Customer." *Journal of Retail Banking*, 1981, *3* (3), 33–40.

Berry, L. L., and Clark, T. "Four Ways to Make Services More Tangible." *Business*, 1986, *36* (Oct.–Dec.), 53–54.

Berry, L. L., Zeithaml, V. A., and Parasuraman, A. "Quality Counts in Services, Too." *Business Horizons*, 1985, *28* (May–June), 44–52.

George, W. R., and Berry, L. L. "Guidelines for the Advertising of Services." *Business Horizons*, 1981, *24* (May–June), 52–56.

Gronroos, C. "Internal Marketing—Theory and Practices." In T. M. Bloch, G. D. Upah, and V. A. Zeithaml (eds.), *Services Marketing in a Changing Environment*. Chicago: American Marketing Association, 1985.

Legg, D., and Baker, J. "Advertising Strategies for Service Firms." Working paper, Texas A&M University, 1987.

Lutz, K. A., and Lutz, R. J. "Imagery—Eliciting Strategies: Review and Implications of Research." In H. K. Hunt (ed.), *Advances in Consumer Research*. Ann Arbor, Mich.: Association for Consumer Research, 1978.

Monroe, K. B., and Krishnan, R. "The Effect of Price on Subjective Product Evaluations." In J. Jacoby and J. Olson (eds.), *Perceived Quality*. Lexington, Mass.: Lexington Books, 1985.

Olshavsky, R. W. "Perceived Quality in Consumer Decision Making: An Integrated Theoretical Perspective." In J. Jacoby and J. Olson (eds.), *Perceived Quality*. Lexington, Mass.: Lexington Books, 1985.

Olson, J. C. "Price as an Informational Cue: Effects in Product Evaluation." In A. G. Woodside, J. N. Sheth, and P. D. Bennet (eds.), *Consumer and Industrial Buying Behavior*. New York: North Holland, 1977.

Parasuraman, A., Zeithaml, V. A., and Berry, L. L. "A Conceptual Model of Service Quality and Its Implications for Future Research." *Journal of Marketing*, 1985, *49* (Fall), 41–50.

Parasuraman, A., Zeithaml, V. A., and Berry, L. L. "SERVQUAL: A Multiple-Item Scale for Measuring Consumer Perceptions of Service Quality." *Journal of Retailing*, 1988, *64* (Spring), 12–40.

Parasuraman, A., Zeithaml, V. A., and Berry, L. L. "An Empirical Test of the Gap Model of Service Quality." Working paper, Texas A&M University, 1989.

Peterson, R. A., and Wilson, W. R. "Perceived Risk and Price-Reliance Schema and Price-Perceived-Quality Mediators." In J. Jacoby and J. Olson (eds.), *Perceived Quality*. Lexington, Mass.: Lexington Books, 1985.

Sawyer, A. G. "Demand Artifacts in Laboratory Experiments in Consumer Research." *Journal of Consumer Research*, 1975, *1* (Mar.), 20–30.

Shostack, G. L. "Breaking Free from Product Marketing." *Journal of Marketing*, 1977, *41* (Apr.), 73–80.

Wolfinbarger, M. F., and Gilly, M. C. "A Conceptual Model of the Impact of Advertising on Service Employees." Working paper, University of California, Irvine, 1988.

Zeithaml, V. A. "How Consumer Evaluation Processes Differ Between Goods and Services." In J. H. Donnelly and W. R. George (eds.), *Marketing of Services*. Chicago: American Marketing Association, 1981.

Zeithaml, V. A. "The Acquisition, Meaning, and Use of Price Information by Consumers of Professional Services." In R. Bush and S. Hunt (eds.), *Marketing Theory: Philosophy of Science Perspective*. Chicago: American Marketing Association, 1982.

Zeithaml, V. A. "Consumer Perceptions of Price, Quality, and Value: A Means-End Model and Synthesis of Evidence." *Journal of Marketing*, 1988, *52* (July), 2–22.

Zeithaml, V. A., Berry, L. L., and Parasuraman, A. "Communication and Control Processes in the Delivery of Service Quality." *Journal of Marketing*, 1988, *52* (Apr.), 35–48.

Zeithaml, V. A., Parasuraman, A., and Berry, L. L. "Problems and Strategies in Services Marketing." *Journal of Marketing*, 1985, *49* (Spring), 33–46.

17

Conclusion: The State of Service Management Knowledge

Richard B. Chase
Deborah L. Kellogg

This book has presented the recent thought and research about management issues for service organizations. In this concluding chapter, we examine the state of our knowledge about this new area of study and provide suggestions for further developing our understanding of it.

Jaikumar and Bohn (1986) have developed a conceptual framework of knowledge acquisition to explain how and where intelligent systems can be used to aid learning in manufacturing environments. Once knowledge is complete—that is, when all aspects of the production process are understood—the process can be operated by procedural control systems. Although procedural control systems are neither the total objective of service management nor generally achievable for many if any services, the process by which one acquires knowledge to achieve this goal is eminently applicable to services. Equally important, the Jaikumar and Bohn model provides a tight structure for evaluating our progress to date along the critical dimension of knowledge acquisition. Jaikumar and Bohn's framework consists of eight stages of knowledge, which we have cast in service terms where appropriate:

1. Recognition of prototypes—the ability to distinguish between good service organizations and bad service organizations
2. Recognition of attributes and relationships among attributes within prototypes—the ability to identify common characteristics that good service organizations share
3. Discrimination across attributes and relationships—the ability to see which attributes and which relationships are critical to success
4. Discrimination within attributes and relationships—the ability to measure, at least qualitatively, the critical attributes and relationships
5. Local control of attributes and relationships—the ability to begin to use the knowledge by writing some procedures
6. Recognition and discrimination of contingencies in control—the ability to find the secondary attributes and relationships that affect the system
7. Control of contingencies—the ability to measure and react to contingencies
8. Complete procedural control—the ability to run the operation flawlessly, controlling or responding to every eventuality with predefined plans

These eight stages may be grouped into three categories: primary development, secondary development, and complete procedure (see Figure 17.1). The first five stages are related to primary development and are concerned with understanding the basic structure of the underlying process—in this case, service organizations. Secondary development is the process of refinement: When a contingency arises, we have to reconstruct theories of action to accommodate it. Thus, secondary processes recur every time a contingency arises and we progressively refine theories. For the resolution of a contingency, we may have to progress sequentially through the five stages of primary development to refine theories of action. Implicit in this definition of the stages of knowledge is the notion that phenomena can be observed, measured, and controlled. Given this frame-

Figure 17.1. Stages of Knowledge.

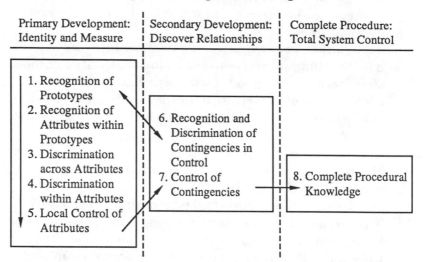

Source: Jaikumar and Bohn, 1986, pp. 169–211. Reproduced by permission.

work, it is possible to determine where we stand in our understanding of service management. It is important to recognize that there are at least two perspectives that can be taken: a broad, global perspective, that of service management in general, and an organization-specific perspective.

Knowledge at the Global Level

From the global perspective, our knowledge of service management is at very primary levels. The popular press continues in stage one, identifying good and bad service organizations and situations (Russell, Grant, and Szonskl, 1987; Zemke and Schaff, 1989). The academic community has been moving into the second and third levels of knowledge, as exemplified by the contributors to this volume.

In her contribution (Chapter Three), Riddle shows the need to consider the functional interdependencies and states that any strategic decision will need to involve at least two of the traditionally defined organizational departments. Heskett

(Chapter Two) states that strategies are not unifunctional. Bateson (Chapter Fourteen) continues this theme and identifies the relationships between the environment, management objectives, and service technology. The ultimate goal of this effort is to measure and eventually develop a contingency approach for ideal structuring of the marketing department within the firm. At the present time, however, the relationships have not been fully specified, nor is adequate measurement possible. In addition to considering the interdependencies of traditionally defined subsystems, Bateson suggests that we may need new definitions. To be sure, the tasks of the traditional marketing, operations, and human resource departments all need to be accomplished. Where, how, and by whom, however, may need to be reevaluated.

In Chapter Nine, Sasser and Fulmer call into question long-held assumptions that increasing production efficiency requires a reduction in personalized services. They identify technology, especially information and communication technology, as mediating the relationship between efficiency and customization. Mills and Moberg (Chapter Five) take a broader view of technology. To them, service technology consists of three types of knowledge—one to produce the service, another to maintain the organization, and a third to manage the client. This perspective, more than any other in this book, demonstrates the basic difference between knowledge acquisition and use in manufacturing and in service: That is, in manufacturing, as represented in the Jaikumar and Bohn (1986) model, technology relates solely to material transformation processes.

This volume is rich with other examples of how researchers are beginning to identify and measure some of the operational relationships that exist in service management. In Chapter Eight, Luthans and Davis show the relationship between human resource management and the application of behavioral techniques to achieve productivity gains. While productivity programs are typically thought to be within the domain of operations departments, Lovelock (Chapter Fifteen) presents a list of operational issues and discusses both how they affect and how they are affected by marketing decisions.

Zeithaml (Chapter Sixteen) states that successful advertising is the responsibility of both operations and marketing.

Heskett, on the other hand, identifies some of the weaknesses and shortfalls in our understanding of relationships. First, we do not understand, nor do most firms begin to measure, the effects of repeat business on profit. There is an assumption that service firms attain leverage through quality and productivity, yet we do not know how these two concepts interact. The management of Japanese manufacturing firms has shown that quality and productivity can go hand in hand. Can this be true for service—specifically, at the point of the encounter? If so, how do we manage for it? Until we can answer these kinds of questions, we will go no further than stage-four knowledge. It is only when we get to stage five that we begin to apply what we know.

Martin (1988) demonstrates the beginnings of a move to a contingency approach (stage six) by examining the effects of risk in franchised service businesses. This work also shows the variety of attributes and relationships that must be considered in the study of service business. Martin not only considers risk but also uses geographical distance, monitoring costs, and sales in his analysis. In his contribution to this volume Tansik (Chapter Seven) also moves to a contingency approach with the recognition that service firms are not all the same. High-contact services require different types of management than low-contact services.

How can we increase our broad-based knowledge of service management? We have not progressed very far along the knowledge-acquisition framework presented above. This framework, however, suggests three ways to increase the level of our current knowledge.

First, although there are an increasing number of collections of case studies of successful, quality-oriented service firms (Zemke and Schaff, 1989; Spechler, 1989), they represent only stage-one knowledge. We recognize that certain service organizations are "good," yet we do not really know why. Such case collections are a valuable source of data, but the common threads must be identified. To move to higher levels of understanding, more compare-and-contrast studies are needed. Schneider (Chapter Six) provides an example of this type of study, comparing two case studies to highlight the important aspects of change in a service orientation. More work using more cases will go far in aiding researchers to identify the crucial attributes and relationships. By using systematic case analysis, we can move to tackling stage-four knowledge.

The second way to increase knowledge is by developing measurement models. The SERVQUAL index referred to by Zeithaml (Chapter Sixteen) and the "service quality map" using LISREL discussed by Collier (Chapter Ten) are examples of the type of measurement needed. In addition, we need tools for measuring service productivity, the value of service, and the value of repeat business, as well as such issues as the effects of training programs or different organizational structures. As pointed out by Heskett in Chapter Two, we have yet to develop an acceptable model of profitability for service businesses. Governmental reporting fails at adequately measuring and accounting for the effects of service in our nation's economy. This has muddied the picture of trends in employment, slowed adequate passage of trade bills affecting service importation and exportation, and dwarfed the growing importance of services to our national well-being. Indeed, the statement that "productivity figures are like hot dogs — you'd be scared to find out what goes into either of them," first coined to describe goods production, is even more apt for services.

The third way to enlarge our knowledge is to develop a service data base. The knowledge base regarding strategy benefited a great deal from the PIMS data base. This collection of data from many diverse companies, including service companies, has allowed researchers to discern the patterns of concepts such as market share, quality, and size and their relationships to overall success and has helped identify the benchmark or prototypical criteria that are associated with success. Service organizations could benefit greatly from a methodical effort of data collection and analysis similar to the PIMS collection. It would be especially useful if it were longitudinal in nature. Such a study should be focused at the issues raised in this volume: the relationships between the marketing, operations, and human resource functions; the frontline-employee–customer interface; service quality; measures of organizational success; and service systems design. Such a data base would provide the data and the means to synthesize them needed to move to stage five on the knowledge framework and begin to apply that knowledge to control our service systems.

Knowledge at the Company Level

It is very difficult to assess how active individual companies are in the first three stages of knowledge acquisition. The stages are cognitive processes and not subject to view by outside observers. The first objective indication that a company is attaining knowledge is its beginning to measure something. Florida Power Light, Paul Revere Insurance, Marriott, and Federal Express are representative of the service organizations that use customer data obtained from surveys, focus groups, and response cards. There is also an increasing amount of competitive benchmarking taking place through customer-service departments and mystery shopping. We anticipate that a great deal more measurement will be undertaken as service firms enter the annual competition for the Malcolm Baldrige National Quality Award sponsored by the U.S. Department of Commerce. This award, modeled somewhat after the Deming prize for quality achievement in Japan, requires companies to provide documentation on all aspects of quality performance. (The impact of this award is being felt in manufacturing. For example, the 1988 winner, Motorola, is requiring all of its 10,000 suppliers, including IBM, to apply for it.)

It is also clear from industry-specific examples that the customer–service provider relationship is a key success factor. Nordstrom and SAS Airlines provide examples of the results of empowering the service employee. The empowering issue, however, also illustrates how much we still need to learn. Under what circumstances and to what degree should the frontline employee be empowered? How would a company measure empowerment and the expected results? Sasser and Fulmer (Chapter Nine) raise the issue of the trade-off between empowering the frontline employee and empowering the customer.

How can we increase knowledge in a company-specific setting? The tasks needed to increase knowledge within a company are similar to those required to increase our more general service management knowledge. First, information acquisition must be systematized. Information technology can play a prominent role in assisting companies to capture information about customers, repeat purchases, profitability, worker productivity, and costs. This information will be useless, however, unless someone in the organization searches for the attributes and relationships that lead to the goals that the company has set. Creative thinking is necessary, and that cannot be provided by the machine. As Jaikumar and Bohn (1986) point out, information systems must be combined with humans in a way that maximizes the strengths of each. Humans can progress along the knowledge acquisition framework much more quickly and accurately if their efforts are augmented by computerization. In Chapter Four, Quinn and Paquette discuss the use of technology to aid in handling complexity. Companies should be developing systems to capture data and then using those data to define relationships and develop measurements for the various critical attributes.

Of particular potential value is sharing information across networks in multisite service firms. Banc-1, a banking chain in the midwest, for example, aggressively seeks inputs on "local experiments" from branch presidents that would help the performance of other branches. It also seeks information on what does not work. However, this type of data sharing is rarely done systematically, even by companies that hold corporatewide annual meetings.

Second, companies need to find ways to force the critical elements for success to the surface. At the preliminary design stage, conjoint analysis and multidimensional scaling have been used to determine what the customer wants (see Wind, Green, Shiffle, and Scarbrough [1989], for their application to Marriott's Courtyard Hotels). Fitzsimmons (Chapter Twelve) provides one possible approach (using the JIT strategy for contin-

ual improvement) to aid in identification of the critical attributes and relationships during the operating stage. The
application of JIT in manufacturing environments is known to
expose problem areas; in the service sector, the use of JIT
principles and waiting-line reduction can help formalize the
learning process and force service companies to provide front-
line employees with problem-solving skills. The important hur-
dle to be overcome is disseminating newly acquired knowledge
throughout the firm as well as to the larger academic
community.

Service firms have ideal conditions in which to experiment with other approaches as well. Different service delivery
options can often be introduced overnight, with very little investment and risk. The multisite location feature of many service firms allows for the application of carefully designed experiments with the effects of experimental groups separated
from those of control groups. Much information can be
gathered with relatively few experimental sites if carefully designed experiments are created.

As service companies move to controlling processes
(stages five through eight), they can apply Taguchi quality-
control techniques—a method for system design using statistical experiments designed to identify the kinds of capabilities
the system must have in order to deal cost effectively with wide
ranges of input variability (Kacker, 1986). As mentioned above
and elsewhere in this book, there is a great deal of uncertainty in
service firms that cannot be adequately controlled merely by
written procedures. The high involvement of the customer in
many service firms requires designing a system that is robust
enough to handle far more "off-the-wall" variations than con-
front goods producers.

When a service firm reaches stage-four knowledge and
can identify what attributes will change with differing relationships and how they will change, it can perform Taguchi
experiments to test various service designs against the range of
environmental factors and measure the resulting service delivery indicators (quality, satisfaction, speed, reliability, and so on).
It will then be possible to identify the best service process

design, the one that is the least costly yet provides the most consistent level of services for any likely set of environmental factors. Before Taguchi methods are applied, a fairly high level of knowledge must exist. Cost information must be known. The target values of the service outcomes must be specified. Relationships between the various design options must be specified. The full range of possible environmental factors must be determined. However, if management is willing to put the effort into learning these things and then run the experiments, Taguchi-designed service systems seem to provide a possible solution to designing flexible, robust, and consistent service delivery systems. The result will be not highly structured, procedure-driven, rigid services focusing on efficiency but services that consistently meet customer needs by focusing on effectiveness of results.

Conclusion

Our knowledge about service management is in its infancy. The immediate goal is to systematize our knowledge acquisition. We must search not only for attributes that are tied with success but for relationships between those attributes. We have no lack of service organizations that are "street smart" in their gathering and use of knowledge. What we need now is the infusion of the concepts from this book to make them "systematically smart." Intelligent use of information technology in particular will be a key success factor in increasing our knowledge. This will be necessary at both an academic and a firm level. Experimentation will be critical to move to a level of knowledge that allows us not only to control our service firms but to make them better for customers and employees. The cross-functional nature of service management must be recognized. At this stage of its development, a generalist viewpoint will be most valuable. This will require a lot from both the academics and the practitioners in service management. They must be well versed in marketing, human resources, and operations. They must also be able to reconcile the conflicts that will inevitably arise.

In many respects, service management is like business

policy in the demands it makes on its students and teachers. Small events—service encounters—must be seen in the context of the big picture. Even disaggregation of subjects into the very broad categories in this book runs the risk of "suboptimization of perspective." As we hear the latest glum news about the United States' lack of competitiveness in manufacturing (Dertouzos, Lester, and Solow, 1989), it should reinforce our resolve to keep the service sector strong. Providing a forum for leading scholars from multiple disciplines to "sing their song" is our contribution to this objective.

References

Dertouzos, M. L., Lester, R. K., and Solow, R. M. *Made in America: Regaining the Production Edge*. Cambridge, Mass.: MIT Press, 1989.

Jaikumar, R., and Bohn, R. E. "The Development of Intelligent Systems for Industrial Use: A Conceptual Framework." In *Research on Technological Innovation, Management and Policy*. Vol. 3. Greenwich, Conn.: JAI Press, 1986.

Kacker, R. N. "Off-Line Quality Control, Parameter Design, and the Taguchi Method." *Journal of Quality Technology*, 1986, 7, 176–188.

Martin, R. E. "Franchising and Risk Management." *American Economic Review*, Dec. 1988, pp. 954–968.

Russell, G., Grant, M., and Szonskl, W. "Pul-eeze! Will Somebody Help Me?" *Time*, Feb. 2, 1987, pp. 48–57.

Spechler, J. W. *When America Does It Right: Case Studies in Service Quality*. Norcross, Ga.: Industrial Engineering and Management Press, 1989.

Wind, J., Green, P. E., Shiffle, D., and Scarbrough, M. "Courtyard by Marriott: Designing a Hotel Facility with Consumer-Based Marketing Models." *Interfaces*, 1989, *19* (1), 25–47.

Zemke, R., and Schaff, D. *The Service Edge: 101 Companies That Profit from Customer Care*. New York: New American Library, 1989.

Name Index

Subject Index